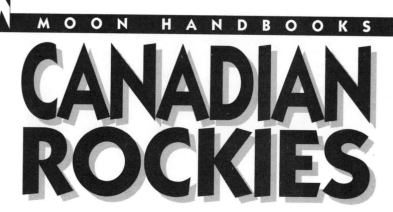

MOON HANDBOOKS

CANADIAN ROCKIES

INCLUDING BANFF
AND JASPER NATIONAL PARKS

SECOND EDITION

ANDREW HEMPSTEAD

AVALON
TRAVEL

MOON HANDBOOKS: CANADIAN ROCKIES
INCLUDING BANFF AND JASPER NATIONAL PARKS
SECOND EDITION

Andrew Hempstead

Published by
Avalon Travel Publishing
5855 Beaudry St.
Emeryville, CA 94608, USA

Printing History
2nd edition—April 2001
5 4 3 2 1

Please send all comments,
corrections, additions,
amendments, and critiques to:

**MOON HANDBOOKS:
CANADIAN ROCKIES
AVALON TRAVEL PUBLISHING
5855 BEAUDRY ST.
EMERYVILLE, CA 94608, USA
email: info@travelmatters.com
www.travelmatters.com**

ISBN: 1-56691-271-7
ISSN: 1531-5622

Editor: Helen Sillett
Series Manager: Erin Van Rheenen
Copyeditor: Jean Blomquist
Index: Helen Sillett
Graphics Coordinator: Erika Howsare
Production: Amber Pirker
Design: Dave Hurst
Map Editors: Naomi Dancis, Mike Ferguson,
Cartography: Chris Folks, Allen Leech, Mike Morgenfeld, Mark Stroud, Eurydice Thomas

Front cover photo: Dick Dietrich, Mt. Robson, Mt. Robson Provincial Park
All photos by Andrew Hempstead unless otherwise noted
All illustrations by Bob Race unless otherwise noted

Distributed in the United States and Canada by Publishers Group West

Printed in USA by R.R. Donnelley

MOON HANDBOOKS

CANADIAN ROCKIES

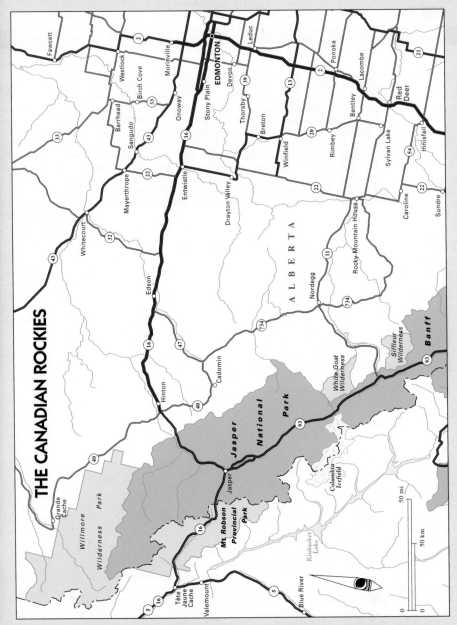

THE CANADIAN ROCKIES

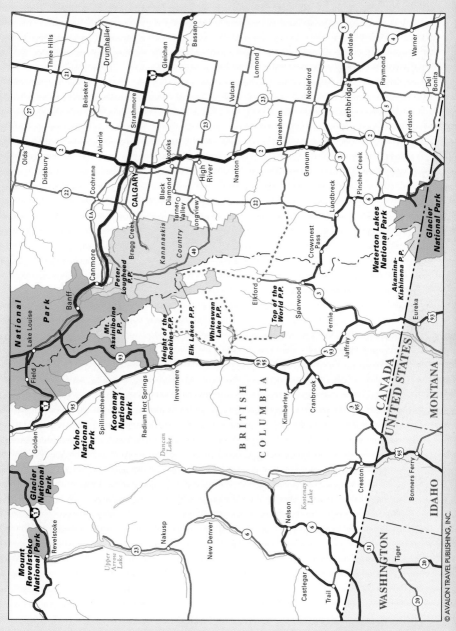

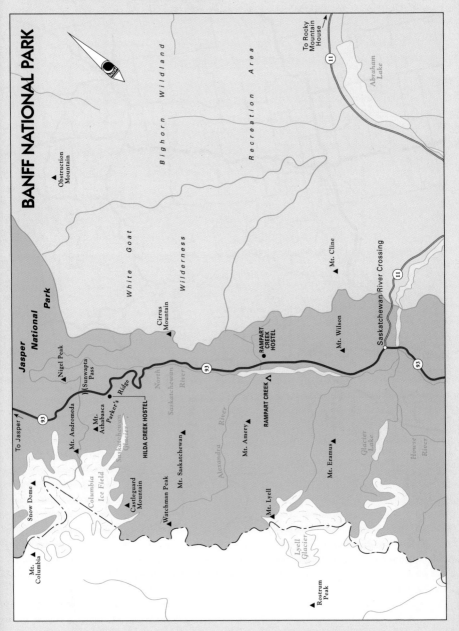

BANFF NATIONAL PARK

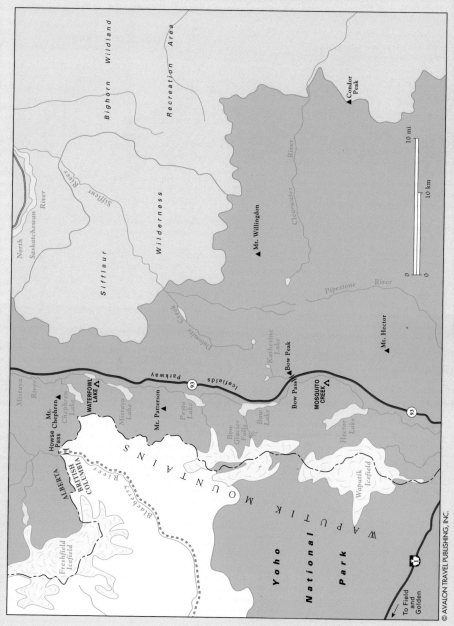

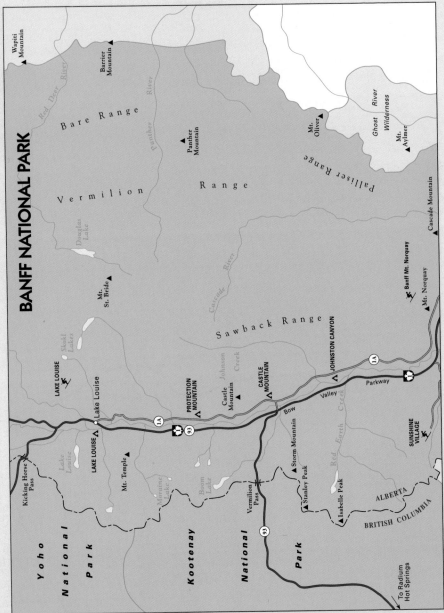

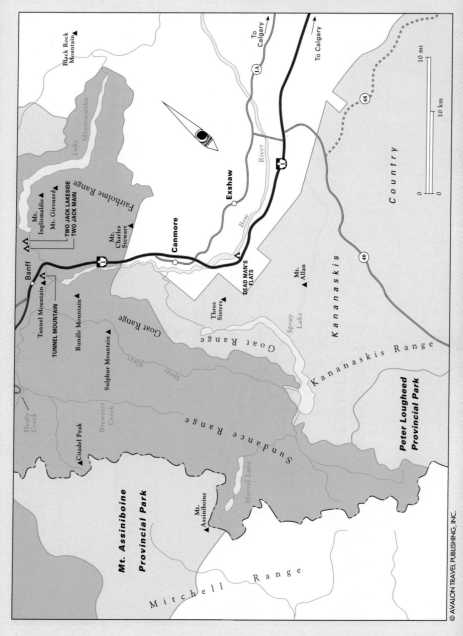

© AVALON TRAVEL PUBLISHING, INC.

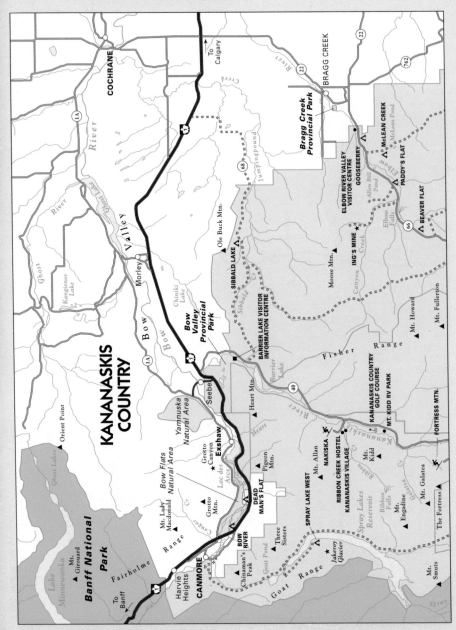

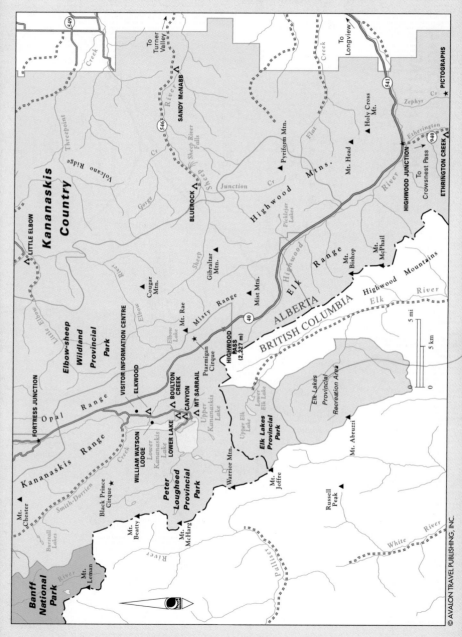

© AVALON TRAVEL PUBLISHING, INC.

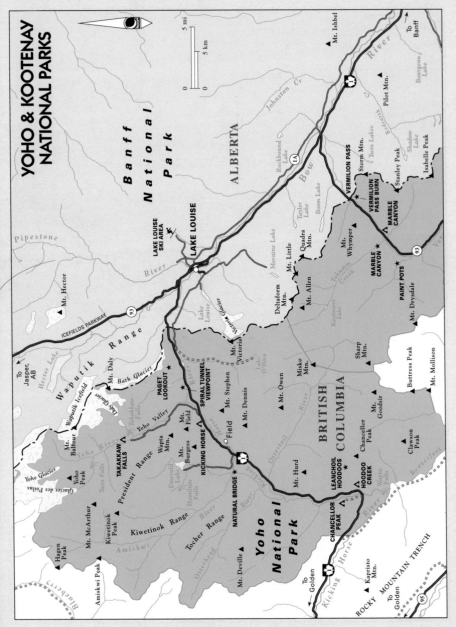

YOHO & KOOTENAY NATIONAL PARKS

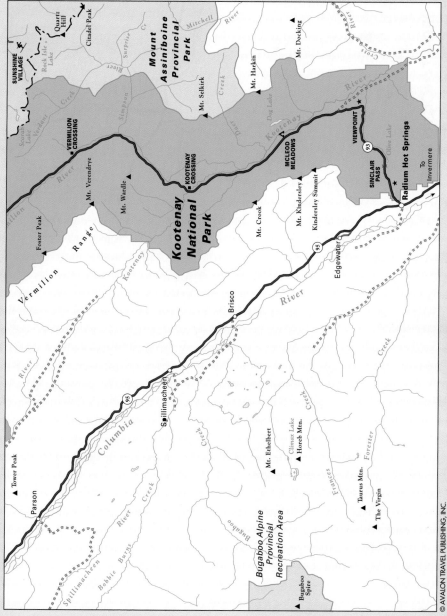

© AVALON TRAVEL PUBLISHING, INC.

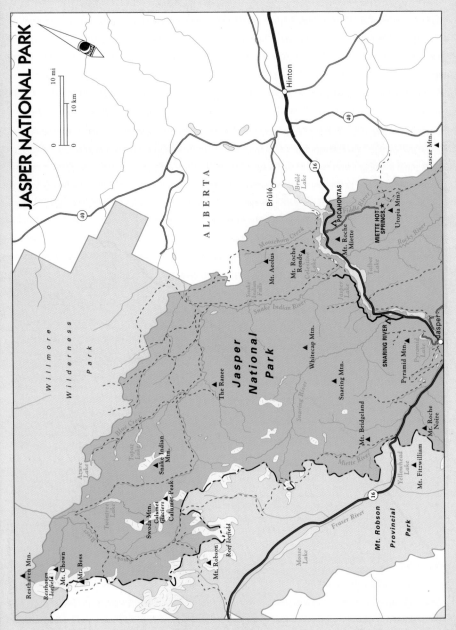

JASPER NATIONAL PARK

10 mi

10 km

ALBERTA

Willmore Wilderness Park

Jasper National Park

Mt. Robson Provincial Park

Hinton

Brûlé

Brûlé Lake

POCAHONTAS

Mt. Roche Miette

MIETTE HOT SPRINGS

Utopia Mtn.

Luscar Mtn.

Mt. Aeolus

Mt. Roche Ronde

Moosehorn Creek

Snake Indian Falls

Snake Indian River

Jasper Lake

Talbot Lake

Rocky River

Whitecap Mtn.

The Ranee

Snaring River

Snaring Mtn.

SNARING RIVER

Pyramid Mtn.

Pyramid Lake

Jasper

Mt. Bridgeland

Mt. Roche Noire

Blue Creek

Azure Lake

Topaz Lake

Twintree Lake

Snake Indian Mtn.

Swoda Mtn.

Calumet Glaciers

Calumet Peak

Miette River

Yellowhead Lake

Mt. Fitzwilliam

Resthaven Mtn.

Resthaven Icefield

Mt. Chown

Mt. Bess

Mt. Robson

Reef Icefield

Smoky River

Fraser River

Moose Lake

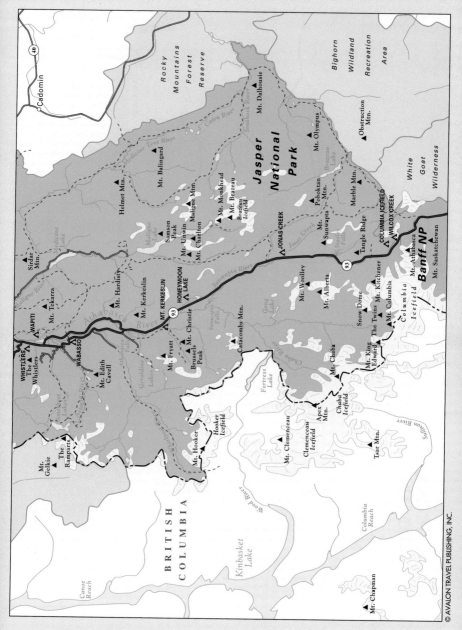

© AVALON TRAVEL PUBLISHING, INC.

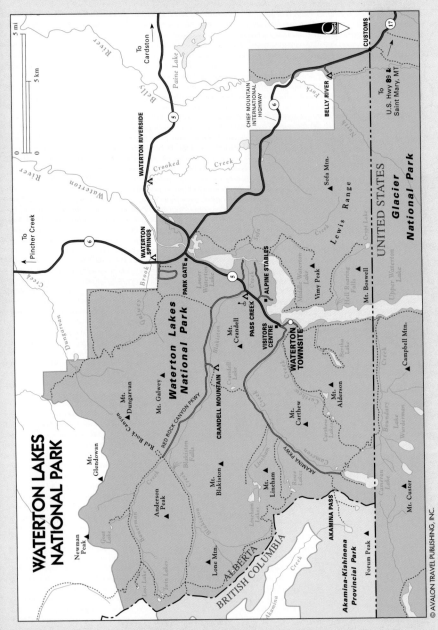

WATERTON LAKES NATIONAL PARK

© AVALON TRAVEL PUBLISHING, INC.

MAP SYMBOLS

▬▬▬	Divided Highway/Road	═══
▬▬▬	Primary Highway/Road	══
▬▬	Secondary Highway/Road	──
▪▪▪▪▪▪▪	Unpaved Road	▪▪▪▪▪▪▪
⋯⋯⋯	Hiking Trail	- - - - -
⌇	Waterfall	⌇
⌒	Glacier/Icefield	⌒
▨	National Park	▨
▢	Provincial/Other Park	▨

🛡	TransCanada Highway	○	City/Town
◯	Provincial/State Highway	∧	Campground
♡	U.S. Highway	▲	Mountain
★	Point of Interest	⌁	Golf Course
•	Accommodation	⛷	Ski Resort
▼	Restaurant/Bar	⟍	Mountain Pass
▪	Other Location	┼─┼	Railroad

CONTENTS

MAPS

For detailed coverage of major national parks within the Canadian Rockies, refer to the color section.

ABBREVIATIONS

AB—Alberta
APEX fare-advance-purchase
  excursion fare
ATV—all-terrain vehicle
B&B—bed-and-breakfast inn
BC/B.C. —British Columbia
C.P.R. —Canadian Pacific
  Railway
d—double occupancy

4WD—four-wheel drive
GPS—Global Positioning
  System
GST—Goods and Services
  Tax
HI—Hostelling International
Hwy.—Highway
km—kilometer
kph—kilometers per hour

NWMP—North West Mounted
  Police
RCMP—Royal Canadian
  Mounted Police
RV—recreational vehicle
s—single occupancy
UNESCO—United Nations
  Educational, Scientific, and
  Cultural Organization

DROP US A LINE

Although we have strived to produce the most up-to-date guidebook
humanly possible, things change–restaurants and accommodations open and close, attractions come and go, and prices go up. If you
come across a great out-of-the-way place, a new restaurant or lodging,
or you think a particular hike warrants a mention, please write to us. Letters from tour operators and people in the tourism and hospitality industries are also appreciated.
Write to:

> Moon Handbooks: Canadian Rockies
> c/o Avalon Travel Publishing
> 5855 Beaudry Street
> Emeryville, CA 94608 USA
>
> e-mail: info@travelmatters.com

ACCOMMODATION PRICE CATEGORIES

Categories are based on high-season, double
occupancy rates. Prices are in Canadian
dollars.

> Under $50
>
> $50–100
>
> $100–150
>
> $150–250
>
> $250 and up

PRICE INFORMATION

All prices are in Canadian dollars, unless otherwise indicated.

ACKNOWLEDGMENTS

It is impossible to spend time in the Canadian Rockies without being affected in some way. Every day I'm here, I gain a greater appreciation of the mountains and their complex environment. This makes writing about them a joy. As a result, most of the work for this book was done by myself, so there's not too many people to thank. A few, however, did help with this new edition, most importantly, the staff at each of the national parks injected ideas and a local perspective that can only be gained from living and working in the parks. And the gang at Avalon did a great job of putting this thing together, as usual.

*Exploring is delightful to look forward to
and back upon, but it is not comfortable at
the time, unless it be of such an easy nature
as not to deserve the name.*

—EREWHON, 1872

Peyto Lake, Banff National Park

INTRODUCTION

Snowcapped peaks by the hundreds, glaciers and icefields, multihued lakes, rushing rivers, an abundance of wildlife—the awe-inspiring Canadian Rockies are one of North America's premier travel destinations. Mother Nature dealt the original winning hand here, which early governments had the foresight to protect for all time in a string of contiguous parks straddling the British Columbia-Alberta border. Banff and Jasper National Parks, on the east side of the Continental Divide in the province of Alberta, are the best known of these. Originally conceived as tourist resorts, the bustling towns of Banff and Jasper serve millions of visitors annually and boast championship golf courses, world-class resorts, hundreds of restaurants, and international shopping.

Two more national parks lie just west of Banff and Jasper, across the Continental Divide in the province of British Columbia. This side of the Canadian Rockies is much less crowded but is no less impressive. Here Kootenay National Park features hot springs and high concentra-

tions of wildlife, while Yoho National Park is famous for multihued Emerald Lake and the superb hiking country around Lake O'Hara. Together, the four national parks make up a complex geological and natural area that has been declared a World Heritage Site by UNESCO.

In addition to these four national parks, several other parks also preserve parts of the Canadian Rockies. On the British Columbia side of the divide, nearby Mt. Assiniboine Provincial Park is favored by backcountry hikers, while at the northern reach of Jasper National Park lies Mt. Robson Provincial Park, which surrounds and is named for the highest peak of the Canadian Rockies. In southern Alberta, Waterton Lakes National Park is a hidden gem that lacks the crowds of its northern counterparts, and Kananaskis Country is a preserve developed as a four-season, multiuse recreation area. Nearby, nestled among the high peaks of the Bow Valley, is Canmore, Alberta, the largest population center of the Canadian Rockies, and offering numerous opportunities for hiking and rock climbing.

THE LAND

The Rocky Mountains rise from the dense forests of central Mexico and run north through the U.S. states of New Mexico, Colorado, Wyoming, and Montana. Continuing north across the 49th parallel (the U.S.-Canada border), the range forms a natural border between the Canadian provinces of British Columbia and Alberta. Mountainous British Columbia is Canada's westernmost province, extending to the Pacific Ocean, while Alberta, to the east, is mostly prairie. The actual provincial boundary is the Continental Divide, an imaginary line that runs along the Rockies' highest peaks. Though it is a subjective matter, perhaps most would agree that this particular stretch of the Rocky Mountains—the Canadian Rockies—is the most spectacular segment anywhere along the entire range. North of British Columbia and Alberta, the Rockies descend to their northern terminus in the boreal forests of northern Canada.

The Canadian Rockies are relatively low compared to other mountain ranges of the world; the highest peak, Mt. Robson, tops out at 3,954 meters. Running parallel to the mountains along their eastern edge is a series of long, rolling ridges known as the foothills. To the west is the Rocky Mountain Trench, a long, wide valley that in turn is bordered to the west by various subranges of the Columbia Mountains.

GEOLOGY

The Rocky Mountains began rising 75 million years ago, making them relatively young compared to the world's major mountain ranges.

But to fully appreciate the geology of the Rockies, you must look back many hundreds of millions of years, to the Precambrian era. At this time, around 700 million years ago, the Pacific Ocean covered most of the western provinces and states. The ocean advanced, then receded, several times over the next half billion years. Each time the ocean flooded eastward it deposited layers of silt and sand on its bed—layers that built up with each successive inundation. Starting approximately 550 million years ago, the oceans began to come alive with marine invertebrates and the first crustaceans. As these creatures died and sank to the ocean floor, they added to the layers of sediment. Over time, the ever-increasing sediment load compressed the underlying layers into sandstone, shale, and quartzite.

Birth of the Rockies

Some 200 million years ago, the stability of the ocean floor began wavering along the West Coast of North America, culminating 75 million years ago as two plates of the earth's crust collided. According to plate tectonics theory, the earth's crust is broken into several massive chunks ("plates") that are always moving and occasionally bump into each other. This isn't something that happens overnight; a plate may move only a few centimeters over a period of thousands of years. In the case of the Rockies, the Pacific Plate butted into the North American Plate and was forced beneath it. The land at this subduction zone was crumpled and thrust upward, creating the Rocky Mountains. Layers of sediment laid down on the ocean floor over the course of hundreds of millions of years were folded, twisted, and squeezed; great slabs of rock broke away, and in places older strata were pushed on top of younger. By the beginning of the Tertiary period, around 65 million years ago, the present form of mountain contours was established and the geological framework of the mountains was in place.

The Ice Ages

No one knows why, but around one million years ago the world's climate cooled a few degrees. Ice caps formed in Arctic regions and slowly moved south over North America and Eurasia. These advances, followed by retreats, occurred four times.

The final major glaciation began moving south 35,000 years ago. A sheet of ice up to 2,000 meters deep covered all but the highest peaks of the Rocky Mountains. The ice scoured the terrain, destroying all vegetation as it crept slowly forward. In the mountains, these rivers of ice carved hollows, known as **cirques,** into the slopes of the higher peaks. They rounded off lower peaks and reamed out valleys from their

The Front Ranges, between the Continental Divide and the foothills, are the most severely folded and faulted. Mt. Kidd (pictured), in Kananaskis Country, is a classic example.

preglacier V shape to a trademark, postglacial U shape. The retreat of this ice sheet, beginning around 12,000 years ago, also radically altered the landscape. Rock and debris that had been picked up by the ice on its march forward melted out during the retreat, creating high ridges known as lateral and terminal **moraines.** Many of these moraines blocked natural drainages, resulting in the formation of lakes. And meltwater drained into rivers and streams, incising deep channels into the sedimentary rock of the plains. Today, the only remnants of this ice age are the scattered icefields along the Continental Divide, including the 325-square-km **Columbia Icefield.**

FOOTHILLS ERRATICS TRAIN

During the last ice age, a sheet of ice up to a kilometer thick crept southward across the area that is now Jasper National Park. A landslide deposited hundreds of large quartzite boulders atop the ice, which continued moving south, carrying the boulders with it. Many thousands of years later, as temperatures warmed and the ice melted, the boulders were deposited far from their source, creating an erratics train through the foothills and extending 650 km south. The largest of these boulders—the world's largest erratic, weighing an estimated 18,000 tons—lies just beyond the foothills, seven kilometers west of Okotoks. The name is difficult to forget; it's called the **Big Rock.**

Waterways

Water in its various forms has had a profound effect on the appearance of the Canadian Rockies. In addition to the scouring action of the glaciers, flowing water in rivers and streams has, over the millennia, deeply etched the landscape. The process continues today.

The flow of water is directly related to **divides,** or high points of land that dictate the direction of water flow. The dominant divide in the Canadian Rockies, and indeed North America, is the Continental Divide. The natural boundary created by this divide forms the Alberta/British Columbia border, while other, less obvious divides form borders of many parks of the Canadian Rockies. The five national parks are classic examples of this scenario. The divides forming the boundaries of Banff National Park encompass the entire upper watershed of the **Bow River.** The Bow flows southward through the park then heads east out of the mountains and into the Saskatchewan River system, whose waters continue east to Hudson Bay and the Atlantic Ocean. The Bow River is fed by many lakes famed for their beauty, including **Bow, Louise,** and **Moraine.** To the south, the rivers of Kananaskis Country and Waterton Lakes National Park also drain into the Saskatchewan River system.

The boundary between Jasper and Banff National Parks is an important north/south divide. The **Columbia Icefield,** a remnant of the last ice age, lies on either side of this divide. Runoff from the south side of the icefield flows south into the

Saskatchewan River system, while runoff from the north side forms the upper headwaters of the **Athabasca River** system. The Athabasca flows north through Jasper National Park and into the Mackenzie River system, which continues north to the Arctic Ocean. All water draining off the western slopes of the Continental Divide ends up in the Pacific Ocean via two major river systems: the **Columbia** and the **Fraser.** The mighty Columbia makes a wide northern loop before heading south into the U.S. state of Washington and draining into the Pacific Ocean. Along the way it picks up the waters of the **Kootenay River,** which begins high in Kootenay National Park and makes a lazy loop south through Montana and Idaho before joining the Columbia at Castlegar, British Columbia, and the **Kicking Horse River,** which flows down from the divides that form the borders of Yoho National Park. The Fraser River, the longest river entirely within British Columbia, begins in the high reaches of Mt. Robson Provincial Park.

CLIMATE

More than any other factor, prevailing moisture-laden westerlies blowing across British Columbia from the Pacific Ocean dictate the climate of the Canadian Rockies. The cold heights of the mountain peaks wring the winds dry, making for clear, sunny skies in southern Alberta; Calgary gets up to 350 hours of sunshine in June alone—good news, unless you're a farmer. In winter, the dry winds blasting down the eastern slopes of the Rockies can raise temperatures on the prairies by up to 40°C in 24 hours. Called **chinooks,** these desiccating blows are a phenomenon unique to Alberta.

Elevation and, to a lesser degree, latitude are two other factors affecting the climate within the mountain ecosystem. Elevations vary from 800 meters above sea level at Radium Hot Springs, to 1,500 meters at Lake Louise, to 3,954 me-

CHINOOK WINDS

On many days in the dead of winter, a distinctive arch of clouds forms in the sky over the southwestern corner of Alberta as a wind peculiar to the Rockies swoops down over the mountains. The warm wind, known as a chinook (a native word meaning "snow eater"), can raise temperatures by up to 20°C in an hour and up to 40°C in a 24-hour period. The wind's effect on the snowpack is legendary. One story tells of a backcountry skier who spent the better part of a day traversing to the summit of a snow-clad peak on the front range of the Canadian Rockies. As he rested and contemplated skiing down, he realized that the slope had become completely bare!

Chinooks originate over the Pacific Ocean when warm, moist air is pushed eastward by prevailing westerlies. The air pressure of these winds is less than at lower elevations, and, therefore, as the air moves down the front ranges of the Canadian Rockies, it is subjected to increased pressure. This increasing of the air pressure warms the winds, which then fan out across the foothills and prairies. The "chinook arch" is formed as the clear air clashes with the warmer cloud-laden winds. The phenomenon is most common in southern Alberta but occurs to a lesser degree as far north as the Peace River Valley. Pincher Creek, the gateway to Waterton Lakes National Park, experiences around 35 chinooks each winter.

PACIFIC OCEAN   ROCKY MOUNTAINS   PRAIRIES

ters at the summit of Mt. Robson. As a general rule, temperatures fall 5°C for every 1,000 meters of elevation gained. Another interesting phenomenon occurring in the Canadian Rockies is the **temperature inversion,** in which a layer of warm air sits on top of a cold air mass. During these inversions, high- and low-country roles are reversed; prairie residents can be shivering and bundling up, while their mountain fellows are sunning themselves in shirtsleeves.

The Seasons

Summer in the mountains is short, but the days are long. With up to 17 hours of daylight around the summer solstice of June 21, this is an ideal time for travel and camping out. The months on either side of summer are ideal for touring, especially September when rainfall is minimal. Winter is cold, but the skiing is fantastic.

January is usually the coldest month, when Banff's average temperature is -10°C. In winter, extended spells of -30°C are not uncommon anywhere in the mountains, and temperatures occasionally drop below -40°C. The coldest temperature recorded was -52°C, in Lake Louise on January 25, 1950. Severe cold weather is often accompanied by sunshine; the cold is a dry cold, unlike the damp cold experienced in coastal regions. Cold temperatures and snow can be expected through mid-March.

Although March, April, and May are, more or less, the official months of spring, snow often falls in May, many lakes may remain frozen until June, and snow cover on higher mountain hiking trails remains until early July. During this period of the year the mountains are often affected by low-pressure weather patterns from the southeast, creating continuous days of rain, especially in the south.

Things warm up in summer; July is the hottest month. On hot days, the temperature will hit 30°C. Again, because of the dryness of the air, these high temperatures are more bearable here than in coastal regions experiencing the same temperatures.

By late September the mountain air begins to have a distinct chill. October brings the highest temperature variations of the year; the thermometer can hit 30°C but also dip as low as -20°C. Mild weather can continue until early December, but generally the first snow falls in October and by mid-November winter has set in.

FLORA

Botanists divide the Canadian Rockies into three distinct vegetation zones (also called biomes): montane, subalpine, and alpine. The boundaries of these zones are determined by a number of factors, the most important being altitude. Latitude and exposure are also factors, but less so. Typically, within any 1,500 meters of elevation, you'll pass through each of the three zones. These changes can be seen occurring most abruptly in Waterton Lakes National Park. Conifers (evergreens) predominate in the montane and subalpine, while above the tree line, in the alpine, only low-growing hardy species survive.

Montane

The foothills, along with most major valleys below an elevation of about 1,500 meters, are primarily cloaked in montane forest. **Aspen, balsam poplar,** and **white spruce** thrive here. **Lodgepole pine** is the first species to emerge after fire. Its hard seed cones are sealed by a resin that is melted only at high temperatures. When fire races through the forest, the resin melts and the cones release their seeds. The lodgepole is named for its straight, slender trunk, which natives used as a center pole for tepees. On dry, south-facing slopes, **Douglas fir** is the climax species. Where sunlight penetrates the forest, such as along riverbanks, flowers like **lady's slipper, Indian paintbrush,** and **saxifrage** are common. Large tracts of **fescue grassland** are common at lower elevations. The montane forest holds the greatest diversity of life of any vegetation zone and is prime winter habitat for larger mammals. But this is the habitat where most development occurs, and therefore is often much changed from its natural state.

Subalpine

Subalpine forests occur where temperatures are lower and precipitation higher than in the montane. In the Canadian Rockies, this is generally from 1,500 to 2,200 meters above sea level. The upper limit of the subalpine zone is the tree line. Approximately half the flora of the mountains falls within this zone. The climax species are **Engelmann spruce** and **subalpine fir** (recognized by its spirelike crown), although extensive forests of **lodgepole pine** occur in areas that have been scorched by fire in the last 100 years. At higher elevations, stands of **larch** are seen. Larches are conifers, but unlike other evergreens, their needles turn a burnt-orange color each fall, producing a magnificent display for photographers.

Alpine

The alpine zone extends from the tree line to mountain summits. The upper limit of tree growth in the Canadian Rockies varies between 1,800 and 2,400 meters above sea level, dropping progressively to the north until it meets the treeless tundra of the Arctic. Vegetation at these high altitudes occurs only where soil has been deposited. Large areas of alpine meadows burst with color for a short period each summer as **lupines, mountain avens, alpine forget-me-nots, avalanche lily, moss campion,** and a variety of **heathers** bloom.

FAUNA

One of the biggest attractions of the Canadian Rockies is the abundance of wildlife, especially large mammals such as elk, moose, bighorn sheep, and bears, which are widespread and easily viewed throughout the mountains.

THE DEER FAMILY

Mule Deer and White-tailed Deer

Mule deer and white-tailed deer are similar in size and appearance. Their color varies with the season but is generally light brown in summer, turning dirty-gray in winter. While both species are considerably smaller than elk, the mule deer is a little stockier than the white-tailed deer. The mule deer has a white rump, a white tail with a dark tip, and large mule-like ears. It inhabits open forests along valley floors. Waterton townsite has a healthy population of mule deer. The white-tailed deer's tail is dark on top. But when the animal runs, it holds its tail erect, revealing an all-white underside. White-tails frequent thickets along the rivers and lakes of the foothills. They are most common on the British Columbia side of the Continental Divide.

Elk

The elk, or **wapiti,** is the most widespread and common of the larger mammals living in the

Elk are the most common of all large mammals in the Canadian Rockies.

WILDLIFE VIEWING: THE BEST SPOTS

Where's the best place to view animals? This is probably the most common question posed by visitors to the Canadian Rockies. While a precise answer is impossible—this isn't a zoo after all—noting a couple of rules of thumb can make your chances of observation more likely. Spring is the best time for viewing wildlife from the roadside; larger mammals come down into the valleys in winter and stay through spring, moving back up to higher elevations as the snow melts. And mammals are most active at dawn and dusk, which are great times of day for scanning the landscape for movement.

In most cases, all species listed below are widespread in their particular habitat throughout the Canadian Rockies. The single location listed below for each species is simply the one that will give you the best chance of seeing that species.

Beaver: Athabasca River wetlands, Jasper National Park

Bighorn sheep: Mt. Norquay Road, Banff National Park

Bison: Buffalo Paddock, Waterton Lakes National Park

Black bear: Icefields Parkway, Banff and Jasper National Parks

Caribou: Bald Hills, Jasper National Park

Cougar: forested valleys around Canmore

Coyote: along Highway 16, east of Jasper townsite, Jasper National Park

Elk: around the outskirts of Banff and Jasper townsites

Grizzly bear (stuffed): Lake Louise Visitor Centre, Banff National Park

Human beings: Banff Avenue, Banff National Park

Lynx: Vermilion Pass, Kootenay National Park

Marmot: around Stanley Glacier, Kootenay National Park

Moose: Peter Lougheed Provincial Park, Kananaskis Country

Mountain goat: Disaster Point, Jasper National Park

Mule deer: Waterton townsite, Waterton Lakes National Park

Porcupine: Yoho Valley Road, Yoho National Park

White-tailed deer: Sheep River Valley, Kananaskis Country

Wolf: Bow Valley (winter only), Banff National Park

Canadian Rockies. It has a tan body with a dark-brown neck, dark-brown legs, and a white rump. This second-largest member of the deer family weighs 250–450 kg and stands 1.5 meters at the shoulder. Beginning each spring, stags grow an impressive set of antlers, covered in what is known as "velvet." The velvet contains nutrients that stimulate antler growth. By fall, the antlers have reached their full size and the velvet is shed. Rutting season takes place between August and October; listen for the shrill bugles of the stags serenading the females. During the rut, randy males will challenge anything with their antlers and can be dangerous. The stags shed their antlers each spring, but don't relax too much—also in spring, females protecting their young can be equally dangerous. Large herds of elk live in around the towns of Banff and Jasper, often nonchalantly wandering along streets and feeding on tasty plants in residential gardens, and always safe from predators.

Moose

The giant of the deer family is the moose, an awkward-looking mammal that appears to have been designed by a cartoonist. It has the largest antlers of any animal in the world, stands up to 1.8 meters at the shoulder, and weighs up to 500 kg. Its body is dark brown, and it has a prominent nose, long spindly legs, small eyes, big ears, and an odd flap of skin called a "bell" dangling beneath its chin. Apart from all that, it's good-looking. Each spring the bull begins to grow palm-shaped antlers that by August will be fully grown. Moose are solitary animals preferring marshy areas and weedy lakes, but they are known to wander to higher elevations searching out open spaces in summer. They forage in and around ponds on willows, aspen, birch, grasses, and all aquatic vegetation. They are not particularly common in the Canadian Rockies, numbering around 350. Although they may appear docile, moose will attack humans if they feel threatened.

Caribou

Small populations of caribou inhabit the backcountry of Banff and Jasper National Parks. Native people named the animal "caribou" ("hoof scraper") for the way in which they feed in winter, scraping away snow with their hooves. Caribou are smaller than elk and have a dark-brown coat with creamy patches on the neck and rump. Both sexes grow antlers—those of the females are shorter and have fewer points. On average males weigh 180 kg, females 115 kg. Like the elk, they breed in fall, with the males gathering a harem.

BEARS

The two species of bears present in the mountains—black bears and grizzlies—can be differentiated by size and shape. Grizzlies are larger than black bears and have a flatter, dish-shaped face and a distinctive hump of muscle behind their neck. Color is not a reliable way to tell them apart. Black bears are not always black. They can be brown or cinnamon, causing them to be confused with the brown-colored grizzly.

Black Bears

If you spot a bear feeding beside the road, chances are it's a black bear. These mammals are widespread throughout all forested areas of the Canadian Rockies, and are good swimmers and climbers. Their weight varies considerably, but males average 150 kg and females 100 kg. Their diet is omnivorous, consisting primarily of grasses and berries but supplemented by small mammals. They are not true hibernators, but in winter they can sleep for up to a month at a time before changing position. During this time, their heartbeat drops to 10 beats per minute, body temperature drops, and they lose up 30 percent of their body weight. Females reach reproductive maturity after five years; cubs, usually two, are born in late winter, while the mother is still asleep.

Grizzly Bears

Grizzlies, second largest of eight recognized species of bears (only polar bears are larger), have disappeared from most of North America but are widespread throughout the Canadian Rockies, numbering around 300 in the region. Grizzlies are only occasionally seen by casual observers; most sightings occur in alpine and subalpine zones, although sightings at lower elevations are not unusual, especially when snow falls early or late. The bears' color ranges from light brown to almost black, with dark tan being

the most common. On average, males weigh 200–350 kg. The bears eat small and medium-sized mammals, and berries in fall. Like black bears, they sleep through most of the winter. When they emerge in early spring, the bears scavenge carcasses of animals that succumbed to the winter, until the new spring vegetation becomes sufficiently plentiful. Females first give birth at four years old, and then every three years, with cubs remaining with their mother for up to 2–3 years.

WILD DOGS AND CATS

Coyotes

The coyote is often mistaken for a wolf when in fact it is much smaller, weighing up to only 15 kg. It has a pointed nose and long bushy tail. Its coloring is a mottled mix of brown and gray, with lighter-colored legs and belly. The coyote is a skillful and crafty hunter, preying mainly on rodents. Coyotes have the remarkable ability to hear the movement of small mammals under the snow, allowing them to hunt these animals without actually seeing them. They are often seen patrolling the edges of highways and crossing open meadows in low-lying valleys.

Wolves

Wolves that inhabit the Canadian Rockies are larger than coyotes, and larger than the wolves of eastern Canada. They weigh up to 60 kg, stand up to a meter high at the shoulder, and resemble large huskies or German shepherds. Their color ranges from snow-white to brown or black; those in the Canadian Rockies are, most often, shades of gray. They usually hunt in packs of up to eight members, traveling, hunting, and resting together, and adhering to a hierarchical social order. As individuals, also, they are complex and intriguing, capable of expressing happiness, humor, and loneliness.

Once the target of a relentless campaign to exterminate the species, the wolf has made an incredible comeback in the Canadian Rockies; today around 120 wolves roam the region.

Cougars

Rarely encountered by casual hikers, cougars (also known as mountain lions, pumas, or catamounts) measure up to 1.5 meters long. The average male weighs 75 kg and the female 40–55 kg. Cougars are versatile hunters whose acute vision takes in a peripheral span in excess of 200 degrees. They typically kill a large mammal such as an elk or deer every 12–14 days, eating part of it and caching the rest. Their diet also includes chipmunks, ground squirrels, snowshoe hares, and occasionally porcupines. Their athletic prowess puts Olympians to shame. They can spring forward more than eight meters from a standstill, leap four meters into the air, and safely jump from a height of 20 meters.

The cougar is a solitary animal with distinct territorial boundaries. This limits its population density, which in turn means that its overall numbers are low. They are most common in the foothills along the eastern slopes of the Canadian Rockies.

Lynx

The elusive lynx is identifiable by its pointy black ear tufts and an oversized "tabby cat" appearance. The animal has broad, padded paws that distribute its weight, allowing it to "float" on the surface of snow. It weighs up to 10 kg, but appears much larger because of its coat of long, thick fur. The lynx, uncommon but widespread throughout the region, is a solitary creature that prefers the cover of subalpine forests, feeding mostly at night on snowshoe hares and other small mammals.

OTHER LARGE MAMMALS

Mountain Goats

The remarkable rock-climbing ability of these nimble-footed creatures allows them to live on rocky ledges or near-vertical slopes, safe from predators. They also frequent the alpine meadows and open forests of the Canadian Rockies, where they congregate around natural licks of salt. The goats stand one meter at the shoulder and weigh 65–130 kg. Both sexes possess a peculiar beard, or rather, goatee. Both sexes have horns. It is possible to determine the sex by the shape of the horns; those of the female grow straight up before curling slightly backward, while those of the male curl back in a single arch. The goats shed their thick coats each summer, making them look ragged. But by fall they've regrown a fine, new white woolen coat.

Bighorn Sheep

Bighorn sheep are some of the most distinctive mammals of the Canadian Rockies. Easily recognized by their impressive horns, they are often seen grazing on grassy mountain slopes or at salt licks beside the road. The color of their coat varies with the season; in summer it's a brownish gray with a cream-colored belly and rump, turning lighter in winter. Fully grown males can weigh up to 120 kg, while females generally weigh around 80 kg. Both sexes possess horns, rather

Bighorn sheep are easily recognized by their long, curled horns

than antlers like members of the deer family. Unlike antlers, horns are not shed each year and can grow to astounding sizes. The horns of rams are larger than those of ewes and curve up to 360 degrees. The spiraled horns of an older ram can measure 115 centimeters and weigh as much as 15 kg. During the fall mating season, a hierarchy is established among the rams for the right to breed ewes. As the males face off against each other to establish dominance, their horns act as both a weapon and a buffer against the head butting of other rams. The skull structure of the bighorn, rams in particular, has become adapted to these head-butting clashes, keeping the animals from being knocked unconscious.

Bighorn sheep are particularly tolerant of humans and often approach parked vehicles; although they are not especially dangerous, as with all mammals, you should not approach or feed them.

Bison
Before the arrival of Europeans, millions of bison roamed the North American plains, with some entering the valleys of the Canadian Rockies to escape harsh winters. A number of factors contributed to their decline, including the combined presence of explorers, settlers, and natives. By the 1800s they were wiped out, and since then a couple of attempts at reintroduction have taken place, including the release of a small herd in Jasper National Park. (No one has sighted them for many years). Today, your best chance of viewing these shaggy beasts is in Waterton Lakes National Park, where a small herd is contained in the "buffalo paddock."

SMALL MAMMALS

Beavers
One of the animal kingdom's most industrious mammals is the beaver. Growing to a length of 50 centimeters and tipping the scales at around 20 kg, it has a flat, rudderlike tail and webbed back feet that enable it to swim at speeds up to 10 kph. The exploration of western Canada can be directly attributed to the beaver, whose pelt was in high demand in fashion-conscious Europe in the early 1800s. The beaver was never

---

WILDLIFE AND YOU

An abundance of wildlife is one of the biggest drawing cards of the Canadian Rockies. To help preserve this precious resource, obey fishing and hunting regulations and use common sense.

Do not feed the animals. Many animals may seem tame, but feeding them endangers yourself, the animal, and other visitors, as animals become aggressive when looking for handouts.

Store food safely. When camping, keep food in your vehicle or out of reach of animals. Just leaving it in a cooler isn't good enough.

Keep your distance. Although it's tempting to get close to animals for a better look or photograph, it disturbs the animal and, in many cases, can be dangerous.

Drive carefully. The most common cause of premature death for larger mammals is being hit by cars.

---

entirely wiped out from the mountains, and today the animals can be found in almost any forested valley with flowing water. Beavers build their dam walls and lodges of twigs, branches, sticks of felled trees, and mud. They eat the bark and smaller twigs of deciduous plants and store branches underwater, near the lodge, as a winter food supply.

Squirrels
Several species of squirrel are common in the Canadian Rockies. The **golden-mantled ground squirrel,** found in rocky outcrops of subalpine and alpine regions, has black stripes along its sides and looks like an oversized chipmunk. Most common is the **Columbian ground squirrel,** which lives in burrows, often in open grassland. It is recognizable by its reddish legs, face, and underside, and a flecked, grayish back. The bushy-tailed **red squirrel,** bold chatterbox of the forest, leaves telltale shelled cones at the base of conifers. Another member of the species, the nocturnal **northern flying fox,** glides through the montane forests of mountain valleys but is rarely seen.

Hoary Marmots
High in the mountains, above the tree line, hoary marmots are often seen sunning themselves on

boulders in rocky areas or meadows. They are stocky creatures, weighing 4–9 kg. When danger approaches, these large rodents emit a shrill whistle to warn their colony. Marmots are only active for a few months each summer, spending up to nine months a year in hibernation.

Porcupines

This small, squat animal is easily recognized by its thick coat of quills. It eats roots and leaves, but is also known as being destructive around wooden buildings and vehicle tires. Porcupines are common and widespread throughout all forested areas, but they're hard to spy since they feed most often at night.

Other Rodents

Widespread throughout western Canada, **muskrats** make their mountain home in the waterways and wetlands of all low-lying valleys. They are agile swimmers, able to stay submerged for up to 12 minutes. They grow to a length of 35 cm, but the best form of identification is the tail, which is black, flat, and scaly. Closely related to muskrats are **voles,** often mistaken for mice. They inhabit grassed areas of most valley floors.

Shrews

A member of the insectivore family, the **furry shrew** has a sharp-pointed snout and is closely related to the mole. It must eat almost constantly as it is susceptible to starvation within only a few hours of its last meal. Another variety present throughout the region, the **pygmy shrew,** is the world's smallest mammal; it weighs just four grams.

Pikas

Pikas, like rabbits, are lagomorphs, which are distinguished from rodents by a double set of incisors in the upper jaw. The small, grayish-colored pika is a neighbor to the marmot, living among the rubble and boulders of scree slopes above timberline.

Weasels

The weasel family, comprising 70 species worldwide, is large and diverse, but in general, all members have long slim bodies and short legs, and all are carnivorous and voracious eaters,

consuming up to one-third of their body weight each day. Many species can be found in the Canadian Rockies, including the **wolverine,** largest of the weasels worldwide, weighing up to 20 kilograms. Known to natives as *carcajou,* meaning "evil one," the wolverine is extremely powerful, cunning, and cautious. This solitary creature inhabits forests of the subalpine and lower alpine regions, feeding on any available meat, from small rodents to the carcasses of larger mammals. Rarely sighted by humans, the wolverine is a true symbol of the wilderness. The **fisher** has the same habitat as the wolverine, but is much smaller, reaching just five kg in weight and growing to 60 cm long. This nocturnal hunter preys on small birds and rodents, but reports of fishers bringing down small deer have been made. Smaller still is the **marten,** which lives most of its life in the trees of the subalpine forest, preying on birds, squirrels, mice, and voles. Weighing just one kg is the **mink,** once highly prized for its fur. At home in or out of water, it feeds on muskrats, mice, voles, and fish. Mink numbers in the Canadian Rockies are low. As well as being home to the largest member of weasel family, the region also holds the smallest—the **least weasel** (the world's smallest carnivore), which grows to a length of just 20 cm and weighs a maximum of 60 grams. Chiefly nocturnal, it feeds mostly on mice and lives throughout open wooded areas, but it not particularly common.

REPTILES AND AMPHIBIANS

Two species of snake, the **wandering garter snake** and the **red-sided garter snake** (North America's northernmost reptile), are found at lower elevations in the Canadian Rockies. **Frogs** are also present; biologists have noted two different species, which are also present at the lower elevations in the Canadian Rockies.

FISH

The lakes and rivers of the Canadian Rockies hold a variety of fish, most of which belong to the trout and salmon family and are classed as "coldwater" species—that is, they inhabit waters where the temperature ranges 4–18 °C. The predominant species, the rainbow trout, is not native to the mountains; it was introduced from more northern Canadian watersheds as a sport fish and is now common throughout lower elevation lakes and rivers. It has an olive-green back and a red strip running along the center of its body. Only three species of trout are native to the mountains. One of these, the **bull trout,** is Alberta's provincial fish. Through the mid-1900s, this truly "native" Canadian trout was perceived as a predator of more favored introduced species, and mostly removed. Today, what was once the most widespread trout east of the Continental Divide, is confined to the headwaters of Canadian Rockies' river systems, and is classed as a threatened species. While the bull trout has adapted to the harsh conditions of its reduced habitat, its continuing struggle for survival can be attributed to many factors, including a scarcity of food and a slow reproductive cycle. Bull trout grow to 70 centimeters in length and weigh up to 10 kilograms. The **lake trout,** which grows to 20 kg, is native to large, deep lakes throughout the mountains. Identified by a slivery-gray body and irregular while splotches along its back, this species grow slowly, taking up to eight years to reach maturity and living up to 25 years. Named for a bright red dash of color that from below the mouth almost to the gills, the **cutthroat trout** is native to southern Alberta's mountain streams, but has been introduced to high elevation lakes and streams on both sides of the Canadian Rockies. **Brown trout,** introduced from Europe in 1924, are found in the Bow and Red Deer Rivers and some slower streams in the eastern zones of Kananaskis Country. Its body is a golden-brown color, and it is the only trout with both black and red spots. The **brook trout** is a colorful fish identified by a dark-green back with pale-colored splotches and purple-sheened sides. It is native to eastern Canada, but was introduced to the mountains as early as 1903 and is now widespread throughout lakes and streams on the Alberta-side of the Continental Divide. **Golden trout** were introduced to a few mountain lakes around 1960 as a sport fish. They are a smallish fish, similar in color to rainbow trout. The **mountain whitefish** (commonly, but incorrectly, called arctic grayling by Albertan anglers) is light gray-colored fish that is native to most lower elevation lakes and rivers of the Canadian Rockies. Also inhabiting the region's waters are **arctic grayling** and **Dolly Varden** (named for a colorful character in a Charles Dickens story).

BIRDS

Bird-watching is popular in the mountains, thanks to the approximately 300 resident bird species and the millions of migratory birds that pass through each year. All it takes is a pair of binoculars, a good book detailing species, and patience. Dense forests hide many species, making them seem less common than they actually are. The Columbia River wetland, between Radium Hot Springs and Golden, lies on the Pacific Flyway and is a major bird-watching area.

Raptors

A wide variety of raptors are present in the Canadian Rockies—some call the mountains home year-round, while others pass through during annual spring and fall migrations. **Golden eagles** migrate across the Canadian Rockies, heading north in spring to Alaska and crossing back over in fall enroute to Midwest wintering grounds. Golden eagles—over 10,000 of them annually—soar high above the mountains on thermal drafts. **Bald eagles** also soar over the Canadian Rockies during annual

Clark's Nutcracker

migrations; mature birds can be distinguished from below by their white head and tail (immature birds resemble the dark brown-colored golden eagle). **Ospreys** spend summers in the region, nesting high up in large dead trees, on telephone poles, or on rocky outcrops, but always overlooking water. They feed on fish, hovering up to 50 meters above water, watching for movement, then diving into the water, thrusting their legs forward and collecting prey in their talons.

Distinct from all species listed above are a group of raptors that hunt at night. Best known as owls, these birds are rarely seen due to their nocturnal habits but are widespread through forested areas of the mountains. Most common is the **great horned owl,** identified by its promi-

nent "horns," which are actually tufts of feathers. Also present is the **snowy owl** and in the north of the region, the largest of the owls, the **great gray owl,** which grows to a length of 75 centimeters.

Others
Bird-watchers will be enthralled by the diversity of eastern and western bird species in the Canadian Rockies. Widespread are **magpies, sparrows, starlings, grouse, ravens,** and **crows. Blackbirds, finches, thrushes, hummingbirds, woodpeckers, flycatchers,** and 28 species of **warblers** are common in forested areas. The popular campground visitor, the cheeky **gray jay,** is similar in appearance to that of the curious **Clark's nutcracker.**

HISTORY

THE EARLIEST INHABITANTS

Human habitation of the Canadian Rockies began at the end of the last Ice Age, around 11,000 years ago. The descendants of the people who migrated from northeast Asia across a land bridge spanning the Bering Strait had fanned out across North America, and as the receding ice cap began to uncover the land north of the 49th parallel, groups of people moved northward with it, in pursuit of large mammals at the edge of the melting ice mass. The mountain landscape then was far different than it is today. Forests were nonexistent; the retreating ice had scoured the land and most of the lower valleys were carpeted in tundra.

The Kootenay
The Kootenay (other common spellings include Kootenai, Kootenae, and Kutenai) were the first human beings to enter the Canadian Rockies. Once hunters of buffalo on the great American plains, they were pushed westward by fierce enemies. As the ice cap melted, they moved north, up the western edge of the Rocky Mountains. This migration was by no means fast—perhaps only 30 or 40 km in each generation—but around 10,000 years ago the first Kootenay arrived in the Columbia River Valley. They were hunters and

gatherers, wintering along the Columbia and Kootenay River valleys, then moving to higher elevations during the warmer months. Over time they developed new skills, learning to fish the salmon-rich rivers using spears, nets, and simple fish weirs. The Kootenay were a serious people with few enemies. They mixed freely with the Shuswap and treated the earliest explorers, such as David Thompson, with respect. They regularly traveled east over the Rockies to hunt—to the wildlife-rich Kootenay Plains or further south to the Great Plains in search of bison. But as the fearsome Blackfoot extended their territory westward to the foothills of present-day Alberta, the Kootenay made fewer trips onto the plains. By the early 1700s, they had been driven permanently back to the west side of the Continental Divide.

The Shuswap
The Shuswap make up only a small chapter in the human history of the Canadian Rockies, although they traveled into the mountains on and off for many thousands of years. They were a tribe of Salish people, who, as the Kootenay did further east, moved north then east with the receding ice cap. By the time the Kootenay had moved into the Kootenay River Valley, the Salish had fanned out across most of southwestern and interior British Columbia, following the

salmon upstream as the glacial ice receded. Those who settled along the upper reaches of the Columbia River became known as the Shuswap. They spent summers in the mountains hunting caribou and sheep, put their fishing skills to the test each fall, then wintered in pit houses along the Columbia River Valley. The descendents of these people live on the Kinbasket Shuswap Reserve, just south of Radium Hot Springs.

The Stoney

The movement of humans into the mountains from the east was much more recent. Around 1650, the mighty Sioux nation began splintering, with many thousands moving north into present-day Canada. Though these immigrants called themselves Nakoda, meaning "people," other tribes called them "Assiniboine," meaning the "people who cook with stones"—their traditional cooking method was to heat stones in a fire, place the hot stones in a rawhide or birchbark basket with water, and cook meat and vegetables in the hot water. The white man translated "Assiniboine" as "Stone People," or "Stoney" for short.

Slowly, generation after generation, smaller groups of the Stoney moved westward along the Saskatchewan River system, allying themselves with the Cree but keeping their own identity. They pushed through the Blackfoot territory of the plains and reached the Rockies' foothills

around 200 years ago. There they split into bands, moving north and south along the foothills and penetrating the wide valleys where hunting was productive. They lived in small family-like groups and developed a lifestyle very different from that of the Plains Indians, diversifying their skills and becoming less dependent on buffalo. Moving with the seasons, they gathered berries in fall and became excellent hunters of mountain animals. They traveled over the mountains to trade with the Shuswap, but rarely ventured onto the plains, home of the warlike Peigan, Blackfoot, and Blood bands of the Blackfoot Confederacy. The Stoney were a steadfast yet friendly people. Alexander Henry the Younger reported in 1811 that the Stoney, "although the most arrant horse thieves in the world,. . . are at the same time the most hospitable to strangers who arrive in their camps."

As the great buffalo herds were decimated, the Stoney were impacted less than the Plains Indians. But the effect of white man's intrusion on their lifestyle was still apparent. The missionaries of the day found their teachings had more effect on the mountain people than on those of the plains, so they intensified their efforts on the Stoney. Reverend John McDougall gained their trust and in 1873 built a small mission church by the Bow River at Morleyville. When the Stoney were presented with Treaty 7 in 1877, they chose to locate their reserve around the Morleyville church. Abandoning their nomadic

a Stoney family, photographed by Mary Schäffer in 1907

lifestyle they quickly became adept at farming; unlike the Plains Indians, who relied for their survival on government rations, the Stoney were almost self-sufficient on the reserve.

Banff Indian Days
In 1889, the staff at the newly opened Banff Springs Hotel asked the Stoneys from the Morleyville reserve to come to the hotel and entertain guests. Around 200 tribe members arrived in Banff, setting up their tepees where the golf course now lies, showing off their horseback-riding skills, dancing, putting on a colorful parade, and inviting hotel guests to inspect their camp. The gathering—called Banff Indian Days—was such a success it became an annual event, attracting the Kootenay from across the mountains, the Sarcee from Calgary, and many thousands of visitors who were able to view customs and traditions of days gone by. As the event got bigger, it moved to a site at the base of Cascade Mountain, with much of the action revolving around a rodeo. But as the years rolled by, times changed. Visitors to the mountains were on tighter schedules than in years past, and park politics and money issues created irremediable problems for the long-running event. As a result, Banff Indian Days was held for the last time in 1978.

EUROPEAN EXPLORATION AND SETTLEMENT

In 1670, the British government granted the Hudson's Bay Company the right to govern Rupert's Land, roughly defined by all the land that drained into Hudson Bay. A vast area of western Canada—including present-day Manitoba, Saskatchewan, Alberta, Northwest Territories, and Nunavut—fell under that definition. The land was rich in fur-bearing mammals, which both the British and the French sought to exploit for profit. The Hudson's Bay Company first built forts around Hudson Bay and encouraged Indians to bring furs to the posts. But soon, French fur traders based in Montreal began traveling west to secure furs, forcing their British rivals to do the same. On one such trip, Anthony Henday became the first white man to view the Canadian Rockies when, on September 11, 1754, he climbed a ridge above the Red Deer River near present-day Innisfail. Henday returned to the east the following spring, bringing canoes loaded with furs and providing reports of snowcapped peaks.

In 1792, Peter Fidler became the first in a long succession of Europeans to actually enter the mountains. The following year Alexander Mackenzie became the first man to cross the continent, traveling the Peace and Fraser River watersheds to reach the Pacific Ocean. Mackenzie's traverse was long and difficult, so subsequent explorers continued to seek an easier

DAVID THOMPSON

One of Canada's greatest explorers, David Thompson was a quiet, courageous, and energetic man who drafted the first comprehensive and accurate map of western Canada. He arrived in Canada from England as a 14-year-old apprentice clerk for the Hudson's Bay Company. With an inquisitive nature and a talent for wilderness navigation, he quickly acquired the skills of surveying and mapmaking. Natives called him Koo-koo-sint, which translates as "the man who looks at stars."

Between 1786 and 1812, Thompson led four major expeditions into western Canada—the first for the Hudson's Bay Company and the last three for its rival, the North West Company. The most important one was the last, during which he traveled up the Athabasca River through what is now Jasper National Park and crossed the Continental Divide at Howse Pass. After descending into the Columbia River Valley, he established Kootenae House on Lake Windermere, using this outpost for a five-year odyssey of exploration of the entire Columbia River system. In the process, he discovered the Athabasca Pass, which for the next 50 years was the main route across the Canadian Rockies to the Pacific Ocean.

In 1813, Thompson began work on a master map covering the entire territory controlled by the North West Company. The map was four meters long and two meters wide, detailing over 1.5 million square miles. On completion it was hung out of public view in the council hall of a company fort in the east. Years later, after his death in 1857, the map was "discovered" and Thompson became recognized as one of the world's greatest land geographers.

route farther south. In 1807, David Thompson set out from Rocky Mountain House, traveling up the North Saskatchewan River to Howse Pass, where he descended to the Columbia River. He established a small trading post near Windermere Lake, but warring Peigan and Kootenay natives forced him to search out an alternate pass to the north. In 1811, he discovered Athabasca Pass, which was used as the main route west for the next 50 years.

In 1857, with the fur trade in decline, the British government sent Capt. John Palliser to investigate the agricultural potential of western Rupert's Land. During his three-year journey he explored many of the watersheds leading into the mountains, including one trip up the Bow River and over Vermilion Pass into the area now encompassed by Kootenay and Yoho National Parks.

The Dominion of Canada

By the 1860s, some of the eastern provinces were tiring of British rule, and a movement was abuzz to push for Canadian independence. The British government, wary of losing Canada as it had lost the U.S., passed legislation establishing the Dominion of Canada. At that time, the North-West Territories, as Rupert's Land had become known, was a foreign land to those in eastern Canada; life out west was primitive with no laws, and no outpost held more than a couple of dozen residents. But in an effort to solidify the Dominion, the government bought the North-West Territories back from the Hudson's Bay Company in 1867. In 1871, British Columbia agreed to join the Dominion as well, but only on the condition that the federal government build a railway to link the fledgling province with the rest of the country.

The Coming of the Railway

The idea of a rail line across the continent, replacing canoe and cart routes, was met with scorn by those in the east, who saw it as unnecessary and uneconomical. But the line pushed westward, reaching Winnipeg in 1879 and what was then Fort Calgary in 1883.

Many routes across the Continental Divide were considered by the Canadian Pacific Railway, but Kicking Horse Pass, surveyed by Maj. A. B. Rogers in 1881, got the final nod. The line

and its construction camps pushed into the mountains, reaching Siding 29 (better known today as Banff) early in the fall of 1883; Laggan (Lake Louise) a couple of months later; then crossing the divide and reaching the Field construction camp in the summer of 1884. The following year, on November 7, 1885, the final spike was laid, opening up the lanes of commerce between British Columbia and the rest of the Canada. In 1914, rival company Grand Trunk Pacific Railway completed a second rail line across the Rockies, at Yellowhead Pass to the north.

PARKS AND TOURISM

The Parks of Today Take Shape

In 1883, three Canadian Pacific Railway (C.P.R.) workers stumbled upon hot springs at the base of Sulphur Mountain, near where the town of Banff now lies. This was the height of the Victorian era, when the great spa resorts of Europe were attracting hordes of wealthy clients. With the thought of developing a similar style resort, the government designated a 26-square-km reserve around the hot springs, surveyed a townsite, and encouraged the Canadian Pacific Railway to build a world-class hotel there. In 1887, Rocky Mountains Park was officially created, setting aside 673 square kilometers as a ". . . public park and pleasure ground for the benefit, advantage, and enjoyment of the people of Canada." The park was later renamed Banff. It was Canada's first national park and only the third national park in the world.

Across the Continental Divide, the railway passed by a small reserve that had been created around the base of Mt. Stephen. This was the core of what would become Yoho National Park, officially dedicated in 1901. In anticipation of a flood of visitors to the mountains along the more northerly Grand Trunk Pacific Railway, Jasper National Park was established in 1907. And Kootenay National Park was created to protect an eight-km-wide strip of land either side of the Banff–Windermere Road, which was completed in 1922. Of the five national parks in the Canadian Rockies, Waterton Lakes National Park was the only one created purely for its aesthetic value. It was established after tireless public campaigning by local resident "Kootenai" Brown, who also became the park's first superintendent.

The First Tourists Arrive

In the era the parks were created, the Canadian Rockies region was a vast wilderness accessible only by rail. The parks and the landscape they encompassed were seen as economic resources to be exploited rather than as national treasures to be preserved. Logging, hunting, and mining were permitted inside park boundaries; all but Kootenay National Park had mines operating within them for many years (the last mine, in Yoho National Park, closed in 1952). To help finance the rail line, the C.P.R. began encouraging visitors to the mountains by building grand mountain resorts: Mt. Stephen House in 1886, the Banff Springs Hotel in 1888, a lodge at Lake Louise in 1890; and Emerald Lake Lodge in 1902. Knowledgeable locals, some of whom had been used as guides and outfitters during railway construction, offered their services to the tourists the railway brought. Tom Wilson, Bill Peyto, Jim and Bill Brewster, the Otto Brothers, and Donald "Curly" Phillips are synonymous with this era, and their names grace everything from pubs to mountain peaks.

Early Mountaineering

Recreational mountaineering has been popular in the Canadian Rockies for over 100 years. Re-ports of early climbs on peaks around Lake Louise spread, and by the late 1880s the area had drawn the attention of both European and American alpinists. Many climbers were inexperienced and ill-equipped, but first ascents were nevertheless made on peaks that today are still considered difficult. In 1893, Walter Wilcox and Samuel Allen, two Yale schoolmates, spent the summer climbing in the Lake Louise area, making two unsuccessful attempts to reach the north peak of Mt. Victoria. The following summer they made first ascents of Mt. Temple and Mt. Aberdeen, extraordinary achievements considering their lack of experience and proper equipment. Accidents were sure to happen, and they did. During the summer of 1896, P. S. Abbot slipped and plunged to his death attempting to climb Mt. Lefroy. In doing so, he became North America's first mountaineering fatality. Following this incident, Swiss mountain guides were employed by the C.P.R. to satisfy the climbing needs of wealthy patrons of the railway and make the sport safer. During the period of their employment, successful climbs were made of Mt. Victoria, Mt. Lefroy, and Mt. Balfour.

In 1906, Arthur O. Wheeler organized the Alpine Club of Canada, which was instrumental in the construction of many trails and backcountry huts still in use today. In 1913, Swiss guide Conrad Kain led a group of the club's members on the successful first ascent of Mt. Robson, the highest peak in the Canadian Rockies. By 1915,

WHYTE MUSEUM OF THE CANADIAN ROCKIES

Feeding bears was one of the early attractions of a visit to the Canadian Rockies.

most of the other major peaks in the range had been climbed as well.

Changing Times

One major change that occurred at the park early on was the shift from railroad-based to automobile-based tourism. Until 1913, motorized vehicles were banned from the mountain parks, allowing the Canadian Pacific Railway a monopoly on tourists. Wealthy visitors to the mountains came in on the train and generally stayed in the C.P.R.'s own hotels for weeks on end and often for the entire summer. The burgeoning popularity of the automobile changed all this; the motor-vehicle ban was lifted and road building went ahead full steam. Many of the trails that had been built for horseback travel were widened to accommodate autos, and new roads were built: from Banff to Lake Louise in 1920, to Radium Hot Springs in 1923, and to Golden in 1930. The Icefields Parkway was finally completed in 1940. Visitor numbers increased, and facilities expanded to keep pace. Dozens of bungalow camps were built specially for those arriving by automobile. Many were built by the C.P.R., far from their rail line, including in Kootenay National Park and at Radium Hot Springs. The company also built lodges deep in the backcountry, including at Mt. Assiniboine and Lake O'Hara.

Another major change that has occurred over the last 90 years is in the way the complex human-wildlife relationship in the parks has been managed. Should the relationship be managed to provide the visiting public the best viewing experience, or rather to provide the wildlife the most wild and natural environment possible? Today the trend favors the wildlife, but early in the history of the Canadian Rockies' parks, the operating strategy clearly favored the visitor. Sixty years ago, you could view a polar bear on display behind the Banff Park Museum. And only 20 years ago, hotels were taking guests to local dumps to watch bears feeding on garbage.

The Victorian concept of wildlife was that it was either good or evil. Although an early park directive instructed superintendents to leave nature alone, it also told them to ". . . endeavor to exterminate all those animals which prey upon others." A dusty century-old philosophy, perhaps. But as recently as the 1960s, a predator-control program led to the slaughter of nearly every wolf in the park.

Amazingly enough, throughout these unsavory sagas, the Canadian Rockies have remained a prime area for wildlife viewing and will hopefully continue to be so for a long time to come.

Bow Lake, Banff National Park

CANADIAN ROCKIES BASICS

RECREATION

The Canadian Rockies are a four-season playground, their great outdoors offering something for everyone. Hiking grabs first place in the popularity stakes; many thousands of km of trails crisscross the entire region. But you can also enjoy skiing, scuba diving, and everything in between. An overview of available outdoor-recreation opportunities is provided below, and you'll find more detail in the individual travel chapters.

National Park Passes

Unless you're passing directly through, passes are required for entry into all five national parks covered in this book. Monies raised from these passes goes directly to Parks Canada for park maintenance and improvements.

A National Parks Day Pass is adult $5, senior $4, child $2 to a maximum of $10 per vehicle. It is interchangeable between parks and is valid until 4 P.M. the day following its purchase. An annual Great Western Pass, good for entry into all 11 of western Canada's national parks, is adult $35, senior $27 to a maximum of $70 per vehicle ($53 for two or more seniors). This pass comes with a Great Western Passbook, which includes a wide variety of discount coupons. Both types of pass can be purchased at park gates (at the entrance to Banff, Kootenay, and Waterton Lakes National Parks), at the tollbooths at either end of the Icefields Parkway, at all park information centers, and at campground fee stations. Day Passes can also be bought at the 24-hour Automated Pass Machines at strategic spots through the mountains. Annual passes can also be bought in advance by calling 800/748-7275 or online at the Parks Canada website, www.parkscanada.gc.ca.

HIKING

The Canadian Rockies are a hiker's paradise. Hiking is free, and the mountains offer some of

SAFE HIKING

When venturing out on the trails of the Canadian Rockies, using a little common sense will help keep you from getting into trouble. First off, don't underestimate the forces of nature—weather can change dramatically anywhere in the mountains at any time. That clear sunny sky that looked so inviting during breakfast can turn into a driving snowstorm within hours. Go prepared for all climatic conditions (always carry food, a sweater, and matches), and take plenty of water—open slopes can get very hot on sunny days.

All national park visitor centers as well as those in Kananaskis Country post daily trail reports and weather forecasts. Check trail conditions before heading out; lingering snow, wildlife closures, or a washed-out trail could ruin your best-laid plans. Also, hikers must register at park information centers for all overnight hikes in national parks.

Topographic maps aren't required for the hikes detailed in this book, but they provide an interesting way to identify natural features. For extended hiking in the backcountry, they are vital. Several series of maps, in different scales, cover the Canadian Rockies. You can purchase them from park information centers, some bookstores, and specialty map shops in the gateway cities of Calgary, Edmonton, and Vancouver.

the world's most spectacular scenery. **Banff National Park** holds the greatest variety of trails. Here you can find anything from short interpretive trails with little elevation gain to strenuous slogs up high alpine passes. Trailheads for some of the best hikes are accessible on foot from the town of Banff. Those farther north begin at higher elevations, from which access to the tree line is less painful. The trails in **Jasper National Park** are oriented more toward the experienced backpacker, offering plentiful routes for long backcountry trips. **Waterton Lakes National Park** is small but has a complex trail system geared especially for the day hiker. Many of the hikes in **Yoho National Park** entail significant elevation gain, but reward your extra effort with spectacular mountain panoramas rivaling those of the more famous parks across the divide. Many less-visited parts of the mountains hold unexpected gems. Examples include Grassi Lakes, near Canmore; Ptarmigan Cirque, Kananaskis Country; Fish Lake, Top of the World Provincial Park; and Grande Mountain, near Grande Cache.

With exceptions made for the most popular overnight hikes, all trails detailed in this book are day hikes. Anyone of moderate fitness could complete them in the time allotted. Strong hikers will need less time, and if you stop for lunch it will take you a little longer. Remember, all distances and times are one-way—allow yourself time at the objective and time to return to the trailhead.

Scrambling

The Canadian Rockies hold many peaks that can be reached without ropes or climbing skills, provided you have a good level of fitness and, more importantly, common sense. Obviously, this type of activity has more inherent dangers than hiking, but these can be minimized by planning ahead. Check weather forecasts, take food, water, and warm clothing, and be aware of the terrain. Routes to the top of the most popular peaks are flagged with tape or marked with rock cairns showing the way, but you should always check with information centers or locals before attempting any ascent. The Bow Valley offers a good selection of well-traveled scrambles. These include Mt. Rundle, Cascade Mountain, and Chinaman's Peak.

Backpacking

Most hikers are just out for the day or a few hours. But staying overnight in the backcountry offers many rewards. Some effort is involved in a backcountry trip—you'll need a backpack, light-weight stove, and tent, among other things. But you'll be traveling through country inaccessible to the casual day hiker, well away from the crowds and far from any road. **Lake O'Hara,** Yoho National Park, is the trailhead for what is generally considered to be Canada's finest backcountry hiking area. The lake is easily accessible—a shuttle bus runs from the highway up an old fire road to this alpine gem. Like select other backcountry destinations, visitors to Lake O'Hara have the choice of camping or staying in a comfortable lodge. **Mt. Assiniboine Provincial Park** is another popular spot far from civilization. And like Lake O'Hara, there's a lodge for hikers not equipped to camp out. Banff and Jasper National Parks also have backcountry lodges. Another option for backcountry accommodations is offered by the **Alpine Club of Canada,** 403/678-3200, www.alpineclubofcanada.ca. The club maintains a series of huts, each generally a full-day hike from the nearest road, throughout the Canadian Rockies.

Heli-hiking

Heli-hiking is an easy way to appreciate high alpine areas without having to gain the elevation on foot. The day starts with a helicopter ride into the alpine, where short, guided hikes are offered and a picnic lunch is served. For details, contact **Alpine Helicopters,** Canmore, 403/678-4802, and **Canadian Mountain Holiday,** 403/762-7100 or 800/661-0252. Expect to pay from $280 for 30 minutes flight time, a guided hike, and a mountaintop lunch.

CLIMBING AND MOUNTAINEERING

The Canadian Rockies are a mecca for those experienced in climbing and mountaineering, but for those who aren't, instruction is available. **Canmore,** in the Bow Valley, is the self-proclaimed capital. Surrounded by towering peaks of limestone, routes to challenge all levels of ability can be found on the immediate outskirts of town and along narrow canyons that open to the valley. The distinctive south face of Yamnuska (easily recognized to the north of the TransCanada Highway as you enter the Bow Valley from the east) is easily the most popular climbing spot in the mountains, with dozens of routes up its sheer 350-meter-high walls. Two books are dedicated solely to its ascent. Experienced climbers should gather as much information as possible before attempting any unfamiliar routes; quiz locals, hang out at climbing stores, and contact park information centers.

Learning the Ropes

For the inexperienced, the Canadian Rockies are the perfect place to learn to climb. Climbers and mountaineers can't live on past accomplishments alone, so to finance their lifestyle some turn to teaching others the skills of their sport. Canmore is home to many qualified mountain guides who operate both in and out of Banff National Park. Basic climbing courses cost $50–80 per day, and instruction is available for all ability levels. The main guiding companies are **M & W Guides,** 403/678-2642, and **Yamnuska,** 403/678-4164, www.yamnuska.com.

ROAD CYCLING AND MOUNTAIN BIKING

The Canadian Rockies are perfect for both road biking and mountain biking. On-road cyclists will appreciate the wide shoulders on all main highways, while those on mountain bikes will enjoy the many designated trails. The most challenging and scenic on-road route is the 290-km **Icefields Parkway** between Lake Louise and Jasper (*Outside* magazine rates it as one of North America's 10 best). Most cyclists allow four to five days, but it's easy to spend a lot longer on the parkway. And with 11 campgrounds and five hostels along the way, you'll have plenty of accommodation options. An extension of the Icefields Parkway is the **Bow Valley Parkway,** the original route between Banff and Lake Louise, which can easily be cycled in one day.

Mountain biking is allowed on designated trails throughout the national parks. Park information centers hand out brochures detailing these trails and give them ratings. The **Canmore Nordic Centre** is home to 70 km of biking trails, some steep enough to hold international downhill competitions each summer. The *Canadian Rockies Bicycling Guide* covers 60 routes through the mountains; pick up a copy from local bookstores. Mountain bikes can be rented throughout the national parks and Kananaskis Country. Basic bikes rent for $5–8 per hour and $24–30 per day. Some shops rent front- and full-suspension bikes; expect to pay up to $15 per hour and $45 per day for these.

Backroads, 801 Cedar Street, Berkeley, CA 94710, USA, 800/462-2848, www.backroads. com, offers a wide variety of trips through the Canadian Rockies. These trips are designed to suit all levels of fitness and all budgets. An average of six hours is spent cycling each day, but there's also always the option of riding in the support van. There's also the option of camping each night (US$1000 for six days) or staying in grand mountain lodges (US$1800 for six days).

HORSEBACK RIDING

Horses were used for transportation in the mountains by the earliest explorers. Even after the completion of the railway, horses remained as the most practical way to get deep into the backcountry; crossing unbridged rivers and carrying large amounts of supplies was impossible on foot. The names of early outfitters—Tom Wilson, Jim and Bill Brewster, Bill Peyto, Jimmy Simpson, and Curly Phillips were the best known—crop up again and again through the mountains. Another legacy of their trade is that many of the main hiking trails began as horse trails.

The tradition of travel by horseback continues today in the Canadian Rockies; some companies have been operating since before the parks were established. Trail riding is available in Banff, Jasper, Waterton Lakes, and Yoho National Parks as well as in Kananaskis Country, Radium Hot Springs, and Grande Cache. Expect to pay around $25 for a one-hour ride (usually covering around three km), $35 for a two-hour ride, and $55–60 for a ride that includes a meal. If you're an experienced rider, consider heading out of the mountains 40 minutes east of Canmore to **Griffin Valley Ranch,** north of Hwy. 1A, 403/932-7433. This sprawling property is one of the few places in western Canada that allows unguided riding. Horse rentals are similarly priced to trail riding; the only additional cost is an annual "membership" (simply sign a waiver and pay a $40 fee). Trails lead through the valley and to high viewpoints where the panorama extends back to the Canadian Rockies.

Overnight pack trips consist of up to six hours of riding per day, with nights spent at a remote mountain lodge or a tent camp, usually in a scenic location where you can hike, fish, or ride further. Rates range $130–160 per person per day, which includes the riding, accommodations, and food. These trips are offered from the Bow Valley by **Brewster Mountain Pack Trains,** 403/762-5454 or 800/691-5085, www.brewsteradventures.com; along the Spray Valley by **Warner Guiding and Outfitting,** 403/762-4551 or 800/661-8352, www.horseback.com; and in Jasper National Park by **Skyline Trail Rides,** 780/852-4215 or 888/852-7787; or **Tonquin Valley Adventures,** 780/852-1188, www.tonquinadventures.com. The remote location of Willmore Wilderness Park makes it a popular destination for those on horseback. Contact the following outfitters for trips into the park: **Sherwood Guides and Outfitters,** 780/922-2266; **U Bar Enterprises,** 780/827-3641; and **Wild Rose Outfitting,** 780/693-2296.

Guest ranches, where accommodations and meals are included in nightly packages, include **Brewster's Kananaskis Guest Ranch,** east of Canmore, 403/673-3737 or 800/691-5085, www.brewsteradventures.com; **Boundary Ranch,** in Kananaskis Valley, 403/591-7171 or 877/591-7177; and **Black Cat Guest Ranch,** on the eastern outskirts of Jasper National Park, 780/865-3084 or 800/859-6840. Expect to pay $120–150 per person per day for accommodations, meals, and trail riding.

Riding through the Canadian Rockies on horseback is both a traditional and relaxing way to enjoy the mountain scenery.

ALBERTA TOURISM

GOLFING

The Canadian Rockies hold special appeal for golfers, as some of the world's most scenic courses lie in their midst. And all the best courses are public, lying in national parks or on provincial land, so anyone can play at any time. The scenery alone stands the courses of the Canadian Rockies apart from others, but there are many other reasons that the region is a golf destination in itself. Stanley Thompson, generally regarded as one of the preeminent golf course architects of the early 1900s (but as most of his work was in Canada, he is little known in the United States), designed three courses in the mountains, typified by holes aligned with distant mountains, elevated tee boxes, and fairways following natural contours of the land.

The jewel in the golfing crown is the **Stanley Thompson 18,** part of a 27-hole layout that graces the grounds of the Banff Springs Hotel and is rated one of the world's most scenic courses. **Jasper Park Lodge Golf Course,** a challenging par-73 course surrounded by spectacular mountain scenery, is of the same high standard. **Kananaskis Country Golf Course,** a 36-hole, Robert Trent Jones–designed course built in the 1980s at a cost of $1 million per hole, was the first of the resort-style courses built in the Canadian Rockies. At Canmore, **Silvertip Resort** set a new standard in golf course difficulty in Canada when it opened in 1998. It promotes itself as an "extreme" experience, and it is: 7,300 yards long, with elevation changes up to 40 meters on any one hole, and a slope rating of 153—the highest of any Canadian course. Across the valley from Silvertip, **Stewart Creek** opened in the summer of 2000, bringing the total number of courses at Canmore to three. With two more courses already cut and slated to open by 2005, Canmore is a good base for keen golfers. Other resort courses are at Radium Hot Springs (36 holes), Panorama Mountain Village, and Bragg Creek, while the towns of Canmore and Golden offer excellent 18-hole layouts, as does Waterton Lakes National Park.

The golfing season is fairly short, from mid-May to early October, depending on snow cover. (The golf courses at Radium Hot Springs and Golden are the first to open each spring.) But with the long days of summer, there's plenty of time for golfing. Greens fees range from $50 at Kananaskis Country (voted by *Golf Digest* as North America's best value course) to $125 for a round at Silvertip or at the Banff course. At the resort courses, greens fees usually include the use of practice facilities and a cart (complete with GPS at Silvertip). The sport's popularity in the mountains is such that tee times need to booked well in advance—up to a month for preferred times at some courses.

ON THE WATER

Canoeing

This traditional form of Canadian transportation is a great way to explore the waterways of the mountains that are otherwise inaccessible—places such as **Vermilion Lakes** in Banff National Park, where beavers, elk, and a great variety of birds can be appreciated from water level. Canoes can be rented on the **Bow River** in the town of Banff, **Lake Louise,** and **Moraine Lake** in Banff National Park; **Pyramid** and **Maligne Lakes** in Jasper National Park; the **Kananaskis Lakes** in Peter Lougheed Provincial Park; **Cameron Lake** in Waterton Lakes National Park; and **Emerald Lake** in Yoho National Park. Expect to pay around $8–15 per hour, and up to $30 per hour on Lake Louise. The more adventurous visitor can rent a canoe and paddle down the Bow River from Lake Louise to downtown Banff.

Whitewater Rafting

The rafting season is relatively short, but the thrill of careening down a river laced with rapids is not easily forgotten. Qualified guides operate on many rivers flowing out of the mountains. The **Kicking Horse River,** which flows through Yoho National Park to Golden, is run by companies based in Golden, Lake Louise, and Banff. This is the most popular river for rafting trips. The **Maligne** and **Sunwapta Rivers** in Jasper National Park are other rivers offering big thrills. For a more sedate river trip, try the **Bow River** in Banff National Park, or the **Athabasca River** in Jasper National Park. Both are run commercially. All companies offer half- and full-day trips, including transportation, wetsuits, and often light snacks.

Scuba Diving

Being landlocked, the Canadian Rockies are not renowned for scuba diving. A few interesting opportunities do exist, however, and rentals are available in Lethbridge, Calgary, and Edmonton. The old townsite of **Minnewanka Landing,** in Banff National Park, has been flooded, and although a relatively deep dive, the site is interesting. **Patricia Lake,** in Jasper National Park, conceals a sunken World War II barge, and due to the high altitude and clear water, visibility is exceptional. Another sunken boat lies at the bottom of Emerald Bay in Waterton Lakes National Park, not far from some wagons that fell through the ice many winters ago. For a list of dive shops and sites, contact Alberta Underwater Council, 780/453-8566.

FISHING

The Canadian Rockies are an angler's delight. Fish are abundant in many lakes and rivers (the exceptions to good fishing are the lakes and rivers fed by glacial run-off, such as Lake Louise) and outfitters provide guiding services throughout the mountains. Many lakes are stocked annually with a variety of trout—most often rainbows—and although stocking was discontinued in the national parks in 1988, populations have been maintained. In Banff National Park, **Lake Minnewanka** is home to the mountains' largest fish—lake trout—as well a variety of other trout and whitefish. This lake, along with **Maligne Lake** in Jasper National Park, are major fishing centers, with boats and tackle for rent and guides offering their services.

Rainbow trout are the fighting fish of the Canadian Rockies; they are to western Canada what bass are to the United States. Although not native, through stocking they are found in lakes and streams throughout the mountains. Wet flies and small spinners are preferred methods of catching these fish. The largest fish found in the region is the lake trout, which grows to 18 kilograms. It feeds near the surface after breakup, and then moves to deeper, colder water in summer. Long lines and heavy lures are needed to hook onto these giants. Brown trout, introduced from Europe, are found in slow-flowing streams in the eastern zones of Kananaskis Country as well as in the Bow River. They are most often caught on dry flies, but are finicky feeders, and therefore difficult to hook. Brook trout are widespread throughout lower elevation lakes and streams. Cutthroat trout inhabit the cold and clear waters of the highest lakes, which generally require a hike to access. Fishing for cutthroat requires using the lightest of tackle as the water is generally very clear; fly-casting is most productive on the still water of lakes, while spinning is the preferred river-fishing method. Arctic grayling, easily identified by their large dorsal fins, are common in cool clear streams throughout the far north, but are not native to the Canadian Rockies; Wedge Pond (Kananaskis Country) is stocked with these delicious fish. Dolly Varden can be caught in many high-elevation lakes on the British Columbia side of the mountains; Whiteswan Lake is a local favorite. Whitefish are a commonly caught fish in lower elevation lakes and rivers (many anglers in Alberta call whitefish "arctic grayling," but they are in fact two distinct species—and grayling aren't native to the mountains). Hydroelectric dams, such as those east of Canmore and in the Spray Valley zone of Kananaskis Valley, are popular with anglers chasing whitefish.

Note: The bull trout is an endangered species, and is a catch-and-release fish. Possession of bull trout—a dark-colored fish with light spots—is illegal. The defining difference between the bull trout and the brook trout, with which it is often confused, is that the bull trout has *no black spots on its dorsal fin;* due to its status, correct identification of this species is especially important.

Regulations

Three different licenses are in effect in the Canadian Rockies—one license covers all the national parks, another Albertan waters, and a third the freshwaters of British Columbia.

National parks: Licenses are available from park offices and some sport shops; $6 for a seven-day license, $13 for an annual license. The brochure *Fishing Regulations Summary,* available from all park information centers, details limits and closures.

Alberta: Alberta has an automated licensing system, with licenses sold from vending machines in sporting stores, hardware stores, and gas stations. To use the machines you'll need a

Wildlife Identification Number (WIN) card. These numbers are sold by all license vendors and cost $8 (valid for five years). Once you have your card, it is swiped through a vending machine to purchase a license. An annual license for Canadian residents over age 16 is $18 (no license required for those under 16 or Albertans over 64); for nonresidents age 16 and older, it is $36, or $20 for a five-day license.

The *Alberta Guide to Sportfishing Regulations,* which outlines all the open seasons and bag limits, is available from outlets selling licenses and from Natural Resource Services offices, or write Natural Resources Services, Alberta Environment, Main Floor, South Tower, Petroleum Plaza, 9915 108th Street, Edmonton, AB T5K 2G8; 780/944-0313; www.gov.ab. ca/env/fw/fishing.

British Columbia: In British Columbia, the cost of a license varies according to your place of residence. British Columbian residents pay $30 for a one-year license, $17 for an eight-day license, or $8 for a single-day license. Residents of other Canadian provinces pay $40, $25, or $15, respectively, while non-Canadians pay $55, $30, or $15, respectively. For more information contact Recreational Fisheries, Ministry of Environment, Lands, and Parks, Parliament Buildings, Victoria, BC V8V 1X4, 250/387-4573.

Make fresh tracks at any one of the half-dozen world-class ski resorts.

WINTERTIME

Downhill Skiing

Six world-class ski areas are perched among the high peaks of the Canadian Rockies. The largest, and Canada's second-largest (only Whistler/Blackcomb is larger), is **Lake Louise,** overlooking the lake of the same name in Banff National Park. The area boasts 1,500 hectares of skiing on four distinct faces, with wide-open bowls and runs for all abilities. Banff's other two resorts are **Sunshine Village,** sitting on the Continental Divide and accessible only by gondola, and **Banff Mt. Norquay,** a resort with heartpounding runs overlooking the town of Banff. Kananaskis Country is home to **Nakiska,** a resort developed especially for the downhill events of the 1988 Winter Olympic Games, and nearby **Fortress Mountain,** in a spectacular location and with runs for all abilities. **Marmot Basin,** in

Jasper National Park, has minimal crowds and a maximum variety of terrain.

Winter is low season in the mountains, so many accommodations reduce their rates drastically. Lift and lodging package deals at many resorts start around $60 per person per night. Sunshine Village and Fortress Mountain have onslope lodging, while the other resorts are served by shuttle buses from the nearest towns. Most major resorts open in early December and close in May.

Heli-Skiing

Helicopters are banned in the national parks of the Canadian Rockies, but two surrounding heliski operators provide transfers from Banff and Jasper. One such company is **R. K. Heli Ski Panorama,** 250/342-3889 or 800/661-0252, www.rkheliski.com, which is based on the west side of the mountains at Panorama, but provides daily transfers from Banff and Lake Louise for a day's helicopter skiing high in the Purcell

Mountains. The cost is $600 per person plus $70 for Banff transfers. The only other company that offers day trips is **Robson Helimagic,** based west of Jasper at Valemont, 250/566-4700, which charges $449 for a day's skiing on the northern boundary of Mt. Robson Provincial Park.

Banff is also headquarters for the world's largest heli-skiing operation, **Canadian Mountain Holidays,** founded by Hans Gmoser. Seven-day packages in British Columbia's interior mountain ranges begin at around $5,600 per person in the high season. For more information contact Canadian Mountain Holidays at 403/762-7100 or 800/661-0252, www.cmhski.com.

Other Winter Activities
Many hiking trails provide ideal routes for **cross-country skiing,** and many are groomed for that purpose. The largest concentration of groomed trails is in Kananaskis Country. Other areas are Banff, Jasper, Kootenay, Waterton, and Yoho National Parks. The Canmore Nordic Centre was developed for the 1988 Winter Olympic Games and is now a public facility. The townsite in Waterton Lakes National Park all but closes down for winter, but this park is one of the most enjoyable spots for a skiing sojourn. Anywhere you can cross-country ski you can **snowshoe,** a traditional form of winter transportation that is making a comeback. **Sleigh rides** are offered in Banff, Lake Louise, and Jasper.

Winter travel brings its own set of potential hazards, such as hypothermia, avalanche, frostbite, and sunburn. Necessary precautions should be taken. All park information centers can provide information on hazards and advice on current weather conditions.

ACCOMMODATIONS AND FOOD

Following is a summary of the types of accommodations and dining choices you can expect to find through the Canadian Rockies. Individual properties are detailed in each travel chapter, along with prices and contact information. Nearly all accommodations now have toll-free numbers, and many have websites, through which you can find more information about each property and make bookings.

For a list of all hotels, motels, lodges, and bed-and-breakfasts in Alberta, pick up a copy of *Alberta Accommodation Guide,* produced by the Alberta Hotel Association. The guide is available from tourist information centers or from **Travel Alberta,** P.O. Box 2500, Edmonton, AB T5J 2Z4, 780/427-4321 or 800/661-8888. The association's website is www.alberta-accommodations.com. The same association produces the *Alberta Campground Guide* (online at www.alberta-campgrounds.com). **Tourism British Columbia** produces the *Accommodations* brochure, which lists all accommodations and campgrounds in the province. Copies are available from Visitor Information Centres, or direct from Tourism British Columbia, P.O. Box 9830, Stn. Provincial Government, Victoria, BC V8V 9W5, 250/387-1642 or 800/435-5622; www.hellobc.com.

Hotels and Motels
Hotels and motels are found throughout the Canadian Rockies. They range from substandard road motels to sublime resorts such as the famous Banff Springs Hotel. Bookings throughout the mountains, but especially in Banff, Lake Louise, and Jasper, should be made as far in advance as possible. Finding inexpensive lodging in the mountain national parks is difficult in summer. By late afternoon, the only rooms left will be in the more expensive categories and by nightfall all of these will go. Hotel rooms in Banff begin around $100; those in Jasper and Waterton are a little less. Accommodation prices are slashed by as much as 70 percent outside summer. Always ask for the best rate available and check local tourist literature for discount coupons. All rates quoted in this handbook are for the cheapest category of rooms during the most expensive time period (summer). To all rates quoted you must add the 7 percent Goods and Services Tax (GST), refundable to nonresidents (keep receipts). Additionally, accommodations in Alberta are subject to a 5 percent provincial room tax, while those in British Columbia are subject to an 8 percent room tax.

Park-at-your-door, single-story road motels are mostly a thing of the past in the mountains,

Staying in a self-contained log cabin is a typical mountain experience. Pictured is a cabin at Castle Mountain Village.

although Radium Hot Springs, just outside Kootenay National Park, still has a large number of these motels (one of which proudly boasts "Electric Heat"). In most cases rooms are fine, but check before paying, just to make sure. Most have a few rooms with kitchenettes, but these fill fast. Expect to pay $50–70 s, $50–85 d. You will also find this style of accommodation in Banff (there's just one left), Canmore, Waterton townsite, and Golden.

Seasonal Accommodations

As roads through the mountains were improved in the 1920s, the number of tourists arriving by automobile increased greatly. To cater to this new breed of traveler, many "bungalow camps" were constructed along the highways. Many remain today, offering a high standard of accommodation away from the hustle and bustle of the towns. Generally they consist of free-standing, self-contained units and are open for the summer only.

Bed-and-Breakfasts

The bed-and-breakfast phenomenon is well entrenched in Canada. Hosts are generally well informed local people and rooms are cozy. Bed-and-breakfasts are located in Banff, Canmore, Bragg Creek, and Jasper. In Jasper National Park, a park bylaw was recently lifted that prevented such establishments from serving breakfast; some have started serving meals, but those that don't are still known as "private home accommodations." The best way to find out about individual lodging is from local tourist information centers or from listings in either the *Alberta Accommodation Guide* or British Columbia Tourism's *Accommodations* guide. Major bed-and-breakfast associations that represent properties in the Canadian Rockies are **Alberta & Pacific B&B Reservation Service,** P.O. Box 15477 M.P.O., Vancouver, BC V6B 5B2, 604/944-1793; **Bed and Breakfast Agency of Alberta,** 410 19th Avenue NE, Calgary, AB T2E 1P3, 403/543-3900 or 800/425-8160; and **Canada-West Accommodations,** P.O. Box 86607, North Vancouver, BC V7L 4L2, 604/990-6730, www.b-b.com.

Backcountry Huts and Lodges

Scattered through the backcountry are 18 huts maintained by the Alpine Club of Canada. The huts are rustic—typically bunk beds, a woodstove, wooden dining table, and an outhouse. Rates are $12–25 per person per night. Reservations should be made in advance by contacting the Alpine Club of Canada, P.O. Box 8040, Canmore, AB T1W 2T8, 403/678-3200, www.alpineclubofcanada.ca.

Privately operated backcountry lodges are found in Banff, Jasper, and Yoho National Parks, as well as Mount Assiniboine Provincial Park. The best known is **Lake O'Hara Lodge** in Yoho National Park. It lies 11 km from the nearest public road—access is on foot or shuttle bus—and is surrounded by some of the finest hiking in all the Canadian Rockies. Banff National Park has two backcountry lodges: **Shadow Lake**

Lodge, northwest of Banff, and **Skoki Lodge,** east of Lake Louise. Jasper National Park is home to **Tonquin Amethyst Lake Lodge.** All require some degree of effort to reach—either on foot or on horseback in summer, or on cross-country skis or snowshoes in winter. **Mount Assiniboine Lodge** is furthest from the road system but can be reached by helicopter. Rates at these lodges begin at $130 per person including three meals. None have television, but all have running water and a congenial atmosphere.

Backpacker Lodges

Hostelling International–Alberta operates 14 hostels in the Canadian Rockies. The curfews and chores are long gone at Hostelling International, a worldwide, 5000-hostel-strong organization, and you don't even need to be a member to stay. Six of these are in Banff National Park, five in Jasper National Park, and one each in Kananaskis Country, Yoho National Park (British Columbia), and Waterton Lakes National Park. A sheet or sleeping bag is required, although many can usually be rented. All the hostels are equipped with a kitchen and lounge room, and some have laundries and private rooms. Those in Banff and Lake Louise are world-class, with hundreds of beds as well as libraries and cafes. The five rustic hostels along the Icefields Parkway are evenly spaced, perfect for a bike trip along one of the world's great mountain highways. Rates for members are $10–22 per night, nonmembers $16–28. Staying in hostels is an especially good bargain for skiers; packages including accommodation and a day pass at a local ski resort start at $48. Whenever you can, make reservations in advance, especially in summer. Book by contacting the individual hostels, or in the case of the rustic hostels, through those in Banff, Lake Louise, or Jasper. Hostelling International–Alberta has its own website at www.hostellingintl.ca/alberta.

If you plan to travel extensively using hostels, join Hostelling International before you leave home. In the U.S., write Hostelling International–American Youth Hostels, Inc., 133 First Street NW, Suite 800, Washington, DC 20005; 202/783-6161; www.hiayh.org. In Canada, contact Hostelling International–Canada, 400-205 Catherine St., Ottawa, ON K2P 1C3, 613/237-7884, www.hostellingintl.ca.

Campgrounds

Camping is the way to stay cheaply in the Canadian Rockies. Each of the five national parks has excellent campgrounds, which, combined, have a total of 6,000 sites plus large areas set aside for overflow camping. Many of the campgrounds consist of nothing more than picnic tables, drinking water, pit toilets, and firewood ($6 per site per night), but at least one campground in each park has hot showers and full hookups. Each park also has an area set aside for winter camping. All national park campgrounds operate on a first-come, first-served basis and often fill by midday in July and August.

Each of the road-accessible provincial parks covered in this handbook provides camping facilities, usually only with drinking water, picnic tables, and pit toilets. The exceptions are Peter Lougheed and Bow Valley Provincial Parks in Kananaskis Country, where hookups and showers are provided. In total, Kananaskis Country holds 30 campgrounds, including the privately operated Mount Kidd RV Park, which boasts a tennis court, recreation room, spa, and sauna.

Alberta Environment manages a string of primitive campgrounds in the foothills along the eastern slopes of the Canadian Rockies, while the Ministry of Forests manages similar facilities along the other side of the divide; camp fees range $6–10 per night.

Commercial campgrounds operate in Canmore, Radium Hot Springs, at the entrance to Waterton Lakes National Park, in Golden, in Mt. Robson Provincial Park, and in Grande Cache. They provide full hookups and have showers, but generally lack the natural surroundings found in national and provincial parks.

Backcountry camping in all national parks is $6 per person per night to a maximum of $30 per person per trip. An Annual Wilderness Pass, $42, is valid for unlimited backcountry travel and camping for 12 months from its purchase date. Before heading out, you must register at the respective park information center (regardless of whether you have an annual pass) and pick up a Wilderness Pass (for those without an annual pass, the nightly camping fee multiplied by the number of nights you'll be in the backcountry). Many popular backcountry campgrounds have quotas, with reservations taken up to three months in advance. The reservation fee is $10 per party per trip. In 1998, Kananaskis Country also introduced a $6 per person backcountry camping fee. Most campgrounds in the backcountry have pit toilets, and some have bear bins for secure food storage. Fires are discouraged, so bring a stove.

FOOD AND DRINK

Although Canada isn't renowned for its culinary delights, there are some dishes to look for. Alberta beef is delicious and is served in most restaurants. And while the mountains are a long way from the ocean, British Columbia is known for its seafood. For a three-course meal in a family-style restaurant, including a steak dish, expect to pay $25 per person—at least double that in the better eateries. Banff holds an astonishing array of restaurants—over 100 at last count.

The best way to eat cheaply if you're camping is with a campstove (those made by Coleman are the most reliable). Don't rely on open fire for cooking—fire bans are often in effect. The two largest supermarkets, Safeway and I.G.A., generally have the least expensive groceries, but prices are still marginally higher than in the United States.

Drink
The Canadian Rockies are home to two small boutique breweries: Grizzly Paw Brewery and Peak Brewing Company, both in Canmore. Grizzly Paw, on Canmore's main street, has a pub on site.

The minimum age for alcohol consumption in both Alberta and British Columbia is 18. From the United States, visitors may bring 1.1 liters of liquor or wine or 24 cans or bottles of beer into Canada free of duty.

TRANSPORTATION

GETTING THERE

The closest city to the Canadian Rockies is Calgary, Alberta, 128 km east of Banff. Vancouver, British Columbia's largest city, is also a major gateway to the mountains. It lies on Canada's West Coast, 830 km west of Banff. Even though Vancouver is a lot further from the Canadian Rockies than Calgary, it is a popular starting point, as the trip across British Columbia by rail, bus, or auto is spectacular.

Air
Calgary and Vancouver International Airports are served by many international carriers. In mid-2000 **Air Canada** took over Canadian Airlines, leaving just one national carrier, and a huge network of routings throughout the world. Air Canada is now one of the world's largest airlines, serving five continents. It offers direct flights to Calgary from all major Canadian cities, as well as from Seattle, Los Angeles, San Francisco, Reno, Las Vegas, Phoenix, Chicago, Boston, Washington, Dallas/Fort Worth, New York, Atlanta, and St. Louis. From Europe, Air Canada flies direct from London to both Calgary and

Vancouver, and from Paris, Frankfurt, and Rome to either Calgary or Vancouver via Toronto. South Pacific and Asian cities served include Sydney, Melbourne, and Brisbane, as well as Auckland, Bangkok, Kuala Lumpur, Hong Kong, Taipei, Nagoya, Beijing, and Tokyo. Air Canada's flights originating in the South American cities of Santiago, Buenos Aires, Sao Paulo, and Rio de Janeiro are routed through Toronto. For information on Air Canada flights, call 604/688-5515 or 800/776-3000, www.aircanada.ca.

U.S. carriers offering service to Calgary and Vancouver are **American Airlines,** 800/443-7300; **Delta Air Lines,** 800/221-1212; **Northwest Airlines,** 800/225-2525; and **United Airlines,** 800/247-2262.

Rail
The original transcontinental line passed through Banff, crossing the Continental Divide at Kicking Horse Pass and continuing to Vancouver via Rogers Pass. But this form of transportation, which opened up the Canadian Rockies to tourists, began to fade with the advent of efficient air services, and the last scheduled services on this line ended in 1991. Today **VIA Rail** provides coast-to-coast rail service using a more

CUTTING FLIGHT COSTS

Ticket structuring for international air travel is so complex that often even travel agents have problems coming to grips with it. The first step when planning your trip to the Canadian Rockies is to contact the airlines that fly to Vancouver or Calgary and ask for the best price they have for the time of year you wish to travel. Then shop around the travel agencies—you should be able to save 30–50 percent of the price you were quoted by the airline. Check the Sunday travel section of most newspapers for an idea of current discount prices. The Internet is another good place to start searching out the cheapest fares.

Many cheaper tickets have strict restrictions regarding changes of flight dates, lengths of stay, and cancellations. A general rule is the cheaper the ticket, the more restrictions. Most travelers today fly on APEX (advance-purchase excursion) fares. These are usually the best value, though some (and, occasionally, many) restrictions apply. These might include minimum and maximum stays, and non-changeable itineraries (or hefty penalties for changes); tickets may also be nonrefundable, once purchased.

Within Canada, **Travel Cuts,** www.travelcuts.com, with offices in all major cities, consistently offers the lowest airfares available. In the U.S., one of the largest consolidators is **Unitravel,** 800/325-2222, www.unitravel.com. The **Flight Centre,** 888/967-5331, www.flightcentre.com, with offices throughout the U.S., guarantees to match any quoted airfare. In London, **Trailfinders,** 194 Kensington High Street, Kensington, 020/7938-3939, www.trailfinders.com, always has good deals to Canada and other North American destinations.

When you have found the best fare, open a **frequent flyer** membership with the airline—**Air Canada** has a very popular program that makes rewards very obtainable.

---

northerly route that passes through Jasper National Park. At Jasper, the westbound transcontinental line divides, with one set of tracks continuing west to Prince Rupert via Prince George and the other heading southwest to Vancouver.

The **Canadian** is a thrice-weekly service between Toronto and Vancouver via Winnipeg, Saskatoon, Edmonton, Jasper, and Kamloops. Service is provided in two classes of travel: **Ecomony** features lots of leg room, reading lights, pillows and blankets, a Skyline Car complete with bar service while **Silver and Blue** is more luxurious, featuring sleeping rooms, daytime seating, all meals, a lounge and dining car, and shower kits for all passengers. At Jasper the westbound transcontinental line divides, with one set of tracks continuing slightly north to Prince Rupert. Along this route, the **Skeena** makes three trips a week. It is a daytime only service, with passengers transferred to Prince George accommodations for an overnight stay. It also offers first-class travel, in **Totem Class.**

Discounts of 25–40 percent apply to travel in all classes October–June. Those over 60 and under 25 receive a 10 percent discount that can be combined with other seasonal fares. Students receive a 50 percent discount year-round. Check for advance-purchase restrictions on all discount tickets. The **Canrailpass** allows unlimited travel anywhere on the VIA Rail system for 12 days within any given 30-day period. During high season (June 1–October 15) the pass is $589; the rest of the year it's $379. Even if you plan limited train travel, the pass is an excellent deal; the regular Toronto-Vancouver one-way fare alone is $570.31. VIA Rail has recently cooperated with Amtrak to offer a North American Rail Pass, with all the same seasonal dates and discounts as the Canrailpass. The cost is CDN$919, US$643 for a high season pass. (For Amtrak information, call 800/872-7245).

Pick up a train schedule at any VIA Rail station or call 800/561-8630 within western Canada; in other Canadian locations, contact your local VIA Rail Station. In the U.S., call any travel agent. The VIA Rail website, www.viarail.ca, provides route, schedule, and fare information as well as links to towns and sights en route.

Rocky Mountaineer Rail Tours, 604/606-2245 or 800/665-7245, www.rkymtnrail.com, runs a luxurious rail trip between Vancouver and Banff or Jasper, through the spectacular interior mountain ranges of British Columbia. Travel is during daylight hours only so you don't miss anything. Trains depart in either direction in the morning (every second or third day), overnight-

BREWSTER

Rail travel opened up the Canadian Rockies to tourism, and today continues as a popular form of transportation in the mountains.

ing at Kamloops. One-way travel in Signature Service, which includes light meals, nonalcoholic drinks, and Kamloops accommodations costs $610 per person from either Banff or Jasper to Vancouver and $670 from Calgary. GoldLeaf Service is the ultimate in luxury. Passengers ride in a two-story glass-domed car, eat in a separate dining area, and stay in Kamloops' most luxurious accommodations. GoldLeaf costs $1,110 from Banff or Jasper to Vancouver and $1,210 from Calgary. During value season (May and the first two weeks of October), fares are reduced $100.

Bus

Greyhound, 800/661-8747, www.greyhound.ca, serves areas throughout Canada and the United States. Travel by Greyhound is simple—just roll up at the depot and buy a ticket. No reservations are necessary. Greyhound bus depots are always close to downtown and generally link up with local public transportation. Always check for any promotional fares that might be available at the time of your travel. Regular-fare tickets are valid for one year and allow unlimited stopovers between paid destinations.

The **Domestic Canada Pass** is valid on all Greyhound routes in Canada. It is sold in periods of seven days ($223.13), 15 days ($294.25), 30 days ($401.25), and 60 days ($508.25). It must be purchased seven days in advance and is nonrefundable. You can buy the pass at any bus depot. In the U.S., the pass can be bought from most travel agents. Outside of North America, it is sold as the **International Canada Pass** with a similar pricing structure except that there is a low season with a 25 percent discount that runs mid-September to mid-June.

From Calgary: Greyhound runs five times daily from their depot at 850 16th Street, Calgary, 403/265-9111, to Canmore and Banff ($18.56 one-way). From Calgary International Airport, Brewster, 403/762-6767, and the Banff Airporter, 403/762-3330, run regular shuttle services to Canmore ($32), Banff ($36), and Lake Louise ($41), with Brewster continuing on to Jasper ($71; summer only). Both companies have booking desks on the Arrivals level.

From Vancouver: The main Greyhound routes from Vancouver include the TransCanada Highway to Golden, Field, and Banff; a northern route along Hwy. 5 through Jasper to Edmonton and beyond; and a southern route on Hwy. 3, through Cranbrook to Radium Hot Springs and on to Banff. The fare between Vancouver and Banff is $101.12 one-way. The bus depot in Vancouver is at 1150 Station Street, 604/482-8747.

From the United States: If you're traveling from the U.S., get yourself to Great Falls, Montana, from which regular services continue north to the Coutts/Sweetgrass port of entry. There you change to a Canadian Greyhound bus for Calgary, where you can make connections to Banff.

GETTING AROUND

Bus

Getting around the Canadian Rockies is easiest with your own vehicle as public transportation is limited. **Brewster,** 403/762-6767, is primarily a tour company, but also runs a scheduled bus service linking Calgary International Airport, Canmore, Banff, and Lake Louise, with a summer-only service between Lake Louise and Jasper. Sample fares: Banff to Lake Louise, $11; Banff to Jasper, $51; Lake Louise to Jasper, $44.

Hostel Shuttle

Between mid-May and the end of October, a shuttle bus runs between all hostels in the Canadian Rockies every second day. The route begins from the hostel in Calgary at 8A.M. and ends at the Mt. Edith Cavell hostel at 4:30 P.M. that same day. The schedule is reversed the following day. Sample fares are Calgary to Banff, $23; Calgary to Lake Louise, $30; Calgary to Jasper, $65; Banff to Lake Louise, $14; Lake Louise to Jasper, $38. Book through the hostels.

Car and RV Rental

All major car rental agencies have outlets at Calgary and Vancouver International Airports. Car rentals are also available in Banff, Canmore, and Jasper. To ensure a vehicle is available for you, book in advance. Generally vehicles can be booked through parent companies in the United States. Rates start at $60 a day for a small economy car, $75 for a mid-size car, and $85 for a full-size car. Most major agencies now offer unlimited mileage, but check to make sure. Cheaper cars are available from agencies such as **Rent-A-Wreck,** 800/327-0116, www.rentawreck.ca, but each km driven over 100 km each day will cost $.15–.30. In all cases insurance is from $15 per day and is compulsory. Rates are often lower outside summer. Charges apply if you need to drop off the car at an agency other than the rental location. All agencies provide free pick-up and drop-off at major city hotels. Major rental agencies include: **Avis,** 800/879-2847, www.avis.com; **Budget,** 800/268-8900, www.budgetcanada.com; **Dollar,** 800/800-4000, www.dollar.com; **Enterprise,** 800/325-8007, www.enterprise.com; **Hertz,** 800/263-0600, www.hertz.com; **National,** 800/227-7368, www.nationalcar.com; and **Thrifty,** 800/847-4389, www.thrifty.com.

Camper-vans, recreational vehicles, and travel trailers are a great way to get around the Canadian Rockies without having to worry about accommodations each night. The downside is cost. The smallest vans, capable of sleeping two people, start at $100 per day with 100 free kilometers per day. Standard extra charges include insurance, a preparation fee (usually around $50 per rental), a linen/cutlery charge (around $60 per person per trip), and taxes. The major agencies, based in Calgary and Vancouver, are **Cruise Canada,** 403/291-4963 or 800/327-7799, or, in the U.S., 800/327-7778, www.cruiseamerica.com; **Canadream,** 604/572-3220 or 800/461-7368, www.canadream.com; and **C.C. Canada Camper,** 604/327-3003, www.canada-camper.com.

Driving in Canada

Driver's licenses from all countries are valid in Canada for up to six months. An **International Driving Permit,** available in your home country, is valid in Canada for one year. You should also carry car registration papers or rental contracts. Proof of insurance must be carried and you must wear seat belts. If coming from the U.S., check that your American insurance covers travel in Canada. All highway signs give distances in kilometers and speeds in kilometers per hour (kph). The speed limit on major highways is 100 kph (62 mph). U.S. motorists are advised to obtain a Canadian Non-resident Inter-provincial Motor Vehicle Liability Insurance Card, available through U.S. insurance companies, which is accepted as evidence of financial responsibility in Canada. Members of the American Automobile Association are entitled to services provided by the Canadian Automobile Association, including travel information.

Note: Drunk-driving laws in Canada are tough.

Tours

For those with limited time, an organized tour is the best way of seeing the Canadian Rockies. **Brewster,** 403/762-6767 or 800/661-1152, www.brewster.ca, offers day tours and overnight tours throughout the mountains, as well as car rental and accommodation packages. Rocky Mountaineer Rail Tours (see "Getting There," above) offer a wide variety of longer tours in conjunction with rail travel between Vancouver and Banff or Jasper. On a smaller scale, **Good Earth Travel Adventures** provides one-on-one consultations for all aspects of travel through the Canadian Rockies—from day tours to accommodation reservations. Contact them at 403/678-9358 or 888/979-9797; www.goodearthtravel.com.

INFORMATION AND SERVICES

VISAS AND OFFICIALDOM

Entry for U.S. Citizens

Citizens and permanent residents of the United States do not need a passport for entry to Canada. Although photo driver's licenses are acceptable forms of identification for entry, it is advisable to carry extra identification such as a birth certificate, passport, or alien card. (The latter is essential for U.S. resident aliens to re-enter the United States.)

Other Foreign Visitors

Visitors from countries other than the U.S. must have a valid passport and, in some cases, a visa for entry to Canada. Presently, citizens of the British Commonwealth and Western Europe do not need a visa, but check with the Canadian embassy in your home country. The standard entry permit is valid for six months; proof of onward tickets and/or sufficient funds is required in order to obtain the permit. Extensions are possible from the Employment and Immigration Canada offices in Calgary and Vancouver ($60 per person).

Employment and Study

Anyone wishing to work or study in Canada must obtain authorization *before* entering Canada. Authorization to work will only be granted if no qualified Canadians are available for the work in question. Applications for work and study are available from all Canadian embassies and must be submitted with a nonrefundable processing fee.

The Canadian government has a reciprocal agreement with Australia for a limited number of **holiday work visas** to be issued each year. Australian citizens under the age of 30 are eligible; contact your nearest Canadian embassy or consulate for more information.

MONEY

As in the United States, Canadian currency is based on dollars and cents. Coins come in denominations of one, five, 10, and 25 cents, and one and two dollars. The one-dollar coin is the 11-sided, gold-colored "loonie," named for the bird featured on it. The unique two-dollar coin, introduced in 1996, is silver with a gold-colored insert. The most common notes are $5, $10, $20, and $50. A $100 bill does exist but is uncommon. Each note features a different bird. Until recently they depicted various Canadian scenes, including Moraine Lake, in Banff National Park (on the $20 note).

All prices quoted in this book are in Canadian dollars unless otherwise indicated. American dollars are accepted at many tourist areas, but the exchange rate will be more favorable at banks. Traveler's checks are the safest way to carry money, but often a fee is charged to cash them if they're in a currency other than Canadian dollars. All major credit cards are honored at Canadian banks, gas stations, and most commercial establishments.

Tips are not usually added to a bill, and in general 15 percent of the total amount is given. Tips are most often given to waiters, waitresses, taxi drivers, doormen, bellhops, and bar staff.

Costs

The cost of living in the mountains is generally higher than in other parts of Canada, especially when it comes to accommodations. Provincially, the cost of living is lower in Alberta than in British Columbia, but higher than in the United States. By planning ahead, having a tent or joining Hostelling International, and being prepared to cook your own meals, it is possible to get by on $50 per person per day. Gasoline is sold in liters (3.78 liters equals one U.S. gallon) and is generally $.65–.75 cents a liter for regular unleaded.

Taxes

Canada imposes a 7 percent **Goods and Services Tax (GST)** on most consumer purchases. Nonresident visitors can get a rebate for the GST they pay on short-term accommodations and on most consumer goods bought in the country and taken home. Items not included in the GST rebate program include: gifts left in Canada, meals and restaurant charges,

CURRENCY EXCHANGE

The Canadian dollar lost value against the greenback through the late 1990s, and at one stage in late 2000 traded at US$1 per CDN$1.56, within two cents of its all time low. At press time the Canadian dollar traded at US$1 per CDN$1.49–1.53.

Current exchange rates (into CDN$) for other major currencies are:

AUS$1 = $.85
DM1 = $.68
EURO = $1.34
HK$10 = $1.95
NZ$1 = $.67
UK£ = $2.18
¥100 = $1.29

HEALTH

Compared to other parts of the world, Canada is a relatively safe place to visit. That said, wherever you are traveling, carry a medical kit that includes bandages, insect repellent, sunscreen, antiseptic, antibiotics, and water-purification tablets. Good first-aid kits are available through most camping shops.

Taking out a travel-insurance policy is a sensible precaution, as hospital and medical charges start at around $1,000 a day. Bring copies of your current prescriptions with you to Canada.

Giardia

Giardiasis, also known as beaver fever, is a real concern for those who drink water from back-country water sources. It's caused by an intestinal parasite, *Giardia lamblia,* that lives in lakes, rivers, and streams. Once ingested, its effects, although not instantaneous, can be dramatic; severe diarrhea, cramps, and nausea are the most common. Preventive measures should always be taken, and include boiling all water for at least 10 minutes, treating all water with iodine, or filtering all water using a filter with a small enough pore size to block the *Giardia* cysts.

Winter Travel

Travel through the mountains during winter months should not be undertaken lightly. Before setting out in a vehicle, check antifreeze levels and always carry a spare tire and blankets or sleeping bags. **Frostbite** is a potential hazard, especially when cold temperatures are combined with high winds (a combination known as **windchill**). Most often it leaves a numbing, bruised sensation, and the skin turns white. Exposed areas of skin, especially the nose and ears, are most susceptible.

Hypothermia occurs when the body fails to produce heat as fast as it loses it. It can strike at any time of year but is more common during cooler months. Cold weather, combined with hunger, fatigue, and dampness, creates a recipe for disaster. Symptoms are not always apparent to the victim. The early signs are numbness, shivering, slurring of words, dizzy spells, and, in extreme cases, violent behavior, unconsciousness, and even death. The best way to

campground fees, services such as dry cleaning and shoe repair, alcoholic beverages, tobacco, automotive fuels, groceries, agricultural and fish products, prescription drugs and medical devices, and used goods that tend to increase in value, such as paintings, jewelry, rare books, and coins. The rebate is available on services and retail purchases that total at least $100 and were paid for within 60 days prior to your exit from the country. Rebates can be claimed any time within one year from the date of purchase. You'll need to include with your claim all receipts and vouchers that prove the GST was paid. Most visitors apply for the rebate at duty-free shops (also called Visitor Rebate Centres) when exiting the country. The duty-free shops can rebate up to $500 on the spot. For rebates over $500, you'll need to mail your completed GST rebate form directly to Revenue Canada, Customs and Excise, Visitors' Rebate Program, Ottawa, Ontario K1A 1J5. You can also submit rebate forms for amounts less than $500 directly to Revenue Canada. Rebate checks from Revenue Canada are issued in Canadian funds. For more information, call toll-free from anywhere in Canada 800/668-4748; from outside Canada phone 902/432-5608; www.rc.gc.ca/visitors.

Provincial Sales Tax applies in British Columbia but not Alberta and ranges 5–12 percent on most goods purchased in shops or restaurants.

dress for the cold is in layers, including a waterproof outer layer. Most importantly, wear headgear. The best treatment is to get the patient out of the cold, replace wet clothing with dry, slowly give hot liquids and sugary foods, and place the victim in a sleeping bag. Warming too quickly can lead to heart attacks.

COMMUNICATIONS AND MEASUREMENTS

All **mail** posted in Canada must have Canadian postage stamps attached. First-class letters and postcards are $.46 to destinations within Canada, $.55 to the U.S., and $.95 to all other destinations. All Canadian post offices offer a General Delivery service. If you would like mail sent to you while traveling in the Canadian Rockies, have it addressed to yourself either c/o General Delivery, Banff, AB T0L 0C0 or c/o General Delivery, Jasper, AB T0E 1E0, and the respective post offices will hold your mail for 15 days before returning it to the sender.

Alberta and British Columbia have two area codes each. The **area code** for southern Alberta is **403**. The area code for northern Alberta, including Jasper National Park, is **780**. The area code for all British Columbia except Vancouver and environs is **250**. The area code for Vancouver is **604**. Unless otherwise noted, all numbers must be dialed with this prefix, including long-distance calls made within the province that you are calling from. The country code for Canada is 1, the same as the United States. Public phones accept five-, 10-, and 25-cent coins. Local calls cost $.25, and most long-distance calls from public phones cost at least $2 for the first minute. Phone cards, available from drug and grocery stores, provide considerable savings for those using public phones.

Electrical voltage is 120 volts, the same as the United States. Canada is on the **metric system** (see the "Metric System" chart at the back of this book), although many people talk in miles and supermarket prices are advertised in ounces and pounds.

Alberta is in the **mountain time zone,** one hour later than Pacific time, two hours earlier than eastern time. The mountain time zone extends west into southern British Columbia, which includes Yoho and Kootenay National Parks as well as the towns of Golden and Radium Hot Springs. The rest of British Columbia, including Mount Robson Provincial Park, is in the **Pacific time zone.**

Shops are generally open Monday–Friday 9A.M.–5P.M., Saturday 9A.M.–noon, and are closed on Sunday. Major shopping centers and those in resort towns are often open till 9P.M. and all weekend. **Banks** are open Monday–Friday 9:30 A.M.–3:30 P.M., and till 4:30 or 5P.M. on Friday.

MAPS AND INFORMATION

Maps
The best sources of maps are the specialist map shops. In Calgary contact **Map Town,** 640 6th Avenue, SW, 403/266-2241. In Vancouver try **International Travel Maps and Books,** 552 Seymour Street, 604/687-3320, www.itmb.com. By request they'll send you a catalog of available maps for hiking (topographical maps), camping (road/access maps), and canoeing (river details such as gradients). Topographic maps are for sale at all park information centers, as well as at some sport and outdoor stores.

Information
Each of the five national parks has at least one **Park Information Centre.** These are the places

---

HEADING FURTHER AFIELD?

Alberta Tourism: 403/427-4321 or 800/661-8888; www.travelalberta.com
Tourism British Columbia: 250/387-1642 or 800/435-5622; www.hellobc.com
Tourism Yukon: 403/667-5340; www.touryukon.com
Alaska Division of Tourism: 907/465-2010; www.dced.state.ak.us/tourism/
Northwest Territories Arctic Tourism: 403/873-7200 or 800/661-0788; www.nwttravel.nt.ca
Nunavut Tourism: 819/979-6551 or 800/491-7910; www.nunatour.nt.ca
Tourism Saskatchewan: 306/787-2300 or 800/667-7191; www.sasktourism.com
Travel Manitoba: 204/945-3777 or 800/665-0040; www.travelmanitoba.com

to head for interpretive displays, all park-related information, trail reports, weather forecasts, and Wilderness Passes. Individual addresses and websites are listed in the relevant travel chapters. The national parks are managed by **Parks Canada,** www.parkscanada.gc.ca. On the Alberta-side of the Canadian Rockies, all other parks are managed by **Alberta Environment,** 780/944-0313, www.gov.ab.ca/env. British Columbia's provincial parks are managed by **BC Parks,** 250/387-4550, www.elp.gov.bc.ca/bcparks.

For general tourism information, the towns of Banff, Canmore, Jasper, Radium Hot Springs, and Golden have information centers that provide advice on local attractions, accommodations, and restaurants. In Calgary, the main information center is in the Calgary Tower Centre, corner of Centre Street and 9th Avenue, SW, 403/263-8510 or 800/661-1678. The Vancouver Visitor Info Centre is at 200 Burrard Street, 604/683-2000. Both Calgary and Vancouver International Airports have information booths.

Crowfoot Glacier

BANFF NATIONAL PARK

INTRODUCTION

This 6,641-square-km national park encompasses some of the world's most magnificent scenery. The snowcapped peaks of the Rocky Mountains form a spectacular backdrop for glacial lakes, fast-flowing rivers, and endless forests. Deer, moose, elk, mountain goats, bighorn sheep, black and grizzly bears, wolves, and cougars inhabit the park's vast wilderness, while the human species is concentrated in the picture-postcard towns of Banff and Lake Louise—two of North America's most famous resorts. Banff is near the park's southeast gate, 128 km west of Calgary. Lake Louise, northwest of Banff along the TransCanada Highway, sits astride its namesake lake, which is regarded as one of the seven natural wonders of the world. The lake is rivaled for sheer beauty only by Moraine Lake, just down the road. Just north of Lake Louise, the Icefields Parkway begins its spectacular course alongside the Continental Divide to Jasper National Park.

One of Banff's greatest drawing cards is the accessibility of its natural wonders. Most highlights are close to the road system. But adventurous visitors can follow an excellent system of hiking trails to alpine lakes, along glacial valleys, and to spectacular viewpoints where crowds are scarce and human impact has been minimal. Summer in the park is busy. In fact, the park receives nearly half of its four million annual visitors in just two months—July and August. The rest of the year crowds outside the town of Banff are negligible. In winter, three world-class ski resorts—Banff Mt. Norquay, Sunshine Village, and Lake Louise (Canada's second-largest ski area) —crank up their lifts. Being low season, hotel rates are reasonable. And if you tire of downhill skiing, you can try cross-country skiing, ice-skating,

See color maps of Banff National Park on pages iv–vii.

PARK ENTRY

Permits are required for entry into Banff National Park. A National Parks Day Pass is adult $5, senior $4, child $2 to a maximum of $10 per vehicle. It is interchangeable between parks and is valid until 4 P.M. the day following its purchase. An annual Great Western Pass, good for entry into all 11 of western Canada's national parks, is adult $35, senior $27 to a maximum of $70 per vehicle ($53 for two or more seniors). This pass comes with a Great Western Passbook, which includes a wide variety of discounts, including to camp fees. Both types of pass can be bought at the eastern park gate on the Trans-Canada Highway, the park information centers in Banff Lake Louise, and campground kiosks. Day Passes can also be bought at the 24-hour Automated Pass Machines at strategic spots through the park. Annual passes can also be bought in advance by calling 800/748-7275 or online at the Parks Canada website, www.parkscanada.gc.ca.

or snowshoeing; take a sleigh ride; soak in a hot spring; or go heli-skiing nearby.

The park is open year-round, although occasional road closures occur on mountain passes along the park's western boundary in winter, due to avalanche-control work and snowstorms.

THE LAND

The park lies within the main and front ranges of the Rocky Mountains, a mountain range that extends the length of the North American continent. Although the mountains are composed of bedrock laid down up to one billion years ago, it wasn't until 100 million years ago that forces below the earth's surface transformed the lowland plain of what is now western Canada into the varied, mountainous topography we see today.

The front ranges lie to the east, bordering the foothills. These geographically complex mountains are made up of younger bedrock that has been folded, faulted, and uplifted. The main ranges are older and higher, with the bedrock lying mainly horizontal and not as severely disturbed as the front ranges. Here the pressures have been most powerful; these mountains are characterized by castle-like buttresses and pinnacles, and warped waves of stratified rock. Most glaciers are found among these lofty peaks. The spine of the main range is the **Continental Divide.** In Canadian latitudes to the east of the divide, all waters flow to the Atlantic Ocean; those to the west flow into the Pacific.

Since rising above the surrounding plains these mountains have been eroding. At least four times in the last million years sheets of ice have covered much of the land. Advancing and retreating back and forth like steel wool across the landscape, they rounded off lower peaks and carved formerly V-shaped valleys into broad U-shaped ones (**Bow Valley** is the most distinctive). Meanwhile, glacial meltwater continued carving ever-deeper channels into the valleys, and rivers changed course many times.

This long history of powerful and even violent natural events over the eons has left behind the dramatic landscape visitors marvel over today. Now forming the exposed sides of many a mountain peak, layers of drastically altered sediment are visible from miles away, especially when accentuated by a particular angle of sunlight or a light fall of snow. Cirques, gouged into the mountains by glacial action, fill with glacial meltwater each spring, creating trademark translucent green lakes that will take your breath away. And the wide sweeping U-shaped valleys scoured out by glaciers past, now create magnificent panoramas that will draw you to pull off the road and gasp in awe; open views are easy to come by here, thanks to a climate that keeps the tree line low.

FLORA

Nearly 700 species of plants have been recorded in the park. Each species falls into one of three distinct vegetation zones, based primarily on altitude. Lowest is the montane zone, which covers the valley floor. Above it, the subalpine zone comprises most of the forested area. Highest of all is the alpine zone, where climate is severe and vegetation cover is limited.

Montane-zone vegetation is usually found at elevations below 1,350 meters but can grow at higher elevations on sun-drenched, south-facing slopes. As fires frequently affect this zone, **lodgepole pine** is the dominant species; its tightly

Castle Mountain, easily recognized driving north from the town of Banff, is one of the park's most distinctive peaks.

sealed cones only open with the heat of a forest fire, thereby regenerating the species quickly after a blaze. **Douglas fir** is the zone's climax species and is found in open stands, such as on Tunnel Mountain. **Aspen** is common in older burn areas, while **limber pine** thrives on rocky outcrops.

Dense forests of **white spruce** and **Engelmann spruce** typify the subalpine zone. White spruce dominates to 2,100 meters; above 2,100 meters to 2,400 meters, Engelmann spruce is dominant. In areas affected by fire, such as west of Castle Junction, lodgepole pine occurs in dense stands. **Subalpine fir** grows above 2,200 meters and is often stunted by the high winds experienced at such lofty elevations.

The transition from subalpine to alpine is gradual and usually occurs around 2,300 meters. The alpine has a severe climate with temperatures averaging below zero. Low temperatures, strong winds, and a very short summer force alpine plants to adapt by growing low to the ground with long roots. Mosses, mountain avens, saxifrage, and an alpine dandelion all thrive in this environment. The best place to view the brightly colored carpet of **alpine flowers** is Sunshine Meadows or Parker's Ridge.

FAUNA

Viewing the park's abundant and varied wildlife is one of the most popular visitor activities in Banff.

In summer, with the onslaught of the tourist hordes, many of the larger mammals move away from the heavily traveled areas. It then becomes a case of knowing when and where to look for them. Spring and fall are the best times of year for wildlife viewing; the crowds are thinner than in summer, and big-game animals are more likely to be seen at lower elevations. Winter also has its advantages. Although bears are hibernating, a large herd of elk winters on the outskirts of the town of Banff, coyotes are often seen roaming around town, bighorn sheep have descended from the heights, and wolf packs can be seen along the Bow Valley Corridor.

Small Mammals
One of the first mammals you're likely to come in contact with is the **Columbian ground squirrel,** seen throughout the park's lower elevations. The **golden-mantled ground squirrel,** similar in size but with a striped back, is common at higher elevations or around rocky outcrops. The one collecting Engelmann spruce cones is the **red squirrel.** The **least chipmunk** is striped, but smaller than the golden-mantled squirrel. It lives in dry, rocky areas throughout the park.

Short-tailed weasels are common, **long-tailed weasels** are rare. Look for both in higher subalpine forests. **Pikas** (commonly called rock rabbits) and **hoary marmots** (well known for their shrill whistles) live among rock slides near high-country lakes—look for them around Moraine

THE ELK OF BANFF NATIONAL PARK

Few visitors leave Banff without having seen elk—a large member of the deer family easily distinguished by its white rump. Though the animals have been reported passing through the park for a century, they've never been indigenous. In 1917, 57 elk were moved to Banff from Yellowstone National Park. Two years later 20 more were transplanted and the new herd multiplied rapidly. At that time, coyotes, cougars, and wolves were being slaughtered under a predator-control program, leaving the elk unfettered by nature's population-control mechanisms. The elk proliferated and soon became a problem as they took to wintering in the range of bighorn sheep, deer, moose, and beaver. Between 1941 and 1969, controlled slaughters of elk were conducted in an attempt to reduce the population.

Today, with wolf packs returning to the park, the elk population has stabilized at about 2,800. In summer, look for them in open meadows along the Bow Valley Parkway, along the road to Two Jack Lake, or at Vermilion Lakes.

Each fall, traditionally, hundreds of elk moved into the town itself, but starting in 2000 Parks Canada has been making a concerted effort to keep them away from areas such as the golf course and recreation grounds. The main reason for this is that fall is rutting season and the libidinal bull elk become dangerous as they gather their harems. The days of seeing elk feeding in downtown Central Park or walking proudly down Banff Avenue may be gone, but they're still there, just a little harder to find.

Lake and along Bow Summit Loop. **Porcupines** are widespread and are most active at night.

Vermilion Lakes is an excellent place to view the **beaver** at work; the best time is dawn or dusk. **Muskrats** and **mink** are common in all wetlands within the park.

Hoofed Residents

The most common and widespread of the park's hoofed residents are elk, which number around 2,800. In 2000, a concerted effort was made to keep them out of Banff's downtown core, but they are still congregating around the outskirts of the town, including up near the Tunnel Mountain campgrounds. They can also be seen along the Bow Valley Parkway. **Moose** were once common around Vermilion Lakes, but competition from an artificially expanded elk population caused their numbers to decline and now only around 100 live in the park. Look for them at Waterfowl Lakes and along the Icefields Parkway near Rampart Creek.

Mule deer, named for their large ears, are most common in the southern part of the park. Watch for them along the Mt. Norquay Road and Bow Valley Parkway. **White-tailed deer** are much less common but seen occasionally at Saskatchewan River Crossing. A small herd of around 20 **woodland caribou** remains in the Dolomite Pass area and Upper Pipestone Valley and is rarely seen.

It is estimated that the park is home to around 900 **mountain goats.** These nimble-footed creatures occupy all mountain peaks, living almost the entire year in the higher subalpine and alpine regions. The most accessible place to view these high-altitude hermits is along Parker's Ridge in the far northwestern corner of the park. The park's **bighorn sheep** have for the most part lost their fear of humans and often congregate at certain spots to lick salt from the road. Your best chance of seeing one of the park's 2,000–2,300 bighorn is at the south end of the Bow Valley Parkway, between switchbacks on the Mt. Norquay Road, and just beyond Lake Minnewanka along the loop road.

Predators

Coyotes are widespread along the entire Bow River watershed. They are attracted to Vermilion Lakes by an abundance of small game, and many have permanent dens there. **Wolves** had been driven close to extinction by the early 1950s, but today at least four wolf packs have been reported in the park. One pack winters close to the townsite and is occasionally seen on Vermilion Lakes during that period. The **lynx** population fluctuates greatly; look for them in the backcountry during winter. **Cougars** are very shy and number less than 20 in the park. They are occasionally seen along the front ranges behind Cascade Mountain.

Bears

The exhilaration of seeing one of these magnificent creatures in its natural habitat is unforgettable. From the road you're most likely to see **black bears,** which range in color from jet black to cinnamon brown and number around 50. Try the Bow Valley Parkway at dawn or late in the afternoon. Farther north they are occasionally seen near the road as it passes Cirrus Mountain. Banff's 70-odd **grizzly bears** spend most of the year in remote valleys, often on south-facing slopes away from the Bow Valley Corridor. During late spring they are occasionally seen in the area of Bow Pass.

The chance of encountering a bear face-to-face in the backcountry is remote. To lessen chances even further, you should take a number of simple precautions. Never hike alone or at dusk. Make lots of noise when passing through heavy vegetation. Keep a clean camp. And read the pamphlets available at all park visitor centers. At the Banff Visitor Centre, 224 Banff Avenue, daily trail reports list all recent bear sightings. Report any bears you see to the Warden's Office, 403/762-4506.

Reptiles and Amphibians

The **wandering garter snake** is rare and found only near the Cave and Basin, where warm water from the mineral spring flows down a shaded slope into Vermilion Lakes. Amphibians found in the park include the widespread **western toad;** the **wood frog,** commonly found along the Bow River; the rare **spotted frog;** and the **long-toed salamander,** which spawns in shallow ponds and spends summer under logs or rocks in the vicinity of its spawning grounds.

Birds

Although over 240 species of birds have been recorded in the park, most are shy and live in heavily wooded areas. One species that definitely isn't shy is the fearless **gray jay,** which haunts all campgrounds and picnic areas. Similar in color, but larger, is the **Clark's nutcracker,** which lives in higher, subalpine forests. Another common bird is the black and white **magpie. Ravens** are frequently encountered, especially around campgrounds.

A number of species of **woodpecker** live in subalpine forests. Several species of grouse are also in residence. Most common is the **downy ruffed grouse** seen in montane forest. The **blue grouse** and **spruce grouse** are seen at higher elevations, as is the **white-tailed ptarmigan,** which lives above the tree line. (Watch for them in Sunshine Meadows or on the Bow Summit Loop.) A colony of **black swifts** in Johnston Canyon is one of only two in the Canadian Rockies.

Good spots to view **dippers** and migrating waterfowl are Hector Lake, Vermilion Lakes, and the wetland area near Muleshoe Picnic Area. A bird blind has been set up below the Cave and Basin but is only worth visiting at dawn and dusk when the hordes of human visitors aren't around. Part of the nearby marsh stays ice free during winter, attracting **killdeer** and other birds.

Although raptors are not common in the park, **bald eagles** and **golden eagles** are present part of the year, and Alberta's provincial bird, the **great horned owl,** lives in the park year-round.

HISTORY

Although the valleys of the Canadian Rockies became ice free nearly 8,000 years ago and native people periodically have hunted in the area since that time, the story of Banff National Park really began with the arrival of the railroad to the area.

The Coming of the Railway

In 1871, Canadian prime minister John A. MacDonald promised to build a rail line linking British Columbia to the rest of the country as a condition of the new province joining the confederation. It wasn't until early 1883 that the line reached Calgary, pushing through to **Laggan,** now known as Lake Louise, that fall. The rail line was one of the largest and costliest engineering jobs ever undertaken in Canada.

Discovery of the Cave and Basin

On November 8, 1883, three young railway workers—Franklin McCabe, and William and Thomas McCardell—went prospecting for gold on their day off. After crossing the Bow River by raft, they came across a warm stream and traced it to its source at a small log-choked basin of warm water that had a distinct smell of sulphur. Nearby they detected the source of the foul smell coming from a hole in the ground. Nervously, one of the three men lowered himself into the hole and came across a subterranean pool of aqua-green warm water. The three men had not found gold, but something just as precious—a hot mineral spring that in time would attract wealthy customers from around the world. Word of the discovery soon got out, and the government encouraged visitors to the Cave and Basin as an ongoing source of revenue to support the new railway.

A 25-square-km reserve was established around the springs on November 25, 1885, and two years later the reserve was expanded and renamed **Rocky Mountains Park.** It was primarily a business enterprise centered around the unique springs and catering to wealthy patrons of the

railway. At the turn of the century, Canada had an abundance of wilderness; it certainly didn't need a park to preserve it. The only goal of Rocky Mountains Park was to generate income for the government and the Canadian Pacific Railway.

A Town Grows

After the discovery of the Cave and Basin just a few kilometers from the railway station (then known as Siding 29), many commercial facilities sprang up along what is now Banff Avenue. The general manager of the C.P.R. (later to become its vice president), William Cornelius Van Horne, was instrumental in creating a hotel business along the rail line. His most recognized

WILD BILL PEYTO

". . . rarely speaking—his forte was doing things, not talking about them." These words from a friend sum up Bill Peyto—one of Banff's earliest characters and one of the Canadian Rockies' greatest guides. In 1886, at the tender age of 18, Ebenezer William Peyto left England for Canada. After traveling extensively he settled in Banff and was hired as an apprentice guide for legendary outfitter Tom Wilson. Wearing a tilted sombrero, fringed buckskin coat, cartridge belt, hunting knife, and six-shooter, he looked more like a gunslinger than a mountain man.

As his reputation as a competent guide grew, so did the stories. While guiding clients on one occasion, he led them to his cabin. Before entering, Peyto threw stones in the front door until a loud snap was heard. It was a bear trap that he'd set up to catch a certain trapper who'd been stealing his food. One of the guests commented that if caught, the trapper would surely have died. "You're damned right he would have," Bill replied. "Then I'd have known for sure it was him."

In 1900, Peyto left Banff to fight in the Boer War and was promoted to corporal for bravery. This was revoked before it became official after they learned he'd "borrowed" an officer's jacket and several bottles of booze for the celebration. Returning to a hero's welcome in Banff, he established an outfitting business and continued prospecting for copper in Simpson Pass. Although his outfitting business thrived, the death of his wife left him despondent. He built a house on Banff Avenue; its name, "Ain't it Hell," summed up his view of life.

In his later years, he became a warden in the Healy Creek–Sunshine district, where his exploits during the 1920s added to his already legendary name. After 20 years of service he retired, and in 1943, at the age of 75, he passed away. One of the park's most beautiful lakes is named after him, as are a glacier and a popular Banff watering hole (**Wild Bill's**—a designation he would have appreciated). His face also adorns the large signs welcoming visitors to Banff.

WHYTE MUSEUM OF THE CANADIAN ROCKIES

achievement was the Banff Springs Hotel, which opened in 1888. It was the world's largest hotel at the time. Enterprising locals soon realized the area's potential and began opening restaurants, offering guided hunting and boating trips, and developing manicured gardens. Banff soon became Canada's best-known tourist resort, attracting visitors from around the world. It was named after Banffshire, the Scottish birthplace of George Stephen, the C.P.R.'s first president.

In 1902, the park boundary was again expanded to include 11,440 square km of the Canadian Rockies. This dramatic expansion meant that the park became not just a tourist resort but home to existing coal-mining and logging operations and hydroelectric dams. Government officials saw no conflict of interest, actually stating that the coal mine and township at Bankhead added to the park's many attractions. Many of the forests were logged, providing wood for construction, while other areas were burned to allow clear sightings for surveyors' instruments.

After a restriction on automobiles in the park was lifted in 1916, Canada's best-known tourist resort also became its busiest. More and more commercial facilities sprang up, offering luxury and opulence amid the wilderness of the Canadian Rockies. Calgarians built summer cottages and the town began advertising itself as a year-round destination. As attitudes began to change, the government set up a Dominion Parks Branch whose first commissioner, J. B. Hawkins, believed that land set aside for parks should be used for recreation and education. Gradually resource industries were phased out. Hawkins's work culminated in the National Parks Act of 1930, which in turn led Rocky Mountains Park to be renamed Banff National Park. Present boundaries, encompassing 6,641 square km, were established in 1964.

Icefields Parkway

Natives and early explorers found the swampy nature of the Bow Valley north of Lake Louise difficult for foot and horse travel. When heading north, they used instead the Pipestone River Valley to the east. Banff guide Bill Peyto led American explorer Walter Wilcox up the Bow Valley in 1896, to the high peaks along the Continental Divide northeast of Lake Louise. The first complete journey along this route was made by Jim Brewster in 1904. Soon after, A. P. Coleman made the arduous journey, becoming a strong supporter for the route aptly known as "The Wonder Trail." During the Great Depression of the 1930s, as part of a relief-work project, construction began on what was to become the Icefields Parkway. The road was completed in 1939 and the first car traveled the route in 1940. In tribute to the excellence of the road's early construction, the original roadbed, when upgraded to its present standard in 1961, was followed nearly the entire way.

Development and the Future

For most of its existence, the town of Banff was run as a service center for park visitors by the Canadian Parks Service in Ottawa, a government department with plenty of economic resources but little idea about how to handle the day-to-day running of a mid-sized town. Any inconvenience this caused park residents was offset by cheap rent and subsidized services. In June 1988, Banff's residents voted to sever this tie, and on January 1, 1990, Banff officially became an incorporated town, no different than any other in Alberta (except that Parks Canada controls environmental protection within the townsite). The town of Banff is the largest urban center in any national park in the world. Demand for housing continues to grow faster than development will allow, real estate prices are high, and each summer 50,000 visitors daily converge on the town, overloading existing facilities. On the surface, Banff's commercialism seems to work against the national park's mandate—visitors park in multistory car parks, shops sell bearskin rugs, and trees are logged for new housing estates. But the situation is admittedly unique, since the park itself has grown from what was originally a moneymaking exercise.

Another subject of often-heated debate is the high percentage of property in the park owned by foreign interests, principally Japanese. Japanese investors bought into the area heavily in the 1980s and today own around a third of Banff's hotel industry, including two of the three largest hotels. Non-English-speaking salespeople are common, and over half of all jobs advertised locally require fluent Japanese.

These issues of continuing development, housing, and foreign ownership of property here in Canada's first national-park town will be debated well into this new millennium.

SIGHTS AND DRIVES

TOWN OF BANFF

Many visitors planning a trip to the national park don't realize that the town of Banff is a bustling commercial center with 7,500 permanent residents. The town's location is magnificent. It is spread out along the Bow River, extending to the lower slopes of Sulphur Mountain to the south and Tunnel Mountain to the east. In one direction is the towering face of Mt. Rundle, and in the other, framed by the buildings along Banff Avenue, is Cascade Mountain. A strip of hotels and motels lines the north end of Banff Avenue,

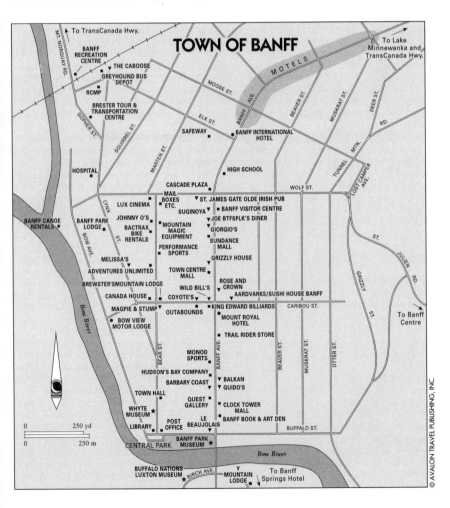

TOWN OF BANFF

© AVALON TRAVEL PUBLISHING, INC.

while a profusion of shops, boutiques, cafés, and restaurants hugs the south end. Also at the south end, just over the Bow River, is the Park Administration Building. Here the road forks—to the right is the historic Cave and Basin Hot Springs, to the left the Banff Springs Hotel and Sulphur Mountain Gondola. Some people are happy walking along the crowded streets or shopping in a truly unique setting; those more interested in some peace and quiet can easily

slip into pristine wilderness just a five-minute walk from town.

Banff Park Museum

Although displays of stuffed animals are not usually associated with national parks, this museum, at 93 Banff Avenue, 403/762-1558, provides an insight into the park's early history. Visitors during the Victorian era were eager to see the park's animals without actually having to venture into

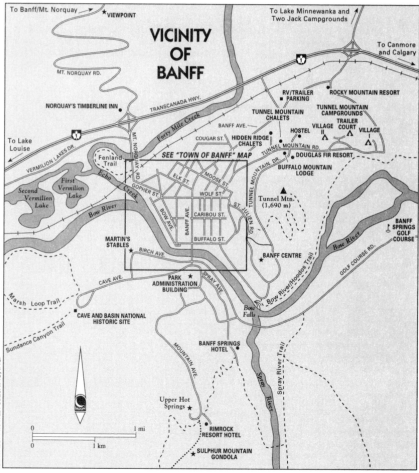

VICINITY OF BANFF

To Banff/Mt. Norquay ★ VIEWPOINT

To Lake Minnewanka and Two Jack Campgrounds

To Canmore and Calgary

MT. NORQUAY RD.

NORQUAY'S TIMBERLINE INN

TRANSCANADA HWY.

RV/TRAILER PARKING

ROCKY MOUNTAIN RESORT

TUNNEL MOUNTAIN CHALETS

TUNNEL MOUNTAIN CAMPGROUNDS

BANFF AVE.

HOSTEL

VILLAGE II

TRAILER COURT

VILLAGE

COUGAR ST.

HIDDEN RIDGE CHALETS

To Lake Louise

VERMILION LAKES DR.

Fenland Trail

SEE "TOWN OF BANFF" MAP

TUNNEL MOUNTAIN RD.

DOUGLAS FIR RESORT

First Vermilion Lake

Echo Creek

ELK ST.

MOOSE ST.

BUFFALO MOUNTAIN LODGE

Second Vermilion Lake

GOPHER ST.

WOLF ST.

ST. JULIEN RD.

Tunnel Mtn. (1,690 m)

Bow River

BOW AVE.

BANFF AVE.

CARIBOU ST.

BANFF SPRINGS GOLF COURSE

MARTIN'S STABLES

BIRCH AVE.

BUFFALO ST.

Bow River

Hoodoos Trail

GOLF COURSE RD.

BANFF CENTRE

Marsh Loop Trail

CAVE AVE.

PARK ADMINISTRATION BUILDING

SPRAY AVE.

Bow River

Bow Falls

Spray River Trail

Sundance Canyon Trail

CAVE AND BASIN NATIONAL HISTORIC SITE

MOUNTAIN AVE.

BANFF SPRINGS HOTEL

Spray River

Moon

Upper Hot Springs ★

RIMROCK RESORT HOTEL

0   1 mi
0   1 km

SULPHUR MOUNTAIN GONDOLA

the bush. A lack of roads and scarcity of large game due to hunting meant that the best places to see animals, stuffed or otherwise, were the game paddock, the zoo, and this museum, which was built in 1903. In its early years, the Banff Zoo and Aviary occupied the grounds behind the museum. The zoo kept over 60 species of animals, including a polar bear. The museum itself was built before the park had electricity, hence the "railroad pagoda" design using skylights on all levels.

As times changed, the museum was considered outdated; plans for its demolition were put forward in the 1950s. Fortunately the museum was spared and later restored for the park's 100th anniversary in 1985. While the exhibits still provide visitors with an insight into the intricate workings of various park ecosystems, they are also an interesting link to the park's past. The museum is open in summer daily 10 A.M.–6 P.M., the rest of the year daily 1–5 P.M. Admission is $2.50. The museum also has a Discovery Room, where "touching" is encouraged, and a reading room stocked with books on the park.

Whyte Museum of the Canadian Rockies
The Whyte Foundation was established in the mid-1950s by local artists Peter and Catherine Whyte to help preserve artistic and historical material relating to the Canadian Rockies. Their museum opened in 1968 and has continued to grow ever since. It now houses the world's largest collection of Canadian Rockies literature and art. Included in the archives are over 4,000 volumes, oral tapes of early pioneers and outfitters, antique postcards, old cameras, manuscripts, and a large photography collection. The highlight is the photography of Byron Harmon, whose black-and-white studies of mountain geography have shown people around the world the beauty of the Canadian Rockies. The downstairs gallery features changing art exhibitions. The museum also houses the library and archives of the Alpine Club of Canada. On the grounds are a number of heritage homes formerly occupied by local pioneers. The Whyte Museum is beside the library at 111 Bear Street, 403/762-2291. It's open in summer Tuesday–Saturday 10 A.M.–9 P.M., Sunday–Monday 10 A.M.–6 P.M.; hours the rest of the year are 10 A.M.–5 P.M. Admission is adult $4, senior and child $2. Don't miss this one.

The Whyte Museum hosts a variety of interesting walking tours through summer. The most popular of these is the Historic Banff Walk, which departs from the museum daily at 11 A.M. and 3 P.M., taking around 90 minutes.

Natural History Museum
Banff's smallest museum, upstairs in the Clock Tower Mall at 112 Banff Avenue, 403/762-4652, is crammed with exhibits displaying the geological evolution of the Canadian Rockies. Highlights include a replica of Castleguard Cave (one of the largest caves in North America), an interesting slide show, rock and fossil displays, and a tacky life-size model of Bigfoot—just what you came to Banff for. It's open daily noon–5 P.M., till 10 P.M. in summer.

Cascade Gardens
One of the earliest entrepreneurs to take advantage of Banff's hot springs was Dr. R. G. Brett. In 1886, he opened a private spa and hospital that became known as Brett's Sanatorium. It accommodated 90 guests, drawn to Banff by the claimed healing qualities of the hot springs' water. The hotel burned down in 1933 and was replaced in 1936 by the **Park Administration Building** that stands today on the south side of the Bow River. Here you'll have a commanding view along Banff Avenue and of Cascade Mountain. And the surrounding gardens are immaculately manicured, making for enjoyable strolling on a sunny day.

Buffalo Nations Luxton Museum
Looking like a stockade, this museum west of the Banff Bridge at 1 Birch Avenue, 403/762-2388, is dedicated to the heritage of the natives who once inhabited the Canadian Rockies and adjacent prairies. It was named for prominent Banff resident Norman Luxton, who had a close relationship with the natives of the area and was involved in the Banff Indian Days. He operated a trading post on the site for many years before opening the museum in 1952 with the help of the Glenbow–Alberta Institute. The museum contains memorabilia from Luxton's 60-year relationship with the Stoney, as well as an elaborately decorated tepee, hunting equipment, a few stuffed animals, a realistic diorama of a buffalo jump, peace pipes, and traditional clothing.

The Indian Trading Post is now one of Banff's better gift shops and is definitely worth a browse. The museum is open in summer daily 9 A.M.–7 P.M., the rest of the year 11:30 A.M.–4:30 P.M. Admission is $6.

Cave and Basin National Historic Site

At the end of Cave Avenue, this historic site is the birthplace of Banff National Park and of the Canadian National Parks system. Here in 1883, three men employed by the C.P.R. stumbled upon the hot springs now known as the Cave and Basin and were soon lounging in the hot water— real luxury in the Wild West. They built a fence around the springs, constructed a crude cabin, and began the long process of establishing a claim to the site. But the government beat them to it, settling their claims for a few thousand dollars and acquiring the hot springs.

Bathhouses were installed in 1887 and bathers paid $.10 for a swim. The pools were eventually lined with concrete, and additions were built onto the original structures. Ironically, the soothing minerals in the water that had attracted millions of people to bathe here eventually caused the pools' demise. The minerals, combined with chlorine, produced sediments that ate away at the concrete structure until the pools were deemed unsafe. After closing in 1975, the pools were restored to their original look at a cost of $12 million. They reopened in 1985 only to close again in 1993 for the same reasons, coupled with flagging popularity.

Although the pools are now closed for swimming, the center is still one of Banff's most popular attractions. Interpretive displays describe the hows and whys of the springs. A narrow tunnel winds into the dimly lit cave, and short trails lead from the center to the cave entrance and through a unique environment created by the hot water from the springs. Interpretive tours begin four times daily in summer. The site is open in summer daily 9:30 A.M.–5 P.M., the rest of the year daily 11 A.M.–4 P.M. Admission to the center is $2.50. For more information, call 403/762-1566.

Upper Hot Springs

These springs on Mountain Avenue, toward Sulphur Mountain Gondola, were first developed in 1901. The present building was completed in 1935, with extensive renovations made in 1996.

Water flows out of the bedrock at 47°C and is cooled to 40°C in the main pool. Once considered for privatization, they are still run by Parks Canada and are popular throughout the year. Swimming is adult $7, senior and child $6, lockers and towel rental extra. Within the complex is **Pleiades Massage & Spa** offering a wide range of therapeutic treatments including massages from $45 for 30 minutes as well as body wraps, aromatherapy, and hydrotherapy. The facility, 403/762-1515, is open in summer daily 9 A.M.–11 P.M., 10 A.M.–10 P.M. the rest of the year. **Brewster,** 403/762-6767, provides shuttle service to the hot springs from downtown hotels for $20 including pool admission.

Sulphur Mountain Gondola

The easiest way to get high above town without raising a sweat is on this newly renovated gondola, 403/762-5438, which rises 700 meters in eight minutes to an elevation of 2,285 meters. From the observation deck at the upper terminal, the breathtaking view includes the townsite, Bow Valley, Cascade Mountain, Lake Minnewanka, and the Fairholme Range. Bighorn sheep often hang around the upper terminal. The short **Vista Trail** leads along a ridge to a restored weather observatory. Between 1903 and 1931, long before the gondola was built, Norman Sanson was the meteorological observer who collected data at the station. During this period he made over 1,000 ascents of Sulphur Mountain, all in the line of duty. **Summit Restaurant** serves mediocre food, inexpensive breakfasts, and priceless views. The gondola runs in summer 7:30 A.M.–9 P.M., shorter hours the rest of the year; closed in December. Adults pay $18, children $12. A 5.5-km trail to the summit begins from the Upper Hot Springs parking lot. Although it's a long slog, views on the way up are good and you'll be rewarded with a free gondola ride down—they don't check tickets at the top. From downtown the gondola is three km along Mountain Avenue. In summer **Brewster,** 403/762-6767, provides shuttle service to the gondola from downtown hotels ($25 includes gondola ride).

Banff Springs Hotel

On a terrace above a bend in the Bow River is one of the largest, grandest, and most opulent

Banff Springs Hotel

mountain-resort hotels in the world. What better way to spend a rainy afternoon than to explore this turreted 20th-century castle, seeking out a writing desk overlooking one of the world's most photographed scenes and penning a long letter to the folks back home?

"The Springs" has grown with the town and is an integral part of local history. William Cornelius Van Horne, vice president of the C.P.R., decided that the best way of encouraging customers to travel on his newly completed rail line across the Rockies was to build a series of luxurious mountain accommodations. The largest of these was begun in 1886, as close as possible to Banff's newly discovered hot springs. The location chosen had magnificent views and was only a short carriage ride from the train station. Money was no object and architect Bruce Price began designing a mountain resort the likes of which the world had never seen. At some stage of construction his plans were misinterpreted, and much to Van Horne's shock the building was built back to front. The best guest rooms faced the forested slopes of Sulphur Mountain while the kitchen had panoramic views of the Bow Valley.

On June 1, 1888 it opened, the largest hotel in the world with 250 rooms beginning at $3.50 per night including meals. Water from the nearby hot springs was piped into the hotel's steam baths. Rumor has it that when the pipes blocked, water from the Bow River was used, secretly supplemented by bags of sulphur-smelling chemicals. Overnight, the quiet community of Banff

became a destination resort for wealthy guests from around the world, and the hotel soon became one of North America's most popular accommodations. Every room was booked every day during the short summer seasons. In 1903, a wing was added, doubling the hotel's capacity. The following year a tower was added to each wing. Guest numbers reached 22,000 in 1911, and construction of a new hotel, designed by Walter Painter, began that year. The original design—an 11-story tower joining two wings in a baronial style—was reminiscent of a Scottish castle mixed with a French country chateau. This concrete-and-rock-faced, green-roofed building stood as it did at its completion in 1928 until 1999 when an ambitious multiyear program of renovations commenced. At first, the most obvious change to those who have visited before will be the new lobby, moved to a more accessible location, but all rooms have also been refurbished and many of the restaurants changed or upgraded. The Canadian Pacific moniker remained part of the Banff Spring's official name until 2000, when the hotel, and all other Canadian Pacific hotels, became part of the Fairmont Hotels and Resorts chain.

Don't let the hotel's opulence keep you from spending time here. Sightseeing is actually encouraged. Visit the hotel between 11:30 A.M. and 1:30 P.M., and enjoy a huge buffet lunch combined with a 30-minute **Historical Hotel Tour** for $19.95 per person. Call 403/762-2211 for details. Otherwise wander through on your own, admiring the 5,000 pieces of furniture and antiques (most "antiques" in public areas are reproductions), paintings, prints, tapestries, and rugs. Take in the medieval atmosphere of Mt. Stephen Hall with its lime flagstone floor, enormous windows, and large oak beams; take advantage of the luxurious spa facility (see "The Solace" under "Indoor Recreation," later in this chapter), or relax in one of 12 eateries or four lounges.

The hotel is a 15-minute walk southeast of town, either along Spray Avenue or via the trail along the south bank of the Bow River. Horse-drawn buggies take passengers from the Trail Rider Store at 132 Banff Avenue to the Springs for $35, while **Banff Transit** buses leave downtown for the Springs twice an hour, $1.

Bow Falls

Small but spectacular Bow Falls is below the Banff Springs Hotel, only a short walk from downtown. The waterfall is the result of a dramatic change in the course of the Bow River brought about by glaciation. At one time the river flowed north of Tunnel Mountain and out of the mountains via the valley of Lake Minnewanka. As the glaciers retreated they left terminal moraines, forming natural dams and changing the course of the river. Eventually the backed-up water found an outlet here between Tunnel Mountain and the northwest ridge of Mt. Rundle. The falls are most spectacular in late spring when runoff from the winter snows fills every river and stream in the Bow Valley watershed.

To get there from town, cross the bridge at the south end of Banff Avenue, scramble down the grassy embankment to the left, and follow a pleasant trail along the Bow River to a point above the falls. This easy walk is one km (30 minutes) each way. By car, cross the bridge and follow Golf Course signs. From the falls a paved road crosses the Spray River and passes through the golf course.

Banff Centre

On the lower slopes of Tunnel Mountain is Banff Centre, whose surroundings provide inspiration as one of Canada's leading centers for postgraduate students in four divisions—Centre for the Arts, Centre for Mountain Culture, Centre for Management, and Centre for Conferences. The Banff Centre opened in the summer of 1933 as a theater school. Since then it has grown to become a prestigious institution attracting artists of many disciplines from throughout Canada. The Centre's **Walter Phillips Gallery,** on St. Julien Road, 403/762-6281, presents changing exhibits of visual arts from throughout the world. Open Tuesday–Thursday noon–5 P.M., Friday–Saturday noon–8 P.M., and Sunday noon–5 P.M.

Activities are held on the grounds of the Banff Centre year-round. Highlights include a summer educational program, concerts, displays, live performances, the Banff Arts Festival, Banff Mountain Book Festival, and Banff Mountain Film Festival, to name a few (see "Festivals and Events" below). Call 403/762-6100 for a program or check the *Crag and Canyon* (published weekly on Wednesday).

VICINITY OF BANFF

Vermilion Lakes

This series of shallow lakes forms an expansive montane wetland supporting a variety of mammals and 238 species of birds. Vermilion Lakes Drive, paralleling the TransCanada Highway immediately west of Banff, provides the easiest access to the area. The level of **First Vermilion Lake** was once controlled by a dam. Since its removal the level of the lake has dropped. This is the beginning of a long process that will eventually see the area evolve into a floodplain forest such as is found along the Fenland Trail. **Second** and **Third Vermilion Lakes** have a higher water level that is controlled naturally by beaver dams. Near First Vermilion Lake is an active osprey nest. The entire area is excellent for wildlife viewing, especially in winter when it provides habitat for elk, coyote, and the occasional wolf.

Mt. Norquay Road

One of the best views of town accessible by car is on this road, which switchbacks steeply to the base of Banff Mt. Norquay, the local ski area. On the way up are several lookouts, including one near the top where bighorn sheep often graze.

To Lake Minnewanka

Lake Minnewanka Road begins where Banff Avenue ends at the northeast end of town. An alternative to driving along Banff Avenue is to take

Buffalo Street, opposite the Banff Park Museum, and follow it around Tunnel Mountain, passing the hostel, campground, and a number of viewpoints of the north face of Mt. Rundle, rising vertically from the forested valley below. This road eventually rejoins Banff Avenue at the Banff Rocky Mountain Resort. The first road to the right after passing under the TransCanada Highway leads to **Cascade Ponds,** a popular day-use area. The next turnout along this road is at **Lower Bankhead.** During the early 1900s, Bankhead was a booming mining town producing 200,000 tons of coal a year. The poor quality of coal and bitter labor disputes led to the mine's closure in 1922. Soon after, all the buildings were moved or demolished. Although for many years the mine had brought prosperity to the park, peoples' perceptions changed. The National Parks Act of 1930, which prohibited the establishment of mining claims in national parks, was greeted with little animosity. From the parking lot at Lower Bankhead, a 1.1-km interpretive trail leads through the industrial section of the town and past an old mine train. The town's 1,000 residents lived on the other side of the road at **Upper Bankhead.** Just before the Upper Bankhead turnoff the foundation of the Holy Trinity Church can be seen on the side of the hill to the right. Not much remains of Upper Bankhead. It is now a day-use area with picnic tables, kitchen shelters, and firewood. Through the meadow to the west of here are some large slag heaps, concealed mine entrances, and various stone foundations.

Lake Minnewanka

Meaning "Lake of the Water Spirit," Minnewanka is the largest body of water in Banff National Park. Mt. Inglismaldie (2,964 meters) and the Fairholme Range form an imposing backdrop. The reservoir was first constructed in 1912, and additional dams were built in 1922 and 1941 to supply hydroelectric power to Banff. Minnewanka Landing was a resort village that was submerged when the most recent dam went in. It's now a popular spot for scuba diving. **Lake Minnewanka Boat Tours,** 403/762-3473, has a 90-minute cruise to the far reaches of the lake. It departs from the dock 3–5 times daily and costs adult $26, child $11. Brewster, 403/762-6767, offers this cruise combined with a bus tour from

Banff for $41 per person. Easy walking trails lead along the western shore. The lake is great for fishing (lake trout to 15 kg) and is the only one in the park where motorboats are allowed.

From Lake Minnewanka the road continues along the reservoir wall—passing a plaque commemorating the Palliser Expedition—to **Johnson Lake,** which offers good fishing and swimming, as well as lakeside picnic facilities.

BOW VALLEY PARKWAY

Two roads link Banff to Lake Louise. The Trans-Canada Highway is the quicker route, more popular with through traffic. The other is the more scenic 51-km Bow Valley Parkway, which branches off the TransCanada Highway five km west of Banff. Cyclists will appreciate this road's two long divided sections and low speed limit (60 kph). Along this route are a number of impressive viewpoints, interpretive displays, picnic areas, good hiking, great opportunities for viewing wildlife, a hostel, three lodges, campgrounds, and one of the park's best restaurants (see "Accommodations" and "Food," below). Between March 1 and late June, the southern end of the parkway (as far north as Johnston Canyon) is closed daily 6 P.M.–9 A.M. for the protection of wildlife.

As you enter the parkway, you pass the quiet, creekside **Fireside** picnic area, where an interpretive display describes how the Bow Valley was formed. At **Backswamp Viewpoint,** you can look upstream to the site of a former dam, now a swampy wetland filled with aquatic vegetation. Farther along the road is another wetland at **Muleshoe.** This wetland consists of oxbow lakes that were formed when the Bow River changed its course and abandoned its meanders for a more direct path. Across the parkway is a one-km trail that climbs to a viewpoint overlooking the valley. (The slope around this trail is infested with wood ticks during late spring/early summer so be sure to check yourself carefully after hiking in this area.) To the east, **Hole-in-the-wall** is visible. This large-mouthed cave was created by the Bow Glacier, which once filled the valley. As the glacier receded, its meltwater dissolved the soft limestone bedrock, creating what is known as a solution cave.

Beyond Muleshoe the road inexplicably divides for only a few meters. A large white spruce stood on the island until it blew down in 1984. The story goes that while the road was being constructed a surly foreman was asleep in the shade of the tree, and not daring to rouse him workers cleared the roadway around him. The road then passes through particularly hilly terrain, part of a massive rock slide that occurred around 8,000 years ago.

Continuing down the parkway you'll pass the following sights.

Johnston Canyon

Johnston Creek drops over a series of spectacular waterfalls here, deep within the chasm it has carved into the limestone bedrock. The canyon is not nearly as deep as Maligne Canyon in Jasper National Park (30 meters at its deepest, compared to 50 meters at Maligne), but the raised boardwalk that leads to the falls has been built through the depths of the canyon rather than along its lip, making it seem just as spectacular. The lower falls are one km from Johnston Canyon Resort. Other falls line the trail as it weaves its way through the canyon to the **Ink Pots,** mineral springs whose sediments reflect sunlight, producing a brilliant aqua color. While in the canyon look for nesting great gray owls and black swifts.

Silver City

At the west end of **Moose Meadows** a small plaque marks the site of Silver City. At its peak this boomtown had a population of 2,000, making it bigger than Calgary at the time. The city was founded by John Healy, who also founded the notorious Fort Whoop-Up in Lethbridge. During its heady days, five mines were operating, extracting not silver but ore rich in copper and lead. The town had a half dozen hotels, four or five stores, two real-estate offices, and a station on the transcontinental rail line when its demise began. Two men, named Patton and Pettigrew, salted their mine with gold and silver ore to attract investors. After selling 2,000 shares at $5 each, they vanished, leaving investors with a useless mine. Investment in the town ceased, mines closed, and the people left. Only one man refused to leave. His name was James Smith, but he was known to everyone as Joe. In 1887 when

Silver City came under the jurisdiction of the National Parks Service, Joe was allowed to remain. And he did so, friend to everyone including Stoney Indians, Father Albert Lacombe who occasionally stopped by, well-known Banff guide Tom Wilson, and of course to the animals who grazed around his cabin. By 1926, he was unable to trap or hunt due to failing eyesight, and many people tried to persuade him to leave. It wasn't until 1937 that he finally moved to a Calgary retirement home, where he died soon after.

Castle Mountain to Lake Louise

After leaving the former site of Silver City, the aptly named Castle Mountain comes into view. It's one of the park's most recognizable peaks and most interesting geographical features. The mountain consists of very old rock (approximately 500 million years old) sitting atop much younger rock (200 million years old). This unusual situation occurred as the mountains were forced upward by pressure below the earth's surface, thrusting the older rock up and over the younger rock in places.

The road skirts the base of the mountain, passes Castle Mountain Village (gas, food, accommodations), and climbs a small hill to Storm Mountain Viewpoint, which provides more stunning views and a picnic area. The next commercial facility is **Baker Creek Chalets and Bistro,** an excellent spot for a meal. Then it's on to another viewpoint at Morant's Curve, from where Temple Mountain is visible. After passing another picnic area and a chunk of Precambrian shield, the road rejoins the TransCanada Highway at Lake Louise.

LAKE LOUISE AND VICINITY

When you see the first flush of morning sun hit Victoria Glacier, and the impossibly steep northern face of Mt. Victoria reflected in the sparkling, emerald-green waters of Lake Louise, you'll understand why this lake is regarded as one of the world's seven natural wonders. And overlooking the magnificent scene, Chateau Lake Louise is without a doubt one of the world's most photographed hotels. Apart from staring, photographing, and video taping, the area has plenty to keep you busy. Nearby you'll find some of

LAKE LOUISE: A LITTLE BIT OF HISTORY

During the summer of 1882, outfitter Tom Wilson was camped near the confluence of the Bow and Pipestone Rivers when he heard the distant rumblings of an avalanche. He questioned Stoney Indian guides and was told the noises originated from "Lake of Little Fishes." The following day Wilson, led by a native guide, hiked to the lake to investigate. He became the first white man to lay eyes on what he named Emerald Lake. Two years later, the name was changed to Lake Louise, honoring Princess Louise Caroline Alberta, daughter of Queen Victoria.

In 1890, as word of the lake's beauty spread, a modest two-bedroom wooden hotel replaced the crude cabin that had been built on the lakeshore. The coming of the transcontinental railroad further increased the lake's popularity. A railway station known as Laggan was built where the rail line passed closest to the lake, six km away. (Until a road was completed in 1926, everyone arrived by train.) The station's name was changed to Lake Louise in 1913 to prevent confusion among visitors. The hotel by the lake continued to prosper. After many additions, a disastrous fire, and the construction of a new concrete wing in 1925, the chateau of today took shape.

The lakes are such marvelous colors. What kind of chemicals do you use?
—ANONYMOUS,
Lake Louise
Visitor Centre

WHYTE MUSEUM OF THE CANADIAN ROCKIES

the park's best hiking, canoeing, and horseback riding. And only a short distance away is Moraine Lake, not as famous as Lake Louise but rivaling it in beauty.

Lake Louise is 51 km northwest of Banff along the TransCanada Highway, or a little bit farther if you take the quieter Bow Valley Parkway. The hamlet of Lake Louise, composed of a small mall, hotels, and restaurants, is in the Bow Valley, just west of the TransCanada Highway. The lake itself is 200 vertical meters above the valley floor, along a winding four-km road. Across the valley is Canada's largest ski area, also called Lake Louise. It's a world-class facility renowned for diverse terrain, abundant snow, and breathtaking views.

From Lake Louise the TransCanada Highway continues west, exiting the park over Kicking Horse Pass (1,647 meters) and passing through Yoho National Park to Golden. Highway 93, the famous Icefields Parkway, also begins at the townsite and heads northwest through the park's northern reaches to Jasper National Park.

Lake Louise

In summer, around 10,000 visitors a day make the journey from the Bow Valley floor up to Lake Louise. By noon the tiered parking lot is often full. An alternative to the road is one of two trails that begin at the townsite and end at the public parking lot (see "Hiking," below). From here a number of paved trails lead to the lake's eastern shore. From these vantage points the dramatic setting can be fully appreciated. The lake is 2.4 km long, 500 meters wide, and up to 90 meters deep. Its cold waters reach a maximum temperature of 4°C in August.

Chateau Lake Louise is a tourist attraction in itself. Built by the C.P.R. to take the pressure off the popular Banff Springs Hotel, the chateau

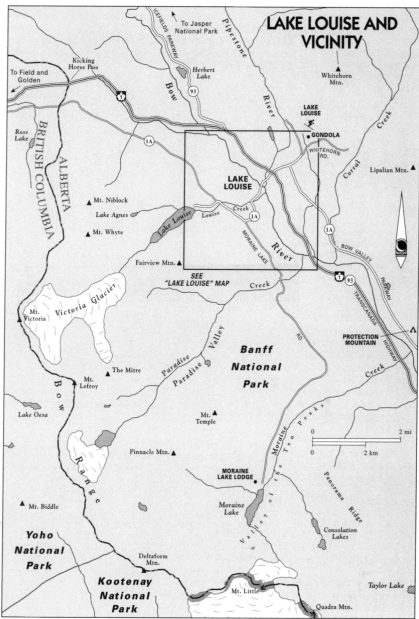

LAKE LOUISE AND VICINITY

To Jasper National Park

ICEFIELDS PARKWAY

Kicking Horse Pass

To Field and Golden

Herbert Lake

Pipestone River

Bow

93

Whitehorn Mtn.

Ross Lake

1

1A

BRITISH COLUMBIA

ALBERTA

LAKE LOUISE

GONDOLA

WHITEHORN RD.

Creek

Corral

Lipalian Mtn.

▲ Mt. Niblock

Lake Agnes

▲ Mt. Whyte

LAKE LOUISE

Lake Louise

Louise

Creek

1A

1A

Fairview Mtn. ▲

SEE "LAKE LOUISE" MAP

Moraine Lake

River

BOW VALLEY

MOON

Mt. Victoria

Victoria Glacier

Creek

1 93

TRANSCANADA

PARKWAY

The Mitre

Mt. Lefroy

Paradise Valley

Paradise

Banff National Park

RD.

PROTECTION MOUNTAIN

HIGHWAY

Λ

Lake Oesa

Bow

Mt. Temple ▲

Creek

B

Range

Pinnacle Mtn. ▲

0   2 mi

0   2 km

▲ Mt. Biddle

Moraine

RD.

Yoho National Park

MORAINE LAKE LODGE

Panorama Ridge

Deltaform Mtn.

Valley of the Ten Peaks

Moraine Lake

Consolation Lakes

Kootenay National Park

Mt. Little

Quadra Mtn.

Taylor Lake

© AVALON TRAVEL PUBLISHING, INC.

has seen many changes in the last 100 years, yet it remains one of the world's great mountain resorts. No one minds the hordes of camera-toting tourists who traipse through each day—and there's really no way to avoid them. The immaculately manicured gardens between the chateau and the lake make an interesting fore-ground for the millions of Lake Louise pho-tographs taken each year. At the lakeshore boathouse, canoes are rented for $30 per hour.

The snow-covered peak at the back of the lake is **Mt. Victoria** (3,459 meters), which sits on the Continental Divide. Amazingly, its base is over 10 km from the eastern end of the lake. Mt. Victoria, first climbed in 1897, remains one of the park's most popular peaks for mountaineers. Although the difficult northeast face (facing the chateau) was first successfully ascended in 1922, the most popular and easiest route to the summit is along the southeast ridge, approached from Abbot Pass.

Moraine Lake

Although less than half the size of Lake Louise, Moraine Lake is just as spectacular and worthy of just as much film. It is located up a winding road 12.5 km off Lake Louise Drive. Its rugged setting, nestled in the Valley of the Ten Peaks among the towering mountains of the main ranges, has provided inspiration for millions of people from around the world since Walter Wilcox became the first white man to reach its shore in 1899. Wilcox's subsequent writings—such as "no scene has given me an equal im-

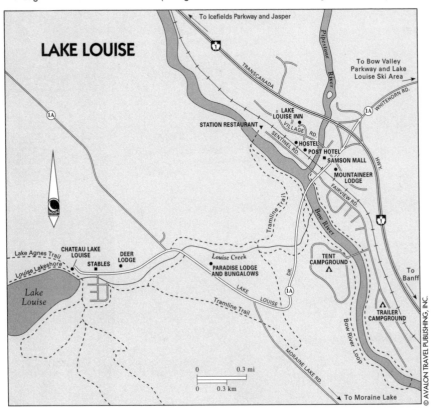

pression of inspiring solitude and rugged grandeur . . ." —guaranteed the lake's future popularity. Although Wilcox was a knowledgeable man, he named the lake on the assumption that it was dammed by a glacial moraine deposited by the retreating Wenkchemna Glacier. In fact, the large rock pile that blocks its waters was deposited by major rockfalls from the Tower of Babel to the south. The lake often remains frozen until June, and the access road is closed all winter. A trail leads along the lake's northern shore, and canoes are rented for $25 per hour from the concession below the lodge.

Lake Louise Sightseeing Gondola

During summer the Friendly Giant quad chairlift at Lake Louise ski area whisks visitors up the face of Mt. Whitehorn to Whitehorn Lodge, at an altitude of over two km above sea level. The view from the lodge—of the Bow Valley, Lake Louise, and the Continental Divide—is among the most spectacular in the Canadian Rockies. Short trails lead through the forests, across open meadows, and, for the energetic, to the summit of Mt. Whitehorn, over 600 vertical meters above. Visitors are free to walk these trails, but guided walks are complimentary and leave regularly from the Nature Centre. After working up an appetite, head to the teahouse in the Whitehorn Lodge, try the outdoor barbecue, or back at the base area, enjoy a meal in the Lodge of the Ten Peaks, the ski area's impressive new day lodge. The lift operates July–August daily 8:30 A.M.–6 P.M., shorter hours June and September; adult $14, senior $12, child $8. For more information, call 403/522-3555. Free shuttles run from Lake Louise accommodations to the lift.

ICEFIELDS PARKWAY

The 230-km Icefields Parkway, between Lake Louise and Jasper, is one of the most scenic, exciting, and inspiring mountain roads ever built. From Lake Louise it parallels the Continental Divide, following in the shadow of the highest, most rugged mountains in the Canadian Rockies. The first 122 km to Sunwapta Pass (the boundary between Banff and Jasper National Parks) can be driven in two hours, and the entire

Moraine Lake

parkway in four. But it's likely you'll want to spend at least a day, probably more, stopping at each of the 13 viewpoints, hiking the trails, watching the abundant wildlife, and just generally enjoying one of the world's most magnificent landscapes. Along the section within Banff National Park are two lodges, three hostels, three campgrounds, and one gas station.

Although the road is steep and winding in places, it has a wide shoulder, making it ideal for an extended bike trip. Allow seven days to pedal north from Banff to Jasper, staying at hostels or camping along the route. This is the preferable direction to travel by bike as the elevation of Jasper townsite is more than 500 meters lower than either Banff or Lake Louise.

The parkway remains open year-round, although winter brings with it some special considerations. The road is often closed for short periods for avalanche control—check road conditions in Banff or Lake Louise before setting out. And fill up with gas—no services are available between November and April.

Lake Louise to Crowfoot Glacier

The Icefields Parkway forks right from the Trans-Canada Highway just north of Lake Louise. The impressive scenery begins immediately. Just three km from the junction is **Herbert Lake,** formed during the last ice age when retreating glaciers deposited a pile of rubble—known as a moraine—across a shallow valley and water filled in behind it. The lake is a perfect place for early morning or evening photography when the Waputik Range and distinctively shaped **Mt. Temple** are reflected in its waters.

Traveling north, you'll notice numerous depressions in the steep, shaded slopes of the Waputik Range across the Bow Valley. The cooler climate on these north-facing slopes makes them prone to glaciation. Cirques were cut by small "local glaciers." On the opposite side of the road, **Mt. Hector** (3,394 meters), easily recognized by its layered peak, soon comes into view.

Hector Lake Viewpoint is 16 km from the junction. Although the view is partially obscured by trees, the emerald-green waters nestled below a massive wall of limestone form a breathtaking scene. **Bow Peak,** seen looking northward along the highway, is only 2,868 meters high but is completely detached from the Waputik Range, making it a popular destination for mountain climbers. As you leave this viewpoint look across the northeast end of Hector Lake for glimpses of **Mt. Balfour** (3,246 meters) on the distant skyline.

Crowfoot Glacier

The aptly named Crowfoot Glacier can best be appreciated from a viewpoint 17 km north of Hector Lake. The glacier sits on a wide ledge near the top of Crowfoot Mountain, from where its glacial "claws" cling to the mountain's steep slopes. The retreat of this glacier has been dramatic. Only 50 years ago, two of the claws extended to the base of the lower cliff.

Bow Lake

The sparkling, translucent waters of Bow Lake are among the most beautiful that can be seen from the Icefields Parkway. The lake was created when moraines deposited by retreating glaciers dammed subsequent meltwater. On still days, the water reflects the snowy peaks, their sheer cliffs, and the scree slopes that run into the

Bow Lake

lake. You don't need a photography class to take good pictures here! At the southeast end of the lake, a day-use area offers waterfront picnic tables and a trail to a swampy area at the lake's outlet. At the upper end of the lake, you'll find a lodge and the trailhead for a walk to Bow Glacier Falls (see "Hiking," below).

The road leaves Bow Lake and climbs to **Bow Summit.** Looking back toward the lake, its true color becomes apparent and the Crowfoot Glacier reveals its unique shape. At an elevation of 2,069 meters, this pass is one of the highest points crossed by a public road in Canada. It is also the beginning of the Bow River, the one you camped beside at Lake Louise, photographed flowing through the town of Banff, and strolled along in downtown Calgary.

Peyto Lake

From the parking lot at Bow Summit, a short paved trail leads to one of the most breathtaking views you could ever imagine. Far below the viewpoint is Peyto Lake, an impossibly intense green lake whose hues change according to season.

Before heavy melting of nearby glaciers begins (in June or early July), the lake is dark blue. As summer progresses, meltwater flows across a delta and into the lake. This water is laden with finely ground particles of rock debris known as "rock flour," which remains suspended in the water. It is not the mineral content of the rock flour that is responsible for the lake's unique color, but rather the particles reflecting the blue-green sector of the light spectrum. As the amount of suspended rock flour changes, so does the color of the lake.

The lake is one of many park landmarks named for early outfitter Bill Peyto. In 1898, Peyto was part of an expedition camped at Bow Lake. Seeking solitude (as he was wont to do), he slipped off during the night to sleep near this lake. Other members of the party coined the name "Peyto's Lake," and it stuck.

A further three km along the parkway is a viewpoint from which **Peyto Glacier** is visible at the far end of Peyto Lake Valley. This glacier is part of the extensive **Wapta Icefield,** which straddles the Continental Divide and extends into the northern reaches of **Yoho National Park** in British Columbia.

Beside the Continental Divide
From Bow Pass the parkway descends to a viewpoint directly across the Mistaya River from **Mt. Patterson** (3,197 meters). Snowbird Glacier clings precariously to the mountain's steep northeast face, and the mountain's lower, wooded slopes are heavily scarred where rock and ice slides have swept down the mountainside.

As the parkway continues to descend and crosses Silverhorn Creek, the jagged limestone peaks of the Continental Divide can be seen to the west. **Mistaya Lake** is a three-km-long body of water that sits at the bottom of the valley between the road and the divide, but it can't be seen from the parkway. The best place to view it is from the Howse Peak Viewpoint at Upper Waterfowl Lake. From here the high ridge that forms the Continental Divide is easily distinguishable. Seven peaks can be seen from here, including **Howse Peak** (3,290 meters). At no point along this ridge does the elevation drop below 2,750 meters. From Howse Peak, the Continental Divide makes a 90-degree turn to the west. One dominant peak that can be seen from Bow Pass to north of Saskatchewan River Crossing is **Mt.**

Chephren (3,268 meters). Its distinctive shape and position away from the main ridge of the Continental Divide make it easy to distinguish. (Look for it directly north of Howse Peak.)

To Saskatchewan River Crossing
Numerous trails lead around the swampy shores of **Upper** and **Lower Waterfowl Lakes,** providing one of the park's best opportunities to view moose, who feed on the abundant aquatic vegetation that grows in Upper Waterfowl Lake. Rock and other debris that have been carried down nearby valley systems have built up, forming a wide alluvial fan, nearly blocking the Mistaya River and creating Upper Waterfowl Lake.

Continuing north is **Mt. Murchison** (3,337 meters), on the east side of the parkway. Although not one of the park's highest mountains, this gray-and-yellow massif of Cambrian rock comprises 10 individual peaks, covering an area of 30 square km.

From a parking lot 14 km northeast of Waterfowl Lake Campground, a short trail descends into the montane forest to **Mistaya Canyon.** Here the effects of erosion can be appreciated as the Mistaya River leaves the floor of Mistaya Valley, plunging through a narrow-walled canyon into the North Saskatchewan Valley. The area is scarred with potholes where boulders have been whirled around by the action of fast-flowing water, carving deep depressions into the softer limestone bedrock below.

The **North Saskatchewan River** posed a major problem for early travelers and later for the builders of the Icefields Parkway. This swiftly running river eventually drains into Hudson Bay. In 1989 it was named a Canadian Heritage River. One km past the bridge you'll come to a panoramic viewpoint of the entire valley. From here the Howse and Mistaya Rivers can be seen converging with the North Saskatchewan at a silt-laden delta. This is also a junction with Hwy. 11 (also known as David Thompson Hwy.), which follows the North Saskatchewan River to Rocky Mountain House and Red Deer. From this viewpoint numerous peaks can be seen to the west. Two sharp peaks are distinctive. **Mt. Outram** (3,254 meters) is the closer. The farther is **Mt. Forbes** (3,630 meters), highest peak in Banff National Park (and sixth-highest in the Canadian Rockies).

To Sunwapta Pass

On the north side of the North Saskatchewan River is the towering hulk of **Mt. Wilson** (3,261 meters), named for Banff outfitter Tom Wilson. The Icefields Parkway passes this massif on its western flanks. A pullout, just past Rampart Creek Campground, offers good views of Mt. Amery to the west and Mounts Sarbach, Chephren, and Murchison to the south. Beyond here is the **Weeping Wall**, a long cliff of gray limestone where a series of waterfalls tumbles more than 100 meters down the steep slopes of Cirrus Mountain. In winter this wall of water freezes, becoming a mecca for ice climbers.

After ascending quickly, the road drops again before beginning a long climb to Sunwapta Pass. Halfway up the 360-vertical-meter climb is a viewpoint well worth a stop (cyclists will definitely appreciate a rest). From here views extend down the valley to the slopes of Mt. Saskatchewan and, on the other side of the parkway, Cirrus Mountain. Another viewpoint, farther up the road, has the added attraction of a view of Panther Falls across the valley. A cairn at **Sunwapta Pass** (2,023 meters) marks the boundary between Banff and Jasper National Parks. It also marks the divide between the North Saskatchewan and Sunwapta Rivers, whose waters drain into the Atlantic and Arctic oceans, respectively.

HIKING

After experiencing the international thrills of Banff Avenue, many people will want to see the *real* park, which is, after all, the reason that millions of visitors flock here, thousands take low-paying jobs just to stay here, and others become so severely addicted that they start families and live happily ever after here.

Although many landmarks can be seen from the roadside, to really experience the park's personality you'll need to go for a hike. One of the best things about Banff's 80-odd hiking trails is the variety. From short interpretive walks originating in town, to easy hikes rewarded by spectacular vistas, to a myriad of overnight backcountry opportunities, Banff's trails offer something for everyone. Before attempting any hikes, you should visit the **Banff Visitor Centre**, 224 Banff Avenue, 403/762-1550, where staff can advise you on the condition of trails and closures. If you are planning an overnight trip into the backcountry you *must* pick up a Wilderness Pass from either of the park information centers before heading out; $6 per person per night.

HIKES AROUND THE TOWN OF BANFF

Fenland

- Length: 2 km (30 minutes) roundtrip
- Elevation gain: none
- Rating: easy

If you've just arrived in town, this short interpretive trail provides an excellent introduction to the Bow Valley ecosystem. It begins at the Forty Mile Creek Picnic Area, 300 meters north of the rail line along Mt. Norquay Road. A brochure, available at the trailhead, explains the various stages in the transition between wetland and floodplain spruce forest, visible as you progress around the loop. This fen environment is prime habitat for many species of birds. The work of beavers can be seen along the trail, and elk are here during winter. This trail is also a popular shortcut for joggers and cyclists heading for Vermilion Lakes.

Tunnel Mountain

- Length: 2.3 km (30–60 minutes) one-way
- Elevation gain: 300 meters
- Rating: easy/moderate

Accessible from town, this short hike is an easy climb to one of the park's lower peaks. The trailhead is on St. Julien Road, 350 meters south of Wolf Street. The trail ascends the western flank of Tunnel Mountain through a forest of lodgepole pine, switchbacking past some viewpoints before reaching a ridge just below the summit. Here the trail turns northward, climbing through a forest of Douglas fir to the summit (which is partially treed, preventing 360-degree views).

Bow River/Hoodoos

- Length: 4.8 km (60–90 minutes) one-way
- Elevation gain: minimal

• Rating: easy

From the Bow River Viewpoint on Tunnel Mountain Drive, the trail descends to the Bow River, passing under the sheer east face of Tunnel Mountain. It then follows the river a short distance before climbing into a meadow where deer and elk often graze. From this perspective the north face of Mt. Rundle is particularly imposing. As the trail climbs you'll hear the traffic on Tunnel Mountain Road long before you see it. The trail ends at hoodoos, strange limestone-and-gravel columns jutting mysteriously out of the forest. An alternative to returning the same way is to catch the **Banff Transit** bus from Tunnel Mountain Campgrounds. It leaves every half hour ($1).

Sundance Canyon

• Length: 4.4 km (90 minutes) one-way
• Elevation gain: 100 meters
• Rating: easy

Sundance Canyon is a rewarding destination accessed from the Cave and Basin National Historic Site. Unfortunately the first three km are along a paved road closed to traffic (but not bikes) and hard on your soles. Occasional glimpses of the Sawback Range are afforded by breaks in the forest. The road ends at a shaded picnic area from where the 2.4-km Sundance Loop begins. Sundance Creek was once a larger river whose upper drainage basin was diverted by glacial action. Its powerful waters have eroded into the soft bedrock, forming a spectacular overhanging canyon whose bed is strewn with large boulders that have tumbled in.

Spray River

• Length: 6 km (2 hours) one-way
• Elevation gain: 70 meters
• Rating: easy/moderate

This trail follows one of the many fire roads in the park. It is not particularly interesting, but it's accessible from downtown Banff and makes a pleasant way to escape the crowds. From the Bow Falls parking lot, walk along Golf Course Road to behind the green of the first golf hole on the right-hand side of the road. From there a trail heads uphill into the forest. It follows the Spray River closely—when not in sight the river can always be heard. For those so inclined, a river crossing one km from the golf course allows for a shorter loop. Continuing south, the trail climbs a bluff for a good view of the Banff Springs Hotel and Bow Valley. The return journey is straightforward with occasional views, ending at a locked gate behind the Banff Springs Hotel, a short walk to Bow Falls.

For serious hikers this trail provides access to the park's rugged and remote southern reaches, but there's another interesting option involving this trail for keen day-hikers. It involves arranging a lift to the trailhead of the Goat Creek hike in Kananaskis Country (see "Hiking" under "Spray Lake" in the Kananaskis Country chapter). From this trailhead, it's 19 km (six hours) one-way back to Banff down the Spray River watershed on a trail that drops over 300 meters in elevation. The trail is most popular with mountain bikers and cross-country skiers.

Western Slope of Mt. Rundle

• Length: 5.4 km (2 hours) one-way
• Elevation gain: 480 meters
• Rating: moderate

At 2,950 meters, Mt. Rundle is one of the park's dominant peaks. Climbing to its summit is possible without ropes, but previous scrambling experience is advised. An alternative is to ascend the mountain's western slope along an easy-to-follow trail that ends just over 1,000 vertical meters before the summit. The trail follows the Spray River Trail (see above) before branching off left 700 meters from Golf Course Road and climbing steadily, breaking out of the enclosed forest after 2.5 km. The trail ends in a gully from which the undefined route to the summit begins.

Stoney Squaw

• Length: 2.4-km loop (1 hour round-trip)
• Elevation gain: 180 meters
• Rating: easy

Looking north along Banff Avenue, Stoney Squaw's 1,884-meter summit is dwarfed by Cascade Mountain, directly behind it. To get to the trailhead of a trail that leads to its easily reached summit, follow Mt. Norquay Road to a parking lot at the ski area. Immediately to the right of the entrance, a small sign marks the trail. The narrow trail passes through a thick forest of lodgepole pine and spruce before breaking out into the open near the summit. The sweeping panorama includes Vermilion Lakes, the Bow Valley, Banff, Spray River Valley, Mt. Rundle, Lake

Minnewanka, and the imposing face of Cascade Mountain (2,998 meters). The return trail follows the northwest slope of Stoney Squaw to an old ski run at the opposite end of the parking lot.

Cascade Amphitheatre
• Length: 6.6 km (2–3 hours) one-way
• Elevation gain: 610 meters
• Rating: moderate/difficult

This enormous cirque and the subalpine meadows directly behind Cascade Mountain are one of the most rewarding destinations for hiking in the Banff area. The demanding trail begins by the Banff Mt. Norquay day lodge at the end of Mt. Norquay Road. From parking lot no. 3, the trail skirts the base of a number of ski lifts, following an old road to the floor of Forty Mile Valley. Keep right at all trail junctions. One km after crossing Forty Mile Creek, the trail begins switchbacking up the western flank of Cascade Mountain through a forest of lodgepole pine. Along the way are breathtaking views of Mt. Louis's sheer east face. After the trail levels off it enters a magnificent U-shaped valley and the amphitheater begins to define itself. The trail becomes indistinct in the subalpine meadow, which is carpeted in colorful wildflowers during summer. Farther up the valley, vegetation thins out as boulder-strewn talus slopes cover the ground. If you sit still long enough on these rocks, marmots, and pikas will slowly appear, emitting shrill whistles before disappearing again.

The most popular route to the summit of 2,998-meter Cascade Mountain is along the southern ridge of the amphitheater wall. It is a long scramble up scree slopes and is made more difficult by a false summit; it should be attempted only by experienced scramblers.

C Level Cirque
• Length: 4 km (90 minutes) one-way
• Elevation gain: 455 meters
• Rating: moderate

This trail begins from Upper Bankhead Picnic Area on the Lake Minnewanka Road and is named for an abandoned mine along its route. It climbs steadily through a forest of lodgepole pine, aspen, and spruce to a pile of tailings and broken-down concrete walls. Soon after is a panoramic view of Lake Minnewanka, then the trail reenters the forest before ending in a small cirque with views down the Bow Valley to Canmore and beyond. The cirque is carved into the eastern face of Cascade Mountain where snow often lingers until July. When the snow melts, the lush soil is covered in a carpet of colorful wildflowers.

Aylmer Lookout
• Length: 12 km (4 hours) one-way
• Elevation gain: 810 meters
• Rating: moderate/difficult

The first eight-km stretch of this trail follows the northern shore of Lake Minnewanka from the day-use area to a junction. The right fork leads to a campground, while the left climbs steeply to the site of an old fire tower on top of an exposed ridge. The deep blue waters of Lake Minnewanka are visible, backed by the imposing peaks of Mt. Girouard (2,995 meters) and Mt. Inglismaldie (2,964 meters). Bighorn sheep often graze in this area. From here a trail forks left and continues climbing to the alpine tundra of Aylmer Pass.

HIKES BETWEEN BANFF AND LAKE LOUISE

Cory Pass
• Length: 5.8 km (2.5 hours) one-way
• Elevation gain: 920 meters
• Rating: moderate/difficult

This strenuous hike from the Fireside Picnic Area at the Banff end of the Bow Valley Parkway has a rewarding objective—a magnificent view of dogtoothed Mt. Louis. The towering slab of limestone rises more than 500 meters from the valley below. Just over one km from the trailhead, the trail divides. The left fork climbs steeply across an open slope to an uneven ridge that it follows before ascending yet another steep slope to Cory Pass—a wild, windy, desolate area surrounded in jagged peaks dominated by Mt. Louis. An alternative to returning along the same trail is continuing down into Gargoyle Valley, following the base of Mt. Edith before ascending to Edith Pass and returning to the junction one km from the picnic area. Total distance for this trip is 13 km, a long day considering the steep climbs and descents involved.

Mount Louis, as seen from a high ridge that is traversed between Cory and Edith Passes

Bourgeau Lake

- Length: 7.6 km (2.5 hours) one-way
- Elevation gain: 730 meters
- Rating: moderate

This trail follows Wolverine Creek from a parking area three km west of Sunshine Village Junction on the TransCanada Highway to a small subalpine lake nestled at the base of an impressive limestone amphitheater. Although the trail is moderately steep, plenty of distractions along the way are worthy of a stop (and rest). Across the Bow Valley, the Sawback Range is easy to distinguish. As the forest of lodgepole pine turns to spruce, the trail passes under the cliffs of Mt. Bourgeau and crosses Wolverine Creek (below a spot where it tumbles photogenically over exposed bedrock). After strenuous switchbacks, the trail climbs into the cirque containing Bourgeau Lake. As you continue around the lake's rocky shore, you'll hear the colonies of noisy pikas, even if you don't see them.

Rock Isle Lake

- Length: 8 km (2.5 hours) one-way
- Elevation gain: 590 meters
- Rating: moderate

Sunshine Meadows, straddling the Continental Divide, is a unique and beautiful region of the Canadian Rockies. Large amounts of precipitation create a lush cover of vegetation during the short summer season—over 300 species of wildflowers alone have been recorded here. For 60 years the meadows have been a favorite area for downhill skiing, though it wasn't until 1984 that summer activities were promoted. Suddenly, instead of a few hundred adventurous souls willing to hike the 6.5-km road into the meadows, tens of thousands of visitors were whisked onto the fragile alpine tundra by gondola. In 1992 Sunshine Village terminated its summer gondola service and the meadows are quiet once again.

To get to the base station from Banff follow the TransCanada Highway nine km west to Sunshine Village Road, which continues another nine km to the Gondola Base Station. The road to the meadows is closed to public traffic and climbs steadily for 6.5 km to Sunshine Village. From there the Rock Isle Lake Trail passes the Strawberry Chairlift and climbs out of the valley into an alpine meadow covered in a colorful carpet of fireweed, glacier lilies, mountain avens, white mountain heather, and forget-me-nots. Mt. Assiniboine (3,611 meters), known as the "Matterhorn of the Rockies," is easily distinguished to the southeast. Various viewpoints punctuate the descent to the lake, which is ringed by benches and an observation deck.

In summer, **White Mountain Adventures** offers a shuttle service for a limited number of hikers to Sunshine Village from Banff (daily at 8:45 A.M., $35 roundtrip) and the Sunshine Village parking lot (daily at 9:30 A.M., 10:30 A.M., 11:30 A.M., and 1:30 P.M., $18 round-trip). If you take the 10:30 A.M. shuttle, a two-hour guided hike is just $8 extra. Advance reservations are required; call 403/678-4099 or 800/408-0005.

Shadow Lake

- Length: 14.3 km (4.5 hours) one-way
- Elevation gain: 440 meters
- Rating: moderate

Shadow is one of the many impressive subalpine lakes along the Continental Divide and a popular base for a great variety of day trips. The trail begins at the Redearth Creek Parking Area, 20 km west of Banff on the TransCanada Highway. It follows the old Redearth fire road for 11 km before forking right and climbing into the forest. The campground is two km beyond this junction, and just 500 meters farther is **Shadow Lake Lodge** (see "Backcountry Huts and Lodges" in the "Accommodations" section, below, for details). The lake is nearly two km long, and from its southern shore trails lead to Ball Pass, Gibbon Pass, and Haiduk Lake.

Castle Lookout
- Length: 3.7 km (90 minutes) one-way
- Elevation gain: 520 meters
- Rating: moderate

However you travel through the Bow Valley, you can't help but be impressed by Castle Mountain rising proudly from the forest below. This trail takes you above the tree line on the mountain's west face to the site of Mt. Eisenhower fire lookout, abandoned in the 1970s and burned in the 1980s. The trailhead is on the Bow Valley Parkway, five km northwest of Castle Junction. The trail follows a wide pathway for 1.5 km to an abandoned cabin in a forest of lodgepole pine and spruce. It then becomes narrower and steeper, switchbacking through a meadow before climbing through a narrow band of rock and leveling off near the lookout site. Magnificent panoramas of the Bow Valley spread out before you in both directions. Storm Mountain can be seen directly across the valley.

Rockbound Lake
- Length: 8.4 km (2.5 hours) one-way
- Elevation gain: 760 meters
- Rating: moderate/difficult

The trailhead for this strenuous hike is just east of Castle Junction on the Bow Valley Parkway. For the first five km the trail follows an old fire road along the southern flanks of Castle Mountain. Early in the season or after heavy rain, this section can be boggy. Glimpses of surrounding peaks ease the pain of the steady climb as the trail narrows. After eight km you'll come to Tower Lake, backed by grassed slopes, which the trail skirts to the right before climbing a steep slope. From the ridge, Rockbound Lake comes into view and the reason for its name immediately

becomes apparent. A scramble up any of the nearby slopes will reward you with good views.

HIKES AROUND LAKE LOUISE

The variety of hiking opportunities in the vicinity of Lake Louise and Moraine Lake is surely equal to any area on the face of the earth. The region's potential for outdoor recreation was first realized in the late 1800s, and it soon became the center of hiking activity in the Canadian Rockies. This popularity continues today; trails here are among the most heavily used in the park. Hiking is best early or late in the short summer season. Head out early in the morning to miss the prams, high heels, dogs, and bear-bells that you'll surely encounter during the busiest periods.

The two main trailheads are at Chateau Lake Louise and Moraine Lake. Two trails lead from the village to the chateau (a pleasant alternative to driving the steep and very busy Lake Louise Drive). Shortest is the 2.7-km **Louise Creek Trail**. It begins on the downstream side of the point where Lake Louise Drive crosses the Bow River, crosses Louise Creek three times, and ends at the Lake Louise parking lot. The other trail, **Tramline,** is 4.5 km longer but not as steep. It begins behind the railway station and follows the route of a narrow-gauge railway that once transported guests from the C.P.R. line to Chateau Lake Louise.

Bow River Loop
- Length: 7 km (1.5–2 hours)
- Elevation gain: minimal
- Rating: easy

This loop follows both banks of the Bow River southeast from the railway station. Used by joggers and cyclists to access various points in the village, the trail also links the station to the hostel, Post Hotel, Samson Mall, both campgrounds, and the Louise Creek and Tramline trails to Lake Louise. Interpretive signs along its length provide information on the Bow River ecosystem.

Louise Lakeshore
- Length: 2 km (30 minutes) one-way
- Elevation gain: none
- Rating: easy

Probably the park's busiest trail, this one follows

*looking back at Chateau
Lake Louise from Louise
Lakeshore Trail*

the north shore of Lake Louise from in front of the chateau to the west end of the lake. Here numerous braided glacial streams empty their silt-filled waters into Lake Louise. Along the trail's length are benches to sit and ponder what English mountaineer James Outram once described as "a gem of composition and of coloring. . . perhaps unrivalled anywhere."

Plain of the Six Glaciers
- Length: 5.3 km (90 minutes) one-way
- Elevation gain: 370 meters
- Rating: easy/moderate

Hikers along this trail are rewarded not only with panoramic views of the glaciated peaks of the main range, but also with a rustic trail's-end teahouse serving homemade goodies baked on a wooden stove. For the first two km, the trail follows Louise Lakeshore Trail to the western end of the lake. From there it begins a steady climb through a forest of spruce and subalpine fir. It enters an open area where an avalanche has come tumbling down (now a colorful carpet of wildflowers), then passes through a forested area into a vast wasteland of moraines produced by the advance and retreat of Victoria Glacier. Views of surrounding peaks continue to improve until the trail enters a stunted forest. After switchbacking up through this forest, the trail arrives at the teahouse.

Built by the C.P.R. at the turn of the century, the teahouse operates the same way now as it did then. Supplies are packed in by horse and all cooking is done in a rustic kitchen. It's open July–early September. After resting, continue one km to the end of the trail on the narrow top of a lateral moraine. From here the trail's namesakes are visible. From left to right the glaciers are Aberdeen, Upper Lefroy, Lower Lefroy, Upper Victoria, Lower Victoria, and Pope's. Between Mt. Lefroy (3,441 meters) and Mt. Victoria (3,459 meters) is Abbot Pass, where it's possible to make out Abbot Hut on the skyline. When constructed in 1922, this stone structure was the highest building in Canada. The pass and hut are named for Phillip Abbot, who died attempting to climb Mt. Lefroy in 1896.

Lake Agnes
- Length: 3.6 km (90 minutes) one-way
- Elevation gain: 400 meters
- Rating: moderate

This moderately strenuous hike is one of the park's most popular. It begins in front of the chateau, branching right near the beginning of the Louise Lakeshore Trail. For the first 2.5 km, the trail climbs steeply, switchbacking through a forest of subalpine fir and Engelmann spruce, crossing a horse trail, passing a lookout, and leveling out at tiny Mirror Lake. Here the old, traditional trail veers right (use it if the ground is wet or snowy) while a more direct route veers left to the Plain of the Six Glaciers. The final elevation gain along both trails is made easier by a flight of steps beside Bridal Veil Falls. The trail ends beside a rustic teahouse overlooking Lake Agnes, a subalpine lake nestled in a hanging valley. The teahouse offers homemade soups, healthy sandwiches, and a wide assortment of teas.

From the teahouse a one-km trail leads to Little Beehive and impressive views of the Bow Valley. Another trail leads around the northern shore of Lake Agnes, climbing to Big Beehive (see below) or joining to the Plain of the Six Glaciers Trail (see above), just 3.2 km from the chateau and 2.1 km from the teahouse at the end of that trail.

Big Beehive
• Length: 5 km (2 hours) one-way
• Elevation gain: 520 meters
• Rating: moderate

The lookout atop the larger of the two "beehives" is one of the best places to admire the uniquely colored waters of Lake Louise, over half a km directly below. The various trails to the summit have one thing in common—all are steep. But the rewards are worth every drop of sweat along the way. The most popular route follows the Lake Agnes Trail for the first 3.6 km to Lake Agnes. From the teahouse, a trail leads to the western end of the lake, then switchbacks steeply up an exposed north-facing ridge. At the crest of the ridge, the trail forks. To the right it descends to the Plain of the Six Glaciers Trail, to the left it continues 300 meters to a log gazebo. This trail is not well defined but scrambling through the large boulders is easy. Across Lake Louise is Fairview Mountain (2,745 meters), and behind this peak is the distinctive shape of Mt. Temple (3,549 meters). Views also extend up the lake to Mt. Lefroy and northeast to Lake Louise Ski Area. Views from the edge of the cliff are spectacular but be very careful—it's a long, long way down. By returning down the Lake Louise side of the Big Beehive, the loop is 11.5 km (4–5 hours).

Saddleback
• Length: 3.7 km (90 minutes) one-way
• Elevation gain: 600 meters
• Rating: moderate

This trail climbs the lower slopes of Fairview Mountain from beside the boat shed on Lake Louise, ending in an alpine meadow with a view of Mt. Temple from across Paradise Valley. Four hundred meters from the trailhead the trail forks.

Keep left and follow the steep switchbacks through a forest of Englemann spruce and subalpine fir until reaching the flower-filled meadow. The meadow is actually a pass between Fairview Mountain (to the northwest) and Saddle Mountain (to the southeast). Although most hikers are content with the awesome views from the pass and return along the same trail, it is possible to continue to the summit of Fairview (2,745 meters), a further climb of 400 vertical meters. The barely discernible, switchbacking trail to the summit begins near a stand of larch trees above the crest of Saddleback. As you would expect, the view from the top is stupendous; Lake Louise is over one km directly below. This option is for strong, experienced hikers only. From the Saddleback, the trail descends into Sheol Valley, then into Paradise Valley. The entire loop would be 15 km.

Paradise Valley
• Length: 18 km (6 hours) round-trip
• Elevation gain: 380 meters
• Rating: moderate

This aptly named trail makes for a long day hike, but it can be broken up by overnighting at the backcountry campground at the far end of the loop. The trailhead is 3.5 km along the Moraine Lake Road in a heavily forested area on the right. The trail climbs steadily for the first five km, crossing Paradise Creek numerous times and passing the junction of a trail that climbs the Sheol Valley to Saddleback (see above). After five km the trail divides again, following either side of the valley to form a 13-km loop. **Lake Annette** is 700 meters along the left fork. It's a typical subalpine lake in a unique setting—nestled against the near-vertical 1,200-meter north face of snow- and ice-capped **Mt. Temple** (3,549 meters), one of the 10 highest peaks in the Canadian Rockies. This difficult face was successfully climbed in 1966, relatively late for mountaineering "firsts." The lake is a worthy destination in itself. Allow yourself four hours round-trip from the trailhead. For those completing the entire loop, continue beyond the lake into an open avalanche area that affords views across Paradise Valley. Look and listen for pikas and marmots among the boulders. The trail then passes through Horseshoe Meadow, crosses Paradise Creek, and heads back down the valley. Keep to the left at all trail crossings and you'll quickly arrive at a series of waterfalls known as the Giant Steps. From the base of these falls, it is eight km back to the trailhead.

Consolation Lakes
- Length: 3 km (1 hour) one-way
- Elevation gain: 65 meters
- Rating: easy/moderate

This short trail begins from the bridge over Moraine Creek at the outlet of Moraine Lake and ends at a pleasant subalpine lake. The first section of the trail traverses a boulder-strewn rock pile—the result of rock slides on the imposing Tower of Babel (3,101 meters) —before entering a dense forest of Engelmann spruce and subalpine fir and following Babel Creek to the lower lake. The wide valley affords 360-degree views of the surrounding jagged peaks, including Mt. Temple back down the valley and Mts. Bident and Quandra at the far end of the lakes. After eating lunch while perched on one of many boulders, you could continue to Upper Consolation Lake by crossing Babel Creek and following a usually wet and muddy trail along the lake's eastern shore.

Larch Valley
- Length: 2.9 km (60–90 minutes) one-way
- Elevation gain: 400 meters
- Rating: moderate

In fall, when the larch trees have turned a magnificent gold and the sun is shining, few spots in the Canadian Rockies can match the beauty of this valley. But don't expect to find much solitude (and don't be too disappointed if the trail is closed in fall—it often is due to wildlife). Although the most popular time for visiting the valley is fall, it is a worthy destination all summer, when the open meadows are filled with colorful wildflowers. The trail begins just past Moraine Lake Lodge and climbs fairly steeply with occasional glimpses of Moraine Lake below. After reaching the junction of the Eiffel Lake Trail, keep right, passing through an open forest of larch and into the meadow beyond. The range of larch is restricted within the park and this is one of the few areas where they are prolific. Mt. Fay (3,235 meters) is the dominant peak on the skyline, rising above the other mountains that make up the Valley of the Ten Peaks.

Sentinel Pass
- Length: 5.8 km (2–3 hours) one-way
- Elevation gain: 725 meters
- Rating: moderate/difficult

Keen hikers should consider continuing through the open meadows of Larch Valley to Sentinel Pass (2,608 meters), one of the park's highest trail-accessible passes. The length and elevation gain listed are from Moraine Lake. Once in Larch Valley, you're halfway there and have made over half of the elevation gain. Upon reaching Larch Valley, take the formed trail that winds through the open meadow. From the end of the meadow, the trail switchbacks for 1.2 kilometers up a steep scree slope to the pass, sandwiched between Pinnacle Mountain (3,067 meters) and Mt. Temple (3,549 meters). From the pass most hikers opt to return along the same trail, although with advanced planning it is possible to continue into Paradise Valley and back to the Moraine Lake access road, a total of 17 km one way.

Eiffel Lake
- Length: 5.6 km (2 hours) one-way
- Elevation gain: 400 meters
- Rating: moderate/difficult

Eiffel Lake is small, and looks even smaller in its rugged and desolate setting, surrounded by the famed Valley of the Ten Peaks. For the first 2.4 km, follow the Larch Valley Trail (see above), then fork left. Most of the elevation gain has already been made, and the trail remains relatively level before emerging onto an open slope from where each of the 10 peaks can be seen, along with Moraine Lake far below. From left to right the peaks are: Fay, Little, Bowlen, Perren, Septa, Allen, Tuzo, Deltaform, Neptuak, and Wenkchemna. The final two peaks are divided by Wenkchemna Pass (2,605 meters), a further four km and 360 vertical meters above Eiffel Lake. The lake itself soon comes into view. It lies in a depression formed by a rock slide from Neptuak Mountain. The lake is named for **Eiffel Peak** (3,085 meters), a rock pinnacle behind it, which with a little imagination could be compared to the Eiffel Tower in Paris.

Skoki Lodge
- Length: 14.4 km (5 hours) one-way
- Elevation gain: 775 meters
- Rating: moderate/difficult

The trail into historic Skoki Lodge is only one of the endless hiking opportunities tucked behind Lake Louise Ski Area, across the valley from all hikes detailed above. Access to the Skoki Valley is from a parking lot on a gravel road that branches right from the ski area access road. The first four km of the trail are along a gravel access road leading to Temple Lodge, part of the Lake Louise Ski Area. From here, the trail climbs to Boulder Pass, passing a campground and Halfway Hut, above Corral Creek. The pass harbors a large population of pikas and hoary marmots. The trail then follows the north shore of Ptarmigan Lake before climbing again to Deception Pass, named for its false summit. It then descends into Skoki Valley, passing the Skoki Lakes and eventually reaching Skoki Lodge (see "Accommodations," below). Just over one km beyond the lodge is a campground, an excellent base for exploring the region.

HIKES ALONG THE ICEFIELDS PARKWAY

Helen Lake
- Length: 6 km (2.5 hours) one-way
- Elevation gain: 455 meters
- Rating: moderate

The trail to Helen Lake is one of the easiest ways to access a true alpine environment from the southern end of the Icefields Parkway. The trailhead is opposite Crowfoot Glacier Lookout, 33 km northwest from the junction with the TransCanada Highway. The trail climbs steadily through a forest of Engelmann spruce and subalpine fir for the first 2.5 km to an avalanche slope, reaching the tree line and the first good viewpoint after three km. The view across the valley is spectacular, with Crowfoot Glacier visible to the southwest. As the trail reaches a ridge, it turns and descends into the glacial cirque where Helen Lake lies. Listen and look for hoary marmots around the scree slopes along the lakeshore.

For those with the time and energy, it's possible to continue an additional three km to Dolomite Pass; the trail switchbacks steeply up a further 100 vertical meters in less than one km, then descends steeply for a further one km to Katherine Lake and beyond to the pass.

Bow Glacier Falls
- Length: 3.4 km (1 hour) one-way
- Elevation gain: 130 meters
- Rating: easy/moderate

This hike skirts one of the most beautiful lakes in the Canadian Rockies before ending at a narrow but spectacular waterfall. The trail begins beside Num-ti-jah Lodge at the north end of Bow Lake and follows the shore through Willow Flats to a gravel outwash area at the end of the lake. Across the lake are reflected views of Crowfoot Mountain and, farther west, a glimpse of Bow Glacier among the jagged peaks of the Waputik Range. The trail then begins a short but steep climb up the rim of a canyon before leveling out at the edge of a vast moraine of gravel, scree, and boulders. This is the end of the trail, although it's possible to reach the base of Bow Glacier Falls by picking your way through the 800 meters of rough ground that remains.

Peyto Lake
- Length: 1.4 km (30 minutes) one-way
- Elevation loss: 100 meters
- Rating: easy

Without doubt the best place to view Peyto Lake is from a popular viewpoint accessible via a short trail from Bow Summit. From here, a trail drops nearly 300 meters in 2.4 km to the lake. An easier 1.4-km trail to the lake starts at a small parking lot 2.4 km north of Bow Summit. The lake's pebbled beach, strewn with driftwood, is the perfect setting for picnicking, painting, or just admiring the lake's quieter side.

Chephren Lake
- Length: 4 km (60–90 minutes) one-way
- Elevation gain: 100 meters
- Rating: easy/moderate

This pale-green body of water is hidden from drivers on the Icefields Parkway. The trailhead is located within Waterfowl Lakes Campground, where the Mistaya River flows into Waterfowl Lake. The trail crosses the Mistaya River, 400 meters from the trailhead, then dives headlong into a subalpine forest until reaching Chephren Lake, nestled under the buttresses of Mt. Chephren. To the left is Howse Peak.

The trail to smaller Cirque Lake (4.5 km from the trailhead) branches left 1.7 km along this trail. It is less heavily used, but this lake is popular with anglers for its healthy population of rainbow trout.

Glacier Lake
• Length: 9 km (2.5–3 hours) one-way
• Elevation gain: 220 meters
• Rating: moderate

This three-km-long lake is one of the park's largest lakes not accessible by road. Although not as scenic as the more accessible lakes along the parkway, it's a pleasant destination for a full-day or overnight trip. The trailhead is in an old gravel pit on the west side of the highway, one km north of the Saskatchewan River Crossing service center. For the first km, the trail passes through an open forest of lodgepole pine to a fancy footbridge across the rushing North Saskatchewan River. From there it climbs gradually to a viewpoint overlooking Howse River and the valley beyond, then turns away from the river for a long slog through dense forest to Glacier Lake. A primitive campground lies just over 300 meters from where the trail emerges at the lake.

Saskatchewan Glacier
• Length: 7.3 km (2 hours) one-way
• Elevation gain: 150 meters
• Rating: moderate

The Saskatchewan Glacier, a tongue of ice from the great Columbia Icefield, is visible from various points along the Icefields Parkway. This hike will take you right to the toe of the glacier. The trailhead is an old concrete bridge on the gravel flats just before the road begins its "big bend," 35 km north of the Saskatchewan River Crossing service center. The trail begins across the bridge, disappearing into the forest to the right, joining an old access road, and continuing up the valley along the south bank of the river. When the toe of the glacier first comes into sight it looks deceptively close, but it's still a long hike away over rough terrain.

Nigel Pass
• Length: 7.4 km (2.5 hours) one-way
• Elevation gain: 365 meters
• Rating: moderate

On the east side of the Icefields Parkway, 2.5 km north of the switchback on the "big bend," is a gravel road that leads to a locked gate. Turn right here and cross Nigel Creek on the bridge.

Saskatchewan Glacier from Parker's Ridge

The trail is obvious, following open avalanche paths up the east side of the valley. In a stand of Engelmann spruce and subalpine fir two km from the trailhead is an old campsite used first by native hunting parties, then by mountaineers exploring the area around the Columbia Icefield. Look for carvings on trees recording these early visitors. From here the trail continues to climb steadily, only increasing in gradient for the last one km to the pass. The pass (2,195 meters) marks the boundary between Banff and Jasper National Parks. For the best view, scramble over the rocks to the left. To the north, the view extends down the Brazeau River Valley, surrounded by a mass of peaks. To the west (left) is Nigel Peak (3,211 meters), and to the southwest are views of Parker's Ridge and the glaciated peaks of Mt. Athabasca.

Parker's Ridge
• Length: 2.4 km (1 hour) one-way
• Elevation gain: 210 meters
• Rating: easy/moderate

This short trail into the alpine begins from a parking lot at the north end of the park, just four km south of Sunwapta Pass. From the trailhead on the west side of the road, the wide path gains elevation quickly through open meadows and scattered stands of subalpine fir. This fragile environment is easily destroyed, so it's very important that you stay on the trail. During the short alpine summer, these meadows are carpeted with red heather, white mountain avens, and blue alpine forget-me-nots. From the summit of the ridge, you look down on the two-km-wide Saskatchewan Glacier spreading out below. Beyond is Castleguard Mountain, renowned for its extensive cave system.

OTHER RECREATION

FAIR WEATHER

Mountain Biking

Whether you have your own bike or you rent one from the many bicycle shops in Banff or Lake Louise, cycling in the park is for everyone. The roads to Lake Minnewanka, Mt. Norquay, through the golf course, and along the Bow Valley Parkway are all popular routes. A number of trails radiating from Banff and ending deep in the backcountry have been designated as bicycle trails. These include Sundance (3.7 km one-way), Rundle Riverside to Canmore (15 km one-way), Spray River Loop (via Goat Creek; 48 km round-trip). Further afield, other trails are at Redearth Creek, Lake Louise, and in the northeastern reaches of the park near Saskatchewan River Crossing. Before heading into the backcountry, pick up the *Trail Mountain Biking Guide* from the Banff or Lake Louise Visitor Centres. Riders are particularly susceptible to sudden bear encounters. Be alert and make loud noises when passing through heavy vegetation.

Bactrax Bike Rentals, 225 Bear Street, 403/762-8177, rents front- and full-suspension mountain bikes for $6–10 per hour and $20–38 per day, the best deal in town. In-line skate rentals are $15 per day. Bactrax also offers mountain-bike tours, including to Vermilion Lakes and along Sundance Canyon. Tours cost $15 per person per hour. The shop is open daily 8 A.M.–8 P.M.

Horseback Riding

Jim and Bill Brewster led Banff's first paying guests into the backcountry on horseback over 100 years ago. Today visitors are still able to enjoy the park on this traditional form of transportation.

Warner Guiding & Outfitting, 403/762-4551, offers a great variety of trips. Their main office is in the Trail Rider Store at 132 Banff Avenue, although most trips depart from either **Martin's Stables,** 403/762-2832, behind the recreation grounds on Birch Ave., or **Banff Springs Corral,** 403/762-2848, along Spray Avenue. One-hour rides are $27, two hours $40, three hours $64. Other day trips include the three-hour **Mountain Morning Breakfast Ride,** featuring a hearty breakfast along the trail, $61; **Explorer,** a seven-hour ride up the Spray River Valley, $115; and the **Evening Steak Fry,** a three-hour ride with a steak dinner along the trail, $61. Overnight trips to established backcountry camps and lodges are also available; rates begin at $437 including all meals, two night's accommodation at Sundance Lodge, and the horse, of course.

Brewster Lake Louise Stables, 403/522-3511, offers hour-long rides (departing on the hour) for $30, 90-minute rides to the end of Lake Louise for $45, half-day rides to Lake Agnes Teahouse for $60, and all-day rides up Paradise Valley, including lunch, for $120.

Whitewater Rafting and Canoeing

Anyone looking for whitewater-rafting action will want to run the Kicking Horse River, which flows down the western slopes of the Canadian Rockies into British Columbia. Many operators provide transportation from Banff and Lake Louise (see "Sights and Recreation" under "Golden" in the Yoho National Park and Vicinity chapter). **Rocky Mountain Raft Tours,** 403/762-3632, offers one-hour ($24) and two-hour ($39) float trips down the Bow River, beginning just below Bow Falls.

On a quiet stretch of Bow River, at the north end of Wolf Street, **Banff Canoe Rentals,** 403/762-3632, rents canoes for use on the river from where it's an easy paddle upstream to the Vermilion Lakes and Forty Mile Creek; $16 per hour or $40 for a full day of paddling. Rentals are available in summer, daily 10 A.M.–7 p.m.

Fishing and Boating

The finest fishing in the park is in Lake Minnewanka, where lake trout as large as 15 kilograms have been caught. One way to ensure a good catch is through **Lake Minnewanka Guided Fishing,** 403/762-3473, which offers fishing trips in a heated cabin cruiser; trolling and downrigging are preferred methods of fishing the lake. A half-day's fishing is $200 for one or two persons. The company also rents small aluminum fishing boats with small outboard motors for $30 per hour. **Adventures Unlimited,** 211 Bear Street, 403/762-4554 or 800/644-8888, offers a wide variety of fishing trips, including drifting down the Bow River in a boat, fishing high alpine lakes from a belly boat, or simply fly-casting from the banks of a river or stream favored by your guide. Rates of $115–165 per person for a full day include guiding, gear, and lessons.

Before fishing anywhere in the park you need a national park fishing license ($6 per week, $13 per year), available from the Banff and Lake Louise visitor centers and sport shops throughout the park.

Golfing

One of the world's most scenic golf courses, the Banff Springs Golf Course, spreads out along the Bow River between Mt. Rundle and Tunnel Mountain. The first course was laid out here in 1911, but in 1928 Stanley Thompson was brought in by the C.P.R. to redesign it into 18 holes and to build what was at the time North America's most expensive course. In 1989 the Tunnel Nine opened (along with a new clubhouse), creating today's 27-hole course.

Between 1997 and 1999 no expense was spared in rebuilding the entire original 18 holes and adding longer tees, while also reverting to Thompson's planned sequence of play, known now as the **Stanley Thompson 18.** The course is typically Thompson, taking advantage of natural contours, and featuring elevated tees, wide fairways, and holes aligned to distant mountains. From the back markers it is 6,938 yards and plays to a par of 71. The course is not only breathtakingly beautiful, it's also challenging for every level of golfer. Pick up a copy of the book *The World's Greatest Golf Holes,* and you'll see a picture of the fourth hole on the Rundle Nine. It's a par three, over Devil's Cauldron 70 meters below, to a small green backed by the sheer face of Mt. Rundle rising vertically more than 1,000 meters above the putting surface. Another unique feature of the course is the abundance of wildlife: there's always the chance of seeing elk feeding on the fairways, or coyotes, deer, or black bears scurrying across.

Greens fees are $125 for 18 holes including a cart (through the first and last months of operation, May and early October, greens fees are reduced to $70). Free shuttle buses run from

Bunkers aren't the only hazard on Banff's golf course.

the Banff Springs Hotel to the clubhouse. (The original 1911 clubhouse still stands, but has been replaced by a modern, circular building in the heart of the course.) There you'll find club rentals ($25), three putting greens, a driving range, pro shop, two chipping greens with surrounding bunkers, and a restaurant. Booking tee times well in advance is essential; call 403/762-6801.

WINTERTIME

From November till May, the entire park transforms itself into a winter playground covered in a blanket of snow. Of Alberta's six world-class ski resorts, three are in Banff National Park. Banff Mt. Norquay is a small but steep hill overlooking the town of Banff; Sunshine Village perches high in the mountains on the Continental Divide, catching more than its share of fluffy white powder; and Lake Louise, Canada's second-largest ski area, spreads over four distinct mountain faces. Apart from an abundance of snow, the resorts have something else in common—spectacular views, which alone are worth the price of a lift ticket.

Other winter activities in the park include cross-country skiing, ice-skating, snowshoeing, dogsledding, or just relaxing. Crowds are nonexistent and hotels reduce rates by up to 70 percent (except Christmas holidays) —reason enough to venture into the mountains. Lift and lodging packages begin at $60 per person.

Banff Mt. Norquay

The steep eastern slopes of Mt. Norquay had been attracting local skiers for 20 years before Canada's first chairlift was installed on its face in 1948. Ever since then, the resort has had an experts-only reputation, mainly because of terrain serviced by the North American Chair (including the famous double-black-diamond Lone Pine run). But an express quad installed in 1990 opened up new intermediate terrain and made the resort a favorite with shredders and cruisers alike. Lift tickets are adult $42, senior $34, child $15; lift, lesson, and rental packages cost about the same. Night skiing is offered on Wednesday. A shuttle bus picks skiers up from Banff hotels for the short, six-km ride up the hill;

$5. For more information on the resort, call 403/762-4421, or in Calgary call the 24-hour Snowphone, 403/221-8259.

Sunshine Village

The skiing at Sunshine has lots going for it— over six meters of snow annually (no need for snowmaking up here), wide-open bowls, a season stretching for nearly 200 days, skiing in two provinces, and the only slope-side accommodations in the park.

The first people to ski the Sunshine Meadows were two local men, Cliff White and Cyril Paris, who became lost going over Citadel Pass in the spring of 1929 and returned to Banff with stories of deep snow and ideal slopes for skiing. In the following years, a C.P.R. cabin was used as a base for skiing in the area. In 1938 the Canadian National Ski Championships were held here, and in 1942 a portable lift was constructed. The White family was synonymous with the Sunshine area for many years, running the lodge and ski area while Brewster buses negotiated the steep narrow road that led to the meadows. In 1980 a gondola was installed to whisk skiers six km from the parking area in Bourgeau Valley to the alpine village. More recently, new high-speed quads have opened up the north face of Goats Eye Mountain, made the trip to the summit of 2,730-meter Lookout Mountain much quicker, and the Wolverine Express, which opened for the 2000–01 season, has made the trip between Goast Eye and the "village" a lot quicker. One of Canada's most infamous runs, Delirium Dive, off the northeast-facing slope of Lookout Mountain, opened after a 20-year closure for the 1998–99 season. To ski this up-to-50-degree run, you must be equipped with a transceiver, shovel, probe, and partner, but you'll have bragging rights that night at the bar (especially if you've skied the Bre-X line).

Aside from Delirium Dive, the area is best known for its excellent beginner and intermediate terrain, which covers 60 percent of the mountain. The area is serviced by a gondola and 10 lifts, including the fastest chairlift in the Canadian Rockies. Lift tickets are $52 per day, seniors $42, and those under six ski free. Two days of skiing and one night's lodging at slopeside Sunshine Inn costs from $125 per person per day. The inn has a restaurant, lounge, game room, and hot tub. For lodging and general resort information, call 403/762-6500 or 800/661-1676. Call the Snow Phone at 403/760-7669. Transportation from Banff, Canmore, or Lake Louise to the hill is $10 roundtrip; call the hill or inquire at major hotels for the timetable.

Lake Louise

Canada's answer to U.S. mega-resorts such as Vail and Killington is Lake Louise. The nation's second-largest ski area (behind only Whistler/Blackcomb) comprises 40 square km of gentle trails, mogul fields, long cruising runs, steep chutes, and vast bowls filled with famous Rocky Mountain powder.

The earliest skiing undertaken in the Lake Louise area was in the 1920s, when groups from Banff went backcountry touring in the Skoki Valley. In 1930, Cliff White and Cyril Paris built a small ski chalet in the valley. The location of this chalet, 20 km from the nearest road, turned out not to be practical, so a closer one was built on the site of today's Temple Lodge. In 1954, a lift was constructed next to Temple Lodge's back door, opening the slopes of Larch Mountain to the ever-increasing number of downhill enthusiasts in the area. A young Englishman who had inherited a fortune from his father saw the potential for a world-class ski resort here and made the completion of his dream a lifelong obsession. Norman Watson, known as the "Barmy Baronet," pulled together a group of financiers and constructed a gondola up the slopes of Whitehorn in 1958. More lifts were constructed and two runs—Olympic Men's Downhill and Olympic Ladies' Downhill—were cut on the south face of Whitehorn in anticipation of a successful bid for the 1968 Winter Olympics. The bid eventually failed due to the opposition of environmentalists (the same reason that the alpine events of the Calgary Winter Olympics were held on a specially built hill outside of the park boundary). Huge development plans for the base area that included rooms for 6,500 guests were scuttled in 1972, but under the supervision of one-time local mountain guide Charlie Locke, the area has continued to improve and grow, and often hosts World Cup skiing events.

The resort is made up of four distinct faces. The front side has a vertical drop of 1,000 meters and is served by eight lifts, including two high-speed quads. The four back bowls are each as big as many mid-size ski areas and are all well above the tree line. Larch and Ptarmigan faces have a variety of terrain, allowing you to follow the sun as it moves across the sky or escape into trees for protection on windy days. "The Jungle" on the front face, is North America's largest snowboard park.

Each of the three day lodges has a restaurant and bar. Ski rentals, clothing, and souvenirs are available in the Lodge of the Ten Peaks, a magnificent log day lodge that overlooks the

If you stay at Chateau Lake Louise, great skiing is on your back doorstep.

front face. Lift tickets are $54 per day, seniors $43, and children under 12 $15. Lifts are open from early November to early May, 9 A.M.–4 P.M. Free guided tours of the mountain are available three times daily—inquire at customer service. Free shuttle buses run regularly from Lake Louise accommodations to the hill. From Banff you pay $15 round-trip for transportation to Lake Louise. For more information on the ski area, call 403/522-3555.

Ski Rentals and Sales

Each resort has rental and sales facilities, but getting your gear down in town is often easier. **Monod Sports,** 129 Banff Avenue, 403/762-4571, has been synonymous with Banff and the ski industry for over half a century, and while the **Rude Boys Snowboard Shop,** downstairs in the Sundance Mall, 215 Banff Avenue, 403/762-8480, has only been around since the 1980s, it is *the* snowboarder hangout. Other shops with sales and rentals include **Abominable Ski,** 229 Banff Avenue, 403/762-2905; **Adventures Unlimited,** 211 Bear Street, 403/762-4554; **Clock Tower Sports,** 110 Banff Avenue, 403/760-3525; **Mountain Magic Equipment,** 224 Bear Street, 403/762-2591; **Ski Stop,** in the Banff Springs Hotel, 403/762-5333; and **Snow Tips,** 225 Bear Street, 403/762-8177. Basic ski packages—skis, poles, and boots—are $20–25 per day, while high performance packages range $30–45. Snowboards and boots rent for $20–40 per day.

Switching Gear, down the valley from Banff in nearby Canmore has an excellent selection of used ski and snowboard equipment, as well as winter clothing at very reasonable prices. It's at 718 10th Street, 403/678-1992.

Cross-Country Skiing

No better way of experiencing the park's winter delights exists than skiing through the landscape on cross-country skis. Many summer hiking trails are groomed for winter travel. The most popular areas are Johnson Lake, Golf Course Road, Spray River, Sundance Canyon, Moraine Lake Road, on Lake Louise, and in Skoki Valley at the back of Lake Louise Ski Area. The booklet *Cross-country Skiing—Nordic Trails in Banff National Park,* is available for $1 from the Banff and Lake Louise Visitor Centres. Weather forecasts

(403/762-2088) and avalanche hazard reports (403/762-1460) are posted at both centers.

Rental packages are available from **Performance Sports** at 208 Bear Street, 403/762-8222; **Snowtips,** 225 Bear Street, 403/762-8177; and **Mountain Magic Equipment** at 224 Bear Street, 403/762-2591. Expect to pay $12–20 per day. **White Mountain Adventures,** 403/678-4099, offer lessons for $50 per person, as well as an ice walk through a frozen Johnston Canyon.

Ice-Skating

Of all the ice-skating rinks in Canada, the one on frozen Lake Louise, in front of the chateau, is surely the most spectacular. Spotlights allow skating after dark, and on special occasions hot chocolate is served. Skates are available in the chateau at **Monod Sports,** 403/522-3837; $10 for two hours. Other rinks are at **Banff High School** on Banff Avenue at Wolf Street; on the **Bow River** along Bow Street; and on the golf course side of the **Banff Springs Hotel.** The latter rink is lighted after dark and a raging fire is built beside it—the perfect place for a hot chocolate. Rent skates from **The Ski Stop** in the Banff Springs Hotel, 403/762-5333; $5 per hour.

Sleigh Rides

Holiday on Horseback offers sleigh rides on the frozen Bow River throughout winter. For reservations, call 403/762-4551 or stop by the Trail Rider Store at 132 Banff Avenue. ($14 per person). **Brewster Lake Louise Sleigh Rides,** 403/762-5454, offers rides in traditional horse-drawn sleighs along the shores of Lake Louise beginning from in front of the chateau. Although blankets are supplied, you should still bundle up. The one-hour ride is $15 per person, $10 for children. Reservations are necessary. The rides are scheduled hourly from 11 A.M. on weekends, from 3 P.M. weekdays.

Other Winter Activities

Without the tourists, dogsledding probably wouldn't take place in the park, but there are tourists and there is dogsledding. **Mountain Mushers,** 403/762-3647, offers half-hour ($75), one-hour ($130), and half-day ($275) tours around the Banff Springs Golf Course. Rates are for two people.

Beside the Banff Springs Hotel ice-skating rink is an unofficial toboggan run; ask at your hotel for sleds or rent them from **The Ski Stop,** in the Banff Springs Hotel; $4 per hour.

Banff Fishing Unlimited offers ice-fishing trips on nearby lakes, 403/762-4936, while curling bonspiels take place at the Banff Recreation Centre on Mt. Norquay Road.

Anyone interested in ice climbing must register at the national park desk in the Banff Visitor Centre or call 403/762-1550. The world famous (if you're an ice climber) **Terminator** is just outside the park boundary.

If none of the above appeals to you, head to **Upper Hot Springs** for a relaxing soak; open Monday–Friday noon–9 P.M., Saturday–Sunday 10 A.M.–11 P.M. ($7). Camping might not be everyone's idea of a winter holiday, but Tunnel Mountain Village II campground remains open year-round.

INDOOR RECREATION

Fitness and Swimming Facilities
Many of Banff's better hotels have fitness rooms and some have indoor pools. A popular place to swim and work out is in the **Sally Borden Building,** at the Banff Centre, St. Julien Road, 403/762-6450, which holds a wide range of fitness facilities and a 25-meter-long heated pool. General admission is $9.50, or pay $3.75 to swim only. It's open daily 6:30 A.M.–11 P.M. In the local high school, on Banff Avenue at Wolf Street, the **Community Fitness Centre,** 403/760-0706, is open daily 3–10 P.M., with extended hours of 10:30 A.M.–6:30 P.M. on Saturday. Admission is only $4, or use the six-meter-high climbing wall for $3. **Mountain Magic Equipment,** one block off the main drag at 224 Bear Street, 403/762-2591, has climbing and bouldering walls (free) with instruction and gear rentals offered for a reasonable price.

The Solace
This luxurious spa facility in the Banff Springs Hotel, 403/762-2211, is the place to pamper yourself. Opened in 1995 at a cost of $12 million, it sprawls over two levels and 3,000 square meters of a private corner of the hotel. The epicenter of the facility is a circular mineral pool capped by a high glass-topped ceiling and ringed by floor-to-ceiling windows on one side and on the other by hot tubs fed by cascading waterfalls of varying temperatures. Other features include outdoor saltwater hot tubs, private solariums, steam rooms, luxurious bathrooms, and separate male and female lounges complete with fireplaces and complimentary drinks and snacks. A great variety of other services are offered, including facials, body wraps, massage therapy, salon services, and hydrotherapy. Entry to the Solace is included in the rates for guests at the hotel. General admission is $50 per day (book in advance), which includes the use of a locker and spa attire, with almost 100 services available at additional cost (most of these include general admission, so, for example, you can spend the day in the Solace and receive a 30-minute massage for $80). The Solace is open daily 6 A.M.–10 P.M.

Other Indoor Recreation
Banff Springs Hotel, 403/762-2211, has a four-lane, five-pin bowling center; games are $3.75 per person. **King Edward Billiards,** upstairs at 137 Banff Avenue, 403/762-4629, is a large, clean pool hall. Tables are $12 per hour. The **Lux Cinema Centre** at 229 Bear Street, 403/762-8595, shows new releases for $9 ($5 on Tuesday).

Banff's only water slide is in the **Douglas Fir Resort** on Tunnel Mountain Drive, 403/762-5591. The two slides are indoors, and the admission price of $7.50 (under five free) includes use of a hot tub and exercise room. It's open Monday–Friday 4–9:30 P.M., Saturday–Sunday 10 A.M.–9:30 P.M.

NIGHTLIFE

Bars and Lounges
Like resort towns around the world, Banff has more than its fair share of bars and nightclubs. **Wild Bill's,** upstairs at 201 Banff Avevue, 403/762-0333, is named for Banff guide Bill Peyto, and is truly legendary. Bands usually play a bit of everything, but generally expect alternative music early in the week and rock or country Thursday–Sunday. The food here is excellent. Just as popular is the **Barbary Coast,** 119 Banff Avenue, 403/762-4616, which also serves good food and has live music in a clean, casual atmosphere. Across the road from Wild Bill's is the **Rose and Crown,** 202 Banff Avenue,

403/762-2121, an English-style pub serving British beers and typical pub meals. It also features a rooftop patio and rock and roll bands a few nights a week. The **Pump and Tap Tavern,** in the lower level of the Sundance Mall, 215 Banff Avenue, 403/760-6610, features "cave-like" furnishings befitting its location. It's a popular locals' hangout, with free pool in the afternoon and nightly drink specials. **St. James Gate Old Irish Pub,** 205 Wolf Street, 403/762-9355, is a large Irish-style bar with a reputation for excellent British-style meals and occasional appearances by Celtic bands. Away from busy Banff Avenue is **Melissa's,** 218 Lynx Street, 403/762-5776, which is a long-time favorite drinking hole for locals. It has a small outdoor patio, a long evening happy hour, pool, and multiple TVs.

Many Banff hotels have small lounges open to the guests and nonguestss alike. They are generally quieter than those listed above and often offer abbreviated menus from adjacent restaurants. The best of these is **Outfitters,** in Brewster's Mountain Lodge, at 208 Caribou Street, 403/762-2900, a casual yet elegant lounge that exudes a stylish western atmosphere. Another of the more stylish places for a quiet drink is the lounge at **Buffalo Mountain Lodge,** Tunnel Mountain Road, 403/762-2400. The **Mount Royal Hotel,** corner Banff Avenue and Caribou Street has a small lounge off the lobby, while below, accessed from further up Banff Avenue, is the **Buffalo Paddock,** 138 Banff Avenue, 403/762-3331, with pool tables. At the opposite end of the style-scale to the hotel bars listed above is the lounge in the **Voyager Inn,** 555 Banff Avenue, 403/762-3301, which is worth listing for the fact that it has the cheapest beer in town and drink specials every night. Just past the Voyager Inn is **Bumpers,** 603 Banff Avenue, a steakhouse with a small bar and pool table upstairs.

Nightclubs

Banff's newest night spot is the cavernous **Aurora,** downstairs in the Clock Tower Mall at 110 Banff Avenue, 403/760-5300. Formerly the infamous Silver City, this place has tried to add some class to Banff's clubbing scene (and is respectable early in the evening), but becomes one obnoxiously loud, over-priced smoky pick-up joint after midnight. The other option is **Outabounds,** 137 Banff Avenue (enter from Caribou St.), 403/762-8434, but watch for anyone diving off the bar. It's open daily 8 P.M.–2 A.M.

Police patrol Banff all night, promptly arresting anyone who even looks like trouble, including anyone drunk or drinking on the streets.

In Lake Louise

Hang out with seasonal workers at **Lake Louise Bar and Grill,** upstairs in Samson Mall, or head to rowdy **Charlie's Pub** in the Lake Louise Inn for dancing to recorded music. Although the bar in the Post Hotel doesn't have mountain views, it has light food, a fireplace, and a distinctive mountain atmosphere. In the Chateau Lake Louise is **The Glacier Saloon,** where on most summer nights a DJ plays music ranging from pop to western.

SHOPPING

It may seem a little strange, but city folk from Calgary actually drive into Banff National Park to shop for clothes. This reflects the number of clothing shops in Banff rather than a lack of choice in one of Canada's largest cities. About the only clothing store that Banff lacks is an army-surplus outlet.

Canadiana and Clothing

Few companies in the world were as responsible for the development of a country as was the **Hudson's Bay Company** in Canada. Founded in 1670, the HBC established trading posts throughout western Canada, many of which attracted settlers, forming the nucleus for towns and cities that survive today, including Alberta's capital, Edmonton. Hudson's Bay Company stores continue their traditional role of providing a wide-range of goods, in towns big and small across the country. In Banff, the Hudson's Bay Company store is at 125 Banff Avenue. Another Canadian store, this one famous for its fleeces, sweaters, and leather goods, is **Roots,** with an outlet at 227 Banff Avenue. For western clothing and accessories, check out the **Trail Rider Store** at 132 Banff Avenue. Pick up your Canadian-made Tilley Hat and other Tilley Endurables from **Piccatilley Square,** on the main floor of the Cascade Plaza at 317 Banff Avenue. The **Rude Boys** is a snowboard and skate shop downstairs in the Sundance Mall, 215 Banff

Avenue, is, well, rude. Take a look—their T-shirts are hilarious (and, unlike anything along Banff Avenue, original), but don't expect to find anything for your grandparents here.

Camping and Outdoor Gear

Inexpensive camping equipment and supplies can be found in **Home Hardware** at 208 Bear Street, and **The Hudson's Bay Company** at 125 Banff Avenue (in the low-ceilinged downstairs section). More specialized needs are catered to at **Mountain Magic Equipment,** 224 Bear Street, 403/762-2591. The store stocks a large range of top-quality outdoor and survival gear (including climbing equipment) and rents tents ($17 per day), sleeping bags ($10), backpacks ($8), and boots ($7.50). Mountain Magic Equipment also sells and repairs all types of bikes.

One of the best places to shop for outdoor apparel is **Outdoor Access** at 201 Banff Avenue; downstairs is a factory outlet with big savings. Other recommended stores are **Monod Sports** at 129 Banff Avenue; **Columbia Mountain Shop,** 202 Caribou Street, and **Helly Hansen,** in the back of Kirby Lane Mall at 119 Banff Avenue.

Gifts and Galleries

Banff's numerous galleries display the work of mostly Canadian artists. **Canada House,** 201 Bear Street, 403/762-3757, features a wide selection of Canadian landscape and wildlife works and native art. The **Quest Gallery,** 105 Banff Avenue, 403/762-2722, offers a diverse range of affordable Canadian paintings and crafts as well as more exotic pieces such mammoth tusks from prehistoric times and Inuit carvings from Nunavut. Across the Bow River from downtown, browse through traditional native arts and crafts at the **Buffalo Nations Luxton Museum Shop,** 1 Birch Avenue, 403/762-2388.

FESTIVALS AND EVENTS

Spring

Most of the major spring events take place at local ski areas, including a variety of snowboard competitions that make for great spectator viewing. At Lake Louise a half pipe and jump are constructed right in front of the day lodge for this specific purpose. One long-running spring event is the **Slush Cup,** which takes place at Sunshine Village in late May. Events include kamikaze skiers who attempt to jump an ice-cold pit of water. While keen skiers are at higher elevations, swooshing down the slopes of some of North America's latest-closing resorts, late spring sees the Banff Springs golf course open for the season.

The **Jasper to Banff Relay** footrace, attracting 120 teams along the 300-km route, is held on the weekend falling closest to June 1. Call 780/497-4680 for entry details.

During the second week of June, the **Banff Television Festival** attracts the world's best television directors, producers, writers, and even actors for meetings, workshops, and awards, with many show screenings are open to the public. For information, call 403/678-9260.

Summer

Summer is a time of hiking and camping, so festivals are few and far between. The main event is the **Banff Arts Festival,** a summer-long extravaganza presented by professional artists studying at the Banff Centre. They perform dance, drama, opera, and jazz for the public at locations around town. Look for details in the *Crag and Canyon* or call 403/762-6300 or 800/413-8368.

On July 1, Banff celebrates **Canada Day** with a parade, fireworks, and events for all the family in Central Park.

Each summer the national park staff presents an extensive **Park Interpretive Program** at locations in town and throughout the park, including downstairs in the visitor center daily at 8:30 P.M. All programs are free and include guided hikes, nature tours, slide shows, campfire talks, and lectures. For details, consult *The Mountain Guide* available at the Banff Visitor Centre, 403/762-1550, or look for postings on campground bulletin boards.

Fall

Fall is the park's quietest season, but busiest in terms of festivals and events. First of the fall events, on the last Saturday in September, **Melissa's Mini-marathon** attracts over 2,000 runners in 3-, 10-, and 22-km races. The following weekend is **Taste of Banff/Lake Louise,** when visitors can take advantage of the park's varied dining opportunities by "testing" samples of cuisine from local restaurants. In the same vein is a **wine and food festival** hosted by the Banff Springs Hotel at the end of October. To encourage tourism during the quietest time of the year, **Winterstart** features cheap lodging and a host of fun events. This coincides with the opening of local ski hills.

Banff Mountain Film Festival

One of the year's biggest events is the Banff Mountain Film Festival, held on the first weekend of November. Mountain-adventure filmmakers from around the world submit films to be judged by a select committee. Films are then shown throughout the weekend to an enthusiastic crowd of thousands. Exhibits and seminars are also presented, and top climbers and mountaineers from around the world are invited as guest speakers.

Tickets go on sale a year in advance and sell out in advance. Tickets for daytime shows start at $40 (for up to 10 films). Night shows are from $25, and all-weekend passes cost around $120 (weekend passes with two nights accommodations and breakfasts start at a reasonable $250). Films are shown in the two theaters of the Banff Centre. For more information, call the Banff Centre for Mountain Culture, 403/762-6675; for tickets, call the Banff Centre box office, 403/762-6301 or 800/413-8368. Tickets can also be purchased online at www.banffcentre.ab.ca/cmc. If you miss the actual festival, it hits the road on the Best of the Festival World Tour. Look for it in your town, or check out the listed website for venues and dates.

Starting in the days leading up to the film festival, then running in conjunction with it, is the **Banff Mountain Book Festival,** which showcases the work of publishers, writers, and photographers whose work revolves around the world's great mountain ranges. Tickets can be bought to individual events ($15–30), as well as a Book Festival Pass and a pass combining both festivals.

Winter

By mid-December all local ski areas are operating. **Santa Claus** makes an appearance on Banff Avenue at noon on the last Saturday in November; if you miss him there, he usually goes skiing at each of the local resorts on Christmas Day. Events at the resorts continue throughout the long ski season, among them **World Cup Downhill** skiing. **First Night** is an alcohol-free New Year's celebration held downtown. **Banff/Lake Louise Winter Festival** is a 10-day celebration at the end of January that has been a part of Banff's history for over 75 years. Look for ice sculpting, the Lake Louise Loppet, barn dancing, and the Town Party, which takes place in the Banff Springs Hotel. The long-running **Lake Louise Loppet,** a Nordic-skiing competition comprises races run at 10-km and 20-km distances, with prizes in 29 age categories. For details, call the Calgary Ski Club at 403/245-9496.

ACCOMMODATIONS

Finding a room in Banff National Park in summer is nearly as hard as trying to justify its price. By late afternoon just about every room and campsite in the park will be occupied, and basic hotel rooms begin at around $100. Fortunately, many alternatives are available. Rooms in private homes begin at around $50 s, $60 d. Canmore, just outside the park boundary, has many hotels and motels. Banff International Hostel has dormitory-style accommodations from $19 per night. Bungalows or cabins can be rented, which can be cost-effective for families or small groups. And around 2,400 campsites in 13 campgrounds accommodate campers. Wherever you decide to stay, it is vital to book well ahead during summer and the Christmas holidays. The park's off-season is from October to May, and hotels offer huge rate reductions during this period. Shop around and you'll find many bargains.

Banff Central Reservations, 403/705-4020 or 877/542-2633, is tied in with Sunshine Village, but has been providing an excellent booking and reservation service for many years. Like the rest of the world, they've gone online, and reservations can be made at www.banffreservations.com.

All rates quoted below are for a standard room in the high season (June–Sept.).

HOTELS, MOTELS, AND LODGES IN BANFF

Banff has a few accommodations right downtown, but most are strung out along Banff Avenue, an easy walk from the shopping and dining precinct. Nearby Tunnel Mountain is also home to a cluster of accommodations.

Under $50

The only beds in town under $50 are at Banff International Hostel (see "Hostels," below) and at the **Y Mountain Lodge**, 102 Spray Ave., 403/762-3560 or 800/813-4138, www.ywca-banff.ab.ca. Along with a recent name change, this accommodation has undergone massive renovations, and although a part of the YWCA organization, is an excellent choice for budget travelers. Facilities include a casual restaurant open throughout the day, a laundry facility, and the Great Room, a huge living area where the centerpiece is a massive stone fireplace with writing desks and shelves stocked with books scattered throughout. A bed in the dormitory is $21 per person, a private room that shares bathroom facilities is $55 s or d, and an ensuite is $72–79 s or d. These rates are reduced outside of summer.

$50–100

Banff's only motel rooms under $100 are at the **Spruce Grove Motel**, 545 Banff Ave., 403/762-2112, the last park-at-your-door style motel left in town. This orange, green, and white dinosaur from the past offers basic rooms for $75; kitchenettes are $95 but are larger and sleep four. (You can get rooms here for $55 in the off season.)

$100–150

Elkhorn Lodge, 124 Spray Ave., 403/762-2299, is halfway up the hill to the Banff Springs Hotel. The small sleeping rooms are $100, while larger rooms with kitchens are $155.

At the far end of the motel strip, the **Banff Voyager Inn**, 555 Banff Ave., 403/762-3301 or 800/879-1991, has an outdoor swimming pool, a restaurant, a bar renowned for the cheapest beer in town, and a liquor store; $120 s or d.

Six blocks along the motel strip from downtown is **Rundle Manor**, 348 Marten St., 403/762-

5544 or 800/661-1272, offering one-bedroom suites for $135, two-bedroom suites for $205, each with a full kitchen.

Bumper's Inn, is at the far end of the strip at 603 Banff Avenue, 403/762-3386 or 800/661-3518. It's best known for its steakhouse, but behind the restaurant are 39 older-style rooms for $135 s or d.

All 52 rooms at the **Red Carpet Inn,** 425 Banff Ave., 403/762-4184 or 800/563-4609, were recently renovated; $120 s, $140 d.

Adjacent to the Red Carpet Inn is the **Irwin's Mountain Inn,** 429 Banff Ave., 403/762-4566 or 800/661-1721, www.irwinsmountaininn.com, which offers rooms of similar standard for $140 s or d, as well as a fitness room and laundry facility.

The **Homestead Inn,** 217 Lynx St., 403/762-4471 or 800/661-1021, is a fairly basic hostelry charging $145 s or d for its 27 guest rooms.

If you have your own transportation, consider **Norquay's Timberline Inn,** away from downtown on the north side of the TransCanada Highway at the base of the Banff Mt. Norquay ski area road, 403/762-2281 or 877/762-2281, www.banfftimberline.com. Standard rooms are $133–153; those on the second floor have private balconies, those on the south-facing side have excellent views. Out in back are chalets that sleep six to eight in three bedrooms. Each chalet has a kitchen and fireplace; $280 per night.

$150–200

Close to both the river and downtown is **Bow View Motor Lodge,** 228 Bow Ave., 403/762-2261 or 800/661-1565, www.bowview.com; rooms are $150 or, with a view of the river, $175.

Close to downtown is **High Country Inn,** 419 Banff Ave., 403/762-2236 or 800/661-1244, www.banffhighcountryinn.com, which has an indoor pool, hot tubs, and a popular Swiss/Italian restaurant and pool; $150 per room.

The rooms at the **Dynasty Inn,** 501 Banff Ave., 403/762-8844 or 800/667-1464, are much more modern than those at the High Country Inn, but town is a five-minute walk away. Each of the 99 rooms has a log-trimmed balcony, and the facade is Rundlestone (quarried locally and named for Mt. Rundle). Rooms are $155 s or d.

Rundlestone Lodge, 537 Banff Ave., 403/762-2201 or 800/ 661-8630, www.rundlestone.com, features an indoor pool, whirlpool, and sauna, and many of the elegantly furnished rooms have balconies, fireplaces, and kitchenettes. Rooms begin at $170; some are wheelchair accessible.

Toward downtown, **Charlton's Cedar Court,** 513 Banff Ave., 403/762-4485 or 800/661-1225, www.charltonresorts.com, has an indoor pool; basic rooms are $180 s or d, loft suites with a fireplace are $205.

Banff Traveller's Inn, 401 Banff Ave., 403/762-4401 or 800/661-0227, www.banfftravellersinn.com, has larger rooms, many with mountain views. A buffet breakfast is served for guests each morning. Rates are $180 s or d.

After undergoing a massive renovation program, the **Banff Ptarmigan Inn,** 337 Banff Ave., 403/762-2207 or 800/661-8310, has reopened as a full-service hotel with tastefully decorated rooms, down comforters on all beds, a restaurant, and a variety of facilities to soothe sore muscles, including a spa, a whirlpool, and a sauna. Rooms start at $178 s, $193 d.

Within easy walking distance of downtown is **Banff Caribou Lodge,** 521 Banff Ave., 403/762-5887 or 800/563-8764, www.banffcaribou properties.com. Its 200 bright airy rooms go for $180 s, $195 d. Facilities include a guest shuttle bus, a steakhouse and bar, and a whirlpool and sauna. The impressive log entrance is not easily missed.

Best Western Siding 29 Lodge, 453 Marten St., 403/762-5575 or 800/528-1234, www.siding29.com, is good value for small groups; rooms are $195 for up to four people.

In the heart of downtown Banff, the venerable **Mount Royal Hotel,** 138 Banff Ave., 403/762-3331 or 800/267-3035, www.mountroyalhotel.com, first opened in 1908. Since its purchase by the Brewster Transport Company in 1912, this distinctive red-brick building has seen various expansions and a disastrous fire in 1967, which destroyed the original wing. Today guests are offered 136 tastefully decorated rooms and the use of a large health club with a newly renovated hot tub. Also on the premises are a restaurant and small lounge. Rates are from $195 s or d.

The following three accommodations are on Tunnel Mountain. Although falling in the same price range as many of those on Banff Avenue, all have self-contained units, making them good for families, small groups, or those who want to cook their own meals. Town is a 15-minute walk away.

Douglas Fir Resort, 403/762-5591 or 800/661-9267, www.douglasfir.com, has 133 large condo-style rooms. Each has a fully equipped kitchen and a lounge with fireplace. Facilities include an indoor pool, two water slides, a hot tub, weight room, squash and tennis courts, a grocery store, and Laundromat. Rates begin at $195 s or d.

Across the road is **Tunnel Mountain Chalets,** 403/762-4515 or 800/661-1859, www.tunnelmountain.com. Each modern unit has a kitchenette, fireplace, and two TVs; some have a whirlpool. One-bedroom units go for $195, two bedrooms $235.

Hidden Ridge Chalets, 403/762-3544 or 800/661-1372, www.banffhiddenridge.com, is just that, hidden, with 83 self-contained cabins spread among stands of Douglas fir and spruce, behind Tunnel Mountain Chalets. Each has a kitchen and fireplace; $195 per night, $225 for larger chalets on the ridge.

$200–250

Over 100 years since Jim and Bill Brewster guided their first guests through the park, their descendants are still actively involved in the tourist industry, opening Banff's most central and stylish accommodations in 1996. **Brewster's Mountain Lodge,** 208 Caribou St., 403/762-2900 or 888/762-2900, www.brewsteradventures.com, features an eye-catching log exterior with an equally impressive lobby and adjoining lounge in a prime downtown location. The Western theme is continued in the 71 upstairs rooms. Superior rooms feature two queen-size beds or one king-size bed ($200), deluxe rooms offer a private balcony ($220), and suites have private hot tubs ($290–400). All rates include breakfast. Rates here in the off season are slashed up to 50 percent.

Banff International Hotel, at 333 Banff Avenue, right at the downtown end of the motel strip, 403/762-5666 or 800/665-5666, www.banffinternational.com, is a full service hotel that underwent extensive renovations inside and out in 1999, including the construction of an impressive cedar and stone lobby. Guests enjoy extensive in-room facilities, as well as a comfortable lounge area, a fitness room, and dining choices. Standard rooms are $209, the much larger lofts are $239, mountain-view rooms $259.

One of Banff's larger hotels, but a 10-minute walk to town, is **Inns of Banff,** 600 Banff Ave., 403/762-4581 or 800/661-1272, www.inns ofbanff.com. Each room has a mini-bar, fridge, and balcony while near the lobby are a pool, lounge, and restaurant; $210–285 s or d.

The first things you'll notice at **Buffalo Mountain Lodge,** a 15-minute walk from town on Tunnel Mountain Road, 403/762-2400 or 800/661-1367, www.crmr/bml, are the impressive log entrance, the hand-hewn construction of the lobby, and the huge stone fireplace. The rooms, chalets, and bungalows all have fireplaces; many have kitchens. And you won't need to go to town to eat—one of Banff's best restaurants, Cilantro Mountain Café, is adjacent to the main lodge. Rooms start at $225. (The lodge takes its name from Tunnel Mountain, which early park visitors called Buffalo Mountain, for its shape).

Also away from the main strip of accommodations is **Banff Rocky Mountain Resort,** at the northeast end of Banff Avenue on the corner of Tunnel Mountain Road, 403/762-5531 or 800/661-9563, www.rockymountainresort.com, is an ideal alternative for groups or families. Over 170 units are spread out across the well-manicured grounds while the main building holds a lounge, restaurant, pool, and exercise room. Tennis courts are available for guest use and cross-country ski trails are set during winter. Many of the one- and two-bedroom suites have kitchens, all have fireplaces; $225 and $300, respectively. A free shuttle runs into town from the resort each hour.

With over 200 rooms, two blocks from the heart of downtown Banff, is **Banff Park Lodge,** 222 Lynx St., 403/762-4433 or 800/661-9266, www.banffparklodge.com, a modern, full-service luxury hotel. Rooms begin at $240, suites with bedside hot tubs are $285.

Over $250

Banff's newest hotel is **Charlton's Royal Canadian Lodge,** 459 Banff Ave., 403/762-3307 or 800/661-1379, www.charltonresorts.com, which opened in the summer of 2000. It features 99 luxuriously appointed rooms, heated underground parking, a lounge and restaurant, a large spa-pool complex, and a landscaped courtyard. Rates start at $290 s or d.

On Mountain Avenue, a short walk from the Upper Hot Springs, is **Rimrock Resort Hotel,** 403/762-3356 or 800/661-1587, www.rim rockresort.com. The original hotel was constructed in 1903 but was fully rebuilt and opened as a 346-room full-service luxury resort in the mid-1990s. Each well-appointed room has a king-size bed, comfortable armchair, writing desk, mini-bar, and hair dryer. This hotel caters to disabled persons are well as any in the park. Since it's set high above the Bow Valley, views for the most part are excellent. Prices range from $265 to $345 depending solely on the views. Regular shuttle buses make the short run to town during summer.

Banff Springs Hotel

This famous landmark, one of the world's great mountain resort hotels, has been undergoing massive renovations in recent years, cementing its position as Banff's premier accommodation. Over $30,000 has been spent installing air-conditioning, updating furnishings, and replacing beds in each of the 840 rooms. Other major changes include moving the lobby to a more accessible side of the hotel, reopening the old lobby as a cavernous lounge area, and changing many of the in-house dining facilities. Through the massive changes, the hotel came under the ownership of Fairmont Hotels and Resorts, losing its century-old tag as a Canadian Pacific hotel and in the process its ties to the historic railway company that constructed the original hotel back in 1888.

Even though the rooms have been modernized, many date to the 1920s, and as is common in older establishments, these are small. But room size is only a minor consideration when staying in this historic gem. With 16 eateries, a luxurious spa facility, a huge indoor pool, an elegant library, a 27-hole golf course, tennis courts, horseback riding, and enough twisting, turning hallways, boardwalks, towers, and shops to warrant a detailed map, you'll not be wanting to spend time in your room. Unless, of course, you are in the presidential suite, located in the central tower. It has eight rooms, a canopy bed, hot tub, baby grand piano, private pool, and your own glass elevator linking each of the three floors.

In the process of changing ownership and undergoing the renovations, the way rooms are charged has also changed. Staying at the Banff

Springs is now *very* expensive through summer, as rooms are charged as part of a package. Guests have a choice of two packages—the **Castle Experience** and the **Canadian Rockies Experience.** The Castle Experience is the less expensive of the two, and includes golfing and golf lessons, horseback riding, guided hiking and climbing, tennis, mountain bike rental, canoeing, unlimited entry to the Solace spa and one spa treatment, tennis, and three meals daily in any of hotel restaurants. This package taken in a Canadian Pacific room costs $979 d, but the CP rooms are fairly small, and for an extra $100 you can stay in a much larger Heritage room. The Canadian Rockies Experience includes all that the Castle Experience does, as well as guided fishing, whitewater rafting, and all Brewster tours. This package starts at $1079 d with accommodations in the smallest rooms. (You may not want to take full advantage of all the activities offered. But if, for example, you decide to take a golf lesson and follow it up with a round on the hotel's course, go for an afternoon horseback ride, spend an evening at the spa, and dine in the hotel, the actual cost of the room will work out at about $300 for the night.) Between October and May, rooms are sold on a bed-and-breakfast basis, and prices start at $190 s, $210 d.

The hotel is at the end of Spray Avenue. For reservations, call 403/762-2211 or 800/441-1414, or click on the relevant link at www.fairmont.com.

LODGES ALONG THE BOW VALLEY PARKWAY

The Bow Valley Parkway is the original route between Banff and Lake Louise. It is a beautiful drive in all seasons and along its length are three lodges, each a viable alternative to staying in Banff.

Johnston Canyon Resort, 403/762-2971 or 888/378-1720, www.johnstoncanyon.com, is 26 km west of Banff at the beginning of a short trail that leads to the famous canyon. The rustic cabins are older, and some have kitchenettes. On the grounds are tennis courts, a barbecue area, and an excellent new restaurant. Basic two-person cabins are $109, two-person cabins with a fireplace are $149, and they go up in price all the way to $245 for a "Classic" cabin complete with

cooking facilities, and luxurious heritage-style furnishings. It's open mid-May to early October.

Six km farther northwest is **Castle Mountain Chalets,** tel. (403) 762-3868, www.castlemountain.com. The older-style cabins have recently been replaced with 22 deluxe log chalets. These spacious chalets have high ceilings, beautifully handcrafted log interiors, three beds, a stone fireplace, full kitchen with dishwasher, a bathroom with hot tub, and satellite TV; $175 for up to four people, $195 for five or six.

Baker Creek Chalets, 403/522-3761, is the next resort along the parkway, 40 km from Banff and 10 km from Lake Louise. Each of the 25 log cabins has a kitchenette, fireplace, and outside deck (complete with cute woodcarvings of bears climbing over the railings). Basic one-room cabins are $140 for two; one-bedroom cabins with loft (sleeps six) are $185; two bedroom cabins (sleeps six) are $240 for four. A new wing has eight luxurious suites, each with a kitchen and hot tub, for $200 s or d. Each additional person $15. The restaurant here is highly recommended.

HOTELS, MOTELS, AND LODGES IN LAKE LOUISE

In summer, accommodations at Lake Louise are even harder to come by than Banff, so it's essential to make reservations well in advance. Any rooms not taken by early afternoon will be the expensive ones.

$100–150
Aside from the Chateau, the **Lake Louise Inn,** 210 Village Rd., 403/522-3791 or 800/661-9237, www.lakelouiseinn.com, is the village's largest lodging, sprawling over two hectares within easy walking distance of Samson Mall. Its 232 rooms start at $148 s or d.

$150–200
Not right in the village, but a good deal for families, small groups, and those who like privacy, is **Paradise Lodge and Bungalows,** 403/522-3595, www.paradiselodge.com. Spread out around well-manicured gardens are 21 self-contained cabins beginning at $165 per night. Bungalows with kitchens are $175 for one bedroom

Paradise Lodge and Bungalows

and $185 for two bedrooms. A few self-contained two-room units with large balconies boast views across the Bow Valley; $195. Twenty-four newly built suites, each with a fireplace, TV, one or two bedrooms, and fabulous mountain views start at $235, or $255 with a kitchen. Honeymoon suites, with all of the above as well as a hot tub, are $280. The lodge is open mid-May to mid-October. To get there from the valley floor, follow Lake Louise Drive toward Chateau Lake Louise for two km.

The historic **Deer Lodge,** 403/522-3747 or 800/661-1595, www.crmr.com/dl, began life in 1921 as a teahouse, with rooms added in 1925. Facilities include a rooftop hot tub, games room, restaurant, and bar. Rooms range $160–220. It's along Lake Louise Drive, up the hill from the village, and just below the lake itself.

Mountaineer Lodge, close to everything at 101 Village Road, 403/522-3844, www.mountaineerlodge.com, charges from $160 s or d for large rooms, each separate sleeping areas. It's only open May–October.

Over $200

Originally called Lake Louise Ski Lodge, the **Post Hotel,** 403/522-3989 or 800/661-1586, www.posthotel.com, is bordered to the east and south by the Pipestone River. It may lack views of Lake Louise, but it is as elegant, in a modern, woodsy way, as the Chateau. Each bungalow-style room is furnished with Canadian pine and has a balcony. Many have whirlpools and fireplaces, while some have kitchens. Other facilities include an indoor pool, steam room, and library. High tea is served in the lobby each afternoon. The hotel has 17 different room types, with 26 different rates depending on the view. Rates start at $300 s or d per night.

Overlooking the famous lake for which it's named, 11 km from the valley floor, is luxurious **Moraine Lake Lodge,** 403/522-3733 or 800/661-8340, www.morainelake.com. Rooms in the main lodge are spacious and well-appointed; guests are pampered with afternoon tea and evening liqueurs. It's only open June–September, with rooms in the lodge going for $350-plus and cabins from $410 in the height of summer.

Chateau Lake Louise

This historic 500-room hotel on the shore of Lake Louise has views equal to any mountain resort in the world. But all this historic charm and mountain scenery comes at a price. During the summer season (June to mid-October), rooms must be booked as a Canadian Rockies Experience or Castle Experience package, costing from $1079 d for a wide range of activities (many of them, such as golf, are back in Banff). This rate is for a standard room, and it rising exponentially for mountainside and lakeside rooms. Rates drop as low as $219 s, $238 d outside of summer, with ski packages often advertised. Children under 17 sharing with parents are free, but if you bring a pet it'll be an extra $20. For reservations–and you'll need one–call 403/522-3511 or 800/441-1414, www.fairmont.com.

LODGES ALONG THE ICEFIELDS PARKWAY

Bow Lake

Pioneer guide and outfitter Jimmy Simpson built **Simpson's Num-ti-jah Lodge** on the north shore of Bow Lake, 40 km north of Lake Louise, as base for his outfitting operation in 1920. In those days, the route north from Lake Louise was nothing more than a horse trail. The desire to build a large structure when only short timbers were available led to the unusual octagonal shape of the main lodge. Simpson remained at Bow Lake, a living legend, until his death in 1972 at the age of 95. Today the lodge offers a variety of facilities for travelers along the highway, as well as 25 rooms. These cost $140 s or d with shared bathrooms, $160 s or d with private bathrooms, and $185 with views. A small coffee shop is open daily 9 A.M.–5:30 P.M., and the **Elkhorn Dining Room** is open for dinner. Horseback rides are offered for guests and nonguests. A one-hour ride along Bow Lake is $25, a three-hour ride to Peyto Lake is $52, and a full-day ride to Helen Lake is $100. Book at 403/522-2167 or online at www.num-ti-jah.com. Closed November.

Saskatchewan River Crossing

Just north of Saskatchewan River Crossing, 45 km south of the Columbia Icefield, is **The Crossing,** 403/761-7000, a well-priced lodging with rooms for $84 s, $89 d (40 percent discount in spring and fall), a self-serve restaurant, cafeteria, lounge, large gift shop, and gas. It's open late March to October.

BED-AND-BREAKFASTS

The Banff/Lake Louise Tourism Bureau in the Banff Visitor Centre, 224 Banff Ave., 403/762-8421, maintains a list of bed-and-breakfasts and private homes that rent rooms or cabins. Standards range from fair to good, but the prices are lower than those of the hotels. Bookings can also be made through **Banff Central Reservations,** 403/705-4020 or 877/542-2633, www.banffreservations.com.

Blue Mountain Lodge, 137 Muskrat St., 403/762-5134, www.bluemtnlodge.com, has rooms for $75 and small cabins from $90. All guests have use of shared kitchen facilities. Better value is **Beaver St. Suites and Cabins,** 220 Beaver St., 403/762-5077, with rooms beginning at $65 and cabins at $75.

Without a doubt, the best bed-and-breakfast in town is **Eleanor's House,** 125 Kootenay Ave., 403/760-2457, www.bbeleanor.com, a lovely guesthouse on a quiet residential street. It has a library, and each of the two luxuriously furnished rooms has a private bathroom. Rates are $135 s, $145 d, which includes a gourmet breakfast and evening drinks.

HOSTELS

All the hostels listed below are linked by a shuttle service that departs Calgary International Hostel daily at 8 A.M. and continues north along the Icefields Parkway to all Jasper National Park hostels. Sample fares are Calgary to Banff, $25; Calgary to Lake Louise, $30; Banff to Lake Louise, $14; Banff to Jasper International Hostel, $45. Reservations can be made through Calgary International Hostel, 403/269-8239, or any of the hostels listed below. The service runs between mid-May and the end of October.

Banff

Banff International Hostel, 403/762-4122, is just off Tunnel Mountain Road three km from downtown. This large, modern hostel sleeps 216 in small two-, four-, and six-bed dormitory rooms. The large lounge area has a fireplace, and other facilities include a recreation room, public Internet access bike and ski workshop, large kitchen, self-service cafe, and laundry. Members of Hostelling International (HI) pay $20 per night, nonmembers $24. During July and August reserve at least a month in advance to be assured of a bed. The hostel is open all day, but check-in isn't until 3 P.M. To get there from town, ride the Banff Transit bus ($1), which passes the hostel twice an hour during summer. The rest of the year the only transportation is by cab, about $6 from the bus depot.

Bow Valley Parkway

Thirty-two km from Banff along the Bow Valley Parkway, **Castle Mountain Hostel** is near a number of interesting hikes. This hostel sleeps 28 and has a kitchen, common room, hot showers, and bike rentals; HI members $13, nonmembers $17. Make reservations through the Banff Hostel.

Lake Louise

With beds for over $100 less than anyplace

else in town, **Canadian Alpine Centre** fills up quickly each day. Of log construction, with large windows and high vaulted ceilings, the hostel was a joint venture between the Alpine Club of Canada and the Southern Alberta Hostelling Association. It opened early in the summer of 1992, and extensions in 1995 brought the total number of beds to 150. Downstairs are a large reception area and **Bill Peyto's Cafe,** the least expensive place to eat in Lake Louise. Upstairs are a large lounge area and guide's room—a quiet place to plan your next hike or browse through the large collection of mountain literature. Hostel members pay $22 per night for a bunk in a two-, four-, or six-bed dorm, while nonmembers pay $26. The hostel is open year-round, with check-in after 3 P.M. In summer and on weekends during the ski season, advance bookings (up to six months) are essential. The hostel is on Village Road, one km from Samson Mall, 403/522-2200.

Along the Icefields Parkway

North of Lake Louise, three hostels dot the Icefields Parkway. The first (at Km 24) is **Mosquito Creek Hostel,** which is near good hiking and offers accommodations for 38 in four cabins. Facilities include a kitchen, wood-heated sauna, and large common room with fireplace. **Rampart Creek Hostel** (at Km 88) is 12 km north of Saskatchewan River Crossing, a long day's bike ride from Mosquito Creek. Like Mosquito Creek, it's near good hiking and has a kitchen and sauna. Its two cabins hold 30 people. After the long climb up to Sunwapta Pass, **Hilda Creek Hostel** (at Km 118) will be a welcome sight for cyclists. This hostel lies just below the glacial moraines left by the retreating Columbia Icefield; a variety of hikes begin from the doorstep. It has 21 dorm beds, a kitchen, sauna, and a common room. Members pay $12–13, nonmembers $16–17.

Mosquito Creek Hostel is open year-round; the other two are open nightly mid-May to mid-October and weekends only mid-December to mid-May (closed the rest of the year). Book ahead during July and August as these hostels fill each night. Rampart Creek requires reservations between November and May. Reservations can be made at the hostels in Banff, 403/762-4122 or Lake Louise, 403/522-2200.

BACKCOUNTRY HUTS AND LODGES

In the backcountry of the national park are two distinct types of accommodations–rustic mountain huts and lodges. The Alpine Club of Canada manages the extensive system of huts. Often of historical significance, each of the huts has a stove, lantern, kitchen utensils, and foam mattresses. For locations and reservations, contact the club at 403/678-3200 or surf the Internet to www.alpineclubofcanada.ca.

Shadow Lake Lodge

Shadow Lake Lodge, 403/762-0116 or 800/691-5085, is 14 km from the nearest road. Access is on foot or, in winter, on skis. The lodge is near picturesque Shadow Lake, and many hiking trails are nearby. The oldest structure has been restored as a dining area; guests sleep in newer, more cozy cabins. The daily rate, including three meals and afternoon tea, is $170 s, $132 per person d per day. The trailhead is along the TransCanada Highway, 19 km from Banff, at the Redearth Creek parking area.

Skoki Lodge

Skoki is a rustic lodge, deep in the backcountry north of Lake Louise Ski Area. Getting there requires an 11-km hike or ski, depending on the season. The lodge is an excellent base for exploring nearby valleys and mountains. It dates to 1930, when it operated as a lodge for skiers. Today it comprises a main lodge and three cabins, sleeping a total of 22 people. Accommodations are rustic–no electricity or indoor plumbing–but comfortable, and the lodge has a reputation for excellent meals, which are included in the nightly rate of $131.40 per person per night. For information and reservations, call 403/522-3555, www.skilouise.com/skoki.

CAMPGROUNDS

Reservations are not taken at any of the campgrounds within Banff National Park. The best way to ensure a site is to arrive in the morning, when other campers are leaving. When these main campgrounds fill, those unable to secure a site will be directed to an "overflow" area. These provide few facilities, and no hookups, but cost less. Open fires are permitted in designated areas throughout all campgrounds, but you must purchase a Firewood Permit ($4 per site per night) to burn wood, which is provided at no cost.

Near the Town of Banff

Although Banff has five campgrounds with over 1,500 sites in its immediate vicinity, all fill by early afternoon. Closest to town are **Tunnel Mountain Village II** and **Tunnel Mountain Trailer Court,** 3.5 km along Tunnel Mountain Road. The former has electrical hookups and is the only campground near Banff open year-round. The latter has full hookups and is open early May to early October. Both have hot showers but little privacy between sites. Sites are $21–24 and no tents are allowed (except when Tunnel Mountain Village I is closed). Less than one km farther along the road is the park's largest campground (622 sites), **Tunnel Mountain Village I,** which has hot showers, private sites, and kitchen shelters, but no hookups. Sites are $17 and it's open early May to early October.

Toward Lake Minnewanka northeast of town is **Two Jack Lakeside,** which has showers and lots of trees; $17 per night. In the same vicinity is the much larger **Two Jack Lake Main;** $13.

Bow Valley Parkway

Along Bow Valley Parkway you'll find **Johnston Canyon Campground, Castle Mountain Campground,** and **Protection Mountain Campground.** Johnson Canyon is largest, with 180 sites, and has hot showers. All sites are $17 and it's open early June to mid-September.

The other two have no showers, and open a few weeks later; $13 per night.

Lake Louise

Lake Louise Campground, within easy walking distance of the village, is divided into two areas by the Bow River. One side has unserviced sites, the other serviced. Individual sites are close together, but some privacy and shade are provided by towering lodgepole pines. The unserviced (tent camping) sites have showers, flush toilets, kitchen shelters, fire rings, and picnic tables; $17 per night. Serviced (trailer camping) sites have showers, power, and flush toilets; $21. A dump station is located near the entrance to the campground ($5 per use). An interpretive program runs throughout summer, nightly at 9 P.M. in the outdoor theater. The Bow River Loop hiking trail leads into the village along either side of the Bow River, crossing at the southern end of the serviced sites and again behind Samson Mall. To get to the campground, take Lake Louise Drive under the railway bridge, turn left on Fairview Drive, and continue past the impressive log staff accommodations to the fee station. The serviced section of this campground is open year-round, the unserviced section mid-May to September.

Along the Icefields Parkway

Campgrounds are located at **Mosquito Creek** (km 24; $10), **Waterfowl Lakes** (km 57; $13), and **Rampart Creek** (km 88; $10). Each has pit toilets (Waterfowl Lakes has flush toilets), kitchen shelters, firewood, and fire rings, but no showers or hookups, and each is open from mid-June to early September. Mosquito Creek also remains open for winter camping.

FOOD

Banff alone has over 100 restaurants. That's more per capita than any town or city across Canada. From lobster to linguini, alligator to à la carte, and fajitas to fudge, anyone who spends time in the park will find something that suits his or her taste and budget. Many of the town's restaurants have been around for decades and attract diners from as far away as Calgary (some of whom have been known to stay overnight just to eat at their favorite haunt). An

eclectic mix of restaurants lines Banff Avenue–most have menus posted out front. The less adventurous can try one of the eateries at the major hotels; the Banff Springs Hotel tops the list with a choice of 15 different dining options. In July and August, the most popular restaurants don't take reservations and you can expect a wait. Various dining guides are available throughout town.

BANFF

Budget Stretchers

The best place to begin looking for cheap eats is the Food Court in the lower level of Cascade Plaza at 317 Banff Avenue. Here you'll find two bakeries and **Edo Japan,** which sells simple Japanese dishes for around $6, including a drink. **Café Alpenglow,** in the Banff International Hostel, Tunnel Mountain Rd., 403/762-4122, features all the usual café-style dishes, such as a pile of nachos for $7; no entrée is over $10. A local bylaw prohibiting obtrusive signs and neon lights means that the fast-food chains are easily missed. For the most expensive Big Macs this side of the Toronto Skydome, head to **McDonald's,** 116 Banff Ave. **KFC** is at 202 Caribou Street. **Aardvarks,** 304 Caribou St., 403/762-5500, is a late-night pizza hang-out open until 4 A.M.

Cafés and Coffee Shops

The **Cake Company,** 220 Bear St., 403/762-2330, serves great coffee, as well as a delicious range of pastries, muffins, and cakes baked daily on the premises. Another Cake Company outlet is on the lower level of Cascade Plaza; a muffin and coffee is $2.50. **Evelyn's,** on Banff Avenue in the Town Centre Mall, has good coffee and huge sandwiches, and is a super place for socializing and people watching. **Jump Start,** opposite Central Park at 206 Buffalo St., 403/762-0332, has a wide range of coffee concoctions as well as delicious homemade soups (from $4.50) and sandwiches ($5).

Bruno's Café & Grill, named for Bruno Engler, renowned photographer, ski instructor, and mountain man, is a cozy little café with a great "mountain" ambience and comfortable couches. It's open daily 7 A.M.–10 P.M.; at 304 Caribou St., 403/762-8115.

Steak and Seafood

Even though **Bumper's,** 603 Banff Ave., 403/762-2622, is away from the center of Banff, it remains one of the town's busiest restaurants. And not just in summer; locals and visitors alike flock to this popular steak house year-round. Large cuts of Alberta beef, efficient service, and great prices keep people coming back. Favorite choices are the prime rib Pile-o-bones, Barbecue

Busy Banff Avenue is lined with restaurants.

Beef Ribs, and of course slabs of juicy beef cooked to your taste. Main entrées run $10.50–27 and include a trip to the small salad bar. Upstairs is the **Loft Lounge,** a good place to wait for a table or relax afterwards with an inexpensive drink. It's open 4:30–10 P.M.

A town favorite that has faithfully served locals for many years is **Melissa's,** 218 Lynx St., 403/762-5511, housed in a log building that dates from 1928 (the original Homestead Inn). For breakfast, the hotcakes, piled high on your plate ($5.50), can't be beat. Or try the bran muffins made from scratch each morning. Lunch and dinner are casual affairs—choose from a wide variety of generously sized burgers, freshly prepared salads, and mouthwatering Alberta beef. Melissa's also features an outside patio and rustic bar with well-priced drinks. Open daily 7:30 A.M.–10 P.M.

Offering tremendous views back across the highway to Mt. Rundle and up the Spray Valley is the **Big Horn Steak House,** in Norquay's Timberline Inn, 403/762-2285. A cut of prime

BREAKFAST FAVORITES

All Banff's coffee shops and cafés open early for coffee and muffins, but for something more substantial to start the day, any one of the following will get you off on the right track.

Outfitter's, in Brewster's Mountain Lodge, 208 Caribou Street, 403/762-5454, is a stylish lounge that opens each morning between 7 A.M. and 10 P.M. for a delicious breakfast buffet, which includes everything from mouth-watering omelets to gourmet yogurts; $12.50. The Rimrock Resort Hotel's **Primrose Restaurant,** Mountain Avenue, 403/762-3356, is an elegant dining room with mountain views and well-spread tables giving a certain amount of privacy. This isn't your usual setting for a buffet, but the breakfast spread here through winter is one of the best in the valley; $15. **The Pines,** Rundlestone Lodge, 537 Banff Avenue, 403/760-6690, serves up a continental breakfast buffet for $8.50, $11 with hot dishes, daily 7–10:30 A.M.

Melissa's, 218 Lynx Street, 403/762-5511, is renowned for hotcakes, piled high on your plate, for $5.50. Or try the bran muffins made from scratch each morning. For traditional diner-style cooked breakfasts, head down to **Craig's Way Station,** 461 Banff Avenue, 403/762-4660; open daily from 6:30 A.M. Cooked breakfasts are all under $7.50.

Alberta beef ranges $18–26, and while the food is good, it's the views that will make you drool here. This restaurant is open daily 7 A.M.–10 P.M., with a sun deck open in summer.

The romantic era of the railway is relived in **Caboose Steak and Lobster Restaurant,** in the old C.P.R. station at the corner of Elk and Lynx Streets, 403/762-3622. Although not the original station, kings, queens, and millions of other visitors have passed through the building. The walls are lined with railway memorabilia, and the elegant atmosphere makes for a memorable dining experience. Seafood and steak dominate the menu, including the very best Alberta beef and Alaskan king crab; expect to pay $18–35 for entrées and around $5 for dessert. All meals include the self-service salad cart that is wheeled to your table. The Caboose is open daily 5–10 P.M.

Other Canadian Classics

In the Banff Caribou Lodge is **The Keg,** 521 Banff Ave., 403/762-4442, part of a western Canada chain noted for its consistently good steak, seafood, and chicken dishes at reasonable prices. All entrées include a 60-item salad bar. The Keg is open daily 7 A.M.–2 A.M. Another Keg location is downtown at 117 Banff Avenue, 403/760-3030. The familiar **Earl's,** upstairs in the heart of the action at 229 Banff Avenue, 403/762-4414, has more of the same at slightly higher prices. This chain has a reputation for a menu of "fusion" cuisine that follows food trends, bright young servers, and a fun atmosphere. The **Old Spaghetti Factory,** upstairs in the Cascade Plaza on Banff Avenue, 403/760-2779, is a family favorite, with a casual rustic décor, and a few tables spread along a balcony. The most you'll pay for any meal is $16, which includes soup or salad and dessert.

Not necessarily a Canadian classic, **Joe Btfsplk's Diner** (pronounced "bi-tif-splik's") is a classic nevertheless. It's a modern 1950s style diner, complete with a jukebox, a counter up back along the kitchen, and a range of tacky souvenirs. The menu is similarly themed with daily specials for around $10 at lunch, $15 at dinner, and everything from Caesar salad to meatloaf on the regular menu. It's at 221 Banff Avenue., 403/762-5529, and is open daily for breakfast, lunch, and dinner.

Upmarket Canadian Dining

Banff's original bistro-style restaurant, which opened in the early 1990s, is **Coyote's,** 206 Caribou St., 403/762-3963. Meals are prepared in full view of diners, and the menu emphasizes health-conscious, Southwestern-style dishes (lots of chili); the salmon, sea bass, broiled chicken, and tempting desserts are favorites. Entrées range $10–19.50. Coyote's is open daily 8 A.M.–10 P.M.

The **Buffalo Mountain Lodge Restaurant** has a distinctive interior of hand-hewn cedar beams and Old World elegance—the perfect setting for a moderate splurge. Expect to pay around $35 per person for soup, an entrée, and dessert. Breakfast is also good. The restaurant is open daily 7 A.M.–11 P.M. Most of Banff's motels have restaurants that combine Canadian and continental cuisine, all similarly priced. The better ones include **Churchill's,** Mount Royal Hotel, 138 Banff Ave., 403/762-7180; **Chinook Restaurant** (with a great Sunday brunch), Banff Park Lodge, 222 Lynx St., 403/762-4433. Another hotel restaurant with an excellent reputation is **The Pines,** in the Rundlestone Lodge, 537 Banff Ave., 403/760-6690. The dinner menu features modern Canadian cuisine in a contemporary setting. The service is excellent and meals well priced.

Mexican and Cajun
The **Magpie & Stump,** 203 Caribou St., 403/762-4067, serves no-frills authentic Mexican food at reasonable prices. Lunch is from $5.50, dinner from $9, and a few outside tables catch the afternoon sun. It's open 11 A.M.–midnight.

Italian
Banff is blessed with fine Italian restaurants. **Guido's,** 116 Banff Ave., 403/762-4002, is known for its homemade pasta, which is cooked to perfection in a variety of sauces that appeal to all tastes and diets. Entrées are $9.50–19. It's open daily from 5 P.M. More trendy (reflected in the prices) is **Giorgio's,** 219 Banff Ave., 403/762-5114, which has a stylish decor and a casual Old World atmosphere. Its chefs prepare as many as 400 meals each afternoon, and the lineup for tables is ever present. Pasta dishes begin at $10. It's open from 4:30 P.M.

If you are staying up on Tunnel Mountain (or even if you're not), **Cilantro Mountain Cafe,** at Buffalo Mountain Lodge, 403/762-2400, is well worth trying. The menu is limited to a few Italian-style dishes, which change as seasonal produce becomes available, and pizza is prepared in a wood-fired oven in full view of diners. The atmosphere is typifies mountain dining: casual, and elegantly rustic. The outside deck is perfect for those hot summer nights. Pizza is around $15, entrées average $25.

Greek
The **Balkan,** 120 Banff Ave., 403/762-3454, is run by Greeks, but the menu blends their heritage with the cuisines of Italy, China, and Canada. Select from Greek ribs (pork ribs with a lemon sauce) for $15.95, the Greek chow mein (stir-fried vegetables, fried rice, and your choice of meat) for $10.50, or Greek spaghetti for $9.50.

But the most popular dishes are souvlakia ($12.95) and an enormous Greek platter that includes a leg of lamb ($39 for two). The Balkan is open daily 11 A.M.–11 P.M.

Swiss-Italian
Once one of Banff's busiest restaurants, **Ticino,** has moved from downtown to the High Country Inn at 415 Banff Avenue, 403/762-3848. It's named for the southern province of Switzerland, where the cuisine has a distinctive Italian influence. The Swiss chef is best known for his beef and cheese fondues, veal dishes, and juicy steaks. Expect to pay around $6 for appetizers and from $14 for entrées; open daily 5–11 P.M.

Japanese
The large number of Japanese visitors in Banff has created the need for good Japanese restaurants. **Shiki Japanese Noodles,** in the back of the Clock Tower Mall, 110 Banff Ave., 403/762-0527, has a choice of *donburi,* various meat cakes, teriyaki, and sushi. Dishes are $5–10 each. It's a casual, café-type place with only a few tables, and is popular for lunch (eat in or take out). Hours are 11 A.M.–9 P.M. daily.

More expensive is **Suginoya,** 225 Banff Ave., 403/762-4773, which has a relaxed atmosphere. Choose from the sushi bar, *ozashiki* booths, or regular tables. Traditional *shabu-shabu* and seafood teriyaki are popular. The number of Japanese diners here is indicative of the quality. Expect to pay at least $13 for entrées, $19–25 for one of the combination dinners. Suginoya is open daily 11 A.M.–10:30 P.M. **Sushi House Banff,** 304 Caribou St., 403/762-2971, is a unique little restaurant where diners sit around a moving miniature railway, picking sushi and other delicacies from a train as it circles the chef, loading the carriages as quickly as they empty. Banff's best Japanese restaurant is the **Samurai,** in the Banff Springs Hotel (see below).

French
Le Beaujolais, 212 Buffalo St. (at Banff Ave.), 403/762-2712, is a Canadian leader in French cuisine and has become one of Banff's most popular fine-dining restaurants for almost 20 years. Its second-floor location ensures great views of Banff, especially from window tables. The dishes feature mainly Canadian produce, prepared

and served with a traditional French flair. Entrées begin at $18, but the extent of your final tab depends on whether you choose à la carte items or the four- or six-course table d'hôte menu ($50 and $66 respectively) —and also on how much wine you consume (from a 10,000-bottle cellar at $20–250 a bottle). The restaurant is open daily from 6 P.M.; reservations are necessary.

The Grizzly House

This unique fondue restaurant at 207 Banff Avenue, 403/762-4055, provides Banff's most unusual dining experience. The decor is, to say the least, eclectic (many say eccentric). Each table has a phone for across-table conversation, or you can call your waiter, the bar, a cab, diners in the private booth, or even those who spend too long in the bathroom. Through all this, the food is good and the service professional. Although traditional Swiss fondues are on the menu, so are buffalo, rattlesnake, alligator, seafood, and Asian dishes. Of course it wouldn't be right to leave without having a chocolate fondue dipped with fresh fruit. Individual fondues are $18–34 (lunch a little cheaper); complete three-course dinners start at $40. Open 11:30 A.M.–midnight.

Banff Springs Hotel

Whether guests or not, most visitors to Banff drop by to see one of the town's biggest tourist attractions. And a meal here might not be as expensive as you think. The hotel itself has more eateries than most small towns—from a deli serving pizza to the finest of fine dining in the Banffshire Club.

If you are in the mood for a light snack or sandwiches to go, head downstairs to the Arcade Level and the **Delicatessen,** which is open 24 hours daily. Named for the adjacent spa facility, **Solace Lite** has a corresponding menu—health-conscious salads and light meals. This café-style eatery also offers stunning mountain views. In the same vicinity of the hotel, the **Bow Valley Terrace** features outdoor summer lunch dining between 11:30 A.M. and 6 P.M.

The **Bow Valley Grill,** with seating for 275, is the hotel's largest dining room. Each morning a large buffet of hot and cold delicacies, including freshly baked bread and seasonal fruits, is laid out for the masses. Lunch is served 11:30

A.M.–5:30 P.M., with a wide-ranging menu featuring everything from salads to seafood. Through the busiest months of summer, a buffet lunch is offered 11:30 A.M.–1:30 P.M., with a free Historical Hotel Tour included in the rate of $19.95 per person. The hotel's Sunday brunch, served in the Bow Valley Grill, is legendary, with chefs working at numerous stations scattered around the dining area, and an enormous spread not equaled for variety anywhere in the mountains. Dinner is served nightly until 10 P.M., with mains running $15–26.50. Reservations are required for Sunday brunch (as far in advance as possible) and dinner.

Through recent hotel renovations, the **Alhambra Room** retained its Old World atmosphere and reputation as an elegant yet casual dining choice. The à la carte dinner menu features a wide variety of beef and seafood dishes. In July and August, this restaurant features Van Horne's Grand Buffet, with chef-attended dining stations offering dishes prepared to order from around the world. Open nightly for dinner, **Castello Ristorante** serves pasta at good prices while also offering a wide range of other Italian specialties and a mouthwatering antipasto bar. The **Samurai Restaurant** is the most expensive of Banff's many Japanese restaurants, but is also the most traditional (and busiest); open for dinner only.

Two restaurants lie within the grounds surrounding the hotel, and both are worthy of consideration. Originally the golf course clubhouse, the **Waldhaus Restaurant** is nestled in forested area of lodgepole pine directly below the hotel. Open daily 6–10 P.M., it features German specialties, with mains from $17. Below this restaurant is a pub of the same name, with a pub-style dinner menu offered in a casual atmosphere. The **Clubhouse Dining Room** is a seasonal restaurant on the golf course proper that serves light breakfasts, casual lunches, and more formal dinners. A shuttle bus runs every 30 minutes between the main lobby and the clubhouse.

The **Rundle Lounge,** is a long, narrow piano bar, where most tables offer views down the Bow Valley. It's open 11 A.M.–midnight, with an à la carte menu on offer. Smoke-free **Grapes** is an intimate yet casual wine bar noted for its fine cheeses and pâtés. More substantial meals such as fondues are also offered. It's open for lunch and dinner.

The hotel's most acclaimed restaurant is the

Banffshire Club, which seats just 76 diners and requires men to wear a jacket. Like its predecessor, the Rob Roy Room, this fine-dining restaurant has quickly become renowned for its excellently prepared Alberta beef. (Try the beef strip loin for two, broiled to order then carved at your table). Many lighter dishes such as chicken and seafood ($18–34) are also offered. It's open daily 6–10 P.M.

For all Banff Springs Hotel dining reservations, call 403/662-6860, or after 5 P.M., call 403/762-2211. During the summer months a desk in the main lobby has all menus posted and takes reservations.

BOW VALLEY PARKWAY

Along the Bow Valley Parkway toward Lake Louise are two excellent restaurants. The first is at Johnston Canyon Resort, 26 km from Banff, 403/762-2971. The resort has always had a restaurant, but in the past it had only opened as a courtesy to resort guests (the resort actually began life as a teahouse). This changed when, after extensive renovations, **Bridges,** with a historic atmosphere and views out to the creek, opened in 2000. It opens nightly at 6 P.M. for a wide ranging menu where most mains are under $20.

A further 14 km along the parkway is **Baker Creek Bistro,** at Baker Creek Chalets, 403/522-2182. This intimate restaurant, housed in a log building, is definitely worth the drive from Banff. Next to the restaurant is a rustic lounge and large outdoor patio. The bistro is open in summer, daily 7 A.M.–10 P.M., shorter hours the rest of the year.

LAKE LOUISE

Start your day with breakfast (summer only) in the grand surroundings of the **Lodge of the Ten Peaks,** at the base of Lake Louise ski area, 403/522-3555. It's a casual affair, eat all you can for $16, or eat and ride the gondola for $20, a good deal considering the gondola ride alone is $14.

On the Cheap
Samson Mall is the center of much activity each afternoon as campers descend on the grocery store to stock up on supplies for the evening meal. Prices are high and by the end of the day stocks are low. **Laggan's Mountain Bakery,** also in the mall, 403/552-2017, is *the* place to hang out with a coffee and one of their delicious freshly baked pastries, cakes, or muffins. If the tables are full and you manage to somehow reach the cake cabinet, order takeout and enjoy your feast on the grassy bank behind the mall. The chocolate brownie ($1.50) is delicious. Order two slices to save having to line up again. The bakery is open daily 6 A.M.–7 P.M.

Forget the Bar and Grill in the mall—much

Baker Creek Bistro.

better is **Bill Peyto's Cafe** in the hostel on Village Road, 403/522-2200. The food is consistent and well priced. A huge portion of nachos is $7. You don't have to be staying in the hostel to eat there. Open daily 7 A.M.–9 P.M. **Legends,** in the Lake Louise Inn, 403/522-3791, is a family restaurant offering typical Canadian fare (including buffalo) and the occasional summer buffet dinner.

Lake Louise Station Restaurant

One hundred years ago visitors departing trains at Laggan Station were keen to get to the Chateau Lake Louise as quickly as possible to begin their adventure. Today guests from the Chateau, other hotels, and even people from as far away as Banff are returning to the restored station to dine in this unique restaurant. Although the menu is not extensive, the ample variety satisfies most tastes. Open for lunch and dinner. For reservations, call 403/522-2600.

Chateau Lake Louise

Within this famous hotel are a choice of eateries and an ice-cream shop. The **Poppy Room** has obscured lake views and is the most casual place for a meal. A continental buffet breakfast is served 7–9 A.M.; $13.50. For dinner a pizza and pasta buffet is offered ($18), or order off the menu. It's open till 8:30 P.M. **Walliser Stube** is an elegant two-story wine bar decorated with oak furniture. It offers a simple menu of German dishes from $15.95 as well as cheese fondue. **Lakeside Lounge** is along floor-to-ceiling windows where Victorian afternoon tea of crumpets, sandwiches, desserts, and drinks is served each afternoon; $16.95. **Victoria Dining Room** is a relaxed but stylish restaurant open for breakfast, a buffet lunch, and evening dining with live entertainment. **Edelweiss Dining Room,** the chateau's signature dining room, has the best view of Lake Louise and offers the Chateau's most elegant setting. Appetizers start at $4.75 while entrées from the fish, game, chicken, and meat menu start at $19.50. For all reservations, call 403/522-3511.

Post Hotel

In 1987, the Post Hotel was expanded to include a luxurious new wing. The original log building was renovated as a rustic, timbered, dining room, linked to the rest of the hotel by an intimate bar. Although the dining room isn't cheap, it's a favorite of locals and visitors alike. The chef specializes in European cuisine, preparing a number of Swiss dishes (such as veal zurichois) to make owner George Schwarz feel homesick. But he's also renowned for his presentation of Alberta beef, Pacific salmon, and Peking duck. Main meals start at $25. The restaurant is open daily 11:30 A.M.–2 P.M. and 6–8:30 P.M. Reservations are essential for dinner; call 403/522-3989.

OTHER PRACTICALITIES

TRANSPORTATION

Getting There

Calgary International Airport is the closest major airport to Banff National Park. **Brewster,** 403/762-6767, is one of many companies offering shuttles between the airport and Banff National Park. Their service leaves the airport three times daily, stopping at Banff and Lake Louise. Calgary to Banff is $36, Calgary to Lake Louise is $41. This shuttle stops at all major Banff hotels as well as the park's main bus terminal, the **Brewster Tour and Transportation Centre,** at 100 Gopher St., Banff. The depot has a ticket office, lockers, a cafe, and gift shop. It's open daily 7:30 A.M.–10:45 P.M. Other airporter buses are **Banff Airporter,** 403/762-3330 or 888/449-2901; **Laidlaw,** 403/762-9102 or 800/661-4946; and **Skyshuttle,** 403/762-1010 or 888/220-7433. All charge $36 one way to Banff and $40–45 to Lake Louise, with the latter two offering door-to-door service. The earliest service back to the airport departs Lake Louise at 5 A.M. and Banff at 6:30 A.M.

Brewster is the only company with a bus service between Banff and Jasper. From Jasper, Brewster offers an express service to Banff, for $51, departing the railway station on Connaught Drive mid-April to mid-October daily at 1:30 P.M. A longer alternative is the nine-hour Jasper-to-Banff tour, which stops at the Columbia Icefield and Lake Louise; $89 one-way, $124 round-trip. In spring and fall the fare is $67 one-way, $89 round-trip. No bus service runs between Banff and Jasper in winter.

Greyhound, 403/762-1092 or 800/661-8747, offers scheduled service from the Calgary bus depot at 877 Greyhound Way SW, five times daily to a terminal in the Banff railway station on Railway Avenue and Samson Mall, Lake Louise. Greyhound buses also leave Vancouver from the depot at 1150 Station St., three times daily for the scenic 14-hour ride to the park.

Getting Around Banff

Most of the sights and many trailheads are within walking distance of town. **Banff Transit,** 403/760-8294, operates bus service along two routes through the Town of Banff: one from the Banff Springs Hotel to the RV and trailer parking area at the north end of Banff Avenue; the other from the Banff Springs Hotel to the Tunnel Mountain Campgrounds. Mid-May to September, buses run twice an hour between 7 A.M. and midnight. From October to December, the two routes are merged as one, with buses running hourly midday to midnight. No local buses run the rest of the year. Travel costs $1 per sector.

Cabs around Banff and Lake Louise are reasonably priced–flag drop is $2.75, then it's $1.50 per km. From the Banff bus depot to the hostel will run around $6, same to the Banff Springs Hotel, more after midnight. Companies are **Banff Taxi,** 403/762-4444; **Taxi Taxi,** 403/762-3111; and **Mountain Taxi,** 403/762-3351.

The days when a row of horse-drawn buggies eagerly awaited the arrival of wealthy visitors at the C.P.R. Station have long since passed. But the **Trail Rider Store,** 132 Banff Avenue, 403/762-4551, offers visitors rides around town in a beautifully restored carriage ($9 per person for 15 minutes). Expect to pay around $38 per carriage between downtown and the Banff Springs Hotel.

As you'd expect, rental cars in the park aren't cheap. The other catch is that none offer unlimited mileage. The most you'll get is a free 150 km, and then expect to pay $.20–.25 cents per km. **Banff Rent-a-car,** 230 Lynx St., 403/762-3352, rents used cars for $50 per day with 150 free km. Other agencies are **Avis,** 403/762-3222 or 800/879-2847; **Budget,** 403/762-4565 or 800/268-8900; **Hertz,** 403/762-2027 or 800/263-

THE BREWSTER BOYS

Few guides in Banff were as well known as Jim and Bill (pictured) Brewster. In 1892, at ages 10 and 12, respectively, they were hired by the Banff Springs Hotel to take guests to local landmarks. As their reputation as guides grew, they built a thriving business. By 1900, they had their own livery and outfitting company, and soon thereafter they expanded operations to Lake Louise. Their other early business interests included a trading post, the original Mt. Royal Hotel, the first ski lodge in the Sunshine Meadows, and the hotel at the Columbia Icefield.

Today, a legacy of the boys' savvy, **Brewster,** a transportation and tour company, has grown to become an integral part of many tourists' stays. The company operates some of the world's most advanced sightseeing vehicles, including a fleet of Snocoaches on Athabasca Glacier.

WHYTE MUSEUM OF THE CANADIAN ROCKIES

0600; and **National,** 403/762-2688 or 800/227-7368. Reservations for cars in Banff should be made well in advance.

Getting Around Lake Louise

The campground, hostel, and hotels are all within easy walking distance of Samson Mall. Chateau Lake Louise is a 2.7-km walk from the valley floor. The only car rental agency in the village is **National,** 403/522-3870 or 800)/387-4747. The agency doesn't have many cars; you'd be better off picking one up in Banff or at Calgary International Airport. **Lake Louise Taxi & Tours,** in Samson Mall, 403/522-2020, charges $2.30 for flag drop, then $1.25 per km. From the mall to Chateau Lake Louise runs around $9, to Moraine Lake $16, and to Banff $85. **Wilson Mountain Sports,** in Samson Mall, 403/522-3636, has mountain bikes for rent from $8 per hour or $34 per day (includes a helmet, bike lock, and water bottle). Inquire here about canoe rentals for float trips along the Bow River to Banff.

Persons with Disabilities

The Banff and Lake Louise Visitor Centres are wheelchair accessible—washrooms, information desks, and theater are all barrier free. Once inside, use the handy Touchsource monitors for a full listing of all barrier-free services within the park. An all-terrain wheelchair is available at the Cave and Basin National Historic Site for use on park trails. To reserve, call 403/762-1566.

Tours

Brewster, 403/762-6767, is the dominant tour company in the area. Their three-hour Discover Banff bus tour takes in downtown Banff, Tunnel Mountain Drive, the hoodoos, the Cave and Basin, and Sulphur Mountain Gondola (gondola fare not included). This tour runs in summer only and departs from the bus depot daily at 8:30 A.M.; call for hotel pick-up times. Adult fare is $44, children half price.

Brewster also runs a number of other tours. A four-hour tour to Lake Louise departs select Banff hotels daily 1:15–1:40 P.M.; $40 one-way, $49 round-trip. In winter this tour departs in the morning, runs five hours, and includes Banff sights; $38 one-way, $44 round-trip.

During summer, the company offers tours from Banff to Upper Hot Springs ($20; includes

pool admission), Sulphur Mountain Gondola ($25; includes gondola ride), Lake Minnewanka ($41; includes two-hour boat cruise), and Columbia Icefield ($89; Snocoach extra).

Brewster also operates nine-hour tours from Calgary to Banff ($88) and Lake Louise ($92).

SERVICES

Banff

The **post office** is on the corner of Buffalo and Bear Streets opposite Central Park; open Monday –Friday 9 A.M.–5:30 P.M. The general-delivery service here is probably among the busiest in the country, with the thousands of seasonal workers in the area, no home mail-delivery service, and a two-year wait for a post box. Address all mail to General Delivery, Banff, AB T0L 0C0. A window is set aside for general delivery pick-ups, speeding things up considerably. For all other postal services try the small and friendly full-service postal outlet in **Cascade Plaza Drug,** in the far corner of the lower level of Cascade Plaza at 317 Banff Avenue. **Mail Boxes Etc.,** 226 Bear St., is a privately run postal outlet and can send and receive facsimiles. Public Internet access is free at the library, but advance bookings are needed. For instant access, head to **Cyber-web,** downstairs in the Sundance Mall at 215 Banff Avenue, 403/762-9226.

Major banks can be found along Banff Avenue and are generally open 9 A.M.–4 P.M. The **Bank of Montreal,** 107 Banff Ave., allows cash advances with MasterCard, while the **C.I.B.C.,** 98 Banff Ave., accepts Visa.

Freya's Currency Exchange is in the Clock Tower Mall at 108 Banff Avenue and also has offices in the Cascade Plaza and Banff Springs Hotel.

Downtown Laundromats are **Johnny O's,** at 223 Bear St., open Monday –Saturday 8 A.M.–11 P.M., Sunday 10 A.M.–10 P.M., and **Cascade Coin Laundry,** on the lower level of the Cascade Plaza, open daily 7:30 A.M.–10 P.M. **Chalet Coin Laundry** is on Tunnel Mountain Road at the Douglas Fir Resort, within walking distance of all Tunnel Mountain accommodations; open daily 8 A.M.–10 P.M.

Along Banff Avenue you'll find a handful of one-hour film labs; check around for the cheapest, as many have special offers. The most competitive and reliable is **Miles High Image Center** at 119 Banff Avenue (beneath the Barbary Coast), 403/762-5221. Drop slide film here on Wednesday and it will be ready for pick-up Friday morning. Get photographic supplies from **Wolf Street Cameras** at 203 Bear St., 403/762-9300.

Mineral Springs Hospital is at 301 Lynx Street, 403/762-2222. **Cascade Plaza Drug** on the lower level of the Cascade Plaza at 317 Banff Avenue is open till 9 P.M., as is **Harmony Drug** at 111 Banff Avenue. (Harmony Drug was once owned by noted Banff photographer Byron Harmon, whose prints, dating from around 1915, adorn the walls and adjacent mall.) **Gourlay's Pharmacy** at 229 Bear Street is open till 8 P.M. For the **RCMP,** call 403/762-2226.

Lake Louise

A small postal outlet in Samson Mall also serves as a bus depot and car rental agency. Although Lake Louise has no banks, there's a currency exchange in the Chateau Lake Louise and a cash machine in the grocery store. The mall also holds a busy Laundromat open in summer, daily 8 A.M.–8 P.M., shorter hours the rest of the year. Camping supplies are available from **Wilson Mountain Sports.** For photographic supplies, try **Pipestone Photo,** 403/522-3617, which offers one-hour photo-developing service and is the only place in the park offering overnight slide developing. The closest **hospital** is in Banff, 403/762-2222. For the **RCMP,** call 403/522-3811.

BOOKS AND BOOKSTORES

Banff Public Library

Banff's library is opposite Central Park at 101 Bear Street, 403/762-2661. The extensive collection of nonfiction books, many about the park and its environs, makes it an excellent rainy-day hangout. It also has a large collection of magazines and newspapers. Internet access is free, but book ahead. Hours are Monday –Thursday 10 A.M.–8 P.M., Friday 10 A.M.–6 P.M., Saturday 11 A.M.–6 P.M., and Sunday 1–5 P.M.

Bookstores

The Canadian Rockies are one of the most written about, and definitely the most photographed, regions in Canada. As a walk along Banff Avenue will confirm, there is definitely no lack of postcards, calendars, and books about the area. For general reading, the guides and coffee-table books produced by **Altitude Publishing** in Canmore are the best. Look for them in all Banff bookstores. Ben Gadd's *Handbook of the Canadian Rockies* is the best all-around source of information for those interested in the geology, climate, ecology, flora, and fauna of the Canadian Rockies.

Banff Book & Art Den, at 94 Banff Avenue, 403/762-3919, stocks a large collection of park literature, wilderness guides, coffee-table books, travel guides, and relevant topographical maps for backcountry trips within the park. Open in summer daily 10 A.M.–9 P.M., till 7 P.M. the rest of the year. Another bookstore is **Cascade Mountain Books,** downstairs in the Cascade Plaza, 403/762-8508.

In Lake Louise, **Woodruff & Blum,** in the Samson Mall, 403/522-3842, offers an excellent selection of books on the natural and human history of the park, as well as animal field guides, hiking guides, and general western Canadiana.

Look for the *Crag and Canyon* each Wednesday. It's been keeping residents and visitors informed about park issues and town gossip for over 90 years. *Wildlife* is a free monthly newspaper that offers entertaining coverage of mountain life and upcoming events.

INFORMATION

Many sources of information are available on the park and its commercial facilities. Once you've arrived, the best place to make your first stop is the **Banff Visitor Centre.** This large complex at 224 Banff Avenue houses information desks for **Parks Canada** and the **Banff/Lake Louise Tourism Bureau** as well a Friends of Banff National Park shop, which stocks a good variety of park-related literature. The center is open mid-June to August daily 8 A.M.–8 P.M., mid-May to mid-June and September daily 8 A.M.–6 P.M., the rest of the year daily 9 A.M.–5 P.M.

National Park Information

On the right hand side of the Banff Visitor Centre is a row of desks manned by Parks Canada staff. They will answer all of your queries and questions regarding Banff's natural wonders and advise you of trail closures. Anyone planning an overnight backcountry trip should register here and obtain a Wilderness Pass ($6 per person per night). Also here, you can pick up the brochure *Banff and Vicinity Drives and Walks* (a compact guide to things to see and do around Banff), view a free slide show and videos about the park. All questions pertaining to the national park itself can be answered here or write Superintendent, Banff National Park, P.O. Box 900, Banff, AB T0L 0C0; call 403/762-1550, or check out the park's www.parks canada.gc.ca/banff.

The park's **Warden's Office** is in the industrial park, 403/762-1470 or 762-4506. The **weather office,** 403/762-2088, offers updated forecasts. A full weather synopsis is available by calling 403/762-3091. Tune into 101 on the FM band to listen to Parks Radio.

Tourism Information
In the Banff Visitor Centre, across the floor from Parks Canada, is a desk for the Banff/Lake Louise Tourism Bureau. This organization rep-resents businesses and commercial establishments in the park. Here you can find out about accommodations and restaurants and have any other questions answered. To answer the most-often-asked question, the washrooms are downstairs. For general tourism information, write the Banff/Lake Louise Tourism Bureau, P.O. Box 1298, Banff, AB T0L 0C0; 403/762-8421; www.banfflakelouise.com. Another good website is www.banff.com, with good general information on the park and links to accommodations and commercial operators.

Lake Louise Visitor Centre
The Lake Louise Visitor Centre, 403/522-3833, is beside Samson Mall on Village Road. This excellent Parks Canada facility has interpretive displays, slide and video displays, and staff on hand to answer questions, recommend hikes suited to your ability, and issue Wilderness Passes to those heading out into the backcountry. Look for the stuffed (literally) female grizzly and read her fascinating, but sad, story. It's open mid-June to August daily 8 A.M.–8 P.M., mid-May to mid-June and September daily 8 A.M.–6 P.M., the rest of the year daily 9 A.M.–4 P.M.

Chinaman's Peak forms a stunning backdrop to Canmore.

CANMORE

INTRODUCTION

Canmore (pop. 11,000) lies in the wide Bow Valley, 97 km west of Calgary, 31 km southeast of Banff, and on the northern edge of Kananaskis Country. Long perceived as a gateway to the mountain national parks, the town is very much a destination in itself these days. Its ideal mountain location and the freedom it enjoys from the strict development restrictions that apply in the nearby parks have made the town one of the fastest-growing resort areas in North America. When the last of Canmore's mines closed in 1979, the population stood at 3,500; in the last 20 years that number has tripled. Half the current residents have lived in town for less than five years. There seems no end to the boom, and the population is estimated to reach 20,000 sometime in the next 20 years.

The surrounding mountains provide Canmore's best recreation opportunities. Hiking is excellent on trails that lace the valley and mountainside slopes, with many high viewpoints easily reached. Nearby, Mt. Yamnuska has become the most developed rock-climbing site in the Canadian Rockies. Canmore also hosted the nordic events of the 1988 Winter Olympic Games and is the home of the Alpine Club of Canada.

THE LAND

Canmore lies in the Bow Valley, flanked by mountains rising up to 1,000 meters above the valley floor. To the south and west are the distinctive peaks of the Three Sisters, Mt. Lawrence Grassi, impressive Chinaman's Peak, and the southeastern extent of Mt. Rundle. Across the valley are the Fairholme Range, Mt. Lady Macdonald, and Grotto Mountain. Like the rest of the Canadian Rockies these mountains began as layers of sedimentary rock laid down on the bed of an ancient sea. The seabed was forced upward over millions of years to create today's lofty peaks, whose sedimentary layers give them a distinct appearance. Through the valley flows the braided Bow River, heading eastward and into the Saskatchewan River system. At the north end of town, the river divides in two, leaving downtown Canmore on a low-lying island that is protected from annual spring flooding by dikes of large boulders.

Flora and Fauna

Even though much of the valley floor is developed, large tracts of land are protected by **Bow Valley Wildland Park** and **Bow Flats Natural Area**, making the surrounding area a delight for nature lovers. Lowlands on either side of the Bow River are lined with stands of poplar, while the drier mountainsides support extensive stands of **Douglas fir, Engelmann spruce,** and **lodgepole pine.**

The forested valley floor provides habitat for many larger mammals, including elk, white-tailed deer, coyotes, black bears, and grizzly bears. Bighorn sheep are often sighted perched on rocky outcrops above Spray Lakes Road. Cougars inhabit the surrounding wilderness, but are rarely sighted. Smaller mammals present in Bow River and its adjacent sloughs include large populations of beaver, muskrat, and mink. Red and Columbian ground squirrels and least chipmunks inhabit the forests around town, while at higher elevations golden-mantled ground squirrels and pikas find a home. Wild rabbits thrive around the residential streets east of Centennial Park.

Bird life around Canmore is prolific. Mallard ducks are a popular attraction on Policeman's Creek in downtown Canmore. A number of active osprey nests can be seen along the banks of the Bow River; other permanent residents include great horned owls, jays, and ravens.

HISTORY

The Hudson's Bay Company explored the Bow Valley corridor and attempted, without success, to establish a fur trade with Stoney natives for most of the 1840s. In 1858, an expedition from the east, led by Capt. John Palliser, sent back discouraging reports about the climate and prospects of agriculture in the valley. A few decades later the Canadian Pacific Railway chose the Bow Valley Corridor as the route through the mountains, and the first divisional point west of Calgary was established at what is now Canmore in 1883.

The C.P.R. was delighted to discover that the valley was rich with coal, which it could use in the steam engines. Mining on the Three Sisters and Mt. Rundle commenced in 1886, attracting hundreds of miners and their families. Within a few years four mines operated around Canmore. Hotels and businesses were established, and a hospital, NWMP post, and opera house were built. The Canmore Opera House—reputed to be the only log movie house in the world—still stands and has been relocated to Calgary's Heritage Park. Georgetown, below the nordic center, and Anthracite, 16 km toward Banff, were both bustling little coal-mining towns that have long since disappeared. In 1899 the C.P.R. moved its divisional point to Laggan (now Lake Louise), but the mines continued to operate, with the most productive mine located on Canmore Creek. Many British and European miners were attracted to the area, and the population continued to increase. A small contingent of Chinese miners also lived in Canmore. They didn't stay long, but their memory lives on in the name Chinaman's Peak. A Chinese cook was bet $50 that he couldn't climb the peak and return to Canmore in less than six hours. He did, and it's been known as Chinaman's Peak ever since.

Recent Times

Just over 100 years after mining commenced and less than 20 years after the last mine closed (in 1979), Canmore experienced its second boom—tourism—which today shows no sign of slowing. Resort and residential projects costing over $2 billion have been planned for the next two decades, and the town's population is estimated to reach 20,000 by the end of that period. The largest and most controversial development, still in its infancy, is the Three Sisters Resort. When completed, the 840-hectare project will include 4,000 residential units, two hotels, and three golf courses—all in an environmentally sensitive area along the Bow River, between Pigeon Mountain and Chinaman's Peak.

Canmore is a popular spot for moviemakers; recent big-budget movies filmed in and around town have included *Shanghai Noon,* *Grizzly Falls, Mystery Alaska, The Edge, Wild America, The Last of the Dogmen,* and *Legends of the Fall.*

SIGHTS AND RECREATION

SIGHTS •

Downtown

Through booming times, downtown Canmore, on the southwestern side of the TransCanada Highway, has managed to retain much of its original charm. Many historical buildings line the downtown streets while other buildings from the coal-mining days are being preserved at their original locations around town. The best way to get downtown from the TransCanada Highway is to take Railway Avenue from Highway 1A and drive down Eighth Street, the main drag (parking is easiest one street back along 7th Street, where one parking lot is designated for RVs). The first building of interest at the east end of Eighth Street is Canmore's original **North West Mounted Police post,** built in 1892. It is one of the few such posts still in its original position, even though at the time of its construction, the building was designed as a temporary structure to serve the newly born coal-mining town. The interior is decorated with period furnishings while out back is a pleasant picnic area. It's open in summer, Monday–Friday 9 A.M.–5 P.M., Saturday–Sunday noon–4 P.M. and admission is free. The post sits beside Policeman's Creek, a shallow body of water alive with ducks. **Ralph Connor United Church,** a little farther down Eighth Strret, was built in 1890 and is now a Provincial Historic Site. The church is named for its first reverend, Charles Gordon, who used the pen-name Ralph Connor for the 35 books he authored. **Canmore Hotel** on the corner of Eighth Street and Seventh Avenue was built in 1891 (at a time when three hotels already operated) and is still open for thirsty townsfolk and travelers alike. **Canmore Centennial Museum,** 801 Seventh Ave., 403/678-2462, houses a collection of artifacts from the area's early coal-mining days and a display from the 1988 Winter Olympic Games. It's open in summer, Monday—Friday 9 A.M.–5 P.M., SAT-URDAY–SUNDAY NOON–4 p.m.; the rest of the year daily noon–4 P.M. Admission is free.

Sights West of Downtown

A number of historic sites lie across the Bow River from downtown. Reach them on foot by following the river north from Eighth Avenue and crossing at the old C.P.R. trestle bridge, which once served the Cochrane Mine. Follow the paved trail downstream, past the **Mine Shareholders' Cabin,** a log structure built in 1914. In the same vicinity, a trail leads off from Three Sisters Drive up Canmore Creek, passing the remains of a mine site that was worked from 1891 to 1979. Continue up to small waterfalls and across Spray Lakes Road to **Quarry Lake.** This small lake lies in an open meadow and is a popular sunbathing and swimming spot.

HIKING

The hiking trails around Canmore are usually passed by in favor of those of its famous neighbors. But some interesting trails do exist. Paved paths around town are suitable for walking, bicycling, and, in winter, skiing. They link Policeman's Creek with the golf course, nordic center, and Riverview Park on the Bow River.

Grassi Lakes
- Length: 2 km (40 minutes) one-way
- Elevation gain: 300 meters
- Rating: easy/moderate

This historical trail climbs to two small lakes below Chinaman's Peak. To get to the trailhead follow Spray Lakes Road past the nordic center and take the first gravel road to the left after the reservoir. This leads to a parking lot and trailhead. The trail forks to the left by a gate and climbs to Grassi Falls. Stairs cut into a cliff face lead up to a bridge over Canmore Creek and to the lakes. A further scramble up a scree slope leads to four pictographs (native rock

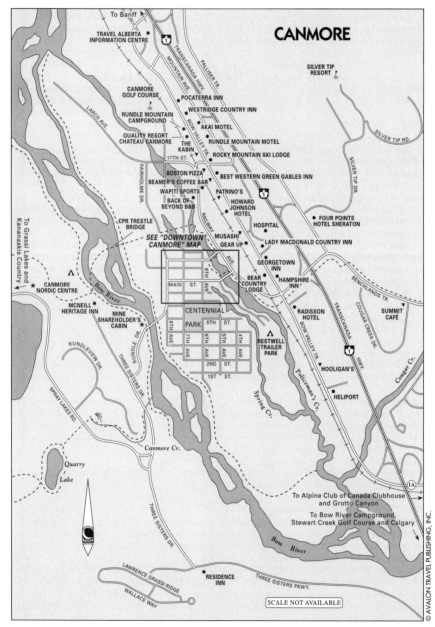

CANMORE

To Banff

TRAVEL ALBERTA
INFORMATION CENTRE

SILVER TIP
RESORT

CANMORE
GOLF COURSE

POCATERRA INN

WESTRIDGE COUNTRY INN

RUNDLE MOUNTAIN
CAMPGROUND

AKAI MOTEL

QUALITY RESORT
CHATEAU CANMORE

RUNDLE MOUNTAIN MOTEL

THE
KABIN

ROCKY MOUNTAIN SKI LODGE

BOSTON PIZZA

BEAMER'S COFFEE BAR

BEST WESTERN GREEN GABLES INN

WAPITI SPORTS

PATRINO'S

BACK OF
BEYOND B&B

HOWARD
JOHNSON
HOTEL

CPR TRESTLE
BRIDGE

FOUR POINTS
HOTEL SHERATON

HOSPITAL

MUSASHI

SEE "DOWNTOWN"
CANMORE" MAP

GEAR UP

LADY MACDONALD COUNTRY INN

CANMORE
NORDIC CENTRE

GEORGETOWN
INN

HAMPSHIRE
INN

SUMMIT
CAFÉ

BEAR
COUNTRY
LODGE

MCNEILL
HERITAGE INN

MINE
SHAREHOLDER'S
CABIN

RADISSON
HOTEL

CENTENNIAL

PARK

5TH ST.

7TH
AVE.

6TH
AVE.

5TH
AVE.

4TH
AVE.

RESTWELL
TRAILER
PARK

2ND ST.

HOOLIGAN'S

1ST ST.

HELIPORT

Quarry
Lake

Canmore Cr.

To Alpine Club of Canada Clubhouse
and Grotto Canyon

To Bow River Campground,
Stewart Creek Golf Course and Calgary

RESIDENCE
INN

THREE SISTERS PKWY.

WALLACE WAY

Bow River

SCALE NOT AVAILABLE

LARCH AVE.

MOUNTAIN AVE.

PALLISER TR.

TRANSCANADA HWY.

BOW VALLEY TR.

17TH ST.

FAIRHOLME DR.

RAILWAY AVE.

SILVER TIP RD.

SILVER TIP DR.

6TH AVE.

MAIN ST.

8TH AVE.

RUNDLEVIEW DR.

THREE SISTERS DR.

SPRAY LAKES RD.

Spring Cr.

Bow Valley Tr.

Policeman's Cr.

BENCHLANDS TR.

COUGAR CREEK DR.

TRANSCANADA HWY.

Cougar Cr.

To Grassi Lakes and
Kananaskis Country

To Banff

Bow River

LAWRENCE GRASSI RIDGE

1A

© AVALON TRAVEL PUBLISHING, INC.

paintings) of human figures. They are on the first large boulder in the gorge. Interpretive signs along the trail point out interesting aspects of the Bow Valley and detail the life of Lawrence Grassi, who built the trail back in the early 1920s.

Chinaman's Peak

- Length: 2.2 km (90 minutes) one-way
- Elevation gain: 740 meters
- Rating: moderate/difficult

Chinaman's Peak is the impressive pinnacle of rock that rises high above Canmore to the southwest. While the sheer eastern face is visible from town, this trail winds up the back side of the mountain and ends with stunning views across the Bow Valley. The unmarked trailhead is along Spray Lakes Road. Leave your vehicle at the Goat Creek Trailhead, cross the road, then walk up to and over the canal to search out the trail, which begins from behind a small workshed. The trail climbs steadily through subalpine forest of Engelmann spruce before breaking out above the tree line,

where views north extend down the glacially carved Goat Creek Valley. The trail then forks; the left fork climbs unforgivingly to Chinaman's Peak, but hikers are rewarded with views no less spectacular by continuing to the right along a lightly marked trail that ends at a saddle. On a clear day, the panorama afforded from this viewpoint is worth every painful step. Take care on the return journey; stay high and to the right and watch for rock cairns and colored flagging to ensure you enter the trees at the right spot.

Cougar Creek

- Length: 9.5 km (four hours) one-way
- Elevation gain: 550 meters
- Rating: moderate

This unofficial trail follows a valley carved deeply into the Fairholme Range by Cougar Creek. To get to the trailhead from downtown, take Bow Valley Trail over the TransCanada Highway and follow Benchlands Trail to the parking lot beside Cougar Creek. The trail follows the northwestern

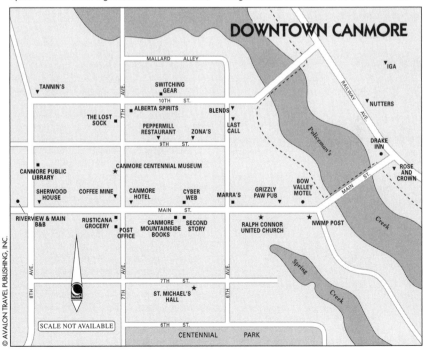

DOWNTOWN CANMORE

bank of the creek past a housing estate and into a lightly forested area. Cross the creek just before the mouth of the canyon. The rough trail crosses the creek 10 times in the first three km to a major fork. Stay left, continuing up the stony creekbed, which winds around the base of Mt. Charles Stewart. From this point, the valley walls close in and it's a steep climb up to a high ridge, which forms the boundary of Banff National Park. On the return journey, continue beyond the parking lot to the Summit Café, where you can relax on the patio with a cool drink.

Mt. Lady Macdonald

• Length: 3.5 km (90 minutes) one-way
• Elevation gain: 850 meters
• Rating: moderate/difficult

Named for the wife of Canada's first prime minister, this peak lies immediately north of Canmore. The trailhead is the same as for the Cougar Creek Trail, detailed above. Follow Cougar Creek to where the canyon begins and

Grassi Lakes is a delightful destination, easily reached from Spray Lakes Road.

look for a faint trail winding up a grassy bank to the left. Once on the trail, take the steepest option at every fork, then a sharp right 400 meters after the trail bursts out into a cleared area. This section is steep, climbing through a rock band to the mountain's southern ridge, which you'll follow the rest of the way. The distance and elevation given above are to a disused helipad below the main summit. It's a steep, unrelenting slog, but views across the Bow Valley are stunning. From the teahouse, the true summit is another 275 vertical meters away, along an extremely narrow ridge that drops away precipitously to the east.

Grotto Canyon

• Length: 2 km (40 minutes) one-way
• Elevation gain: 60 meters
• Rating: easy

This is one of the most interesting trails around Canmore. It begins from Grotto Pond, along Highway 1A east of town, first following a powerline road that winds behind the Baymag plant. Then at a signed intersection it takes off through the woods to the mouth of the canyon. No official trail traverses the canyon; hikers simply follow the creekbed through the towering canyon walls. Around 400 meters into the canyon, look for pictographs to the left. At the two-km mark, the canyon makes a sharp left turn at Illusion Rock, where water cascades through a narrow chasm and into the main canyon. Many hikers return from this point, but through the next section of canyon, the valley opens up, passing hoodoos and a cave. It's 6.5 km from the trailhead to the end of the valley, with most of the 680 meters of elevation gained in the last two km.

Heart Creek

• Length: 2 km (40 minutes) one-way
• Elevation gain: 80 meters
• Rating: easy

This well-formed trail is signposted from the Lac des Arcs interchange, 15 km east of Canmore along the TransCanada Highway. The trail parallels the highway eastward until reaching a fork. The trail to the right follows Heart Creek for just over one km, crossing the creek seven times on narrow log bridges. It ends at a cleared area below a spot where Heart Creek is forced through a narrow cleft. Those tempted to continue further can cross the creek, scramble up a steep, forest-

The Three Sisters rise high above town.

ed ridge, then descend the other side to link up with the creek upstream of the gorge. Cross the creek again for views of another narrow chasm.

Heli-hiking

Heli-hiking is the summer alternative to heli-skiing—a helicopter does the hard work, and you get to hike in a remote, alpine region that would usually entail a long, steep hike to access. **Alpine Helicopters,** 403/678-4802, offers a variety of options starting at $225 per person, which includes 15 minutes of flight time and two to three hours hiking. The company is flexible, with ground-time and destinations chosen by the clients. Flight-seeing (no landing) costs $120 for 25 minutes airtime. The heliport is along Highway 1A south of downtown. (Try and book ahead for these trips—they're very popular with travelers staying in Banff, where there is no flight-seeing).

OTHER RECREATION

Canmore Nordic Centre

This remarkable complex was built at a cost of $15 million for the 1988 Winter Olympic Games. The cross-country skiing and biathlon (combined cross-country skiing and rifle shooting) events were held here, and today the center remains a world-class training ground for Canadian athletes. The operation was privatized in 1997 and pronounced a provincial park in 2000. Even in

summer, long after the snow has melted, the place is worth a visit. An interpretive trail leads down to the banks of the Bow River where Georgetown, an old coal-mining town, once stood. Many other trails lead around the grounds and it's possible to hike or bike to the Banff Springs Hotel. Mountain biking is extremely popular on 70 km of trails. Events are held throughout summer and bike rentals are available at **Trail Sports,** 403/678-6764, at the center; $8 per hour and $30 per day for a front suspension bike. The day lodge has lockers, a lounge area, cafeteria, and an information rack with maps and brochures. It's open daily 8 A.M.–4:30 P.M. For more information, call 403/678-2400.

Fishing

The Bow River has good fishing for rainbow and brook trout. Also try Gap Lake for brown and brook trout; Grotto Pond for rainbow trout; and Ghost Lake for lake, rainbow, and brown trout. **Wapiti Sports,** 1506 Railway Ave., 403/678-5550, stocks bait and tackle and sells fishing licenses.

Climbing

Hundreds of climbing routes have been laid out around Canmore. **Mt. Yamnuska,** which rises 900 meters above the valley floor east of town along Highway 1A, is the most developed site. Climbers also flock to Chinaman's Peak, Cougar Creek, and Grotto Canyon. Canmore is home to

THE ALPINE CLUB OF CANADA

The Alpine Club of Canada (ACC), like similar clubs in the United States and Great Britain, is a nonprofit mountaineering organization whose objectives include the encouragement of mountaineering through educational programs, the exploration and study of alpine and glacial regions, and the preservation of mountain flora and fauna.

The club was formed in 1906, mainly through the tireless campaign of its first president, Arthur Wheeler. A list of early members reads like a Who's Who of the Canadian Rockies—Bill Peyto, Tom Wilson, Byron Harmon, Mary Schäffer—names familiar to all Canadian mountaineers. Today the club membership includes 3,000 alpinists from throughout Canada.

The original clubhouse was near the Banff Springs Hotel, but in 1980 a new clubhouse was built in Canmore to serve as the association's headquarters. The club's ongoing projects include operating the Lake Louise Hostel, maintaining a system of 18 huts throughout the backcountry, and publishing the annual *Canadian Alpine Journal*—the country's only record of mountaineering accomplishments. A reference library of the club's history is kept at the Whyte Museum of the Canadian Rockies in Banff.

For further information and membership details, contact the Alpine Club of Canada, P.O. Box 8040, Canmore, AB T1W 2T8; 403/678-3200; www.alpineclubofcanada.ca.

WHYTE MUSEUM OF THE CANADIAN ROCKIES

many qualified mountain guides. **Yamnuska,** 403/678-4164, www.yamnuska.com, offers basic rock-climbing courses, as well as instruction for all ability levels on ice climbing, mountaineering, and trekking. A good introduction to rock climbing is the weekend-long Basic Rock course, which costs $185. Unique to the company are three-month-long courses that take in all aspects of mountain-oriented skills. Other local guiding companies are **Kiska Adventures,** 403/678-5657 and **M & W Guides,** 403/678-2642.

Golfing

Canmore has three golf courses, including two that have opened in the last few years. As with golfing elsewhere in the Canadian Rockies, book all tee times well in advance. **Canmore Golf Course,** built in 1929 as a nine-hole course, has developed into an 18-hole course with a modern clubhouse and a practice facility that includes a driving range and chipping greens. It is an interesting layout, with one hole running along the Bow River and water on many holes. Greens fees are $45, a cart is $28; for tee times, call 403/678-4784. **Silvertip Resort,** 403/678-1600 or 877/877-5444, opened in the summer of 1998 on a wide bench between the valley floor and the lower slopes of Mt. Lady Macdonald. It was quickly recognized as one of Canada's finest resort courses, but more tellingly, it boasts a Slope Rating of 153, the highest of any course in North America. Needless to say, the layout is very challenging, with the most distinct feature being elevation changes of up to 40 meters on any one hole, and a total 200-meter elevation difference between the lowest and highest points on the course. Adding to this challenge are narrow, sloping, tree-lined fairways, numerous water hazards, 74 bunkers, and a course length of a frightening 7,300 yards from the back markers. Greens fees are $125, which includes a mandatory cart (each cart has GPS to help golfers judge distances). Four hours before sunset greens fees drop to $85. **Stewart Creek Golf Club,** 403/609-6360, 877/993-4653, another new layout, lies across the valley in the Three Sisters development. It is shorter than Silvertip, but still measures over 7,000 yards from the back tees. The fairways are relatively wide, but positioning of tee shots is important, and the course is made more interesting by hanging greens, greenside exposed rock, and historic mine shafts. Greens fees are $105, with power carts an additional $30; twilight rates are just $55. These rates include use of a practice facility. Two more 18-hole courses are planned for the Three Sisters development.

ARTS AND ENTERTAINMENT

Drinking and Dancing

Canmore doesn't have anywhere near the number of bars that nearby Banff is so famous for, but no one ever seems to go thirsty. The **Sherwood House,** 838 Eighth St., 403/678-5211, has a beer garden that catches the afternoon sun and is especially busy on weekends. At the other end of the main street is the **Drake Inn,** 909 Railway Ave., 403/678-5131, with a small outdoor patio and a non-smoking section with comfortable lounges. Across the road, at the **Rose and Crown,** 749 Railway Ave., 403/678-5168, you'll find a beer garden. All these bars have midweek drink specials and a couple of pool tables. The **Grizzly Paw Pub,** 622 Eighth St., 403/678-9983, brews its own beer, with six ales produced in-house (look for special winter brews around Christmas). Most are heavy, English-style beers, but the lighter Grumpy Bear Honey Wheat Ale suits most tastes. Wondering where the cheapest beer in town is? Head to the **Last Call,** 637 10th St., 403/678-3934, where you'll find $1.75 bottled beer on Thursday nights. The rest of the week, it's happy hour 4–8 P.M., daily drink specials, and a bunch of pool-playing locals. See you there.

Canmore's only nightclub is **Hooligan's,** along the Bow Valley Trail, and there's live music somewhere in town every weekend. The Drake Inn has a band playing Thursday–Saturday nights, as does the Rose and Crown, and the Sherwood House has a Sunday afternoon jam session.

Check out the large wine selection at **Alberta Spirits,** 737 10th St., 403/678-2451.

Festivals and Events

Canmore's small town pride lives on through a busy schedule of festivals and events, which are nearly always accompanied by parades of flag-waving kids, free downtown pancake breakfasts, and an evening shindig somewhere in town.

Canmore's annual **Winter Carnival** is a two-week celebration including an ice-sculpture demonstration, ice-fishing derby, and pancake breakfasts. The highlight is the **International Dogsled Race** held at Canmore Nordic Centre, where up to 100 teams of four, six, eight, and 10 dogs are harnessed up and compete in various heats. (Organizers are always looking for volunteers; ask around if you'd like to help). The festival takes place the last two weeks of January.

Voices on the Wilderness, held every Saturday night through summer, is a nature-oriented program of talks, audio-visuals, and slide presentations hosted by knowledgeable locals; call 403/678-2622 for venues and times. **Canada Day** is celebrated with a pancake breakfast, parade, various activities in Centennial Park, and 11 P.M. fireworks. Canmore Nordic Centre hosts one leg of mountain biking's **World Cup** each year on the first weekend of July. The following weekend the nordic center plays host to a stop on the **Cactus Cup** tour, which comprises a variety of stages held over the weekend. Another biking event on the local calendar is a 24-hour endurance race in late July. For a full listing of mountain bike races, contact the nordic center at 403/678-2400. On the Heritage Day long weekend, the first weekend of August, Canmore hosts a **Folk Music Festival,** 403/678-2524, which starts on Sunday and runs through Monday evening. This event, which attracts over 10,000 fans, features national and international acts performing in Centennial Park, musical workshops, and a free pancake breakfast beside the post office on Heritage Day.

The first Sunday of September is the **Canmore Highland Games,** 403/678-9454, a day of dancing, eating, caber tossing, and tug-of-war, culminating in a spectacular and noisy parade of pipe bands through the grounds of Centennial Park that attracts upwards of 10,000 spectators. After the fireworks, a *ceilidh,* a traditional Scottish celebration involving drinking and dancing takes place in a beer garden set up in the park for the occasion.

ACCOMMODATIONS AND CAMPING

Canmore's population boom has been mirrored by the construction of new hotels and motels. Most of the new lodgings are on Bow Valley Trail (Hwy. 1A), the traditional "strip." As with all resort towns in the Canadian Rockies, reservations should be made as far in advance as possible in summer. Outside this busy period, room rates are slashed considerably, with many ski packages (and the option of skiing at either the Banff or Kananaskis ski areas) offered.

HOTELS, MOTELS, AND LODGES

Under $50
The **Alpine Club of Canada Clubhouse** is an excellent hostel-style accommodation at the base of Grotto Mountain. The clubhouse overlooks the Bow Valley and can sleep 30 in the dormitories. It has a kitchen, an excellent library, a laundry, bar, sauna, and a lounge area with a fireplace. Rates are $15 per night for Alpine Club members, $20 otherwise. Club membership is inexpensive and includes a discount at the Lake Louise Hostel. For reservations and more information, call 403/678-3200, www.alpineclubof canada.ca. To get there from the east, take the first Canmore exit and follow Highway 1A toward Exshaw (to the northeast). The clubhouse is signposted to the left after 400 meters.

$50–100
Akai Motel, 1717 Mountain Ave., 403/678-4664, is a little run-down, but each room is air-conditioned and has a small kitchenette; $75 s, $85 d. This is Canmore's least expensive motel.

In the heart of downtown is **Bow Valley Motel,** 610 Eighth St., 403/678-5085 or 800/665-8189, www.bowvalleymotel.com, offering 25 rooms right on the main shopping strip. The rooms are nothing special, but the price is right, $90 s, $95 d, kitchenettes an extra $10. **Rundle Mountain Motel,** 1723 Mountain Ave. (facing the Trans-Canada Hwy., but can be accessed from the Bow Valley Trail), 403/678-5322 or 800/661-1610, www.rundlemontain.com, has small but comfortable rooms, a small indoor pool, an outdoor whirlpool, and a small Swiss restaurant open for a breakfast buffet each morning. Rates range $95–135 s or d.

The **Drake Inn,** 909 Railway Ave., 403/678-5131 or 800/461-8730, www.drakeinn.com, is at the end of Canmore's main street. It has an outdoor hot tub, some rooms with a private balcony overlooking Policeman's Creek, and an adjoining bar is open daily for the best-value breakfast in town. Rates are $88 s, $98 d.

$100–150
Rocky Mountain Ski Lodge, Bow Valley Trail, 403/678-5445 or 800/665-6111, www.rockymtn skilodge.com, is a sprawling complex of 22 large but standard motel rooms and over 50 self-contained one- and two-bedroom, some with loft bedrooms. Also on the property is a playground, barbecue and picnic area, and a Laundromat. The motel rooms are $95 s, $110 d, while the suites cost from $160.

The newest hotel along the "Strip" is the **Hampshire Inn,** 815 Bow Valley Trail, 403/609-0075 or 877/609-6266, a small lodging with 29 comfortable rooms, some with private balconies; $119 s, $129 d.

Diagonally opposite the Hampshire Inn is **Bear Country Lodge,** 1002 Bow Valley Trail, 403/678-1000 or 888/678-1008, another of Canmore's many new hotels. It features 30 medium-sized rooms, each comfortable and with mountain views. Summer rates are $119 s, $129 d, which includes breakfast.

Named for one of the valley's original coal-mining communities, the **Georgetown Inn,** 1101 Bow Valley Trail, 403/678-3439 or 800/657-5955, www.georgetowninn.ab.ca, is run by a friendly English couple who have set the place up as a country inn of times gone by, complete with a private guest-only lounge bar. Each of the 24

*Lady Macdonald
Country Inn*

rooms has its own individual charm and a delicious cooked breakfast is included in the rate of $129 d (from $89 in winter).

Across the street from the Georgetown Inn is **Lady Macdonald Country Inn,** 1201 Bow Valley Trail, 403/678-3665 or 800/567-3919, www.ladymacdonald.com, which exudes the same atmosphere. Its 11 rooms are all individually furnished, extending the Victorian-era charm upon which the exterior is styled. The nicest of the rooms is the Three Sisters, which has a two-way fireplace and hot tub. Rates range $130-185 s or d, which includes a hearty hot breakfast.

Westridge Country Inn, 1719 Bow Valley Trail, 403/678-5221 or 800/268-0935, www.westridgecountryinn.com., has new, comfortable rooms, each with a balcony and fireplace; rates of $145 s or d include a light breakfast.

Also at the top end of this price category is the **Howard Johnson Hotel,** 1402 Bow Valley Trail, 403/678-3625 or 800/263-3625. It is an elongated complex of 202 rooms with a small indoor pool and waterslide, and a restaurant; $145 s or d.

$150–200
Best Western Green Gables Inn, 1602 Second Ave., 403/678-5488 or 800/661-2133, www.bestwestern.com, offers a whirlpool in many of the 61 rooms, private balconies, fireplaces, and a fine-dining French restaurant. Rooms are $155 s or d, and ski packages start at $85 per person.

Further north along the Bow Valley Trail is another Best Western property, the **Pocaterra Inn,** 1725 Mountain Ave., 403/678-4334 or 888/678-6786, www.pocaterrainn.com. It features a large indoor pool, a fitness room, sauna, and 83 guestrooms, each with a fireplace. Summer rates from $160 s or d include a light breakfast.

In the same price range as the two Best Western properties is **Radisson Hotel,** 511 Bow Valley Trail, 403/678-3625 or 800/333-3333, www.radissoncanmore.com, a large complex that features an excellent restaurant (the Sunday brunch here is one of the best in the valley), an indoor pool, a fitness facility and 232 spacious rooms set around landscaped gardens. Rooms range $159–209 s or d.

Similarly priced, and of the same high standard, is **Quality Resort Chateau Canmore,** 1720 Bow Valley Trail, 403/678-6699 or 800/228-5151, www.chateaucanmore.com. Even the standard rooms at this full-service lodging have a fireplace, fridge, and microwave; $165 s or d. The one- and two-bedroom suites also have a fireplace, as well as a full kitchen and separate living area; $205 s or d. Other facilities include a large fitness facility with an indoor pool, a non-smoking bar, and a restaurant.

The **Residence Inn** is a new hotel across the river from town at 91 Three Sisters Dr., 403/678-3400, www.marriott.com. It offers 119 luxurious suites, each with a kitchen, as well as indoor and outdoor pools. A light breakfast is included in the rates of $175–245 s or d.

Over $200

At the base of Silvertip Resort, across the Trans-Canada Hwy. from all the accommodations listed above, is **Four Points Hotel Sheraton Canmore,** Silvertip Trail, 403/609-4422 or 888/609-4422, www.fourpoints.com, is Canmore's most luxurious lodging. It is a full service hotel, complete with a fitness room, Italian restaurant, gift store, and complimentary shuttle to downtown Canmore and Banff. Rates start at $240 s or d.

BED-AND-BREAKFASTS

Over 40 bed-and-breakfasts operate in Canmore. Most are small, family-run affairs, with only one or two rooms. During summer, they fill every night. For a full list of B&Bs in the area, ask at the Travel Alberta Information Centre or check the *Alberta Accommodation Guide.*

Canmore's finest bed-and-breakfast is **McNeill Heritage Inn,** across the Bow River from downtown at 500 Three Sisters Drive, 403/678-4884 or 877/626-3455, www.mcneillinn.ab.ca. Set on a secluded one-hectare property set above the river, this historic 1907, one-time mine manager's residence offers five heritage-styled guest rooms, each with a private bathroom. Guests also enjoy full bar service, a comfortable lounge, a reading room, and outdoor seating set along a riverside veranda. Rates of $150–175 (reduced outside of summer) include a sumptuous breakfast and many special touches, such as chocolates upon arrival. Another choice is **Back of Beyond B&B,** corner Birchwood Place and Railway Avenue, 403/678-6606, is really quite central, linked to downtown by a pleasant creekside trail. The two rooms share a bathroom and are $60 s, $65 d.

ACCOMMODATIONS IN THE VICINITY OF CANMORE

Harvie Heights

Lodging in Harvie Heights, eight km west of Canmore and 23 km from Banff, may seem a little more pricey than Canmore, but most units are self-contained.

The least expensive option is the **Gateway Inn,** 403/678-5396 or 877/678-1810, which com-prises 15 standard motel rooms and three self-contained cabins. The rooms are basic, but well priced from $70 s, $80 d.

Rundle Ridge Chalets, 403/678-5387 or 800/332-1299, www.chalets.ab.ca, is one of the mountains' original bungalow camps, with 38 self-contained log cabins set in a pleasant wooded area. Rates range $99–139 s or d.

Next door to Rundle Ridge, **Stockade Log Cabins,** 403/678-5212 or 800/330-3824, www.stockadecabins.com, is a smaller but similar setup. Only some of the cabins have kitchens, but guests have use of barbecues; from $108 per unit.

Newest of Harvie Heights accommodations is **Banff Boundary Lodge,** 403/678-9555 or 877/678-9555, www.banffboundarylodge.com. The 42 units each have two bedrooms, a comfortable lounge area with TV/VCR, and a full kitchen. In summer, rooms are $189 per night, but the rest of the year rates drop as low as $100 (excellent value).

Deadman's Flats

Deadman's Flats, seven km southeast of Canmore, is little more than a truck stop but has three motels and dining at a Husky gas station. Best of the bunch is the **Big Horn Motel,** 403/678-2290 or 800/892-9908, www.bighornmotel.com. It offers 24 clean and comfortable rooms, each with a balcony. Rates start at $65 s, $69 d.

The other two choices are **Pigeon Mountain Motel,** 403/678-5756, which charges $70 s, $75 d, and **Green Acres Motel,** 403/678-5344 or 800/820-5344, decorated with colorful flowers each summer, and offering spacious rooms for $75 s, $89 d.

Brewster's Kananaskis Guest Ranch

Built in 1923, this historic lodge 10 minutes east of Canmore has been owned and operated by five generations of the Brewster family, a name synonymous with tourism in Banff. The lodge is set on a picturesque lake in the Bow Valley, close to the mountain parks. A traditional Western atmosphere prevails; the emphasis is on horseback riding and the outdoors, although amenities include an indoor hot tub, cocktail lounge, pool table, dining room, and lounge. Chalets and cabins are basic but comfortable. Rates are $125 per person per day, which includes three meals and one hour of trail riding.

For more information, call 403/673-3737 or 800/691-5085, www.brewsteradventures.com.

CAMPGROUNDS

Commercial Campgrounds

Restwell Trailer Park enjoys a great creekside location off Eighth Street in downtown Canmore, 403/678-5111. It is mainly suited to RVs, but tents are allowed along a stretch of grass that parallels Policeman's Creek. Unserviced sites are $22, hookups $24–28, self-contained cabins $120 s or d. Along the Bow Valley Trail toward Banff is **Rundle Mountain Campground,** opposite the motel of the same name, 403/678-1893. Like Restwell, it offers showers, laundry facilities, and hookups. Sites range $19–24.

Other Campgrounds

East of Canmore are three government campgrounds operated by Bow Valley Campgrounds, 403/673-2163, www.bowvalleycampgrounds.com. Each has pit toilets, kitchen shelters, and firewood for sale at $6 per bundle. **Bow River Campground** is three km east of Canmore at the Three Sisters Parkway overpass; **Three Sisters Campground** is accessed from Deadman's Flats, a further four km east, but has a pleasant treed setting, while **Lac des Arcs Campground** is a large lake of the same name a further seven km toward Calgary. These campgrounds are open May–September and all sites are $17.

South of Canmore, 16 km along the Smith-Dorrien/Spray Trail in Kananaskis Country, is a primitive campground on Spray Lake; $12 per night.

OTHER PRACTICALITIES

FOOD

Breakfast

The **Drake Inn,** 909 Railway Ave., 403/678-5131, has the best breakfast deals in town. A hearty breakfast of eggs, bacon, hash browns, and toast will set you back around $5, and you can finish off with a beer or shooter. Open from 7 A.M. The **Summit Café** (see below) is another popular breakfast spot, with an outdoor patio catching the first rays of the sun as it rises over Grotto Mountain.

Cheap Eats

IGA is a large supermarket on Railway Avenue; especially good are the Chicken Pot Pies, which come heated and ready to eat for $4. A smaller supermarket, open till late each evening, is **Marra's,** 638 Eighth Street. In front of IGA, **Nutter's,** 900 Railway Ave., 403/678-3335, is chock-full of bulk bins—a great place to stock up for hiking trips. Along Bow Valley Trail, you'll find **A&W, Wendy's, McDonalds,** and the Canadian donut chain franchise, **Tim Horton's.** At **Boston Pizza,** 1704 Bow Valley Trail, 403/678-3300, Pasta Tuesday is good value—$6 for a large serving, in either the bar or restaurant.

Cafés and Coffee Shops

The best coffee in town is served up at the **Coffee Mine,** 802 Eighth St., 403/678-2241, a small café with a large local following and a sunny outlook. One block from the main street is **Blends,** 637 10th St., 403/678-2688, a tiny café with good coffee and light snacks. Out on the Bow Valley Trail (between Dairy Queen and Boston Pizza) is **Beamer's Coffee Bar,** 403/678-3988. Always busy, this place has a huge following through great coffee, a friendly owner, and a long comfortable couch wrapped around a fireplace—the perfect place to relax with one of Beamer's complimentary daily papers.

Away from downtown, near where Cougar Creek enters Canmore from the Fairholme Range, is **Summit Café,** 1001 Cougar Creek Drive., 403/609-2120. It features a health-conscious menu including lots of salads, but many come just to soak up the sun on the outside deck or relax with the daily paper and a cup of coffee. Open for breakfast, lunch, and dinner.

Restaurants

The restaurant scene has come a long way in Canmore in the last few years. While you can still get inexpensive bar meals at each of the many pubs, other choices run the gamut, from the lively atmosphere of dining in front yard of a converted residence to a sophisticated French restaurant.

Tucked away behind the main street is **Zona's**, 710 Ninth St., 403/609-2000, a great little bistro with a laid-back atmosphere. The menu is only small, but all dishes are healthy, freshly prepared, and delicious. It also serves homemade lemonade, and a wide selection of wines and beers. Eat inside at the rustic tables or out on tables spread around the yard. Open daily 11 A.M.–midnight.

Patrino's, at 1602 Bow Valley Trail, 403/678-4060, is a longtime local favorite, especially renowned for its steaks. The casual, family-style restaurant section has a few outdoor tables, and a menu of entrées ranging $9–20. The bar area features the same menu, as well as an abbreviated menu of snacks and an extremely popular $.20 Wing Night every Thursday. They do a good pizza, eat-in or take-out, from $14 for a medium. Also along the Bow Valley Trail, at 1306, is **Musashi**, 403/678-9360, an inexpensive Japanese restaurant open Monday –Saturday from 5:30 P.M.

The Sherwood House, 838 Eighth St., 403/678-5211, on one of Canmore's busiest downtown corners, is open daily 11 A.M.–10 P.M. You can dine outdoors on a deck or inside in a simply furnished restaurant and lounge. The menu is mainly pasta and grills ranging $14–24, but the bar menu is less expensive. Two blocks north of the Sherwood House is **Tannin's**, 838 10th St., 403/609-9200, is a city-style wine bar offering an extensive menu of appetizers that are perfect for sharing. Choices change with the season, but usually include a cheese fondue and multiple seafood choices. It's open for lunch Wednesday –Saturday and for dinner Tuesday –Sunday. The **Peppermill**, 726 9th St., 403/678-2292, serves excellent homemade pasta and lots of beef. Try daily specials such as lamb or Arctic char, and finish with a bowl of delicious homemade ice cream. It's open daily 5 10 P.M.

The Kabin, 1712 Bow Valley Trail (just across the railway line), 403/678-4878, is a two-story log structure at the eastern end of a strip of motels. The menu is small but varied. Expect to pay $15–20 for a main meal. The restaurant also offers an appetizing brunch buffet on Sunday, 10:30 A.M.–2 P.M.; $16.95, including dessert. Nearby, in the Best Western Green Gables Inn,

is **Chez Francois**, 1602 2nd Ave., 403/678-6111, an upmarket French restaurant offering gourmet breakfasts (from $7.50) and a dinner menu highlighted by beef, lamb, and duck dishes prepared with traditional French flair.

TRANSPORTATION

Getting There
Brewster, 403/762-6767, and the **Banff Airporter**, 403/762-3330, both run between Calgary International Airport and Banff four to six times daily, the former stopping at Canmore's Radisson Hotel, and the latter providing a door-to-door service. Adjacent desks at the airport's Arrivals level take bookings. **Greyhound** stops behind Rusticana Grocery, 801 Eighth St., 403/678-4465, and offers regular services to Calgary, Banff, and beyond. Local bus companies have come and gone in recent years. The latest to come is **Link Transit**, 403/762-3795, which makes a loop through downtown and past the hotels along Bow Valley Trail, stops at Harvie Heights, then heads off to Banff. This is a summer-only service; $7 one way.

Getting Around
The most enjoyable way to get around Canmore is on foot or bike, on the extensive trail network winding throughout the town. **Gear Up**, 1302 Bow Valley Trail, 403/678-1636, rents front- and full-suspension mountain bikes, as well as canoes and kayaks. For a cab, call **Canmore Taxi**, 403/678-0888 or **Apex**, 403/609-0030. **Avis**, based at Frontier Auto, 403/678-9700, is Canmore's only rental car outlet.

SERVICES AND INFORMATION

The **post office** is on Seventh Ave., beside Rusticana Grocery. **The Lost Sock** Laundromat, open 8 A.M.–9:30 P.M., is in the small mall on Seventh Avenue. **Canmore Hospital** is along Bow Valley Trail, 403/678-5536. For the **RCMP**, call 403/678-5516.

Canmore Public Library, 700 Ninth St., 403/678-2468, is open Monday–Thursday 11 A.M.–8 P.M., Friday –Sunday 11 A.M.–5 P.M. Send and receive email from the library (book in advance) or at **Cyber Web,** down the alley at 722 8th St., 403/609-3400. Across the road, **Canmore Mountainside Books,** 721 8th St., 403/678-4482, stocks a small selection of local literature. Upstairs at 713 8th Street, **Second Story,** 403/609-2368, stocks thousands of used books, including a large selection of nonfiction Canadiana.

The best source of pre-trip information (apart from this book, of course) is the website www.tourismcanmore.com, which is maintained by the local chamber of commerce. A **Travel Alberta Information Centre** on the west side of town, just off the TransCanada Highway, provides plenty of information on Canmore and Banff. Open May–September 8 A.M.–8 P.M., and October 9 A.M.–6 P.M.; 403/678-5277.

Mt. Yamnuska, as seen from Bow Valley Provincial Park.

KANANASKIS COUNTRY

INTRODUCTION

Lying along the east side of the Continental Divide south of Banff National Park and less than an hour's drive from Calgary, this sprawling 4,250-square-km area of the Canadian Rockies (pronounced Can-AN-a-skiss) has been extraordinarily successful in balancing the needs of the 2.4 million outdoor enthusiasts that visit annually while keeping the region in a relatively natural state. Although the area lacks the famous lakes and glaciated peaks of Banff and Jasper National Parks, the landscape in many ways rivals those parks. As well as the areas set aside for recreation, large tracts of land give full protection to wildlife. Throughout Kananaskis Country, wildlife is abundant and opportunities for observation of larger mammals are superb.

Geographically, Kananaskis Country can be divided into eight areas, each with its own distinct character. They include **Bow Valley Provincial Park,** a small park beside the TransCanada Highway; **Kananaskis Valley,** home to a golf course, a

ski resort, and the accommodations of Kananaskis Village; **Peter Lougheed Provincial Park** (pronounced LAW-heed), which rises from fish-filled lakes to the glaciated peaks of the Continental Divide; **Spray Lake,** named for a massive body of water nestled below the Continental Divide; **Sibbald,** an integrated recreation area where horseback riding is permitted; **Elbow River Valley** and adjacent **Sheep River Valley,** sections of the foothills that rise to Elbow-Sheep Wildland Provincial Park; and in the far south **Highwood/Cataract Creek** areas, where the rugged landscape ranges from forested valleys to snowcapped peaks. Within its boundaries are six provincial parks, 1,300 km of trails, a complex network of bike paths, areas for horseback riding (and some for ATVs), a world-class 36-hole golf course, boat and bike

See color maps of Kananaskis Country on pages vii–ix.

rentals, and 30 lakes stocked annually with over 150,000 fish. The downhill-skiing events of the 1988 Winter Olympic Games were held here at the specially developed Nakiska ski area, now open to the public. And deeper in the mountains, Fortress Mountain provides more downhill skiing. Meanwhile, nordic skiers can glide over hundreds of cross-country skiing trails in the region.

The accommodations and restaurants of **Kananaskis Village** is the centerpiece of the Kananaskis Country's facility area, but also contained within the region are two other lodges, 31 frontcountry campgrounds holding 2,300 sites, 15 backcountry campgrounds, and five information centers. In addition to Canmore, at the northern entrance to Kananaskis Country, the foothills to the east hold many well-established towns, such as Bragg Creek, with interesting histories, quaint teahouses, holiday ranches, and sprawling properties that enjoy the inspiring Canadian Rockies as a backdrop.

THE LAND

Within Kananaskis Country are two distinct ecosystems: the high peaks of the Continental Divide to the west, and the lower, rolling foothills to the east. The glacier-carved **Kananaskis Valley** separates the two. The Elbow and Sheep River Valleys rise in the west to Front Ranges, which formed around 85 million years and have eroded to half their original height. The Main Ranges, which form part of the Continental Divide, are composed of older, erosion-resistant quartzite and limestone, giving them a more jagged appearance.

Flora and Fauna
Kananaskis Country occupies a transition zone between foothills and mountains, and as a result it harbors a wide variety of plant species. In the east, the relatively low-lying Sheep, Elbow, and Sibbald valleys are dominated by stands of **aspen,** interspersed with open meadows. Climbing gradually to the west, you'll pass through the montane zone, with its forests of **Douglas fir, lodgepole pine, white spruce,** and **balsam poplar,** then enter the subalpine zone, where stands of **Engelmann spruce, subalpine fir,** and occasionally **larch** lead up to tree line. Above the tree line, which here occurs at around 2,300 meters, lie

the open meadows of the alpine zone. These meadows lie under a deep cover of snow for most of the year, but come alive with color during July when wildflowers bloom. Highwood Pass, along Highway 40, is one of the most accessible areas of alpine terrain in the Canadian Rockies; look for **forget-me-nots, Indian paintbrush,** and **western anemone** along the interpretive trail.

These hills, valleys, and forests are home to an abundance of wildlife, including large populations of **moose, mule deer, white-tailed deer, elk, black bear, bighorn sheep,** and **mountain goat.** Also present, but less likely to be seen, are **wolves, grizzly bears,** and **cougars.**

HISTORY

In 1858, Capt. John Palliser bestowed the name "Kananaskis" on the valley, a pass, and two lakes. Kananaskis was a native who, legend had it, suffered a vicious blow to the head by an enemy but survived. The word itself is thought to mean "the meeting of the water." Aside from Palliser, the region was visited by many names synonymous with exploration of the Canadian Rockies: David Thompson in 1787 and 1800, Peter Fidler in 1792, and James Sinclair leading Scottish settlers to the Oregon Territory in 1841. Through these times, and until recent times, the valley remained mostly uninhabited. Logging took place from 1883, mostly in the foothill valleys of the Elbow and Sheep Rivers. Coal was mined at various sites, including Ribbon Creek, by Kananaskis Village, but never on a large scale. To serve these industries, roads were built—including the Forestry Trunk Road (Hwy. 40), which traverses the entire foothills parallel to the Continental Divide.

During Alberta's oil-and-gas boom of the 1970s, oil revenues collected by the provincial government were placed into the Heritage Savings Trust Fund, from where they were channeled into various projects aimed at improving the lifestyle of Albertans. One lasting legacy of the fund is Kananaskis Country, officially designated by premier Peter Lougheed in 1977 as Kananaskis Country Provincial Recreational Area. The mandate was to accommodate a multitude of uses, including most importantly recreational pursuits, but Kananaskis Country also holds 21 active oil and gas leases, 14 grazing permits, 75,000 cubic meters of timber held under lease, and a hydroelectric dam on the Kananaskis River. Since 1997 the government has pumped over $250 into Kananaskis Country, with private investors spending a little over $60 million in that same period. The first major boundary change since 1977 occurred in early 1996 when Elbow-Sheep Wildland Provincial Park was established; at 769 square km it is Alberta's largest provincial park. User demand for more facilities led to the 1999 Kananaskis Country Recreation Policy, but this was roundly rejected by Albertans and there is currently a development moratorium, which has put on hold grand plans for a ski area, more golf courses, and a boat cruises on Spray Lake. The latest area of Kananaskis Country to be declared a provincial park is the Spray Valley, which has created a continuous stretch of protection for the Canadian Rockies from Willmore Wildness Park in the north to Peter Lougheed Provincial Park in the south.

PRACTICALITIES

Services within Kananaskis Country include an information center at each of the main entrances, high-class accommodations in **Kananaskis Village,** 2,300 campsites in 31 campgrounds, and accommodations for the physically challenged at William Watson Lodge. Gas is available at Fortress Junction and Highwood Junction. For more information, write Alberta Environment, Suite 201, Provincial Building, 800 Railway Ave., Canmore, AB T1W 1P1; call 403/678-5508; or surf the Internet to www.gov.ab.ca/env, and click on the "Parks" link. Another good source of information is **Friends of Kananaskis Country,** www.kananaskis.org, a nonprofit organization that promotes educational programs, is involved in a variety of hands-on projects, and promotes Kananaskis Country in partnership with Alberta Environment.

The main access to Kananaskis Country is 76 km west of Calgary off the TransCanada Highway. Other points of access are immediately south of Canmore; at Bragg Creek on the region's northeast border; west from Millarville, Turner Valley, and Longview in the southeast; or along the Forestry Trunk Road from the south.

BOW VALLEY PROVINCIAL PARK

This provincial park at the north end of Kananaskis Country has recently had its boundaries extended from the confluence of the Kananaskis and Bow Rivers straddling the TransCanada Highway to take in a stretch of the Kananaskis River as far south as, and including, Barrier Lake. Calgary is 80 km to the east and Canmore is 26 km to the west.

The Bow Valley was gouged by glaciers during a succession of ice ages, leaving the typical U-shaped glacial valley surrounded by towering peaks. Three vegetation zones are found within the park, but evergreen and aspen forest predominates. To the casual motorist driving along the highway, the park seems fairly small (and is easily missed), but over 300 species of plants have been recorded and 60 species of birds are known to nest within its boundaries. The abundance of wildflowers, birds, elk, and smaller mammals can be enjoyed along short interpretive trails. Other popular activities in the park include fishing for a variety of trout and whitefish in the Bow River, bicycling along the paved trail system, and attending interpretive programs presented by park staff.

HIKING

Montane Trail
• Length: 2.2 km (40 minutes) roundtrip
• Elevation gain: minimal
• Rating: easy
The Montane Trail begins from behind the main information center just off the highway. As the name suggests, it traverses montane forest of aspen and Douglas fir, as well as skirting an open meadow and a number of eskers, low ridges left behind by retreating glaciers during the last ice age.

Many Springs Trail
• Length: 2.8 km (50 minutes) round-trip
• Elevation gain: minimal
• Rating: easy
From the trailhead just beyond Elk Flats day-

use area, this well-formed trail makes a loop around a wetland fed by underground springs. The spring water is relatively warm, creating a microclimate in the immediate vicinity. Look for orchids around damp areas.

Flowing Water Interpretive Trail
• Length: 1.4 km (30 minutes) round-trip
• Elevation gain: minimal
• Rating: easy

This trail begins from the furthest corner of Willow Rock Campground, on the eastern side of Highway 1X, traversing a montane forest along a bench above the Kananaskis River and passing a beaver pond. Interpretive panels along the way explain the importance of water and its relationship to the ecosystem.

PRACTICALITIES

Campgrounds
Facilities at the two campgrounds within the park,

Bow Valley and Willow Rock, are as good as any in the province. Both have showers, flush toilets, firewood sales ($6), and kitchen shelters. Continue beyond the information center to Reach Bow Valley Campground, which has a grocery store, bike rentals, and a nightly interpretive program; $20–23 per night. Willow Rock has a few powered sites (but these are open to the elements) and a coin laundry and is open for winter camping; sites are $17–20. For more information, or for reservations at Bow Valley, contact **Bow Valley Campgrounds,** 403/673-2163, www.bowvalleycampgrounds.com.

Information
A **Visitor Information Centre** at the park entrance on Highway 1X, 403/673-3663, offers general information on the park and Kananaskis Country, as well as interpretive displays. The 2.2-km Montane Trail (see above) begins here. The center is open in summer Monday–Friday 8 A.M.–8 P.M.; the rest of the year Monday–Friday 8:15 A.M.–4:30 P.M.

KANANASKIS VALLEY

This is the most developed area of Kananaskis Country, yet summer crowds are minimal compared to Banff. Highway 40 follows the Kananaskis River through the zone between the TransCanada Highway and Peter Lougheed Provincial Park.

SIGHTS

Make your first stop the Barrier Lake Visitor Information Centre, nestled between Highway 40 and the Kananaskis River near the north boundary of Kananaskis Country. Across the road is Tim Horton's Children's Ranch, set up by a Canadian hockey great to help underprivileged kids enjoy summer camp.

The first main body of water Highway 40 passes is **Barrier Lake,** dominated to the south by the impressive peak of Mt. Baldy (2,212 meters). The lake is manmade, but still a picture of beauty. Two picnic areas and short interpretive trails can be found along its shoreline. The

next stop of interest, especially for anglers, is **Mt. Lorette Ponds,** a string of five small lakes created by diverting the flow of the Kananaskis River. The ponds are stocked annually with rainbow trout.

Kananaskis Village lies just off Highway 40 a few km south of the ponds. The village was the epicenter of action during the 1988 Winter Olympic Games. Developed specially for the games, it sits on a high bench below Nakiska—where the downhill events of the games were held—and overlooks a golf course. The village comprises three hotels, restaurants, and other service shops set around a paved courtyard complete with waterfalls and trout-stocked ponds.

From the village, it's 15 km further south to the border of Peter Lougheed Provincial Park. Just beyond the village is **Wedge Pond,** originally dug as a gravel pit during golf course construction, it is now filled with water and encircled by a one-km trail offering fantastic views across the river to towering 2,958-meter Mt. Kidd.

Highwood Pass is one of the most accessible alpine regions in all the Canadian Rockies.

HIKING

Prairie View

- Length: 6.5 km (2–2.5 hours) one-way
- Elevation gain: 420 meters
- Rating: moderate

This trail provides a variety of options; the most straightforward leads to a high viewpoint atop McConnell Ridge. From the parking lot at the north end of Barrier Lake, cross the Kananaskis River at the Barrier Dam. Take the right fork at the first junction and go left at the second. From this point the trail climbs steadily along an old fire lookout road to the summit, where views extend south across Barrier Lake to Mt. Baldy. The actual site of the fire lookout is a further one km and 80 vertical meters from the main trail along the ridge. The additional climb to the lookout is well worth the effort; you'll be rewarded with views across Bow Valley to Mt. Yamnuska and east across the prairies to Cal-

gary. Back on the main trail, at the 6.5-km mark you'll come to Jewell Pass, a major trail junction. The options from this point are to descend along Jewell Creek to the shore of Barrier Lake, passing picturesque Jewell Falls (14 km round-trip from the parking lot; allow four hours) or continue north into the Quaite Valley and to the Heart Creek trailhead in the Bow Valley (a further eight km one-way).

Baldy Pass

- Length: 4.5 km (1.5–2 hours) one-way
- Elevation gain: 520 meters
- Rating: moderate

This trail traverses Elbow-Sheep Wildland Provincial Park to a 1,990-meter divide separating the Kananaskis River and Jumpingpound Creek watersheds. Park at the small lot three km south of Barrier Lake along Highway 40 and cross the road, entering the woods at the marked trailhead. After 500 meters, at a marked intersection, the trail enters a usually dry watercourse, which it follows the entire way to the pass. Only the last 500 meters are particularly steep, across an avalanche slope. An even better view than that afforded at the pass can be had by following the northern ridge from the pass. It's a steep scramble, though, gaining as much elevation in one km as the whole trail gains between the trailhead and pass.

Ribbon Falls

- Length: 9 km (3–4 hours) one-way
- Elevation gain: 335 meters
- Rating: moderate

Minimal elevation gain and a well-formed trail make this one of the more popular day hikes in the Kananaskis Valley. It begins from the upper parking lot at Ribbon Creek, just off the Kananaskis Village access road. Following Ribbon Creek through a narrow valley between Mt. Kidd and Ribbon Peak, it passes chunks of iron from an old logging camp and the remains of two abandoned log cabins. Beyond the second cabin, the trail enters Dipper Canyon, dotted with pools of water, then climbs across an avalanche slope to a lookout over Ribbon Falls.

Two km beyond the falls is Ribbon Lake, but reaching it requires some rock-climbing skills. From the falls, the trail switchbacks up a scree slope to a sheer cliff face. Three lengths of chain and a series of narrow ledges need to be negotiated to reach the cliff top, then it's a straightforward hike through a subalpine forest to the lake.

Mt. Allan (Centennial Ridge)
• Length: 11 km (4–5 hours) one-way
• Elevation gain: 1,350 meters
• Rating: difficult

This is the highest maintained trail in the Canadian Rockies and one of the few that actually reaches a mountaintop. Its final destination is the summit of Mt. Allan, upon whose slopes the Ski Nakiska ski area lies. The trail starts at the upper parking lot at Ribbon Creek. It branches to the right, through the Hidden Ski Trail, then left through an open meadow that was the site of the Ribbon Creek Coal Mine. And then the fun starts—the trail gains 610 meters of elevation in the next two km. At the end of this climb the trail arrives atop Centennial Ridge and at the top of the Olympic Platter, starting point for the Men's Downhill at the 1988 Winter Olympic Games. It follows the ridge past a group of intriguing 25-meter-high hoodoos known as the Rock Garden, passes a false summit, then, finally, reaches the top of 2,990-meter-high Mt. Allan.

Galatea Creek
• Length: 5.9 km (two hours) one-way
• Elevation gain: 425 meters
• Rating: moderate

Galatea Creek flows from high in the Kananaskis Range through a narrow valley bordered to the north by Mt. Kidd and to the south by Fortress Ridge. From the parking lot along Highway 40 just south of Wedge Pond, the trail descends to the Kananaskis River, crossing via a long suspension bridge. Take the left fork once across the river. The trail is easy to follow as it parallels the north bank of Galatea Creek beneath the sheer southern wall of Mt. Kidd. It traverses a wide avalanche slope before reaching the final steep ascent to tree-encircled Lillian Lake, which is stocked with rainbow trout. Behind the lake's backcountry campground, a trail continues a further two km to Upper Galatea Lake.

Fortress Lake
• Length: 5 km (1.5 hours) one-way
• Elevation gain: 280 meters
• Rating: easy/moderate

This trail is unmarked, but easy enough to follow. It begins from the Fortress Mountain ski area parking lot—the unofficial trailhead is the cat track—and descends to Aussie Creek. Once across the creek, the trail begins the ascent to the lake, crossing under a T-bar and continuing up to Fortress Ridge. From the upper terminal of Farside chairlift, go left at the fork to reach the lake, a deep blue body of water nestled under the cliff for which the ski area is named. The right fork at the top of the chairlift leads along Fortress Ridge, climbing above the tree line for panoramic views across the Kananaskis Valley. The high point of the ridge is 5.5 km from the parking lot, with a more strenuous elevation gain of 530 meters.

OTHER RECREATION

In Kananaskis Village, **Peregrine Sports,** 403/591-7453, rents a wide variety of sporting equipment including mountain bikes (from $7 per hour, $30 per day), scooters ($13 per hour, $60 per day), fishing rods ($10 per day), canoes ($35 per day), and various downhill and cross-country skiing equipment.

Kananaskis Country Golf Course
Regularly voted "Best Value in North America" by *Golf Digest,* this 36-hole layout comprises two 18-hole courses: **Mt. Kidd,** featuring undulating terrain and an island green on the 197-yard fourth hole, and the shorter (which is a relative term—both courses measure over 7,000 from the back markers) **Mt. Lorette,** where water comes into play on 13 holes. The course opened in 1983 at a cost of almost $1 million per hole. No expense was spared in course construction. The bunkers alone—filled with pure-white silica from British Columbia—cost $350,000. Renowned golf-course architect Robert Trent Jones, who designed the layout, described the Kananaskis River Valley as ". . . the best spot I have ever seen for a golf course." After marveling at the surrounding mountains, few will disagree with his statement. Just don't let the 142 sand traps, water that comes into play on over half the holes, or the large rolling greens distract you. Greens fees are $50–75 and a cart is an additional $25. Golfers enjoy complimentary valet parking and use of the driving range, as well as a restaurant and bar with

Golfing in Kananaskis Country is a spectacular experience.

awesome mountain views, and a well-stocked golf shop. For tee times, call 403/591-7272 or 877/591-2525.

WINTERTIME

Nakiska

This state-of-the-art ski area was built on Mt. Allan to host the alpine skiing events of the 1988 Winter Olympic Games. Originally the Olympic events were to be held on existing ski slopes in Banff National Park. Environmentalists succeeded in keeping the games out of the park, but their victory soon turned sour when alternate plans were unveiled to spend $25.3 million creating a new Olympic hill on the slopes of Mt. Allan.

The project was controversial right from the start, but environmental politics wasn't the only problem faced here. Anyone familiar with these mountains knows the devastating effect the area's warm, dry chinook winds have on the snow cover—the idea of building a ski hill here seemed ludicrous. The answer was snowmaking. A computerized snowmaking system covering 85 percent of the runs was installed at a cost of five million dollars. With 40 km of piping and 343 hydrants, the system is capable of pumping 24 million liters of water a day. So who needs Mother Nature?

In the end, the Olympics came off without a glitch, and Nakiska is now open to the public. Great cruising and fast fall-line skiing on runs cut

specially for racing will satisfy the intermediate-to-advanced crowd. And the Bronze Chairlift accesses a novice area below the main area. The area has a total of 28 runs and a vertical rise of 735 meters. Lift tickets are $42 for adults, $34 for seniors and students, $15 for children. Kids five and under ski free. Packages are offered in Kananaskis Village, which is linked to Nakiska by shuttle from Canmore, 40 km to the northwest.

For more ski resort information, call 403/591-7777 or the Snowphone at 403/229-3288. For accommodation reservations, call 800/258-7669.

Fortress Mountain

Fortress is a sleeping giant as ski areas go. It's a 30-minute drive farther into Kananaskis Country than Nakiska but the rewards are uncrowded slopes, more snow, on-hill accommodations, a longer season, and spectacular views. The resort has had a checkered history since opening as Snowridge Ski Area in 1969, but since coming under the umbrella of Resorts of the Canadian Rockies, it is much improved. Runs are short, but with skiing on three distinct faces there's something for everyone. With a little hiking, experienced powderhounds can ski untracked snow days after a storm. Facilities include three chairlifts and three T-bars serving a vertical rise of 330 meters, and a large day lodge with cafeteria, restaurant, and bar. Lift tickets are $32 per day or $24 for the afternoon; seniors and students $25. For more information, call 403/264-5825 or the Snowphone at 403/245-4909. On-hill lodging is

at **Fortress Mountain Lodge,** 403/256-8473 or 800/258-7669. Package deals in the height of the season start at $120 for two nights' accommodation in a motel-style room and two lift tickets. The latest addition to the base area is a string of comfortable, self-contained three-bedroom chalets that cost $175 during the week and $225 on weekends.

Cross-Country Skiing
The most accessible of Kananaskis Country's 200 km of cross-country trails are in the Ribbon Creek area. Most heavily used are those radiating from Kananaskis Village and those around the base of Nakiska. Most trails are easy to intermediate, including a five-km track up Ribbon Creek. Rentals are available in the Village Trading Post in Kananaskis Village.

KANANASKIS VILLAGE

This modern alpine resort 100 km from Calgary was built for the 1988 Winter Olympic Games. Today it serves as headquarters for those who want to experience the wilds of Kananaskis Country while still enjoying the comforts of hotels and fine restaurants. The village sits on a narrow plateau, with magnificent mountain vistas in all directions and two ski areas a short drive away.

Accommodations
Of the two hotels in the village, the **Kananaskis Inn,** 403/591-7500 or 888/591-7501, www.kananaskisinn.com, is the least expensive. Some of the 90 rooms are bedroom lofts with fireplaces, kitchenettes, and sitting rooms ($180); the others are standard hotel rooms that begin at $160. The inn also offers an exercise room, indoor pool, and the Alpine Garden Cafe.

The other accommodation in the Village is the upmarket **Delta Lodge at Kananaskis.** It offers two distinctly different types of rooms. In the main lodge are 251 moderately large rooms, many with mountain views, balconies, and fireplaces as well as a shopping arcade. The John Palliser Manor holds 70 "Signature Club" (a Delta designation) rooms, each boasting a mountain view, a luxurious bathroom complete with bathrobes, extra large beds, and many extras,

such as CD players. Guests in this wing also enjoy a private lounge. All guests have use of the Summit Spa and Fitness Centre, which comprises a full-facility health club, an indoor swimming pool, whirlpool, steam room, sauna, and a beauty salon with tanning beds. Rooms in the main lodge start at $205 s or d while those in the John Palliser Manor, where rates include a light breakfast, start at $295. Rates drop dramatically outside of summer; good ski packages are offered all winter. For information and reservations, call 403/591-7711 or 800/268-1133. Online, visit www.deltahotels.com.

Food
The lodge contains six restaurants and bars. For a warm, relaxed atmosphere, head to the **Bighorn Lounge,** near the arcade's main entrance. It features a warm, relaxed atmosphere and a bistro-style menu highlighted by a wide variety of appetizers perfect for sharing, such as cheese platters. It's open daily from 11 A.M. and offers occasional live evening entertainment. Also in the arcade is **Peaks Restaurant** (open daily 6 A.M.–10 P.M.), with a casual western-style atmosphere, floor-to-ceiling windows, and an adjoining outdoor patio used during summer. It's open daily 6 A.M.–10 P.M., with a buffet breakfast offered until 10 A.M. The country-style **Brady's Market** features seasonal produce prepared in traditional European dishes. **L'Escapade,** in the John Palliser Manor, is the village's most elegant restaurant. French-Canadian cuisine is served on sterling silver, as a pianist plays in the background. It's open for dinner only; expect to pay $18–30 for an entrée. For reservations, call 403/591-7711.

Food is also available at the Alpine Garden Café, at Kananaskis Inn, or at the golf course, where the restaurant offers a casual atmosphere and stunning valley views. Near the entrance to the village is the **Village Trading Post,** a post office, and an information center (open in summer daily 9 A.M.–5 P.M.).

OTHER ACCOMMODATIONS AND INFORMATION

Hostel
Originally the schoolhouse for the short-lived coal-mining town of Kovach, **Ribbon Creek**

Hostel lies alongside Ribbon Creek, just off the access road to nearby Kananaskis Village. The 47-bed hostel has hot showers, a kitchen, family rooms, a lounge room with fireplace, an outdoor barbecue, and a laundry. Cost to members is $13, nonmembers $17. For reservations, call Calgary 403/269-8239 or the Banff hostel at 403/762-4122. Check-in is between 5 P.M. and 11 P.M. A daily shuttle service drops hostelers at Ribbon Creek on the run between Calgary and Banff. Book through the Calgary or Banff hostels.

Campgrounds

Mount Kidd RV Park, 403/591-7700, is arguably the finest RV park in Canada. It's nestled below the sheer eastern face of Mt. Kidd in a forest of spruce and lodgepole pine, 26 km south of the TransCanada Highway. The campground's showpiece is the Campers Centre. Inside are all the usual bathroom facilities as well as whirlpools, saunas, a wading pool, game room, lounge, groceries, a concession, and laundry. Outside are tennis courts, picnic areas by the river, and many paved trails. Tent sites are $19, hookups $23–29. It's open year-round.

Those who can survive without such luxuries have the choice of three other campgrounds along Highway 40; all charge $16 per site per night. No reservations are taken.

Information

At the zone's north entrance, **Barrier Lake Visitor Information Centre,** 403/673-3985, is a good place to start your trip into Kananaskis Country. It's open in summer daily 9 A.M.–6 P.M., the rest of the year daily 9 A.M.–4 P.M. A small information booth operates in Kananaskis Village through the months of summer.

PETER LOUGHEED PROVINCIAL PARK

This park, originally named Kananaskis Provincial Park, was renamed in 1986 after Peter Lougheed. Lougheed was the Albertan premier who, with the help of oil-money-based Heritage Savings Trust Fund, began the development of Kananaskis Country as a multiuse recreation area. The 500-square-km wilderness is the second-largest provincial park in Alberta. The high peaks of the Continental Divide form the eastern and southern boundaries of the park, making a spectacular backdrop for the Kananaskis River and Upper and Lower Kananaskis Lakes. Captain John Palliser passed by the Kananaskis Lakes in 1858, summed up the beauty of the lakes in 1858 by writing "We came upon a magnificent lake, hemmed in by mountains, and studded by numerous islets, very thickly wooded. This lake, about four miles long and one-and-a-half miles wide, receives water from the glacier above, and is a favorite place of resort to the Kootenie Indians."

Highway 40 is the main route through the park, with Kananaskis Lakes Trail branching off into the main recreation areas which are centered around Upper and Lower Kananaskis Lakes. The lakes are the center of boating and fishing in the park and opportunities abound for hiking and camping nearby.

Highwood Pass

In the southeastern corner of the park, Highway 40 climbs to Highwood Pass (2,227 meters), the highest road pass in Canada. On the way up to the pass, a pleasant detour is Valley View Trail, a five-km paved road whose route higher up the slopes of the Opal Range allows views across the entire park to the Continental Divide. The pass itself is right at the tree line, one of the most accessible alpine areas in all the Canadian Rockies. Simply step out of your vehicle and follow the interpretive trails through the **Highwood Meadows.** From the pass, Highway 40 descends into the Highwood/Cataract Creek areas of Kananaskis Country. Highwood Pass is in critical wildlife habitat and is closed December 1–June 15.

HIKING

The park offers a number of interesting interpretive trails and more strenuous hikes. Most trailheads are located along Kananaskis Lakes Trail. Many trails feature interpretive signs; others require an interpretive booklet available from the Visitor Information Centre. **Rockwall Trail,** from the Visitor Information Centre, and **Marl Lake Trail,** from Elkwood Campground, are

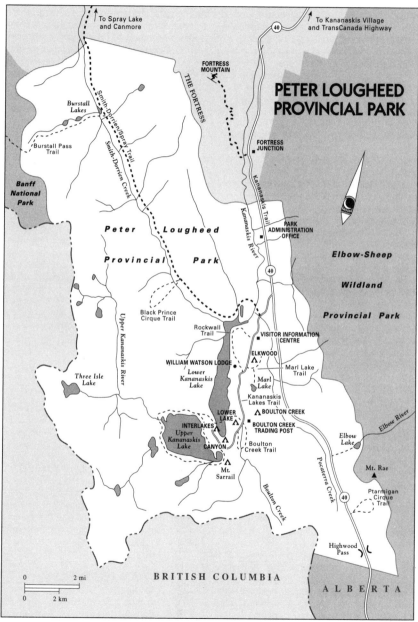

To Spray Lake
and Canmore

To Kanaskis Village
and TransCanada Highway

40

FORTRESS
MOUNTAIN

THE FORTRESS

PETER LOUGHEED
PROVINCIAL PARK

Burstall
Lakes

Smith-Dorrien/Spray Trail

FORTRESS
JUNCTION

Burstall Pass
Trail

Smith-Dorrien Creek

Kananaskis Trail

*Banff
National
Park*

PARK
ADMINISTRATION
OFFICE

Kananaskis River

40

Elbow-Sheep

Peter   Lougheed

Wildland

Provincial   Park

Provincial   Park

Black Prince
Cirque Trail

Rockwall
Trail

VISITOR INFORMATION
CENTRE

Upper Kananaskis River

ELKWOOD

WILLIAM WATSON LODGE

*Lower
Kananaskis Lake*

Marl Lake
Trail

*Three Isle
Lake*

*Marl
Lake*

Kananaskis
Lakes Trail

Elbow River

LOWER
LAKE

BOULTON CREEK

INTERLAKES

BOULTON CREEK
TRADING POST

Elbow
Lake

*Upper
Kananaskis
Lake*

CANYON

Boulton
Creek Trail

Mt. Rae

Mt.
Sarrail

Pocaterra Creek

Ptarmigan
Cirque
Trail

Boulton Creek

40

BRITISH COLUMBIA

ALBERTA

Highwood
Pass

0   2 mi

0   2 km

wheelchair accessible and barrier-free, respectively. Below are some of the park's more popular interpretive and day-hikes.

Boulton Creek

- Length: 4.9 km (90 minutes) round-trip
- Elevation gain: minimal
- Rating: easy

This trail starts where Kananaskis Lakes Trail crosses Boulton Creek. A booklet, available at the trailhead or at the Visitor Information Centre, corresponds with numbered posts along the trail. The highlighted stops emphasize the valley's human history. After a short climb, the trail reaches a cabin built in the 1930s as a stopover for forest-ranger patrols. The trail then follows a high ridge and loops back along the other side of the creek to the trailhead.

Elbow Lake

- Length: 1.3 km (30 minutes) one-way
- Elevation gain: 135 meters
- Rating: easy

The trailhead to this picturesque body of water lies along Highway 40 at the Elbow Pass day-use area, a few km before Highwood Pass. The official trail is a wide road that climbs quickly into the bowl holding shallow Elbow Lake. The lake is a popular spot, especially for summer picnics; campsites are spread around the south shore. An interesting side trip is to Rae Glacier, a small glacier on the north face of Mt. Rae. The trail starts on the east shore of the lake, gaining 400 meters of elevation in just over two km.

Elbow Lake is the source of the Elbow River, which flows eastward through the foothills. The short hiking trail from Highway 40 up to the lake is part of a much longer historic route that ran between the two valleys and is still passable for backcountry adventurers.

Ptarmigan Cirque

- Length: 5.6 km (2 hours) round-trip
- Elevation gain: 230 meters
- Rating: moderate

The trailhead for this steep interpretive walk is across the road from the parking lot at Highwood Pass, 17 km south of Kananaskis Lakes Road on Highway 40. A booklet, available at the trailhead or at the Visitor Information Centre, corresponds with numbered posts along the trail.

As you climb into the alpine zone, magnificent panoramas unfold. Along the trail you are likely to see numerous small mammals. Columbian ground squirrels, pikas, least chipmunks, and hoary marmots are all common. At higher elevations the meadows are home to bighorn sheep, mountain goats, and grizzly bears. Another short walk, the **Rock Glacier Trail,** two km north of Highwood Pass, leads 150 meters to a unique formation of moraine rock.

Black Prince Cirque

- Length: 5.6 km (90 minutes) round-trip
- Elevation gain: 210 meters
- Rating: easy/moderate

Follow the Smith-Dorrien/Spray Trail for eight km beyond the Kananaskis Lakes Trail to access the trailhead for this interesting and relatively easy hike. Numbered posts along the trail correspond to a booklet available at the trailhead or at the Visitor Information Centre. The trail begins by climbing steadily to an area that was logged in the early 1970s. Then it winds through a forest of Engelmann spruce and subalpine fir, crossing Old Creek and emerging at a high mountain cirque scoured out by a glacier. Each spring the cirque fills with water, forming a small, emerald-green lake.

Burstall Pass

- Length: 7.4 km (2.5 hours) one-way
- Elevation gain: 480 meters
- Rating: moderate/difficult

From a trailhead on the west side of the Smith-Dorrien/Spray Trail, at the south end of Mud Lake, this trail begins with a three-km climb up an old logging road to Burstall Lakes. After traversing some willow flats, it begins climbing again through heavy forest and across avalanche paths to a large cirque. The final ascent to the pass is a real slog, but the view across the Upper Spray Valley (which is in Banff National Park) is worth it. From the pass it is possible to continue to Palliser Pass (two days one-way) and Banff townsite (three days one-way).

OTHER RECREATION

Hiking is the most popular activity in the park but by no means the only one. The **Bike Trail,** a

20-km paved trail designed especially for bicycles, begins behind the Visitor Information Centre and follows Lower Kananaskis Lake to Mt. Sarrail Campground. Many other trails are designated for mountain-bike use; inquire at the Visitor Information Centre, 403/591-6344. **Boulton Creek Trading Post,** 403/591-7678, rents mountain bikes; $8 per hour, $32 per day.

Fishing is fair in Upper and Lower Kananaskis Lakes, where a variety of trout and whitefish tease anglers. A nightly interpretive program takes place in campground amphitheaters throughout the park. Look for schedules posted on bulletin boards or check with the Visitor Information Centre.

In winter Highwood Pass is closed to traffic, but Highway 40 entering the park from the north is cleared, and cross-country skiing is excellent.

PRACTICALITIES

William Watson Lodge

This special facility is available to disabled persons and Albertan seniors. It provides a wide range of barrier-free facilities, including hiking trails, a picnic area, and a stocked trout pond. Guests stay in either a campground or one of 22 private cabins, and they must supply their own bedding and food. The main lodge has a kitchen, lounge, library, laundry room, and a sundeck with gas barbecues. Disabled guests may bring up to three family members or friends. The cost is $5–15 per person per night. Reservations are essential and can be made up to four months in advance by Albertans and up to two months in advance by non-Albertans. Write William Watson Lodge, Peter Lougheed Provincial Park, P.O. Box 130, Kananaskis Village, AB T0L 2H0, or call 403/591-7227.

Campgrounds

Within the park are six auto-accessible campgrounds that hold a total of 507 sites. They are operated by Kananaskis Camping Inc., www.kananaskiscamping.com. All are on the Kananaskis Lakes Trail and are linked by bicycle and hiking trails. Firewood is available at each campground for $6 per bundle.

Mt. Sarrail Campground, at the southern end of Upper Kananaskis Lake, is for tenters only. It has pit toilets and bear-proof food caches. Sites are $13 per night and it's open mid-June to early September. **Canyon, Lower Lake,** and **Interlakes Campgrounds** have pit toilets and are open mid-May to early October; $17 per night. **Elkwood Campground** is the largest of the park's campgrounds with 130 sites. It offers showers ($1 for five minutes), flush toilets, and an interpretive amphitheater. All sites are $17 and it's open mid-May to early September. **Boulton Creek Campground** has showers ($1 for five minutes), flush toilets, powered sites, an interpretive amphitheater, and is within walking distance of a grocery store; $17 per night. Boulton Creek is the only campground that takes reservations (403/591-7226) and that is open year-round.

Services and Information

Boulton Creek Trading Post, on the Kananaskis Lakes Trail, 403/591-7678, sells groceries, basic supplies, fishing tackle, and souvenirs. The store also rents bikes. Next door is a small café serving hamburgers and light meals. The ice cream is good, although expensive.

At the excellent **Visitor Information Centre,** three km along Kananaskis Lakes Trail, 403/591-6322, exhibits catalogue the natural and cultural history of the park through photographs, videos, and hands-on displays, and a great display opened in 2000 telling the story about the bears of Kananaskis Country. The knowledgeable staff hides hordes of literature under the desk–you have to ask for it. Also ask them to put a movie or slide show on in the theater; most revolve around the park. The movie *Bears and Man* is a classic 1970s flick dealing with public attitude toward bears–one of the first documentaries to do so. A large lounge area that overlooks the valley to the Opal Range is used mainly in winter by cross-country skiers but is always open for trip planning or relaxing. It's open in summer daily 9 A.M.–7 P.M., the rest of the year Monday –Friday 9 A.M.–5 P.M. and Saturday –Sunday 9 A.M.–5 P.M.

SPRAY LAKE

The Spray Lake area of Kananaskis Country is bordered by Peter Lougheed Provincial Park to the south, the Kananaskis Valley zone to the east and the Continental Divide and Banff National Park to the west. The dominant feature is Spray Lake Reservoir, a 16-km-long body of water that is an integral part of a massive hydroelectric scheme. The Smith-Dorrien/Spray Trail is the only road through the zone. This 60-km-long unpaved (and often dusty) road links Peter Lougheed Provincial Park in the south to Canmore in the north.

From the south, the road climbs up the Smith-Dorrien Creek watershed, passing Mud Lake and entering the Spray Lake zone just before Mt. Engadine Lodge, 403/678-4080, www.mountengadine.com. Around three km further north is Buller Pond (on the west side of the road), from where the distinctive "Matterhorn" peak of Mt. Assiniboine can be seen on a clear day. The road then parallels Spray Lake, which is lined by three picnic areas and a campground. The Spray Development began in 1948 with the construction of a road between Canmore and the Spray River. The next stage was damming the river, creating a reservoir of approximately 2,000 hectares, then diverting its course through Whiteman's Pass and using the water flow as it drops into the Bow River to generate hydroelectric power. The water drops a total of 300 meters and passes through three power plants, which, combined, generate enough electricity to power a city of 100,000.

HIKING

Watridge Lake
- Length: 3.5 km (one hour) one-way
- Elevation gain: 50 meters
- Rating: easy

Most of the hiking in the Spray Lake zone requires some route finding; Watridge Lake is the exception and is open to mountain bikes. Park at the Mt. Shark staging area, five km west of the main road and south of Spray Lake. The trail begins from behind the information board at the entrance to the main parking lot, skirting a maze

of cross-country ski trails and quickly reaching the muddy shoreline of the lake, which is known for excellent cutthroat trout fishing. Dedicated anglers stop here; most other hikers cross the lake's outlet and continue 900 meters (allow 20 minutes one-way) to a delightful spring that bursts from the forested slopes of Mt. Shark and flows along a riverbed carpeted in moss.

Jakeroy Glacier
- Length: 4 km (1.5–2 hours) one-way
- Elevation gain: 600 meters
- Rating: moderate/difficult

This small, hidden glacier is nestled in the shadow of the Goat Range. Reaching it entails some route finding, but the rewards are ample. The trailhead is in Spray Lake Campground, on the west shore of Spray Lake. Follow the road

Even the Canadian Rockies have beaches. This one can be found on the eastern shore of Spray Lake.

through the campground to where it crosses a small creek (beside Site 17, 1.5 km from the end of the dam wall). At the No Camping sign on the upstream side of the road, search out the trail that disappears into a forest of lodgepole pine. The trail parallels the creek for much of the way—making a minimal elevation gain through a moss-carpeted valley—until emerging in an open area where the creek flows through a willow-choked meadow. The headwall and hanging valley are now in clear view straight ahead. Continue a little further, crossing the creek below a waterfall. From this point onward, the trail becomes indistinct, climbing steeply up the scree slope between the cliff face and the tree line. Most of the elevation gain is made in this last one km. The final steep pitch is through a forest of Engelmann spruce and larch into a hanging valley. A moraine running along the left side of the valley affords the best views of the glacier.

Goat Creek
- Length: 19 km (six hours) one-way
- Elevation loss: 370 meters
- Rating: easy/moderate

With prearranged transportation, this is an easy trail that gives hikers a real sense of achievement—walking from Kananaskis Country to downtown Banff. Beginning from the north end of the Spray Lake zone, the trail closely parallels Goat Creek for nine km to the confluence of the Spray River, which it then follows all the way to the grounds of the Banff Springs Hotel. This is also a good trail for mountain biking or cross-country skiing. It's downhill all the way.

PRACTICALITIES

Mount Engadine Lodge
This small lodge is south of Spray Lake near the Mt. Shark staging area. It comprises 12 rooms in the main lodge and two cabins set on a ridge overlooking an open meadow and small creek. The main lodge has a dining room, a comfortable lounge area, and a beautiful sundeck holding a hot tub. Breakfast is served buffet style, lunch can be taken at the lodge or packed for a picnic, and dinner is served in multiple courses of European specialties. Rates range from $110 per person for a room with a shared bathroom to $130 for a private bathroom. All meals are included in these nightly rates. The lodge is open mid-June to mid-October, over the Christmas break, and mid-February to mid-April.

Campground
As the name suggests, **Spray Lake West Campground,** the only campground in the Spray Lake zone, spreads out along the western shoreline of Spray Lake. Many of the 50-odd sites are very private, but facilities are limited to picnic tables, fire pits, and pit toilets. Sites cost $12 per night with firewood an additional $6 per bundle. It's open from when the snow clears (usually late May) to early September.

SIBBALD

This small area in the north of Kananaskis Country protects the rolling foothills that descend to the rich grazing land west of Calgary. Access is along Highway 68, which branches south off the TransCanada Highway 17 km west of the Cochrane intersection. Highway 68 climbs to the Jumpingpound Creek watershed, then crosses a low divide and descends to Highway 40, the main route through Kananaskis Country. It ends right by Barrier Lake. Sibbald is linked to the Elbow River Valley by the 35-km Powderface Trail—a rough, unsealed road usually passable by two-wheel drive.

Fishing is a popular activity in Sibbald. Sibbald Lake is stocked with rainbow trout and gets busy. To the west, Sibbald Meadows Pond is a quieter body of water, also stocked and surrounded by reeds. A couple of short trails leave from the picnic area at Sibbald Lake.

HIKING

Ole Buck Loop
- Length: 4.4 km (90 minutes) round-trip
- Elevation gain: 170 meters

• Rating: easy/moderate

This trail makes a loop around the south-facing slopes of Ole Buck Mountain, which rises to the northeast of Sibbald Lake. From the day-use area at Sibbald Lake, follow the trail that begins from the Sibbald Forestry Exhibit sign for one km. The Ole Buck Loop Trail branches to the left at this point, crossing a small stream from where the 2.4 km loop begins. Views from high points along the trail extend south to Moose Mountain.

Deer Ridge Circuit
• Length: 6 km (two hours) round-trip
• Elevation gain: 210 meters
• Rating: easy/moderate

From Sibbald Lake day-use area, take the trail south following the road for 100 meters, then skirting the south shore of Moose Pond to a trail junction. The left fork is the Eagle Hill Trail, while the trail to the right climbs steadily up Deer Ridge.

A short spur from the ridge leads to a lookout with views south to Moose Mountain. Returning to the main trail, turn left, descending along the north face of the ridge and back to the trailhead.

PRACTICALITIES

Sibbald Lake Campground offers 134 sites spread around five loops (Loop D comes closest to the lake). Amenities include pit toilets, drinking water, and a nightly interpretive program; $17 per site. Equestrian campers can park and camp at **Dawson Equestrian Campground,** a few km down Powderface Trail. This is a staging area for many horse trails; $17 per night. Both are open mid-May to mid-October.

For information, stop in at **Barrier Lake Visitor Information Centre,** in Kananaskis Valley, 403/673-3985; open daily 9 A.M.–6 P.M.

ELBOW RIVER VALLEY AND VICINITY

The Elbow River has its source at Elbow Lake (see "Hiking" in the Peter Lougheed Provincial Park section of this chapter), among the high peaks of Elbow-Sheep Wildland Provincial Park. As it cuts east through the foothills, the Elbow River Valley gradually opens up, ending near the picturesque hamlet of Bragg Creek. At higher elevations elk, bighorn sheep, and bears make their home. The main access is Elbow Falls Road (Hwy. 66) west from Bragg Creek. This road follows the Elbow River its entire 42-km length. It enters the zone after eight km, at Elbow River Valley Visitor Centre. Close to the eastern boundary lie two good fishing spots: **McLean Pond** and **Allen Bill Pond.** Both are stocked with rainbow trout. Moose Mountain, home to a fire lookout since 1929, can be seen north of the highway. Continuing west is six-meter-high **Elbow Falls,** the highest waterfall in Kananaskis Country. Just before the falls an unpaved road leads north to **Ing's Mine,** where a small coal mine operated 1915–20. Beyond the falls, the road first ascends through an area charred by a 1981 wildfire, then descends to its end at a camping spot and picnic areas.

HIKING

Sulphur Springs
• Length: 2 km (40 minutes) one-way
• Elevation gain: 200 meters
• Rating: easy/moderate

Park at Sulphur Springs Creek (just east of Paddy's Flat Campground) and follow the north bank of the small creek upstream, veering left at the cutline to reach the springs. Fed by sulphur-rich water, the springs were diverted through an iron casing in the 1930s.

Moose Mountain
• Length: 7 km (2.5–3 hours) one-way
• Elevation gain: 670 meters
• Rating: moderate/difficult

Rising to an elevation of 2,437 meters, Moose Mountain is the dominant peak in the Elbow River Valley area. Its summit provides 360-degree views over the entire region. To access the trailhead, find the unmarked gravel road 700 meters west of Paddy's Flat Campground. Follow this road north for seven km (if you reach a gate across the road, backtrack 500 meters to the trailhead). The trail follows an old fire-lookout road for four km, climbing steadily just below the ridgeline. It then descends before climbing again into an open meadow. Here begins the relentless slog to the domelike lower summit, from where it's another 100 vertical meters, via switchbacks or a direct climb up a ridge, to the upper summit and fire lookout.

Paddy's Flat
- Length: 2.2 km (40 minutes) round-trip
- Elevation gain: minimal
- Rating: easy

This interpretive trail begins from the end of the road in Loop B of Paddy's Flat Campground. It passes through a forest of lodgepole pine interspersed with white spruce before looping back around and following the Elbow River downstream, back to the trailhead. Numbered posts correspond with a brochure available at the trailhead.

Little Elbow
- Length: 2.5 km (50 minutes) one way
- Elevation gain: minimal
- Rating: easy

This interpretive trail explores a short stretch of the Little Elbow River, just before its confluence with the Elbow River. From the trailhead, at Forget-me-not Pond near the end of Elbow Falls Road, the trail passes between the road and the river then it continues upstream looping past interpretive boards that describe the river and the mammals that live along its length.

PRACTICALITIES

Campgrounds
Five campgrounds, with a combined total of 551 sites, lie along the Elbow River Valley, In 1998 the operation of these campgrounds was privatized, and as a result the cost of camping rose considerably.

The most-developed of the five is **McLean Creek Campground,** 12 km west of Bragg Creek and just south of Highway 66, by McLean Creek. At the campground entrance is a Camper Centre with groceries, coin showers, and firewood ($6 per bundle). Unpowered sites are $20 per night, powered sites $23. This is also the only camp-

ground along the valley that takes reservations; call **Elbow Valley Campgrounds,** 403/949-3132, or book online at www.evcamp.com. The other campgrounds and their distances from Bragg Creek are **Gooseberry** (10 km), **Paddy's Flat** (20 km), **Beaver Flat** (30 km), and, at the very end of the road, **Little Elbow** (50 km). The latter has facilities for campers with horses. Each of these campgrounds has only basic facilities—pit toilets and hand-pumped drinking water—but, still, sites are $17 per night. As at McLean Creek, firewood is available at $6 per bundle.

Information
Elbow Valley Visitor Information Centre, 403/949-4261, is at the entrance to the zone, 10 km from Bragg Creek. It's open May–September, 9 A.M.–5 P.M.

BRAGG CREEK

Bragg Creek is a rural hamlet nestled in the foothills of the Canadian Rockies, 40 km west of Calgary. It lies on the edge of Kananaskis Country, at the entrance to the Elbow River Valley. The town and its quiet, tree-lined streets are a far cry from the hustle and bustle of nearby Canmore and Banff, and provide an ideal retreat to kick back and relax in one of the mountains' true gems. The **Stoney Trail,** an Indian trading route that passed through the area, had been in use for generations when the first white people arrived in the early 1880s. The first settlers were farmers, followed by Calgarians who built weekenders in town. Today many of Bragg Creek's 900 residents commute daily to nearby Calgary. The ideal location and quiet lifestyle have attracted artists and artisans—the town claims to have more painters, potters, sculptors, and weavers than any similarly sized town in Alberta.

Sights and Recreation
White Ave., also known as **Heritage Mile** and originally the main commercial strip, is lined with craft shops, antique emporiums, and restaurants. This road continues southwest to 122-hectare **Bragg Creek Provincial Park,** a day-use area alongside the Elbow River, before continuing along the Elbow River Valley in Kananaskis Country.

© AVALON TRAVEL PUBLISHING, INC.

Wintergreen, 403/949-5105, is a four-season sporting facility six km north of town. It's immaculately manicured golf course features water hazards on 14 of the 18 holes, and four sets of tees designed to fit all levels of golfer. Greens fees are $55 on weekends, $45 weekdays, which includes use of an excellent practice facility. (The twilight rate of $50, which includes a cart and a steak dinner, is one of the better golfing deals in the Canadian Rockies.) A huge log clubhouse that overlooks the course is the epicenter for a great variety of other activities, including swimming in the outdoor pool, and mountain biking the adjacent ski slopes ($7 for an all-day trail pass; lifts operate in summer Thursday–Sunday 10:30 A.M.–8:30 P.M.), and a base of whitewater rafting and horseback riding. In winter a small ski area with five lifts and a vertical rise of 190 meters operates. Night skiing is offered on Friday and Saturday. Lift tickets are $28.

Accommodations and Food

Although lacking motels and campgrounds (closest camping is along the Elbow River Valley in Kananaskis Country), Bragg Creek has bed-and-breakfasts and a restaurant that attracts folk from Calgary. **Four Point Crossing,** 11 Elton Court, 403/949-2247, is a large country-style house nestled among stands of trees, yet is within walking distance of restaurants and shops. The home has a guest lounge with fireplace, a sundeck, and a hearty breakfast is included in the rates of $55 s, $70 d. Another option, this one out of town, is **Little Moose Mountain B&B,** 403/949-3564 or 877/949-3564, www.littlemoose mountain.com, which features two downstairs suites, each with separate entrances. Rates of $75 s, $85 d include a *huge* cooked breakfast of your choice served in your room. Call ahead for directions.

The **Steak Pit,** 43 White Ave., 403/949-3633, is a fantastic restaurant. The decor is early Canadian, yet realistic and elegant. The dining room, decorated with hand-hewn cedar furniture, is only a small part of the restaurant, which also has a café, lounge, sports bar, and gift shop. Eating here isn't cheap but *is* comparable to Calgary restaurants. The menu features mostly Alberta beef but has enough choices to please everyone. Open daily from 11:30 A.M. Bragg

Creek Shopping Centre holds a wide variety of eateries as well as most services. **Pies Plus,** 403/949-3450, specializes in meat and fruit pies at reasonable prices. Also in the shopping center is the **Powderhorn Saloon,** 403/949-3946, which serves good food and has a few pool tables, including a 10-pocket Fusion table shaped like a double diamond. Ask the manager how to play and he'll probably buy you a game. Across the river, out at Wintergreen, the clubhouse is open in summer for Sunday brunch 10 A.M.–2 P.M.

SHEEP RIVER VALLEY

The Sheep River Valley lies immediately south of the Elbow River Valley, in an area of rolling foothills between open ranchlands to the east and the high peaks bordering Elbow-Sheep Wildland Provincial Park to the west. Access is from the town of Turner Valley (take Sunset Blvd. west from downtown), along Highway 546. The Kananaskis Country boundary lies 25 km west of Turner Valley through rolling ranching land, from which point the highway follows the Sheep River for another 21 km to its confluence with Bluerock Creek. Much of the way, the highway passes through 54-square-km **Sheep River Wildlife Sanctuary,** set aside in 1973 to protect the winter range of bighorn sheep. The sheep spend summer further up the valley, and for hundreds of years have migrated down to the open slopes alongside the Sheep River each fall. Sheep are the most common large mammal in the valley; explorer David Thompson reported that the natives also named the valley for its sheep ("itou-kai-you" in their language).

Sheep River Falls, a few km before the end of the road, is reached by a short walk.

HIKING

Price's Camp
• Length: 5 km (1.5–2 hours) one-way
• Elevation gain: 50 meters
• Rating: easy/moderate
Although the trail itself is easy, it requires a fording of the Sheep River, is reached through a maze of cutlines and old logging roads, and can be muddy after rainfall. If all that hasn't put you off, head for the Sandy McNabb day-use area and wade across the river upstream of Coal Creek to reach the trailhead. Head west (to the right), following a grassy bench along the river, from which the trail enters a forest of lodgepole pine. When the trail crosses March Creek, head a few hundred meters up the north bank of the creek to this abandoned logging camp, a pleasant destination for a picnic lunch.

Foran Grade Ridge
• Length: 2.5 km (50 minutes) one-way
• Elevation gain: 190 meters
• Rating: easy/moderate
The trail up Foran Grade Ridge begins from a small pullout 1.5 km west of the winter closure gate at Sandy McNabb day-use area (between a Texas Gate–a cattle grid–and the Sheep River Wildlife Sanctuary sign). Climbing steadily, it traverses an open field and passes through an aspen forest before reaching the high point of the ridge. From here, views extend up the Sheep River Valley all the way to the Opal Range. The distance given above is to this first vantage point. An alternative to returning along the same route is to continue along the ridge for another 2.5 km, then descend the west side of the ridge to Windy Point Creek, which the trail follows downstream to Highway 40. Either walk back to the trailhead along the highway, or cross the road and link up with a trail running through the valley floor for a total trail length of 11 km.

PRACTICALITIES

Campgrounds
Along Highway 546 are two campgrounds. **Sandy McNabb Campround** is the first you'll come to, a short walk from the river right by the entrance to Kananaskis Country. It's named for an Albertan oil man who made an annual pilgrimage to this spot with his family. At the end of Highway 546, 21 km further west, is **Bluerock Campground,** where some sites are set aside for equestrian campers. Both campgrounds are primitive, with pit toilets

Sheep River Falls

and hand-pumped water. All 180 sites cost $17 per night and are open mid-May to early October. For reservations at Sandy McNabb Campground, call **Elbow Valley Campgrounds,** 403/949-3132, or visit www.evcamp.com.www.evcamp.com

Information
A small information center is in the ranger station at the entrance to the Sheep Valley zone. It opens in July and August only, daily 9 A.M.–5 P.M.; 403/933-7172.

HIGHWOOD/CATARACT CREEK

The Highwood/Cataract Creek areas stretch from Peter Lougheed Provincial Park to the southern border of Kananaskis Country. This is the least developed zone in Kananaskis Country. The jagged peaks of the Highwood Mountains are its most dominant feature; high alpine meadows among the peaks are home to bighorn sheep, elk, and grizzlies. Lower down, spruce and lodgepole pine forests spread over most of the zone, giving way to grazing lands along the eastern flanks. The main access from the north is along Highway 40, which drops 600 vertical meters in the 35 km between Highwood Pass and Highwood Junction. From the east, Highway 541 west from Longview joins Highway 40 at Highwood Junction. A lesser-used access is Highway 532, that branches west from Highway 22 37 km south of Longview. This unpaved road passes Indian Graves Campground then begins a steep climb to **Plateau Mountain,** high above the tree line and with stunning views back across to the Porcupine Hills. The main summer activities in this area of Kananaskis Country are hiking,

horseback riding, climbing, and fishing. Winter use is primarily by snowmobilers.

HIKING

Only a few formal hiking trails are signposted. The rest are traditional routes that aren't well traveled; many require river crossings.

Picklejar Lakes
• Length: 4.2 km (90 minutes) one-way
• Elevation gain: 470 meters
• Rating: moderate

The name of these lakes was coined by early anglers, who claimed fishing them was as "easy as catching fish in a pickle jar." The name stuck, and it's still mostly anglers who are attracted to the four lakes. They lie at the southern end of Elbow-Sheep Wildland Provincial Park. To access the trail, park at the Lantern Creek day-use area (not Picklejar day-use area), three km south of the Mist Creek day-use area, then cross the road and walk up the hill 100 meters. The trail is unmarked but easy to follow as it passes through a lightly forested area and open meadows to a ridge above Picklejar Creek. Descend and cross the creek, following its north bank up a steep, open slope, or stay high and right across a scree slope to reach the pass at 2,180 meters. The first lake is 300 meters beyond the pass. The trail continues past two more lakes before ending at the fourth, which is the largest and has incredibly clear water. A lightly marked trail encircles the fourth lake.

Zephyr Creek

- Length: 4.5 km (90 minutes) one-way
- Elevation gain: 180 meters
- Rating: moderate

The walk itself along Zephyr Creek is easy enough, but the trail only commences after a difficult ford of the Highwood River from Sentinel day-use area, east of Highwood Junction along Highway 541. From the picnic area, descend and wade across the river to an old logging road. Turn right, then keep left, climbing slowly into the valley through which Zephyr Creek flows. The trail crosses the creek twice before reaching a small cairn marking the entrance into Painted Creek Valley. Where the valley walls close in, 800 meters from Zephyr Creek, pictographs can be found on the rocky canyon wall, one meter up from the ground.

PRACTICALITIES

Campgrounds

All three campgrounds in the Highwood/Cataract Creek areas are south of Highwood Junction. **Etherington Creek** is seven km south of the junction, while **Cataract Creek** is a further five km south. Both offer primitive facilities including water, pit toilets, firewood, fire pits, and picnic tables; $17 per night. In the far south of the zone, along Highway 532, is **Indian Graves Campground.**

Services and Information

Highwood House, at Highwood Junction, has gas and a grocery store. It's open May–June, Friday –Sunday 9 A.M.–5 P.M.; July–September, daily 9 A.M.–8 P.M.; and October –April, weekends only 9:15 A.M.–5 P.M. The **Highwood Ranger Station,** also at the junction, is open in summer only, Thursday –Monday 10 A.M.–6 P.M.; 403/558-2151.

Step back in time at the Brisco General Store.

KOOTENAY NATIONAL PARK AND VICINITY

INTRODUCTION

Shaped like a lightning bolt, this narrow 140,600-hectare park lies on the British Columbia side of the Canadian Rockies. The park's northern section is bordered by Banff National Park and Assiniboine Provincial Park to the east and Yoho National Park to the north. Highway 93, extending for 94 km through the park, provides spectacular mountain vistas, and along the route you'll find many short and easy interpretive hikes, scenic viewpoints, hot springs, picnic areas, and roadside interpretive exhibits. The park isn't particularly noted for its day-hiking opportunities, but backpacker destinations such as Kaufmann Lake and the Rockwall rival almost any other area in the Canadian Rockies.

Kootenay has the fewest services of the four contiguous mountain national parks. Day-use areas, a gas station and lodge, and three campgrounds are the only roadside services inside the park. The small service town of Radium Hot Springs, at the junction of Highway 93 and 95 near the park's west gate, has a population under 600 but offers a range of accommodations, cafés and restaurants, gas stations, and grocery stores. Radium and its surroundings are covered in their own section at the end of this chapter. The park is open year-round, although you should check road conditions in winter, when avalanche-control work and snowstorms can close Highway 93 for short periods of time.

See color map of Kootenay National Park on pages x–xi.

PARK ENTRY

Permits are required for entry into Kootenay National Park. A National Parks Day Pass is adult $5, senior $4, child $2 to a maximum of $10 per vehicle. It can be used in Banff National Park and beyond, if that is your direction of travel, and is valid until 4 P.M. the day following its purchase. An annual Great Western Pass, good for entry into all 11 of western Canada's national parks, is adult $35, senior $27 to a maximum of $70 per vehicle ($53 for two or more seniors). Both types of pass are available from the western park gate, both park information centers, and campground kiosks. Annual passes can also be bought in advance by calling 800/748-7275 or online at the Parks Canada website, www. parkscanada.gc.ca.

THE LAND

Kootenay National Park lies on the western side of the Continental Divide, straddling the Main and Western Ranges of the Canadian Rockies. As elsewhere in the Canadian Rockies, the geology of the park is complex. Over the last 70 million years, these mountains have been pushed upward—folded and faulted along the way—by massive forces deep beneath the earth's surface. They've also been subject to erosion that entire time, particularly during the ice ages, when glaciers carved U-shaped valleys and high cirques into the landscape. These features, along with glacial lakes and the remnants of the glaciers themselves, are readily visible in the park today.

The park protects the upper headwaters of the **Vermilion** and **Kootenay Rivers,** which drain into the Columbia River south of the park.

Flora

In the lowest areas of the park, in the Kootenay River Valley, **Douglas fir** and **lodgepole pine** find a home. Along the upper stretches of the Vermilion River Valley, where the elevation is higher, **Engelmann spruce** thrive, while immediately above lie forests of **subalpine fir.** The tree line in the park is at around 2,000 meters above sea level. This is the alpine, where low-growing species such as **willow** and **heather** predominate. For a short period each summer, these elevations come alive with color as **forget-me-nots, avens,** and **avalanche lilies** flower. Of special interest is the Vermilion Pass Burn, where fire destroyed 24 square km of forest in 1968. Lodgepole pine is the dominant species here.

Fauna

Large mammals tend to remain in the Kootenay and Vermilion River Valleys. **White-tailed deer, mule deer, moose, black bears,** and **elk** live year-round at these lower elevations, as do **bighorn sheep,** which can be seen at mineral

Marmots inhabit boulder-strewn slopes throughout alpine areas of the Canadian Rockies. The area around the end of the Stanley Glacier Trail has a particularly large population.

licks along Highway 93. The most common large mammal present in Kootenay is the **mountain goat,** but these flighty creatures stay at high elevations, feeding in alpine meadows through summer. **Grizzlies** number around 10 within the park; they range throughout the backcountry, and occasionally are sighted in spring high on roadside avalanche slopes.

HISTORY

Although their traditional home was along the river valley to the south, the indigenous Kootenay people regularly came to this area to enjoy the hot springs—a meeting place for mountain and Plains bands. Natives called the springs Kootemik, meaning "Place of Hot Water." Early European visitors warped "Kootemik" into "Kootenay" and applied the name to the local residents. The natives traveled as far east as the Paint Pots area, to collect ocher for ceremonial painting purposes.

In 1905 Randolph Bruce, an Invermere businessman, persuaded the Canadian government and Canadian Pacific Railway to build a road linking the Columbia River Valley to the prairie transportation hub of Calgary so that western produce could get out to eastern markets. Construction of the difficult **Banff-Windermere Road** began in 1911. But with three mountain ranges to negotiate and deep, fast-flowing rivers to cross, the money ran out after the completion of only 22 km. In order to get the highway project going again, the provincial government agreed to hand over an eight-km-wide section of land along both sides of the proposed highway to the federal government. In return, the federal government agreed to finance completion of the highway. Originally called the Highway Park, the land became known as Kootenay National Park in 1920. The highway was finally completed in 1922 and the official ribbon-cutting ceremony was held at Kootenay Crossing in 1923; a plaque marks the spot.

SIGHTS AND RECREATION

ROAD-ACCESSIBLE SIGHTS

West from the Continental Divide

The eastern access to Kootenay National Park is Highway 93 (still known locally as the Banff-Windermere Highway), which branches west from the TransCanada Highway at Castle Mountain Junction, 29 km northwest of Banff and 27 km southeast of Lake Louise. From this point, Highway 93 climbs steadily for 11 km to the Continental Divide, crossing it at an elevation of 1,640 meters. The divide marks the border between Kootenay National Park to the west and Banff National Park to the east.

Immediately west of the divide is the **Vermilion Pass Burn.** Lightning started the fire that roared through this area in 1968, destroying thousands of hectares of trees. Lodgepole pine, which require the heat of a fire to release their seeds, and fireweed were the first plant species to sprout up through the charred ground. From the highway everything seems pretty dead, but along the 0.8-km **Fireweed Trail** you'll see the growth of a new forest on the floor of the old.

Marble Canyon

Be sure to stop and take the enjoyable self-guided trail, one km each way, which leads along this ice-carved, marble-streaked canyon. The walk takes only about 30 minutes or so, yet as one of several interpretive plaques says, it takes you back over 500 million years.

From the parking lot, the trail follows a fault in the limestone and marble bedrock through Marble Canyon, which has been eroded to depths of 37 meters by fast-flowing Tokumm Creek. As the canyon narrows, water roars down through it in a series of falls. The trail ends at a splendid viewpoint where a natural rock arch spans a gorge. Marble Canyon is also the trailhead for the Kaufmann Lake Trail (see "Hiking," below).

Paint Pots

A scenic one-km trail (20 minutes each way) leads over the Vermilion River to this unique natural wonder: three circular ponds stained red, orange, and mustard yellow by oxide-bearing springs. The natives, who believed that animal spirits resided in these springs, collected ocher from around the pools. They mixed it with animal fat or fish oil then used it in ceremonial body and rock painting. The ocher had a spiritual association and was used in important rituals. Europeans, seeing an opportunity to "add to the growing economy of the nation," mined the ocher in the early 1900s and shipped it to paint manufacturers in Calgary.

Several much longer hiking trails lead off the Paint Pots trail, including one of many routes to the Rockwall (see "Hiking," below).

To Kootenay Valley

Leaving the hot springs, the road parallels Sinclair Creek, crests 1,486-meter Sinclair Pass, and passes small Olive Lake, which is ringed with bright yellow wildflowers in summer. At **Kootenay River Viewpoint** you'll have a splendid view of the wild Kootenay River Valley 250 vertical meters below and the snowcapped mountains along the Continental Divide.

The highway then descends to the valley floor, passes two riverside picnic areas, and crosses the pretty Kootenay River at **Kootenay Crossing.** This was where the official ribbon-cutting ceremony opening the Banff-Windermere Road took place in 1923. Today you'll find a roadside historical exhibit, a number of hiking trails, and a warden's station. As you cross the river and pass small, green Kootenay Pond, your eyes will revel in views of milky-green rivers, lush grassy meadows, tree-covered hills, and craggy, snowcapped peaks; keep your eyes peeled for mountain goats. A bit further on, you'll come to a particularly nice picnic spot at Wardle Creek.

Radium Hot Springs

This was a popular destination for the early Kootenay people, who, like today's visitors, came to enjoy the odorless mineral water that gushes out of the foot of Redstreak Mountain at 44°C. Englishman Roland Stuart purchased the springs for $160 in 1890 and built rough concrete pools to contain the water. Development continued when a visiting millionaire—impressed by the improvement in his paralysis after soaking in the springs—contributed more money to the project. Originally known as Sinclair Hot Springs, after an early settler, the name was changed to Radium in 1915 for the high level of radioactivity in the water. With the declaration of Kootenay National Park in 1922, ownership reverted to

Relax in the pools of Radium Hot Springs.

the government. The latest renovations took place in the late 1990s, when the park information center was relocated to the grounds and the main pool was relined.

Today the water is diverted from its natural course into the commercial pools. Steep cliffs tower directly above the hot pool, whose waters are colored a milky blue by dissolved salts, which include calcium bicarbonate and sulfates of calcium, magnesium, and sodium. The hot pool is particularly stimulating in winter when it's edged by snow and covered in steam—your head is almost cold in the chill air, but your submerged body melts into oblivion.

The pools are open year-round. Summer hours are daily 9 A.M.–11 P.M.; the rest of the year noon–9 P.M. Admission is $6 for adults (day pass $8.25), $5 for seniors and children (day pass $7.25). Towel and locker rentals are available. Three short trails lead from the springs to Redstreak Campground. For information, call 250/347-9485.

From the hot springs, Highway 93 passes

through narrow **Sinclair Canyon,** descending quickly to the town of Radium Hot Springs.

HIKING

Some 200 km of trails lace Kootenay National Park. Hiking opportunities range from short interpretive walks (see "Sights," above) to challenging treks through remote backcountry. All trails start from Highway 93 on the valley floor, so you'll be facing a strenuous climb to reach the park's high alpine areas, especially those in the south. For this reason, many hikes require an overnight stay in the backcountry. The following hikes are listed from east to west.

Stanley Glacier
• Length: 4.6 km (two hours) one-way
• Elevation gain: 365 meters
• Rating: moderate
Although this glacier is no more spectacular than those alongside the Icefields Parkway just a few km away, the sense of achievement of traveling on foot makes this trail well worth the effort. From the trailhead on Highway 93, three km west of the park's eastern boundary, the trail crosses the higher reaches of the Vermilion River. It passes through an area burned by devastating fires in 1968 and climbs steadily until reaching a narrow rock-filled basin and the main glacier viewpoint. It's possible to continue another km up the valley to within 500 meters of the glacier's toe, but the going gets rough.

Kaufmann Lake
• Length: 15 km (five hours) one-way
• Elevation gain: 570 meters
• Rating: moderate
The overnight backpack trip to this beautiful lake in the extreme north end of the park begins at Marble Canyon parking lot. The trail follows Tokumm Creek the entire distance, passing through a forest of lodgepole pine before entering an open meadow and crossing many small waterways. Most elevation gain is made in the final two km, as the trail switchbacks up to the glacial cirque holding Kaufmann Lake. The exquisite lake is surrounded by peaks jutting as high as 3,400 meters. Two campgrounds lie at the end of the trail.

Marble Canyon is along the trail to Kaufmann Lake, but also makes a worthwhile destination in itself.

The Rockwall
• Length: 54 km (three days) round-trip
• Elevation gain: 760 meters
• Rating: moderate/difficult
This is one of the classic hikes in all the Canadian Rockies. The Rockwall is a 30-km-long east-facing escarpment that rises over 1,000 meters from an alpine environment. Four different routes provide access to the spectacular feature; each begins along Highway 93 and traverses a steep valley to the Rockwall's base.

The most popular trail starts at the Paint Pots and follows Helmet Creek 12 km to spectacular 365-meter Helmet Falls. A further 2.4 km takes you to the beginning of the Rockwall trail and a campground, the first of five along the route. The trail then follows the Rockwall in a southeasterly direction for 30 km, passing magnificent glaciers, waterfalls, and lakes, before ending at Floe Lake (see below), 10.4 km from the highway.

The Tumbling Creek and Numa Creek drainages provide alternative access routes to the Rockwall and require similar elevation gains. The elevation gain noted above is for the initial climb from the highway; along the route ascents are made to four additional passes, with elevation gains ranging 280–830 meters.

Hikers will need to make arrangements for shuttle transportation between the beginning and end of this route—about 13 km apart—or allow extra time to hike back. As elsewhere in the park, all hikers spending the night in the backcountry must register and pick up a permit ($6 per person per night) at either of the park information centers.

Floe Lake

- Length: 10.4 km (3.5 hours) one-way
- Elevation gain: 730 meters
- Rating: moderate/difficult

Of all the lakes in Kootenay National Park, this would have to be the most beautiful. Unfortunately, reaching it requires a strenuous day-trip or an overnight expedition. From the parking lot 70 km up Highway 93 from Radium Hot Springs, the trail follows Floe Creek, ascending the watershed through a forest of lodgepole pine and making many switchbacks before leveling off 400 meters before the lake. Nestled in a glacial cirque, the gemlike lake's aquamarine waters reflect the Rockwall, a sheer limestone wall rising 1,000 meters above the far shore. In fall, stands of stunted larch around the lakeshore turn brilliant colors, adding to the incredible beauty.

Dog Lake

- Length: 2.6 km (40 minutes) one-way
- Elevation gain: 80 meters
- Rating: easy

Dog Lake is no Mona Lisa, but it is a popular and easily reached destination, especially for those staying in McLeod Meadows Campground (if you're not camping, park at the picnic area 500 meters to the south). The trail first crosses the wide Kootenay River by footbridge. Then it hops a low ridge over to the shallow lake, which is fringed by marshes at the north end.

Kindersley Summit

- Length: 10 km (four hours) one-way
- Elevation gain: 1,050 meters
- Rating: difficult

The elevation gain on this strenuous day-hike will be a deterrent for many, but views from the summit will make up for the pain endured along the way. The trailhead is 10 km up Highway 93 from the park's west gate. From this point the trail climbs through a valley for about three km, then switchbacks up across a number of avalanche paths and through more forest before emerging at an alpine meadow on Kindersley Pass. The final two-km slog gets you 200 meters higher, to an elevation of 2,400 meters at Kindersley Summit, a saddle between two slightly higher peaks. This is where the scenery makes the journey worthwhile. You'll enjoy views west to the Purcell Mountains, east to the Continental Divide, and, most spectacularly, north over the Kootenay River Valley. An alternate return route to the valley floor follows Sinclair Creek down from Kindersley Summit. This cuts a couple of km off the return distance.

Juniper Trail

- Length: 3.2 km (one hour) round-trip
- Elevation gain: 90 meters
- Rating: easy

Named for the abundance of juniper along one section, this trail traverses a variety of terrain in a relatively short distance. You'll pass Sinclair Creek, an avalanche slope, and a lookout offering views of the Windermere Valley and the Purcell Mountains. The trail begins on the north side of the road just beyond the park information center and rejoins the highway 1.5 km farther into the park. There you can retrace your steps back to the start or return along the highway.

PRACTICALITIES

ACCOMMODATIONS AND CAMPING

Accommodations within the park are limited, but the town of Radium Hot Springs (see below) has a wide range of accommodations to suit all budgets.

Kootenay Park Lodge
This small lodge at Vermilion Crossing, 65 km from Radium Hot Springs, 403/762-9196, www.kootenayparklodge.com, is the only accommodation in the heart of the park. Although no railway passes through the park, the lodge was built by the C.P.R. in 1923. It consists of 10 log cabins, a restaurant, and a gas station/grocery store. Rates are $80–100, depending on cabin size. The lodge is open mid-May to September.

Addison's Bungalows
If you'd like the freedom of cooking your own meals and relaxing on a private balcony, consider staying at Addison's Bungalows, across the road from the hot springs, a few km east of the park gate on Highway 93, 250/347-9545 or 800/794-5024, www.addisonsbungalows.com. Each freestanding cabin contains a fully equipped kitchen, fireplace, balcony, and a barbecue, and some have hot tubs, making them good value at $90–120 s or d.

Campgrounds
The park's largest camping area is **Redstreak Campground** in the extreme southwest (vehicle access from Highway 93/95 on the south side of Radium Hot Springs township), which holds 242 sites, showers, and kitchen shelters. Trails lead from the campground to the hot springs, town, and a couple of lookouts. Unserviced sites are $17, hookups $22. Fire permits cost $4 per site per night. This facility is open mid-May through September.

The park's two other campgrounds—**McLeod Meadows,** 27 km from the west gate, and **Marble Canyon**—are much smaller and offer fewer facilities (no hookups or showers). They're open June–August and all sites are $13.

Hikers planning overnight trips in the back-country must register at either of the park information centers and pick up a Wilderness Pass ($6 per person per night).

INFORMATION

Kootenay Park Information Centre, at the hot springs, 250/347-9505, is an essential first stop. Here you can collect a free map with hiking-trail descriptions; find out about trail closures and campsite availability; get the weather forecast; buy topographical maps ($10 each) and national park fishing licenses ($6 for seven days); and register for overnight backcountry trips. The center is open in summer daily 9 A.M.–7 P.M., in June daily 9:30 A.M.–4:30 P.M., and in the early part of September Friday–Sunday 9:30 A.M.–4:30 P.M. A smaller visitor center, operated out of **Kootenay Park Lodge,** in the middle of the park, is open April–May, Friday–Sunday 11 A.M.–6 P.M.; June–September, daily 10 A.M.–6:30 P.M.; and the early part of October Friday –Sunday 11 A.M.–6 P.M.

For further park information, write the Superintendent, Kootenay National Park, P.O. Box 220, Radium Hot Springs, BC V0A 1M0, or call 250/347-9615; www.parkscanada.gc.ca/ kootenay. For park road conditions, call 403/ 762-1450.

Interpretive Program
In the peak summer months park naturalists present season free slide shows and talks four nights a week (usually Monday, Tuesday, Friday, and Saturday) at **Redstreak Campground** (see "Campgrounds" under "Accommodations and Camping," above). The programs usually start around dusk and typically feature topics such as wolves, bears, the park's human history, or the effect of fire. Dates and details are posted at campgrounds and information centers.

RADIUM HOT SPRINGS

The small service center of Radium Hot Springs (pop. 600) sits at the southwest entrance to Kootenay National Park, 103 km southwest of Castle Mountain Junction (Banff National Park). Its setting is spectacular; most of town lies on benchlands above the Columbia River, from which the panoramic views take in the Canadian Rockies to the east and the Purcell Mountains to the west. As well as providing accommodations and other services for park visitors and highway travelers, Radium is a destination in itself for many. The town is just three kilometers from the hot springs for which it is named, and boasts a wildlife-rich wetland on its back doorstep, two excellent golf courses, and many other recreational opportunities.

SIGHTS AND RECREATION

Columbia River Wetland
Radium sits in the Rocky Mountain Trench, which has been carved over millions of years by the Columbia River. From its headwaters south of Radium, the Columbia flows northward through a 180-km-long wetland to Golden, continuing north for a similar distance before reversing course and flowing south into the United States. The wetland by Radium holds international significance, not only for its size (26,000 hectares and up to two km wide), but also for the sheer concentration of wildlife it supports. Over 100 species of birds live among the sedges, grasses, dogwoods, and black cottonwoods surrounding the convoluted banks of the Columbia. Of special interest are blue herons in large numbers and ospreys in one of the world's highest concentrations.

The wetland also lies along the Pacific Flyway, so particularly large numbers of ducks, Canada geese, and other migratory birds gather here in spring and autumn. The northbound spring migration is celebrated with the **Wings over the Rockies Bird Festival,** which is held in the first week of May in conjunction with International Migratory Bird Day. The festival features a variety of ornithologist speakers, field trips on foot and by boat, workshops, and events

tailored especially for children, all of which take place in Radium and throughout the valley. For details, call 888/933-3311.

Golfing
The Columbia River Valley supports many golf courses and is marketed around western Canada as a golfing destination. Aside from the excellent resort-style courses and stunning Canadian Rockies scenery, golfers here enjoy the area's mild climate. Warm temperatures allow golfing as early as March and as late as October—a longer season than is typical at other mountain courses.

The 36-hole **Springs at Radium Golf Resort** is a highlight of golfing the Canadian Rockies, comprising two very different courses. One of them, the 6717-yard, par 72 Springs Course, is generally regarded as one of British Columbia's top 10 resort courses. It lies between the town and steep cliffs that descend to the Columbia River far below. Immaculately groomed fairways following the land's natural contours, near-perfect greens, and over 70 bunkers filled with imported sand do little to take away from the surrounding mountainscape. Greens fees are $55 for 18 holes (discounted after 2:30 P.M. Mon.-Thurs.). Call 250/347-6200 or 800/667-6444 for tee times. The resort's second course, the Resort Course, is much shorter, but tighter and still challenging. It is nestled in the shadow of the Rockies to the south of Radium, circling the resort's other facilities, which include accommodations (see below), tennis courts, and many other exercise facilities. Greens fees are $40. For tee times, call 250/347-6212 or 800/667-6444.

Other Recreation
The town of Radium Hot Springs is a base of operations for recreation opportunities outside the park. In summer, locals and visitors enjoy fishing and boating on nearby Windermere Lake. Whitewater-rafting trips are offered by **Kootenay River Runners,** 250/347-9210; from $68 for a half-day trip, $105 full-day. Horse fanciers can rent a ride at **Longhorn Stables,** one km north of town, 250/347-9755.

ACCOMMODATIONS AND CAMPING

Radium, with a population of just 600, has over 30 motels, an indication of its importance as a highway stop for overnight travelers. Those that lie along the access road to Kootenay National Park come alive with color through summer as each tries to outdo the other with floral landscaping.

$50–100

Kootenay Motel is along Highway 93, up the hill from the junction of Highway 95, 250/347-9490. The air-conditioned rooms are decorated simply and rent from $48 s, $55 d, $10 extra for a kitchenette. Also on-site is a barbecue area and pleasant gazebo.

Up the hill a little, across the road, and similarly priced, is **Valley View Motel,** 250/347-9565, with a pleasant outdoor barbecue area; from $50 s, $55 d.

Back across the road from the Valley View is the **Alpen Motel,** 250/347-9823 or 888/788-3891, which is probably the best-value accom-

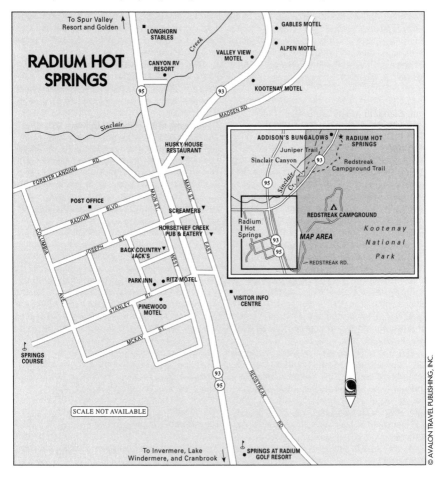

RADIUM HOT SPRINGS

To Spur Valley Resort and Golden

LONGHORN STABLES

GABLES MOTEL

ALPEN MOTEL

VALLEY VIEW MOTEL

CANYON RV RESORT

Creek

95

93

KOOTENAY MOTEL

Sinclair

MADSEN RD.

HUSKY HOUSE RESTAURANT

ADDISON'S BUNGALOWS

RADIUM HOT SPRINGS

Juniper Trail

Sinclair Canyon

93

Redstreak Campground Trail

95

Sinclair Cr.

FORSTER LANDING RD.

POST OFFICE

RADIUM BLVD.

MAIN ST.

SCREAMERS

REDSTREAK CAMPGROUND

Radium Hot Springs

Kootenay

HORSETHIEF CREEK PUB & EATERY

MAP AREA

National

COLUMBIA AVE.

JOSEPH ST.

BACK COUNTRY JACK'S

WEST ST.

EAST ST.

93

Park

95

REDSTREAK RD.

PARK INN

RITZ MOTEL

STANLEY

PINEWOOD MOTEL

VISITOR INFO CENTRE

MCKAY ST.

SPRINGS COURSE

93

95

REDSTREAK RD.

MOON

SCALE NOT AVAILABLE

To Invermere, Lake Windermere, and Cranbrook

SPRINGS AT RADIUM GOLF RESORT

© AVALON TRAVEL PUBLISHING, INC.

modation in town. The rooms are modern and the rates right; from $59 s or d.

Furthermost along this strip is the **Gables Motel,** Highway 93, 250/347-9866 or 877/387-7007, where each of the 19 rooms has mountain views and is well-furnished; $79 s or d.

A number of older motels lie in the residential streets west of Highway 93/95, and a couple are real cheapies. Least expensive of these is the **Pinewood Motel,** 4870 Stanley St., 250/347-9529 or 888/557-5567, which charges from $50 s or d.

The **Ritz Motel,** 4883 Stanley St., 250/347-9644 or 877/347-9644, is an older motel but the rooms are large, with separate sleeping areas. Some have kitchens and are air-conditioned. Rates range $50–60 s, $55–65 d.

The best of the bunch on the west side of the highway is the **Park Inn,** 4873 Stanley St., 250/347-9582 or 800/858-1155, www.parkinn.bc.ca, which features an indoor pool, a barbecue area. Standard rooms are $70 s, $80 d while those with kitchenettes are $90 s, $95 d.

$100–150

At the top end of the scale, **The Springs at Radium Golf Resort,** 250/347-9311 or 800/667-6444, www.springsresort.bc.ca, features one of the province's top golf courses as well as a health club, indoor pool, restaurant, and lounge. Regular motel rooms range $139–155, while kitchen-equipped condos sleeping up to six people start at $225 per night. Golf and ski packages lower rates considerably, especially before and after summer's peak season.

Campgrounds

Within Kootenay National Park, but accessed from Highway 93/95, is **Redstreak Campground** (see "Campgrounds" in the section on the park proper, above). The closest commercial camping is at **Canyon RV Resort,** on Highway 95, 300 meters north of the Highway 93/95 junction, 250/347-9564. Sites are spread along a pleasant creek and all facilities are provided; $17–22 per night. **Spur Valley Resort,** 18 km north of Radium along Highway 95, 250/347-9822, has sites set around a large grassy area; campsites are $14–20 per night, self-contained cabins $60. Tennis and golf facilities are available for guests.

FOOD

The town of Radium Hot Springs holds several good choices for a food break. Give all the fast-food places out by the highway junction a miss and head to **Springs at Radium Restaurant,** at the golf course on Stanley Street (on the west side of the highway), 250/347-9311. The view from the deck, overlooking the Columbia River and Purcell Mountains, is nothing short of stunning. The food is good and remarkably inexpensive; in the morning, for example, an omelette with hash browns and toast is just $7. Lunch and dinner are also well-priced, with a massive Caesar salad for $7 and main meals $10–18.50.

Back in town, **Back Country Jack's,** Main St. W., 250/347-0097, serves up well-priced steak, ribs, and chicken. And they'll deliver anywhere in Radium. Across the road, **Horsethief Creek Pub and Eatery,** Main St. E., 250/347-6400, serves up good pub-style fare. As always, **Husky House Restaurant,** at the corner of Highways 93 and 95, 250/ 347-9811, serves a good solid menu of typical Canadian fare at reasonable prices. This one is open daily 7 A.M. –11 p.m. Just around the corner is **Screamer's,** the place to hang out with an ice cream on a hot summer's afternoon. The ice cream here has been researched many times, most often when returning from camping trips in the Invermere area.

INFORMATION

On the east side of the Highway 93/95 junction is **Radium Hot Springs Visitor Info Centre,** 250/347-9331 or 800/347-9704, www.rhs.bc.ca. It's open weekdays year-round and in the busier summer months Monday–Thursday 9 A.M.–5 P.M., Friday 9 A.M.–8 P.M., Saturday–Sunday 10 A.M.–6 P.M.

NORTH FROM RADIUM ALONG ON HIGHWAY 95

From Radium, Highway 95 follows the Columbia River north for 105 km to Golden, from which the TransCanada Highway heads east, through Yoho National Park and across the Continental

Divide to Banff National Park. Between Radium and Golden are a number of small, historic towns worthy of a stop. The first is **Edgewater,** where a farmers market is held each Saturday. Continuing north is **Brisco,** gateway to the mountaineering mecca of Bugaboo Provincial Park. Named for a member of the 1859 Palliser expedition, Brisco was founded on the mining industry and later grew as a regional center for surrounding farmland. Brisco General Store is a throwback to those earlier times, selling just about everything. Nearby **Spillimacheen,** meaning "whitewater" to the natives, sits at the confluence of the Spillimacheen River and Bugaboo Creek.

SOUTH ALONG HIGHWAY 93/95

The highway south from Radium takes you 140 km to the city of Cranbrook, which sits on Highway 3, a major transprovincial route across the southern portion of British Columbia. This highway accesses four provincial parks, **Whiteswan, Top of the World, Elk Lakes,** and **Height of the Rockies;** these are covered in the chapter "Lesser-Traveled Parks of the Canadian Rockies."

Invermere and Vicinity
The commercial center of the Columbia River Valley is Invermere (population 3,000), 15 km south of Radium. Off the Invermere access road, toward Wilmer, a small plaque marks the site of Kootenae House. Established by David Thompson in 1807, it was the first trading post on the Columbia River. The valley's first permanent settlement, known as Athalmer, was alongside the outlet of Lake Windermere, but continual flooding led to the town's expansion on higher ground. The old townsite is now a popular recreation area, where a pleasant grassy area dotted with picnic tables runs right down to a sandy beach and the warm, shallow waters of the lake. It's on the left as you travel along the Invermere access road. As you approach the town itself, consider a stop at **Windermere Valley Museum,** 622 Third St., 250/342-9769, where the entire history of the valley is contained in seven separate buildings.

Golfers have been flocking to the Columbia Valley since the early 1990s, to 36-hole courses

at Radium and south of Invermere at Fairmont Hot Springs, but two courses have opened in consecutive years at Invermere, expanding their choices even further. **Eagle Ranch Golf Course,** between Highway 93/95 and Invermere, opened to much acclaim in the summer of 2000. The front nine is relatively short, with the longer back nine culminating in the 18th hole, where golfers are forced to hit over a deep ravine and then pitch to an elevated green overlooking Lake Windermere. Greens fees are $100. For bookings, call 250/342-0820 or 877/977-3889. Measuring a monstrous 7,140 yards from the back markers, **Greywolf Golf Course,** west of Invermere, 250/342-0820 or 800/663-2929, opened for the summer of 1999 and was voted best new Canadian course for that year by *Golf Digest.* Water comes into play on 14 holes, including the signature 6th hole, the "Cliffhanger." Greens fees are $90. Greywolf is part of a much larger development, **Panorama Mountain Village,** which is centered around a ski area that boasts the third-highest vertical rise of all North American ski areas (1,200 meters). Despite the impressive relief, Panorama offers slopes suitable for all levels of expertise including an additional 800 hectares that have opened since the 1995/96 season. Lift tickets are adult $45, child $28. For snow reports, call 250/345-6413. The village is also home to **R. K. Heli-ski,** 250/342-3889 or 800/661-6060, who can drop experienced skiers at the top of over 120 named runs spread through 2,000 square kilometers of the Purcell Mountains. This company is one of the few heli-ski operations that offers day trips.

Invermere holds motels, eateries, grocery stores, gas stations, a Greyhound bus depot, and a laundry. The motels downtown are a bit overpriced; the best option is **Delphine Lodge,** 250/342-6851, a couple of kilometers north in the small village of Wilmer. Restored to its former glory, this 19th-century hotel has been converted to a boutique bed-and-breakfast. The six guest rooms share bathrooms but are comfortable, and guests have the use of a private garden, lounge, and library. Rates of $55 s, $65–80 d include breakfast. If you prefer motel-style lodging, **Best Western Invermere Inn,** 1310 7th Ave., 250/342-9246 or 800/661-8911, offers the best rooms in town, as well as a restaurant and bar; from $85 s, $95 d. Accommodations in Panorama Mountain Village are all relatively new, and can be booked through the resort, as can all summer activities; call 250/342-6941 or 800/663-2929, www.panoramaresort.com.

The usual array of fast food joints line the access road into town, but Invermere is also home to **Strand's,** one of the best noncity restaurants in the province. It's contained in a restored 1912 heritage house set on landscaped gardens, with diners seated in small intimate rooms and offered an immaculately presented seasonal menu that often includes delicacies such as trout, salmon, and venison that are served with a wide selection of vegetables. It's at 818 12th Street (up the hill from 7th Ave.), 250/342-6344, and opens daily at 5 P.M.

Along the main drag, on the corner of 5th Street and 7th Ave., is **Invermere Visitor Info Centre,** 250/342-2844; open July–August, daily 9 A.M.–5 P.M. The website www.adventurevalley. com provides information about local recreational opportunities.

The everchanging gradient of the Kicking Horse River allows for an easy float or a heart-pounding ride down churning rapids.

YOHO NATIONAL PARK AND VICINITY

INTRODUCTION

Yoho, a Cree word of amazement, is a fitting name for this 1,313-square-km national park in British Columbia on the western slopes of the Canadian Rockies. The TransCanada Highway bisects the park on its run between Lake Louise (Alberta) and Golden (British Columbia). Banff National Park borders Yoho to the east, while Kootenay National Park lies immediately to the south.

Yoho is the smallest of the four contiguous Canadian Rockies national parks, but its wild and rugged landscape holds spectacular waterfalls, extensive icefields, a lake to rival those in Banff, and one of the world's most intriguing fossil beds. In addition, you'll find some of the finest hiking in all of Canada on the park's 300-km trail system.

Within the park are four lodges, four camp-grounds, and the small railway town of **Field,** where you'll find basic services. The park is open year-round, although road conditions in winter can be treacherous and occasional closures occur on Kicking Horse Pass. The road out to Takakkaw Falls is closed through winter, and it often doesn't reopen until mid-June.

THE LAND

The park extends west from the Continental Divide to the western main ranges of the Rocky

See color maps of Yoho National Park on pages x–xi.

PARK ENTRY

Unless you're traveling straight through and not stopping, a permit is required for entry into Yoho National Park. A National Parks Day Pass is adult $5, senior $4, child $2 to a maximum of $10 per vehicle. It can be used in the other national parks, and is valid until 4 P.M. the day following its purchase. An annual Great Western Pass, good for entry into all 11 of western Canada's national parks, is adult $35, senior $27 to a maximum of $70 per vehicle ($53 for two or more seniors). Both types of pass are available from the Field Visitor Centre and campground kiosks. Annual passes can also be bought in advance by calling 800/748-7275 or online at the Parks Canada website, www.parkscanada.gc.ca.

Mountains. The jagged peaks along this section of the Continental Divide—including famous Mt. Victoria, which forms the backdrop for Lake Louise—are some of the park's highest. But the award for Yoho's loftiest summit goes to **Mt. Goodsir** (3,562 meters), southwest of the Continental Divide in the Ottertail Range.

The park's only watershed is that of the **Kicking Horse River,** which is fed by the Wapta and Waputik Icefields. The Kicking Horse, wide and braided for much of its course through the park, flows westward, joining the mighty Columbia River at Golden. The park's many individual geological features of interest—such as Takakkaw and Twin Falls, Natural Bridge, Leanchoil Hoodoos, Emerald Lake, and Lake O'Hara—are covered under Sights and Recreation, below.

Flora

Elevations within the park cover a range of more than 2,500 meters, making for distinct vegetation changes, and over 600 recorded species of plants. **Douglas fir** is the climax species at lower elevations, but **lodgepole pine** dominates areas affected by fire. **Western red cedar, hemlock,** and the delightful **calypso orchid** can be found in the damp valley around Emerald Lake. At higher elevations, where temperatures are lower and precipitation is higher, the familiar subalpine forests of **Engelmann spruce** and **subalpine fir** thrive. The northernmost extent of **larch** exists around Lake O'Hara. Larch is a conifer (ever-

green), but its needles turn a stunning orange in fall—a photographer's delight. Above the tree line, where wind and rain have deposited soil, wildflowers such as **heather, Indian paintbrush,** and **arnica** create a carpet of color for a few short weeks midsummer.

Fauna

The animals for which Yoho is best known are fossilized in beds of shale and have been dead for over 500 million years. But they still create great interest for the role their remains have played in our understanding of life on earth in prehistoric times. (See the special topic, "Burgess Shale.")

Large mammals are not as common in Yoho as in the other parks of the Canadian Rockies, simply because the terrain is so rugged. Valleys are inhabited by **mule deer, elk, moose,** and **black bears,** as well as a wide variety of smaller mammals. **Porcupines** are common along Yoho Valley Road. The park has a healthy population of **grizzly bears,** but sightings are relatively rare as the grizzly tends to remain in remote valleys far from the busy TransCanada Highway corridor. Much of the park is above the tree line; here noisy **marmots** and **pikas** find a home, along with an estimated 400 **mountain goats.** Over 200 bird species have been recorded within the park.

HISTORY

The Kootenay and Shuswap tribes of British Columbia were the first humans to travel through the rugged area that is now the national park. It's believed the men hid their families in the mountains before crossing over to the prairies to hunt buffalo and to trade with other tribes. On their return they set up seasonal camps along the Kicking Horse River to dry the buffalo meat and hides. They used a more northern route than that taken by travelers today, crossing the divide at Howse Pass and descending to the Kootenay Plains beyond the present-day junction of Highways 93 and 11.

The first Europeans to explore the valley of the Kicking Horse River were members of the 1858 Palliser Expedition, which set out to survey the west and report back to the British government on its suitability for settlement. The party approached from the south, climbing the Kootenay and Vermilion watersheds of present-day Kootenay National Park before descending to Wapta Falls. It was here that the unfortunate expedition geologist, Dr. James Hector, inadvertently gave the Kicking Horse River its name. While walking his horse over rough ground, he was kicked unconscious and took two hours to come to, by which time, so the story goes, other members of his party had begun digging his grave.

Guided by outfitter Tom Wilson, Major A. B. Rogers (for whom Rogers Pass to the west is named) surveyed Kicking Horse Pass in 1881. His favorable report to the Canadian Pacific Railway led to this route being chosen for the much awaited transcontinental railway. The railbed was laid in 1884 and its grade was terribly steep; the first train to attempt the run suffered a brake failure and derailed, killing three workers. In 1909, after dozens more wrecks and derailments, the C.P.R. rerouted the steepest section of the line through the Spiral Tunnels (see below). The highway now follows the original rail grade.

The small township of Field started as a railway maintenance depot at the bottom of treacherous "Big Hill." In 1886 the Canadian Pacific Railway opened Mt. Stephen House in Field, both to encourage visitors to this side of the mountains and as a dining stop for customers of the railway. The C.P.R. then built lodges at several natural attractions in the area, including

BURGESS SHALE

High on the rocky slopes above Field is a layer of sedimentary rock known as the Burgess Shale, which contains what are considered to be the world's finest fossils from the Cambrian Period. The site is famous worldwide, for it has unraveled the mysteries of a major stage of evolution.

In 1909, Smithsonian Institute paleontologist Charles Walcott was leading a pack train along the west slope of Mt. Field, on the opposite side of the valley from the newly completed Spiral Tunnel, when he stumbled across these fossil beds. Encased in the shale, the fossils here are of marine invertebrates around 530 million years old. Generally fossils are the remains of vertebrates, but at this site some freak event—probably a mud slide—suddenly buried thousands of soft-bodied animals (invertebrates), preserving them by keeping out the oxygen that would have decayed their delicate bodies. Walcott excavated an estimated 65,000 specimens from the site. Today paleontologists continue to uncover perfectly preserved fossils here—albeit in far fewer numbers than in Walcott's day. They've also uncovered additional fossil beds, similar in makeup and age, across the valley, on the north face of Mt. Stephen.

Protected by UNESCO as a World Heritage Site, the two research areas are open only to those accompanied by a licensed guide. The Yoho–Burgess Shale Foundation guides trips to both sites between July and September. The access to "Walcott's Quarry" is along a strenuous 10-km trail that gains 780 meters in elevation. Trips leave Friday–Monday at 8 A.M. from the trading post at the Field intersection, returning at 6:30 P.M. $45 per person. Trips to the more easily reached Mt. Stephen Fossil Beds depart Saturday and Sunday at 10 A.M., returning at around 4:30 P.M.; $25 per person. The trail to the Mt. Stephen beds gains 520 meters of elevation in three km. The trails to both sites are unrelenting in their elevation gain—you must be fit. Reservations are a must; call 800/343-3006 Monday–Friday between 9 A.M. and noon. For further information, write Yoho–Burgess Shale Foundation, P.O. Box 148, Field, BC V0A 1G0, 250/343-6006.

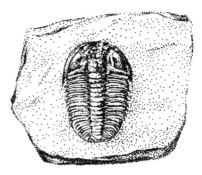

Bathyuriscus *fossil from neighboring Mt. Stephen*

Emerald Lake Lodge in 1902, **Lake O'Hara Lodge** in 1913, and **Wapta Lodge Bungalow Camp** in 1921.

Like adjacent Banff, the coming of the railway was a prime catalyst in the formation of Yoho National Park. Upon opening of the railway line in 1886, 26 square km of land around the base of Mt. Stephen was set aside as Mt. Stephen Park Reserve, Canada's second national park. In 1901 the reserve was expanded, and after three further boundary changes, the park of today came into being in 1930. Mining of lead, zinc, and silver continued until 1952, and today remnants of the Monarch and Kicking Horse mines can still be seen on the faces of Mt. Stephen and Mt. Field, respectively.

SIGHTS AND RECREATION

ROAD-ACCESSIBLE SIGHTS

As with all other parks of the Canadian Rockies, you don't need to travel deep into the backcountry to view the most spectacular features—many are visible from the roadside. The sights below are listed from east to west, starting at the park boundary (the Continental Divide). An alternative to taking the TransCanada Highway over Kicking Horse Pass is to travel Highway 1A, which begins from the road up to Lake Louise, rejoining the main highway just a couple of kilometers into the park. Along this road is **Divide Creek,** which does exactly that—the creek splits in two, with one side flowing west to the Pacific Ocean and the other east to the Atlantic Ocean.

Spiral Tunnel Viewpoint

The joy C.P.R. president William Van Horne felt upon completion of his transcontinental rail line in 1886 was tempered by massive problems along a stretch of line west of Kicking Horse Pass. "Big Hill" was less than five km long, but its gradient was so steep that runaway trains, crashes, and other disasters were common. A trail from Kicking Horse Campground takes you past the remains of one of those doomed trains.

Nearly a quarter century after the line opened, railway engineers and builders finally solved the problem. By building two spiral tunnels down through two km of solid rock to the valley floor, they lessened the grade dramatically and the terrors came to an end. Today the TransCanada Highway follows the original railbed. Along the way is a viewpoint with interpretive displays telling the fascinating story of Big Hill.

Yoho Valley

Fed by the Wapta Icefield in the far north of the park, the **Yoho River** flows through this spectacularly narrow valley, dropping more than 200 meters in the last kilometer before its confluence with the Kicking Horse River. The road leading up the valley passes the park's main campground, climbs a *very* tight series of switchbacks, and emerges at **Upper Spiral Tunnel Viewpoint,** which offers a different perspective on the tunnel described above. A further 400 meters along the road is a pull-out for viewing the confluence of the Yoho and Kicking Horse Rivers—a particularly impressive sight as the former is glacier-fed and therefore silty, while the latter is lake-fed and clear.

Yoho Valley Road ends 14 km from the main highway at **Takakkaw Falls,** the most impressive waterfall in the Canadian Rockies. The falls are fed by the Daly and Des Poilus Glaciers of the Waputik Icefield, which straddles the Continental Divide. Meaning "wonderful" in the language of the Cree, Takakkaw tumbles 254 meters over a sheer rock wall at the lip of the Yoho Valley, creating a spray bedecked by rainbows. It can be seen from the parking lot, but it's well worth the easy 10-minute stroll over the Yoho River to appreciate the sight in all its glory.

Natural Bridge

Three km west of Field is the turnoff to famous Emerald Lake (see below). On your way out to the lake, you'll first pass another intriguing sight. At Natural Bridge, two km down the road, the Kicking Horse River has worn a narrow hole through a limestone wall, creating a bridge. Over time, the bridge will collapse and, well, it won't be such an intriguing sight anymore. A trail leads to several viewpoints—try to avoid

Natural Bridge

the urge to join the idiots clambering over the top of the bridge.

Emerald Lake

Outfitter Tom Wilson stumbled upon stunning Emerald Lake while guiding Major A. B. Rogers through the Kicking Horse River Valley in 1881. He was led to the lake by his horse, which had been purchased from natives. He later surmised that the horse had been accustomed to traveling up to the lake, meaning that the horse's former owners must have known about the lake before the white man arrived.

One of the jewels of the Canadian Rockies, the beautiful lake is surrounded by a forest of Engelmann spruce, as well as many peaks over 3,000 meters. It is covered in ice most of the year, but comes alive with activity for a few short months in summer when hikers, canoeists, and horseback riders take advantage of the magnificent surroundings. **Emerald Lake Lodge** is the grandest of Yoho's accommodations, offering a restaurant, cafe, lounge, and recreation facilities for both guests and nonguests (see "Other Recreation" and "Accommodations and Camping," below).

LAKE O'HARA HIKING

"In all the mountain wilderness the most complete picture of natural beauty is realized at O'Hara Lake." So said alpinist Walter Wilcox in 1904, after having traveled throughout the Canadian Rockies. Visitors today are no less in awe of the lake. Nestled in a high bowl of lush alpine meadows, Lake O'Hara is surrounded by dozens of smaller alpine lakes and framed by spectacular peaks permanently mantled in snow. As if that weren't enough, the entire area is webbed by a network of hiking trails established over the last 90 years by luminaries such as Lawrence Grassi. Trails radiate from the lake in all directions; the longest is just 7.5 km, making Lake O'Hara an especially fine hub for day-hiking. The best area day hikes are detailed below.

The lake has been a popular destination since the early 1900s, when the C.P.R. began constructing trails and built a small lodge in a lakeside meadow. The lodge has since been moved and now sits right on the lakeshore, providing comfortable accommodations (see "Accommodations and Camping," below). Also at the lake are a campground and warden's cabin. Trail maps are available for $8 at the Lake O'Hara Lodge or the park information center.

Access to the lake is by shuttle bus from a parking lot 15 km east of Field and three km west of the Continental Divide. Buses run four times daily between mid-June and early October. Reservations are taken up to three months in advance at the Field Visitor Centre, 250/343-6433. The reservation fee is $10 and the fare is $12 per person round-trip. Six places are allotted each day on a first-come, first-served basis. Show up the day *before* you want to go, but be at the visitor center before it opens at 8:30 A.M. as there's usually a line for these tickets. You can also walk up the 13-km access road to the lake in about 3.5–4 hours; the elevation gain is 420 meters.

Lake Oesa
• Length: 3 km (one hour) one-way
• Elevation gain: 250 meters

Rating: easy/moderate
With the Continental Divide peaks of Mt. Victoria (3,464 meters) and Mt. Lefroy (3,423 meters) as a backdrop, this small aqua-colored lake surrounded by talus slopes is one of the area's gems. The trail begins on the north side of Lake O'Hara, nearly opposite the lodge, and climbs past a number of small lakes before entering the cirque in which Lake Oesa lies.

Opabin Plateau Circuit

• Length: 5.9 km (two hours) round-trip
• Elevation gain: 250 meters
• Rating: easy/moderate

Separated from Lake Oesa by 2,848-meter Mt. Yukness, this plateau high above tree line is dotted with small lakes. The time given above is an absolute minimum, for it's easy to spend an entire day exploring the alpine plateau and scrambling around the surrounding slopes. From the trailhead, 300 meters southeast of Lake O'Hara Lodge, the trail passes Mary Lake, climbing steeply and reaching the plateau in a little over two kilometers. The trail loops through the plateau before descending back into the subalpine forest and finishing on the Lakeshore Trail 600 meters from the lodge.

Lake McArthur

• Length: 3.5 km (80 minutes) one-way
• Elevation gain: 300 meters
• Rating: easy/moderate

This trail begins along the main access road, 200 meters north of Lake O'Hara Lodge. It crosses an open meadow, disappears into a dense forest of Engelmann spruce and subalpine fir, then climbs up to Schäffer Lake. At a junction beyond that lake, the left fork leads to Lake McArthur and the right fork to McArthur Pass. It's a steep final ascent to the lake, but the trail levels off and slopes gently down for the final 400 meters. Surrounded on two sides by steep cliffs, the large lake is fed by McArthur Glacier and reaches depths of over 80 meters. Check the status of this trail and the one up to and across the Odaray Plateau as recent changes have seen unofficial quotas put in place and frequent closures.

Odaray Plateau

• Length: 2.6 km (one hour) one-way
• Elevation gain: 280 meters

Rating: easy/moderate
For a panoramic overview of the Lake O'Hara area with a minimum of energy output, it's hard to beat Odaray Plateau, immediately west of the lodge. From the warden's cabin, the trail crosses open meadows and climbs steadily the entire distance to the lofty perch below Odaray Mountain. This trail is often closed as it passes through critical grizzly habitat; check the current trail status before heading out

Cathedral Basin

• Length: 7.5 km (2.5 hours) one-way
• Elevation gain: 300 meters
• Rating: moderate

The trail out to Cathedral Basin is the longest in the Lake O'Hara area, yet it's still an easy day trip for most people. From the Lake O'Hara campground the trail heads northwest, crossing Morning Glory Creek at the 2.4-km mark then passing large Linda Lake. The final ascent to Cathedral Basin makes a wide loop through an area of ancient rock slides. From this point, the magnificent panorama of the Lake O'Hara area and the backdrop of the Continental Divide are laid out to the southeast.

YOHO VALLEY HIKING

The valley for which the park is named lies north of the TransCanada Highway. As well as the sights discussed above, it provides many fine opportunities for serious day-hikers to get off the beaten track.

Twin Falls

• Length: 8 km (2.5 hours) one-way
• Elevation gain: 300 meters
• Rating: moderate

This trail takes over where the road through the Yoho Valley ends. Starting at the Takakkaw Falls parking lot, it continues up the Yoho River to Twin Falls, passing many other waterfalls along the way. At spectacular Twin Falls, water from the Wapta Icefield divides in two before plunging off an 80-meter-high cliff. Mother Nature may work in amazing ways, but some times she needs a helping hand—or so the Canadian Pacific Railway thought. In the 1920s, the company dynamited one of the channels to make the falls more

TAKAKKAW FALLS

Much discussion is made of which is Canada's highest waterfall. Della Falls, on Vancouver Island, also in British Columbia, is 440 meters high, but this drop is broken by a ledge. Takakkaw Falls is considerably lower, at 254 meters, but the drop is unbroken, which, officially, makes it Canada's highest. There is one thing of which there is no doubt: Takakkaw Falls will leave you breathless, much as it did famous alpinist Sir James Outram, and everyone who has viewed the spectacle since.

The torrent, issuing from an icy cavern, rushes tempestuously down a deep, winding chasm till it gains the verge of the unbroken cliff, leaps forth in sudden wildness for a hundred and fifty feet, and then in a stupendous column of pure white sparkling water, broken by giant jets descending rocketlike and wreathed in volumed spray, dashes upon the rocks almost a thousand feet below, and, breaking into a milky series of cascading rushes for five hundred feet more, swirls into the swift current of the Yoho River.

—Sir James Outram,
In the Heart of the Canadian Rockies

symmetrical. **Twin Falls Chalet** was built below the falls by the C.P.R. in 1923 and today offers hikers light snacks through the middle of the day.

Yoho Pass
- Length: 4.7 km (two hours) one-way
- Elevation gain: 530 meters
- Rating: moderate

The trail to Yoho Pass, which can be combined with the Iceline Trail (see below), begins on the west side of Whiskey Jack Hostel, 500 meters before the Takakkaw Falls parking lot. It leads 3.7 km to picturesque, spruce-encircled Yoho Lake, then continues another easy kilometer to the pass. The pass is below tree line, so views are limited. But from this point it's 5.5 km and

an elevation loss of 530 meters down to Emerald Lake; six km and an elevation gain of 300 meters to spectacular Burgess Pass; or 2.4 km north, with little elevation gain or loss, to an intersection with the Iceline Trail.

Iceline Trail
- Length: 6.4 km (2.5 hours) one-way
- Elevation gain: 690 meters
- Rating: moderate/difficultConstructed in 1987, this is one of the most spectacular day hikes in the Canadian Rockies. The length given above is from the trailhead at Whiskey Jack Hostel to the highest point along the trail. In the middle of this stretch you'll reach the trail's highlight—the four-km traverse of a moraine below Emerald Glacier. Views across the valley improve as the trail climbs to its 2,220-meter crest. Many day-hikers return from this point, although officially the trail continues into Little Yoho River Valley. Another option is to continue beyond Celeste Lake and loop back to Takakkaw Falls and the original trailhead, a total distance of 18 km.

EMERALD LAKE HIKING

Emerald Lake Loop
- Length: 5.2 km (1.5–2 hours) round-trip
- Elevation gain: minimal
- Rating: easy

One of the easiest yet most enjoyable walks in Yoho is around the park's most famous lake. The trail encircles the lake and can be hiked in either direction. The best views are from the western shoreline, where a massive avalanche has cleared away the forest of Engelmann spruce. Across the lake from this point, Mt. Burgess can be seen rising an impressive 2,599 meters. Park staff lead a guided hike around the lake every Saturday morning, departing at 10 A.M. from the parking lot trailhead.

Hamilton Falls
- Length: 800 meters (40 minutes) one-way
- Elevation gain: 60 meters
- Rating: easyThe trail to these falls begins from the Emerald Lake parking lot, down the hill from the bridge to the lodge. It's an easy walk through a forest of Engelmann spruce and subalpine fir to a viewpoint at the base of the falls. A little farther

along, the trail begins switchbacking steeply and offers even better views of the cascade.

The trail continues beyond the waterfall to **Hamilton Lake,** which lies in a small glacial cirque a steep 880 vertical meters above Emerald Lake. Total distance from Emerald Lake to Hamilton Lake is 5.5 km (2.5 hours) one-way.

Emerald Basin

- Length: 4.5 km (1.5–2 hours) one-way
- Elevation gain: 280 meters
- Rating: easy/moderate

The trail to the delightful Emerald Basin begins from the west shore of Emerald Lake, 1.5 km from the main parking lot. From there it's a steady three-km climb through a subalpine forest to the basin, which, chances are, you'll have to yourself. The most impressive sight awaiting you there is the south wall of the President Range, towering 800 vertical meters above.

HIKES IN OTHER AREAS OF THE PARK

Aside from Ross Lake, which is accessed from Highway 1A, the hikes detailed below are along the TransCanada Highway. The hike to the world-famous Burgess Shale is detailed in the corresponding special topic, **Burgess Shale.**

Ross Lake

- Length: 1.3 km (20 minutes) one-way
- Elevation gain: minimal
- Rating: easy

This small lake is easily reached from a trail that begins along Highway 1A just west of the Great Divide and two km east of the TransCanada Highway. The trailhead is relatively high, making the short trip an easy way to access a subalpine lake.

Paget Lookout

- Length: 3.5 km (90 minutes) one-way
- Elevation gain: 520 meters
- Rating: moderate

Beginning from a trailhead at the Wapta Lake picnic area five km west of the Continental Divide, the trail to this viewpoint is moderately strenuous but worthwhile for the panorama of the Kicking Horse River Valley. The first kilometer traverses a forest of Engelmann spruce. Then the

trail breaks out above tree line just below the lookout, the site of an abandoned fire tower. As an alternative, branch right 1.4 km along the trail and continue two km to **Sherbrooke Lake,** which is fed by the Waputik Icefield.

Hoodoo Trail

- Length: 3 km (60–90 minutes) one-way
- Elevation gain: 460 meters
- Rating: moderate

Hoodoos are found in varying forms throughout the Canadian Rockies, but this outcrop, officially known as the Leanchoil Hoodoos, is among the most impressive. Hoodoos are formed by the erosion of relatively soft rock from beneath a cap of harder, more weather-resistant rock. Although these examples require some effort to reach, their intriguing appearance makes the trip worthwhile. The trail begins from Hoodoo Creek Campground, 23 km southwest of Field. The first half of the trail is relatively flat, leaving all the elevation gain to be made in the last, painful 1.5 km.

Wapta Falls

- Length: 2.4 km (45 minutes) one-way
- Elevation loss: minimal
- Rating: easy

This trail begins from the end of a two-km access road leading south off the TransCanada Highway in the park's extreme southwestern corner. It follows an old fire road for a bit, then narrows for the easy stroll through thick forest to a viewpoint above the falls. A steep descent leads to a lower viewpoint.

OTHER RECREATION

Boating and Fishing

No river or stream is particularly well known for fishing, mainly because most of the water is glacially derived and therefore heavily silt-laden. Species present in the park's lakes and rivers include Dolly Varden and rainbow, lake, and cutthroat trout. A national park **fishing permit** costs $6 for seven days or $13 annually. **Emerald Sports,** on the shore of Emerald Lake, 250/343-6000, rents canoes and small boats for $30 per hour or $45 all day. Fishing in Emerald Lake isn't world-class, but there are some trout in the waters and Emerald Sports offers a range of fishing tackle for rent or sale.

Horseback Riding
Emerald Lake Stables, at the lake of the same name, rents horses. A one-hour trip around Emerald Lake costs $28. Two-hour rides are $44, three-hour rides $60, lunch rides $80, and all-day rides with dinner go for $105.

Wintertime
The TransCanada Hwy. through the park is open year-round, but facilities are only open June through mid-September. Some of the trails at higher elevations are impassable until July. Wintertime attracts cross-country skiers who happily slide along the Yoho Valley to frozen Takakkaw Falls, or follow the Lake O'Hara trails.

PRACTICALITIES

ACCOMMODATIONS AND CAMPING

Emerald Lake Lodge
The extensive grounds of this grand, luxury-class accommodation lie along the southern shore of one of the Canadian Rockies' most magnificent lakes. The original lodge was built in 1902 in the same tradition as the Chateau Lake Louise and Banff Springs Hotel—as a playground for wealthy railway travelers. No original buildings remain (although the original framework is made use of in the main building). In 1986 the lodge underwent considerable renovation and expansion. It now boasts 85 units, as well as a hot tub and sauna, swimming pool, restaurant, lounge, and café. Guests can also go horseback riding, or go boating and fishing on Emerald Lake. The rooms are large and many of the more expensive ones are on the lakefront. Rates range $300–460 per night, with sharp discounts in the off-season. For bookings, call 250/343-6321 or 800/663-6336, or visit www.crmr.com.

Kicking Horse Lodge
In the small railway town of Field, simple yet elegant Kicking Horse Lodge, 100 Centre St., 250/343-6303 or 800/659-4944, offers 14 well-furnished rooms, a large comfortable lounge, and a restaurant (open in summer only). In summer, rates are $112–132 s or d (discounted as low as $60 s or d in the off-season) —a great alternative to higher-priced Lake Louise or Banff for skiers.

Cathedral Mountain Lodge and Chalets
Comprising 20 rustic cabins set around a main lodge alongside the Kicking Horse River, this is the most basic of the park's accommodations. Each unit has a fully equipped kitchen and some have private bathrooms. A restaurant and grocery store are on the premises. The chalets are open in summer only; rates range $139–189 s or d. For bookings, call 250/343-6442. In the off-season, call 403/762-0514. The lodge's website is www.cathedralmountain.com.

Lake O'Hara Lodge
This lodge set around beautiful Lake O'Hara allows hikers not equipped for overnight camping the opportunity to explore the backcountry on leisurely day hikes. Located 13 km from the road, the lodge transports guests via shuttle bus to and from a parking lot three km west of the Continental Divide and 15 km east of Field. The 15 cabins, each with a private bathroom, are spread around the lakeshore while within the main lodge are eight rooms, most of which are twins and share bathrooms. Rates of $350 d for a room in the main lodge (shared bathrooms) and $475 d for lakeside cabin include all meals mid-June to September. Between February and April, the eight rooms in the main lodge are available for cross-country skiers at a reduced rate. The lodge books up well in advance; for reservations, call 250/343-6418 (call 403/678-4110 in the off-season), or visit www.lakeohara.com.

Hostel
Hostelling International operates **Whiskey Jack Hostel** near Takakkaw Falls. Formerly cabins used by the C.P.R., then staff quarters for a privately run lodge that was destroyed by an avalanche, the hostel provides basic dormitory accommodations for up to 27 guests,

who have use of a communal kitchen and showers. Members of Hostelling International pay $15 per night, nonmembers $19. Book through Banff International Hostel at 403/762-4122. The daily shuttle service between Calgary and Jasper via the Icefields Parkway makes a detour via Whiskey Jack Hostel. Check in is 5–11 P.M. This hostel is only open mid-June to September.

Campgrounds

The park's main camping area is **Kicking Horse Campground**, five km northeast of Field along the road to Takakkaw Falls. Facilities include showers, flush toilets, and kitchen shelters. Unserviced sites are $14, hookups $18. The campground is open mid-May to mid-October. Back toward the TransCanada Highway, an overflow area with more limited facilities is also open for winter camping. At the end of the same road, **Takakkaw Falls Campground** is designed for tent campers only. Park at the very end of the road and load up the carts with your gear for a pleasant 400-meter walk along the valley floor. No showers are provided, and the only facilities are pit toilets and picnic tables; $13 per site.

Hoodoo Creek Campground, along the TransCanada Highway 23 km southwest of Field, provides sheltered private spots among the trees; $15 per night. A few hundred meters farther west is the turnoff to **Chancellor Peak Campground,** beside the Kicking Horse River; $13 per night.

Just north of Lake O'Hara is a 30-site campground with two kitchen shelters and woodstoves. Camping is $6 per person per night plus a daily fee of $4 per site for firewood. Reservations for sites can be made at 250/343-6433 up to 30 days in advance. A few sites are left open on a first-come, first-served basis.

Primitive wilderness campsites are scattered throughout the backcountry. Users must obtain a permit from the Park Information Centre; $6 per person per night.

FOOD

Overlooking Emerald Lake, **Cilantro on the Lake** is a casual-style café featuring magnifi-

Cilantro on the Lake, at Emerald Lake Lodge

cent views from tables inside and out. The menu is varied—you can sit and sip a coffee or have a full lunch. Pastas range $8–15, grills are around $20, and sandwiches and salads $6–10. (The corn and potato chowder is particularly good.) Within the main lodge you'll find a more formal dining room and a bar.

In Field, the **Kicking Horse Lodge,** 250/343-6303, has a small restaurant which has views over the valley floor. It features a short but varied menu, and is open throughout the day. Across the road is a general store offering hot takeout meals.

The final option for park dining is the restaurant at **Cathedral Mountain Chalets,** 250/343-6442, a casual, inexpensive restaurant open daily through summer 7 A.M.–10 P.M. Breakfast comprises healthy choices such as fresh fruit, croissants, and home-baked bread, then it's soup and sandwiches through to the evening, when a basic menu of chicken, beef, and seafood is offered.

TRANSPORTATION

Transportation to and around the park is limited. **Greyhound,** 403/762-6767 or 800/661-8747, stops in Field daily on its route between Banff and Golden, from where it continues west to Vancouver. **Brewster,** 403/762-6767, offers a 3.5-hour tour of the park, departing Lake Louise daily at 12:35 P.M. (summer only). This tour takes in both the Yoho Valley and Emerald Lake. The cost is $53 per person. Brewster's Mountain Lakes and Canyons Tour is an extended version of the above tour, combining the best of Banff National Park with a trip over the divide into Yoho. It departs the Banff depot mid-May to mid-October daily at 8:10 A.M. through summer. The tour takes 9.5 hours and costs $76 per person.

INFORMATION

The main source of information about the park is the **Field Visitor Centre** on the TransCanada Highway at Field, 250/343-6783. This is also the place to book the bus trip up to Lake O'Hara, pick up backcountry camping permits, buy topographical maps, and find out schedules for the interpretive programs. The center is open in peak summer season, daily 8:30 A.M.–7 P.M.; May–June and September, daily 9 A.M.–5 P.M.; the rest of the year 9 A.M.–4 P.M. For more information, write Yoho National Park, P.O. Box 99, Field, BC V0A 1G0; or surf the Internet to the park's website, www.parkscanada.gc.ca/yoho. For park road conditions, call 403/762-1450; for avalanche reports, call 762-1460.

GOLDEN

From the western boundary of Yoho National Park, the TransCanada Highway meanders down the beautiful Kicking Horse River Valley to the railway and service town of Golden (pop. 5,200), which lies at the confluence of the Kicking Horse and Columbia Rivers. The town makes a good central base for exploring the region, being just a short drive from both Yoho and Glacier National Parks. Golden is an industrial town through and through, with three local mines and huge logging operations, including a new lumber mill that opened in 1999, but it's also gaining a reputation for local outdoor-recreation opportunities, most notably for whitewater-rafting trips down the Kicking Horse River and its new four-season resort.

SIGHTS AND RECREATION

Take Highway 95 off the TransCanada Highway and you'll find yourself in the old section of town, a world away from the commercial strip along the main highway. There's not really much to see in town, although you may want to check out the small museum on 14th Street. The **Columbia River Wetlands** (see "Sights and Recreation" under "Radium Hot Springs" in the Kootenay National Park and Vicinity chapter) extend as far north as Golden. One easily accessible point of the wetlands is **Reflection Lake,** on the southern outskirts of Golden. Here you'll find a small shelter with a telescope for viewing the abundant bird life.

Whitewater Rafting

Anyone looking for whitewater-rafting action will want to run the Kicking Horse River. The rafting season runs late May–mid-September, with river levels at their highest in late June. The Lower Canyon, immediately upstream of Golden, offers the biggest thrills, including a three-km stretch of continuous rapids. Upstream of here the river is tamer but still makes for an exciting trip, while even further upstream, near the western boundary of Yoho National Park, it's more a float—a good adventure for the more timid visitor. The river is run by a number of companies, most of which offer the option of half-day ($55–74) or full-day ($80–100) trips. The cost varies with inclusions such as transportation from Banff and lunch.

Whitewater Voyageurs, based at the Golden Rim Motor Inn, 1416 Golden View Road (just off the TransCanada Hwy. east of downtown), 250/344-7335 or 800/667-7238, is one of the original operators. They offer half- and full-day trips as well as transportation from Lake Louise. **Alpine Rafting,** 250/344-6778 or 888/599-5299, has an office by the Husky gas station in Golden. They offer a wide variety of trips, including an

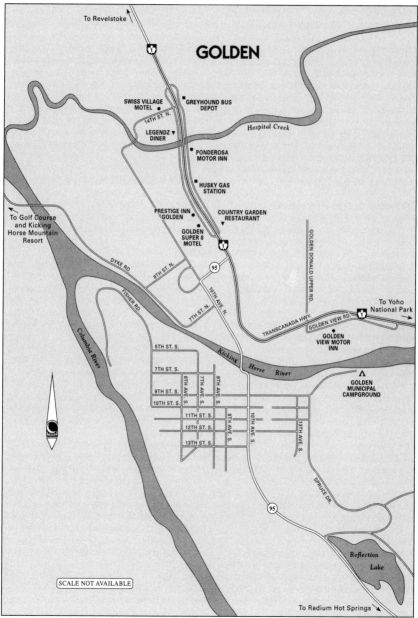

GOLDEN

To Revelstoke

Hospital Creek

SWISS VILLAGE MOTEL

GREYHOUND BUS DEPOT

14TH ST. N.

LEGENDZ DINER

PONDEROSA MOTOR INN

HUSKY GAS STATION

PRESTIGE INN GOLDEN

COUNTRY GARDEN RESTAURANT

GOLDEN SUPER 8 MOTEL

To Golf Course and Kicking Horse Mountain Resort

DYKE RD.

9TH ST. N.

FISHER RD.

7TH ST. N.

10TH AVE. N.

95

GOLDEN DONALD UPPER RD.

TRANSCANADA HWY.

GOLDEN VIEW RD.

To Yoho National Park

GOLDEN VIEW MOTOR INN

Columbia River

Kicking Horse River

5TH ST. S.

7TH ST. S.

9TH ST. S.

10TH ST. S.

6TH AVE. S.

7TH AVE. S.

8TH AVE. S.

11TH ST. S.

12TH ST. S.

13TH ST. S.

9TH AVE. S.

10TH AVE. S.

13TH AVE. S.

GOLDEN MUNICIPAL CAMPGROUND

MOON

SPRUCE DR.

95

SCALE NOT AVAILABLE

Reflection Lake

To Radium Hot Springs

© AVALON TRAVEL PUBLISHING, INC.

easy float and a trip down the Lower Canyon. Transportation from Banff and Lake Louise is an extra charge. Also based in Golden is **Wet 'n' Wild Adventures,** 250/344-6546 or 800/668-9119. This company offers transportation from Banff, but at an extra charge and only for their full-day trips. **Rocky Mountain Rafting Company,** 250/344-6979 or 888/518-7238, offers a variety of combinations, as well as providing transportation from as far away as Canmore. From Lake Louise, **Wild Water Adventures,** 403/522-2211 or 888/647-6444, leads half-day trips down the river for $64, including a narrated bus trip to the put-in point and a light snack. Departures are from Lake Louise at 8:30 A.M. and 1:30 P.M.

Other Summertime Recreation

Golden Golf and Country Club is a challenging 18-hole course set in a forested section of the valley through town and to the north. This course is generally in excellent condition, with water coming into play on many holes, and numerous streams and lakes to catch wayward shots. Greens fees are $48, or there's a $28 twilight rate. For tee times, call 250/344-2700.

Willow Ridge Riding, along Neville Road (off Blaeberry School Rd.), 250/344-7365, is a small horseback riding operation offering 1.5-, 2-, and 3-hour rides along the lower eastern slopes of the Canadian Rockies.

Adventurous souls are drawn to Golden for its thermals, perfect for hang-gliding and paragliding, and to the steep face of Jubilee Mountain, a renowned sport-climbing destination. A different type of Canadian, cowboys, descend on town the first weekend of August for **Golden Rodeo Days.**

Check out the offices of **Golden Mountain Adventures,** beside the Husky gas station, 250/344-6281 or 800/433-9533, for the full range of activities available. This company can also book packages using local operators and accommodations.

Wintertime

What was formerly locally owned Whitetooth Ski Area, spread across the lower slopes of the Purcell Mountains (the runs are easily spotted across the valley as you enter town from the east) is currently undergoing a massive redevelopment program slated for completion in 2007. As well as a new name, **Kicking Horse Mountain Resort,** the old area is basically being rebuilt from scratch, with $75 million invested in new lifts, luxurious ski-in, ski-out hotels, condominiums, restaurants, and other facilities that will make the resort a year-round destination. The first stage of the development, the 8-person Golden Eagle Express, opened for the 2000/01 ski season. Tickets are $40 for adults, $32 seniors and students, $14 children.When completed the resort will have a vertical rise of 1,250 meters (second highest in North America) and over 1,600 hectares of terrain.

ACCOMMODATIONS AND CAMPING

It's easy to find a place to stay in Golden—the town holds over 20 motels, most of which lie right along the TransCanada Highway.

$50–100

Ponderosa Motor Inn, on the TransCanada at the west entrance to town, 250/344-2205, www.ponderosamotorinn.bc.ca, has older rooms, but is set on two-hectares of landscaped gardens, with impressive mountain views, a hot tub, a picnic area, and a playground, making it good value at just $55 s, $60 d.

Similarly priced, and on the same side of town, is **Swiss Village Motel,** 250/344-2276; $56 s, $62 d, with kitchenettes an additional $8.

Golden Super 8 Motel, 1047 TransCanada Highway, 250/344-0888 or 800/800-8000, www.super8.com, is a modern air-conditioned facility where breakfast is included in the rates of $90 s or d.

Blaeberry Mountain Lodge, nine km north of Golden along Highway 1 then seven km farther north along Moberly School Road, 250/344-5296, is set on a 62-hectare property among total wilderness. Rooms are in the main lodge or self-contained cabins, with plenty of activities available to guests. Standard rooms with shared bathroom are $60 s or d, ensuite rooms $75, and the cabins, which sleep four, are $120. Breakfast and dinner are offered for $10 and $20 respectively.

$100–150

Next door to the Super 8 is **Prestige Inn Golden,** 1049 TransCanada Highway, 250/344-7990 or 877/737-8443, www.prestigeinn.com, where you'll find the town's highest-standard rooms, along with views that extend well down the Columbia Valley. Amenities include an indoor pool, hot tub, fitness center, lounge, and restaurant. Rates range $110–150 s or d.

Campgrounds
Down beside the Columbia River you'll find **Golden Municipal Campground,** on 9th Street S. (turn at the one traffic light in town), 250/344-5412. It's a quiet place with adequate facilities, including a pool and tennis court next door. Unpowered sites are $13, powered sites $15. Golfers can stay out at the golf course in a specially developed area for $12 per night.

OTHER PRACTICALITIES

Food
All the usual fast-food places line the Trans-Canada Highway, but the best option is **Legendz Diner,** on the west side of the Trans-Canada Highway, 250/344-5059. As the name suggests, it's a 1950s-style diner complete with attentive staff and good, filling meals from $8. Across the road, **Country Garden Restaurant,** 1002 Trans Canada Highway, 250/344-5971, is a large, casual family-style restaurant with an excellent range of buffets throughout the day, including dinner for $17.

Transportation
Greyhound buses stop four times daily in Golden, utilizing an ATCO trailer tucked away beside the ESSO gas station as a depot, 250/344-6172.

Information
Golden Visitor Info Centre is in the old railway station building at 500 10th Avenue, 250/344-7125 or 800/622-4653. It's open year-round, weekdays 8:30 A.M.–4:30 P.M.

Athabasca Glacier, Columbia Icefield

JASPER NATIONAL PARK

INTRODUCTION

Snowcapped peaks, vast icefields, beautiful glacial lakes, soothing hot springs, thundering rivers, and the most extensive backcountry trail system of any Canadian national park make Jasper a stunning counterpart to its sister park, Banff. Lying on the Albertan side of the Canadian Rockies, Jasper protects the entire upper watershed of the Athabasca River, extending to the Columbia Icefield (and Banff National Park) in the south. To the east are the foothills, to the west the Continental Divide (which marks the Alberta/British Columbia border) and Mt. Robson Provincial Park. Encompassing 10,900 square km, Jasper is a haven for wildlife; much of its wilderness is traveled only by wolves and grizzlies.

The park's most spectacular natural landmarks can be admired from two major roads. The **Yellowhead Highway** runs east-west from Edmonton to British Columbia through the park. The **Icefields Parkway,** regarded as one of the world's great mountain drives, runs north-south,

connecting Jasper to Banff. At the junction of these two highways is the park's main service center—the townsite of Jasper. Run by Parks Canada, Jasper has half the population of Banff, and its setting—at the confluence of the Athabasca and Miette Rivers, surrounded by rugged, snowcapped peaks—is a little less dramatic, though still very beautiful. But the town is also less commercialized than Banff and its streets a little quieter—a major plus for those looking to get away from it all.

Many of the park's campgrounds are accessible by road, while others dot the backcountry. Fishing, boating, downhill skiing, golfing, horseback riding, and whitewater rafting are all popular here.

The park is open year-round, although road

See color maps of Jasper National Park on pages xii–xiii.

PARK ENTRY

Permits are required for entry into the park. A National Parks Day Pass is adult $5, senior $4, child $2 to a maximum of $10 per vehicle. It can be used in Banff if you're traveling down the Icefields Parkway, and is valid until 4 P.M. the day following its purchase. An annual Great Western Pass, good for entry into all 11 of western Canada's national parks, is adult $35, senior $27 to a maximum of $70 per vehicle ($53 for two or more seniors). Both types of pass can be purchased at the park information center, at the booth along the Icefields Parkway a few km south of Jasper townsite, and at campground kiosks. Day Passes can also be bought at the 24-hour Automated Pass Machines at strategic spots through the park. Annual passes can also be bought in advance by calling 800/748-7275 or online at the Parks Canada website, www.parkscanada.gc.ca.

closures do occur on the Icefields Parkway during winter months due to avalanche-control work and snowstorms.

THE LAND

Although the peaks of Jasper National Park are not particularly high, they are among the most spectacular along the range's entire length. About 100 million years ago, layers of sedimentary rock—laid down here up to a billion years ago—were forced upward, folded, and twisted under tremendous pressure into the mountains seen today. The land's contours were further altered during four ice ages that began around a million years ago. The last ice age ended about 10,000 years ago, and the vast glaciers began to retreat. A remnant of this final sheet of ice is the huge Columbia Icefield; covering approximately 325 square km and up to 400 meters deep, it's the most extensive icefield in the Rocky Mountains. As the glaciers retreated, piles of rock melted out and were left behind. Meltwater from the glaciers flowed down the valleys and was dammed up behind the moraines. **Maligne Lake,** like many other lakes in the park, was created by this process. The glacial silt suspended in the lake's waters produces amazing emerald, turquoise, and amethyst colors; early artists who

painted these lakes had trouble convincing people that their images were real.

In addition to creating the park's gemlike lakes, the retreating glaciers carved out the valleys that they ever-so-slowly flowed through. The Athabasca River Valley is the park's largest watershed, a typical example of a U-shaped, glacier-carved valley. The Athabasca River flows north through the valley into the Mackenzie River System and ultimately into the Arctic Ocean. The glacial silt that paints the park's lakes is also carried down streams into the Athabasca, giving the river a pale-green "milky" look. Another beautiful aspect of the park's scenery is its abundance of waterfalls. They vary from the sparkling tumble of Punchbowl Falls, where Mountain Creek cascades down a limestone cliff into a picturesque pool, to the roar of Athabasca Falls, where the Athabasca River is forced through a narrow gorge.

FLORA

Elevations in the park range from 980 meters to over 3,700. That makes for a wide range of resident plant life.

Only a small part of the park lies in the montane zone. It is characterized by stands of Douglas fir (at its northern limit) and lodgepole pine, while balsam poplar, white birch, and spruce also occur. Savannalike grasslands occur on drier sites in valley bottoms. Well-developed stretches of montane can be found along the floors of the Athabasca and Miette River Valley, providing winter habitat for larger mammals such as elk.

The subalpine zone, heavily forested with evergreens, extends from the lower valley slopes up to the tree line at an elevation of around 2,200 meters. The subalpine occupies 40 percent of the park's area. The dominant species in this zone is lodgepole pine, although Engelmann spruce, subalpine fir, poplar, and aspen also grow here. The park's extensive stands of lodgepole pine are inhabited by few large mammals as the understory is minimal. Wildflowers are common in this zone and can be found by the roadside, in clearings, or on riverbanks.

Timberline here lies at an elevation between 2,050 and 2,400 meters above sea level. Above this elevation is the alpine zone, where the climate is severe (the average yearly temperature is below freezing), summer is brief, and only a few stunted trees survive. The zone's plant species grow low to the ground, with extensive root systems to protect them during high winds and through the deep snow cover of winter. During the short summer, these open slopes and meadows are carpeted with a profusion of flowers such as golden arnicas, bluebells, pale columbines, and red and yellow paintbrush. Higher still are brightly colored heathers, buttercups, and alpine forget-me-nots.

FAUNA

Wildlife is abundant in the park and can be seen throughout the year. During winter many larger mammals move to lower elevations where food is accessible. February and March are particularly good for looking for animal tracks in the snow. By June, most of the snow cover at lower elevations has melted, the crowds haven't arrived, and animals can be seen feeding along the valley floor. In fall, tourists move to warmer climates, the rutting season begins, bears go into hibernation, and a herd of elk moves into Jasper townsite for the winter.

While the park provides ample opportunities for seeing numerous animals in their natural habitat, it also leads to human/animal encounters that are not always positive. For example, less than 10 percent of the park is made up of well-vegetated valleys. These lower areas are essential to the larger mammals for food and shelter but are also the most heavily traveled by visitors. Game trails used for thousands of years are often bisected by roads—hundreds of animals are killed each year by speeding motorists. Please drive slowly in the park.

Campground Critters

Several species of small mammals thrive around campgrounds, thanks to an abundance of humans who are careless with their food. **Columbian ground squirrels** are very bold and will demand scraps of your lunch. **Golden-mantled ground squirrels** and **red squirrels** are also common. The **least chipmunk** (often confused with the golden-mantled ground squirrel

thanks to similar stripes) can also be seen in campgrounds; they'll often scamper across your hiking trail then sit boldly on a rock waiting for you to pass.

Aquatic Species

Beaver dams are common between the townsite and the park's east gate. Dawn and dusk are the best times to watch these intriguing creatures at work. Wabasso Lake, a 2.6-km hike from the Icefields Parkway, was created by beavers; their impressive dam has completely blocked the flow of Wabasso Creek. Also common in the park's wetlands are **mink** and **muskrat;** search out these creatures around the lakes on the benchland north of Jasper townsite.

Ungulates

Five species of deer inhabit the park. The large-eared **mule deer** is commonly seen around the edge of the townsite or grazing along the north end of the Icefields Parkway. **White-tailed deer** can be seen throughout the park. A small herd of **woodland caribou** roams throughout the park; they are most commonly seen during late spring, feeding in river deltas. The town of Jasper is in the home range of around 500 **elk,** which can be seen most of the year around the townsite or along the highway northeast and south of town. **Moose,** although numbering under 100 in all of Jasper, can occasionally be seen feeding on aquatic plants along the major drainage systems.

In summer, **mountain goats** browse in alpine meadows. A good place for goat watching is Goat Lookout on the Icefields Parkway. Unlike most of the park's large mammals, these surefooted creatures don't migrate to lower elevations in winter, but stay sheltered on rocky crags where wind and sun keep the vegetation snow free. Often confused with the goat is the darker **bighorn sheep.** The horns on the males of this species are very thick and often curl 360 degrees. Bighorns are common in the east of the park at Disaster Point and will often approach cars. An estimated 2,500 bighorn reside in the park.

Bears

Numbering around 80 within Jasper National Park, **black bears** are widespread the park and occasionally wander into campgrounds looking for food. They are most commonly seen along

Mountain goats inhabit high elevations throughout the park.

the Icefields Parkway in spring, when they first come out of hibernation. **Grizzly bears** are occasionally seen crossing the Icefields Parkway at higher elevations early in summer. For the most part they remain in remote mountain valleys, and if they do see, smell, or hear you, they'll generally move away. Read *Keep the Wild in Wildlife* before setting out into the woods; the pamphlet is available at information centers throughout the park.

Reclusive Residents
Several of the park's resident species keep a low profile, usually out of sight of humans. Populations of the shy and elusive **lynx** fluctuate with that of their primary food source, the snowshoe hare. The largest of the big cats in the park is the **cougar** (also called the mountain lion), a solitary carnivore that inhabits remote valleys. Jasper's **wolves** are one of the park's success stories. After being driven to near extinction, the species has rebounded. Five packs now roam the park, but they keep to the deep wilderness rarely traveled by people. While not common in the park, **coyotes** can be seen in cleared areas alongside the roads; usually at dawn and dusk.

Other Mammals
The **pine marten** is common, but shy; look for them in subalpine forests. The **short-tailed weasel**—a relative of the marten—is also common, while the **long-tailed weasel** is rare. At higher elevations look for **pikas** in piles of fallen

rock. **Hoary marmots** live near the upper limits of vegetation growth, where their shrill warning whistles carry across the open meadows; The Whistlers area, accessed by tramway, supports a healthy population of these noisy creatures.

Birds
The extensive tree cover in the lower valleys hides many species of birds, making them seem less abundant than they are. A total of 248 species have been recorded. The two you're most likely to see are the **gray jay** and **Clark's nutcracker,** which regularly joins picnickers for lunch. Also common are black-and-white **magpies,** raucous **ravens,** and several species of **ducks,** which can be seen around lakes in the Athabasca River Valley. Harlequin ducks nest in the park during early summer. A stretch of the Maligne River is closed during this season to prevent human interference.

The colony of **black swifts** in Maligne Canyon is one of only two in Alberta. Their poorly developed legs make it difficult for them to take off from their nests in the canyon walls—they literally fall before becoming airborne. High alpine slopes are home to **white-tailed ptarmigans,** a type of grouse that turns white in winter. Also at this elevation are flocks of **rosy finches** that live under overhanging cliffs. In subalpine forests the songs of **thrushes** and the tapping of **woodpeckers** can be heard.

At dusk, **great horned owls** swoop silently through the trees, their eerie call echoing through the forest. **Golden eagles** and **bald eagles** can be seen soaring high above the forests, and 15 pairs of **ospreys** are known to nest in the park, many along the Athabasca River between town and the east park gate.

HISTORY

In the summer of 1810, David Thompson, one of Canada's greatest explorers, became the first white man to enter the Athabasca River Valley. The following winter, when Thompson was making the first successful crossing of the Continental Divide, some of his party remained in the Athabasca River Valley and constructed a small supply depot east of the present townsite. The depot grew into a small trading post named Henry House and was used for many years by the North West Company. Other trading posts were built along the Athabasca River, including one that became known as "Jasper's House," for the clerk Jasper Hawse. This particular post was first established in 1813, then moved to the outlet of Jasper Lake in 1829.

By 1865, with the fur trade over and the Cariboo goldfields emptying along routes easier than over Yellowhead Pass, the Athabasca River Valley had no permanent residents. One prospector who did return over Yellowhead Pass was Lewis Swift, who in 1892 made his home in the abandoned buildings of Jasper's House, farming a small plot of land beside the Athabasca River. "Old Swift" became known to everyone, providing fresh food and accommodations for travelers and generating many legendary tales, such as the day he held the Grand Trunk Pacific Railway at gunpoint until they agreed to reroute the line away from his property.

In 1907, aware that the coming of the railway would mean an influx of settlers, the federal government set aside 5,000 square miles as Jasper Forest Park, buying all the land, save for the parcel owned by Lewis Swift. A handful of homesteaders continued to live in the valley, but the land upon which they lived was leased. The threat of oversettlement of the valley had been abated, but as a designated forest park, mining and logging were still allowed.

In 1908, Jasper Park Collieries staked claims in the park. By the time the railway came through in 1911, mining activity was centered at Pocahontas (near the park's east gate), where a township was established and thrived. During an extended miners' strike, the men spent their spare time constructing log pools at Miette Hot Springs, which were heavily promoted to early park visitors. The mine closed in 1921 and many families relocated to Jasper, which had grown from a railway camp into a popular tourist destination. By this time the park boundaries had changed dramatically. In 1911, the park had been reduced to two-thirds its original size, then in 1914 enlarged to include Maligne Lake and Columbia Icefield, then enlarged yet again in 1928 to take in Sunwapta Pass. Today's borders were set in 1930, when Jasper was officially designated a national park.

And what of "Old Swift"? Well after working as the park's first game warden for four years, he hung onto his land until 1935. The government of the day made various offers, but Swift ended up selling to a wealthy Englishman who operated a dude ranch on the site until finally selling the land to the government in 1962.

Jasper Townsite

In 1911, a construction camp was established for the Grand Trunk Pacific Railway near the present townsite of Jasper. When the northern line was completed, visitors flocked into the remote mountain settlement, and its future was assured. The first accommodation for tourists was 10 tents on the shore of Lac Beauvert that became known as Jasper Park Camp. In 1921, the tents were replaced and the original Jasper Park Lodge was constructed. By the summer of 1928, a road was completed from Edmonton and a golf course was built. As the number of tourists to the park continued to increase, existing facilities were expanded. In 1940 the Icefields Parkway opened, and in the 1960s Marmot Basin Ski Area opened and the downtown core of the townsite was developed.

SIGHTS AND DRIVES

COLUMBIA ICEFIELD

The largest and most accessible of 17 glacial areas along the Icefields Parkway is 325-square-km Columbia Icefield, beside the Icefields Parkway the south end of the park, 103 km south from Jasper and 189 km north from Banff. It's a remnant of the last major glaciation that covered most of Canada 20,000 years ago, and it has survived because of the elevation (1,900–2,800 meters above sea level), cold tem-

peratures, and heavy snowfalls. From the main body of the ice cap, which sits astride the Continental Divide, six glaciers creep down three main valleys. Of these, **Athabasca Glacier** is the most accessible and can be seen from the Icefields Parkway; it is one of the world's few glaciers that you can drive right up to. It is an impressive six square kilometers in area and up to 100 meters deep. The speed at which glaciers advance and retreat varies with the long-term climate. Athabasca Glacier has retreated to its current position from across the highway, a

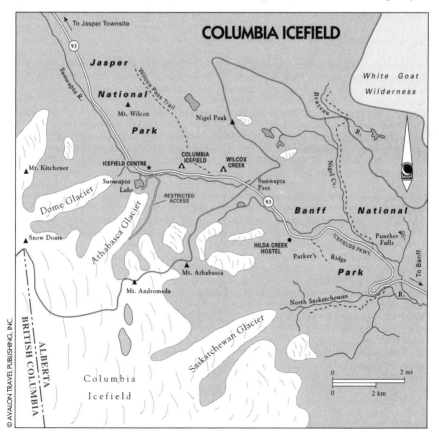

COLUMBIA ICEFIELD

To Jasper Townsite

93

Sunwapta R.

Jasper

Wilcox Pass Trail

White Goat Wilderness

National

Mt. Wilcox

Nigel Peak

Brazeau R.

Park

Mt. Kitchener

ICEFIELD CENTRE

COLUMBIA ICEFIELD

WILCOX CREEK

Sunwapta Lake

Dome Glacier

RESTRICTED ACCESS

Sunwapta Pass

93

Nigel Cr.

Banff   National

Snow Dome

Athabasca Glacier

HILDA CREEK HOSTEL

Parker's   Ridge

ICEFIELDS PKWY.

Panther Falls

To Banff

Mt. Athabasca

Park

Mt. Andromeda

North Saskatchewan   R.

© AVALON TRAVEL PUBLISHING, INC.

ALBERTA · BRITISH COLUMBIA

Saskatchewan Glacier

Columbia Icefield

0   2 mi

0   2 km

distance of over 1.5 km, in 100 years. Currently it retreats two to three meters per year. The rubble between the toe of Athabasca Glacier and the highway is a mixture of rock, sand, and gravel known as "till," deposited by the glacier as it retreats. A road leads down to a parking area from where a short hiking path leads through this area to the toe of the glacier.

The icefield is made more spectacular by the impressive peaks that surround it. **Mt. Athabasca** (3,491 meters) dominates the skyline, and three glaciers cling to its flanks. **Dome Glacier** is also visible from the highway; although part of Columbia Icefield it is not actually connected. Instead it is made of ice that breaks off the icefield 300 meters above, supplemented by large quantities of snow each winter.

Exploring the Icefield
The icefield can be very dangerous for unprepared visitors. Like all glaciers, the broken surface of the Athabasca is especially hazardous, as snow bridges can hide its deep crevasses. The crevasses are uncovered as the winter snows melt. The safest way to experience the glacier firsthand is on specially developed vehicles with balloon tires that can travel over the crevassed surface. These Snocoaches are operated by **Brewster,** 403/762-6767. The 90-minute tour of Athabasca Glacier includes time spent walking on the surface of the glacier. The tour, which begins with a bus ride from the Icefield Centre, costs $26 for adults, $13 for children, and operates from late May to early October 9 A.M.–5 P.M. (try to plan your tour for after 3 P.M., after the tour buses have departed for the day). No reservations are taken. Early in the season the glacier is still covered in a layer of snow and is therefore not as spectacular as during the summer months. Brewster operates day trips to Columbia Icefield from Banff (10 hours; $89 per person, excluding Snocoach) and Calgary (15 hours; $112 excluding Snocoach) through summer.

Icefield Centre
The magnificent Icefield Centre, which opened in the summer of 1996, is nestled at the base of Mt. Wilcox, overlooking the Athabasca Glacier. Costing over $16 million, the building is as environmentally friendly as possible: lights work motion sensors to reduce electricity, some water is reused, suppliers must take their packaging with them after deliveries, and the entire building freezes in winter.

The center is the staging point for Snocoach tours, but before heading out on to the icefield, don't miss the **Glacier Gallery** on the lower floor. This large display area details all aspects of the frozen world, including the story of glacier formation and movement. The centerpiece is a scaled-down fiberglass model of the Athabasca Glacier, which is surrounded by hands-on displays and audio-visual presentations. On the main floor of the center you'll find a Parks Canada desk (780/852-6288), Snocoach booking area, and a reception for the upstairs hotel rooms. Upstairs you'll find a cavernous snack bar with an outdoor seating section and the Glacier Dining Room, open daily for dinner. The complex (including display area) is open daily 9 A.M.–11 P.M.

ICEFIELDS PARKWAY

Sunwapta Pass (2,040 meters), four km south of the Columbia Icefield, marks the boundary between Banff and Jasper National Parks. The following sights along the Icefields Parkway are detailed from south to north, from Icefield Centre to the townsite of Jasper, a distance of 104 km. The scenery along this stretch of road is no less spectacular than the other half through Banff National Park, and it's easy to spend a few days en route. Along this section of the parkway are lodges, hostels, campgrounds, and a gas station.

Between the Columbia Icefield and Sunwapta Falls
Sunwapta Lake, at the toe of the Athabasca Glacier, is the source of the **Sunwapta River,** which the Icefields Parkway follows for 48 km to Sunwapta Falls. Eight km north from the Icefield Centre, the road descends to a viewpoint for **Stutfield Glacier.** Most of the glacier is hidden from view by a densely wooded ridge, but the valley floor below its toe is littered with till left by the glacier's retreat. The main body of the Columbia Icefield can be seen along the clifftop high above, and south of the glacier you can see Mt. Kitchener. Six km farther down the road is **Tangle Ridge,** a grayish-brown wall of lime-

Tangle Ridge

stone over which Beauty Creek cascades. At this point the Icefields Parkway runs alongside the Sunwapta River, following its braided course through the **Endless Range,** the eastern wall of a classic glacier-carved valley.

A further 40 km along the road a one-km gravel spur (at Sunwapta Falls Resort) leads to Sunwapta Falls. Here the Sunwapta River changes direction sharply and drops into a deep canyon. Two km downstream the river flows into the much-wider Athabasca Valley.

Goat Lookout
After following the Athabasca River for 17 km, the road ascends to a lookout with picnic tables offering panoramic river views. Below the lookout is a steep bank of exposed glacially ground material containing natural deposits of salt. The local mountain goats spend most of their time on the steep slopes of Mt. Kerkeslin, to the northeast, but occasionally cross the road and can be seen searching for the salt licks along the riverbank, trying to replenish lost nutrients.

Athabasca Falls
Nine kilometers beyond Goat Lookout and 32 km south of Jasper townsite, the Icefields Parkway divides when an old stretch of highway crosses the Athabasca River and continues along its west side for 25 km before rejoining the Parkway seven km south of the townsite. At the southern end of this loop the Athabasca River is forced through a narrow gorge and over a cliff into a cauldron of roaring water below. Old river channels can be seen along the west bank. As the river slowly erodes the center of the riverbed, the falls will move upstream. Trails lead from a day-use area to various viewpoints above and below the falls.

Continuing North to Jasper
Take Highway 93A beyond Athabasca Falls to reach Mt. Edith Cavell (see below), or continue north along the Icefields Parkway to access the following sights. The first worthwhile stop along this route is **Horseshoe Lake,** reached along a 350-meter trail from a parking lot three km north of Athabasca Falls. The southern end of this delightful little body of water is ringed by a band of cliffs (popular with locals in summer as a cliff-diving spot), but many private (unofficial) picnic spots line its western shoreline. Two km farther north are a couple of lookouts with spectacular views across the Athabasca River to Athabasca Pass, used by David Thompson on his historic expedition across the continent. To the north of the pass lies Mt. Edith Cavell. From this lookout it is 26 km to Jasper townsite.

MT. EDITH CAVELL

This 3,363-meter peak is the most distinctive and impressive in the park. Known to Indians as the "White Ghost" for its snowcapped summit, the mountain was given its official name in honor of a British nurse who was executed for helping prisoners of war escape German-occupied Belgium during World War I. The peak was first climbed that same year; today the most popular route to the summit is up the east ridge (to the left of the summit). The imposing north face (facing the parking lot) has been climbed, but is rated as an extremely difficult climb.

For those less adventurous, several vantage

Horseshoe Lake

points—including the townsite and golf course—provide good views of the peak. But the most impressive place to marvel at the mountain is from directly below the north face. A 14.5-km road winds up the Astoria River Valley from Highway 93A, ending right below the face. This steep, narrow road has many switchbacks. Trailers must be left in the designated area at the bottom. Highway 93A was the original Icefields Parkway, following the southeast bank of the Athabasca River. The route has now been bypassed by the more direct one on the other side of the river.

From the parking lot at the end of the road, you must strain your neck to take in the magnificent sight of the mountain's 1,500-meter north face and **Angel Glacier,** which lies in a saddle on the mountain's lower slopes. On warm days, those who are patient may be lucky enough to witness an avalanche tumbling from the glacier, creating a roar that echoes across the valley. From the parking area, the **Path of the Glacier Trail** (one hour round-trip) traverses barren

moraines deposited by the receding Angel Glacier and leads to some great viewpoints. For other hiking opportunities in the vicinity of Mt. Edith Cavell, see "Hikes near Mt. Edith Cavell" below.

SIGHTS IN AND AROUND JASPER TOWNSITE

Downtown
With all the things to do and see in the park it's amazing how many people hang out in town. July and August are especially busy; much-needed improvements to the parking situation have had little impact on the traffic. The best way to avoid the problem is to avoid town during the middle of day. The Park Information Centre, on Connaught Drive, is the only real reason to be in town. The shaded park in front of the center is a good place for people -watching, but you may get clobbered by a wayward Hacky Sack. Connaught Drive, the town's main street, parallels the rail line as it curves through town. In addition to the Park Information Centre, along this road you'll find the bus depot, rail terminal, restaurants, motels, and a parking lot. Behind Connaught Drive is Patricia Street (one-way), which has more restaurants and services and leads to more hotels and motels on Geikie Street. Behind this main core are rows of neat houses—much less pretentious than those in Banff—and all the facilities of a regular town, including a library, school, post office, museum, swimming pool, and hospital.

At the back of town is the excellent **Jasper-Yellowhead Museum and Archives,** 400 Pyramid Lake Road, 780/852-3013. A new gallery opened here in 1998, featuring exhibits that take visitors through a time line of Jasper's human history through the fur trade, the coming of the railway, and the creation of the park. The museum also features extensive archives, including hundreds of historical photos, manuscripts, documents, maps, videos. Admission is $3. It's open mid-June to September, daily 10 A.M.–9 P.M., the rest of the year Thursday –Sunday 10 A.M.–5 P.M.

If you like taxidermy, visit **The Den Wildlife Museum,** which exhibits around stuffed animals in their "natural setting." You'll find it down a dark stairway beneath the Whistlers Inn. Yep, they even charge you for it—$3. Open year-round, daily 9 A.M.–10 P.M.

Patricia and Pyramid Lakes

A winding road heads through the hills at the back of town to these two picturesque lakes, formed when glacial moraines dammed shallow valleys. The first, to the left, is Patricia; the second, farther along the road, is Pyramid, backed by **Pyramid Mountain** (2,765 meters). Both lakes are popular spots for picnicking, fishing, and boating. Boat rentals are available at **Pyramid Lake Boat Rentals,** at Pyramid Lake Resort, 780/852-3536. Canoes, rowboats, paddleboats, and kayaks are $15 for the first hour and $10 for each additional hour. The resort also rents motorboats for $30 per hour. From the resort, the road continues around the lake to a bridge, which leads to an island popular with picnickers. The road ends at the quieter end of the lake.

Jasper Tramway

This tramway climbs more than 1,000 vertical meters up the steep north face of **The Whistlers,** named for the hoary marmots that live on the summit. The tramway operates two 30-passenger cars that take seven minutes to reach the upper terminal, during which time the conductor gives a narrated lecture about the mountain and its environment. From the upper terminal, a 1.4-km trail leads to the summit (2,470 meters). The view is breathtaking; to the south is the Columbia Icefield, and on a clear day you can see Mt. Robson (3,954 meters) —the highest peak in the Canadian Rockies—to the northwest. Free two-hour guided hikes leave the upper terminal for the true summit daily at 10 A.M., 11 A.M., 2 P.M., and 3 P.M. Round-trip fare is $18; allow two hours on top and, on a clear summer's day, two more hours in line at the bottom. The tramway is three km south of town on Highway 93 (Icefields Parkway) and then three km up Whistlers Road. It operates in summer daily 8:30 A.M.–10 P.M.; shorter hours April–June and September –October; closed the rest of the year. For more information, call 780/852-3093.

Edith and Annette Lakes

These two lakes along the road to Jasper Park Lodge—across the Athabasca River from town—are perfect for a picnic, swim, or pleasant walk. They are remnants of a much larger lake that once covered the entire valley floor. The lakes are relatively shallow, therefore the sun warms the water to a bearable temperature; in fact, they have the warmest waters of any lakes in the park. The 2.5-km **Lee Foundation Trail** encircles Lake Annette and is wheelchair accessible. Both lakes have day-use areas with beaches and picnic areas.

Jasper Park Lodge

Accommodations are not usually considered "sights," but then this is the Rockies, where grand railway hotels attract as many visitors as the more legitimate natural attractions. Jasper Park Lodge has been the premier accommodation in the park since it opened in 1921. Back then it was a single-story structure, reputed to be the largest log building in the world. It burned to the ground in 1952 but was rebuilt. Additional bungalows were erected along Lac Beauvert, forming a basis for today's lodge. Rows of cabins radiate from the main lodge, which contains restaurants, lounges, and the town's only covered shopping arcade. Today up to 900 guests can be accommodated

Mt. Edith Cavell is one of Jasper's most recognizable peaks.

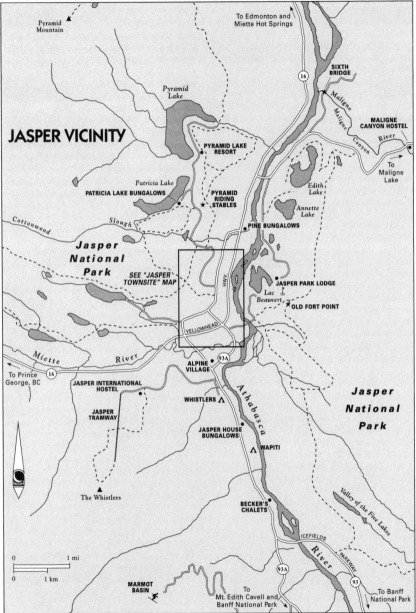

JASPER VICINITY

Pyramid Mountain

To Edmonton and Miette Hot Springs

SIXTH BRIDGE

16

MALIGNE CANYON HOSTEL

Pyramid Lake

Maligne River

To Maligne Lake

PYRAMID LAKE RESORT

Patricia Lake

Edith Lake

PATRICIA LAKE BUNGALOWS

PYRAMID RIDING STABLES

Annette Lake

Cottonwood

Slough

PINE BUNGALOWS

Jasper National Park

SEE "JASPER TOWNSITE" MAP

HWY

JASPER PARK LODGE

Lac Beauvert

OLD FORT POINT

YELLOWHEAD

Miette River

16

To Prince George, BC

ALPINE VILLAGE

93A

JASPER INTERNATIONAL HOSTEL

WHISTLERS

Athabasca

Jasper National Park

JASPER TRAMWAY

JASPER HOUSE BUNGALOWS

WAPITI

The Whistlers

Valley of the Five Lakes

BECKER'S CHALETS

ICEFIELDS

River

0   1 mi

0   1 km

MARMOT BASIN

93A

To Mt. Edith Cavell and Banff National Park

93

To Banff National Park

PARKWAY

© AVALON TRAVEL PUBLISHING, INC.

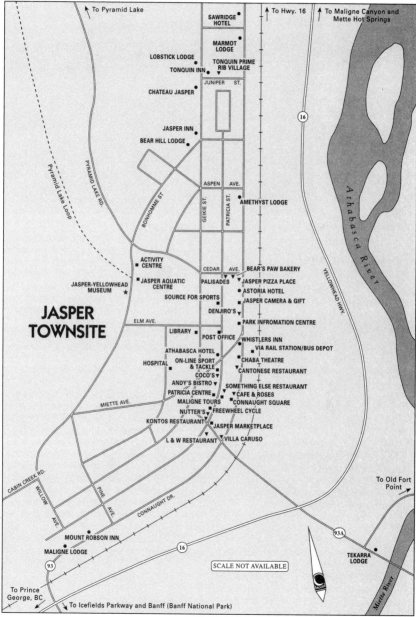

To Pyramid Lake

To Hwy. 16

To Maligne Canyon and
Mette Hot Springs

SAWRIDGE
HOTEL

MARMOT
LODGE

LOBSTICK LODGE

TONQUIN PRIME
RIB VILLAGE

TONQUIN INN

JUNIPER ST.

CHATEAU JASPER

JASPER INN

BEAR HILL LODGE

ASPEN AVE.

AMETHYST LODGE

GEIKIE ST.

PATRICIA ST.

Athabasca River

Pyramid Lake Loop

PYRAMID LAKE RD.

BONHOMME ST.

ACTIVITY
CENTRE

JASPER-YELLOWHEAD
MUSEUM

JASPER AQUATIC
CENTRE

CEDAR AVE.

BEAR'S PAW BAKERY

PALISADES

JASPER PIZZA PLACE

ASTORIA HOTEL

SOURCE FOR SPORTS

JASPER CAMERA & GIFT

DENJIRO'S

JASPER
TOWNSITE

ELM AVE.

PARK INFROMATION CENTRE

LIBRARY

POST OFFICE

WHISTLERS INN

VIA RAIL STATION/BUS DEPOT

ATHABASCA HOTEL

HOSPITAL

ON-LINE SPORT
& TACKLE

CHABA THEATRE

CANTONESE RESTAURANT

COCO'S

ANDY'S BISTRO

SOMETHING ELSE RESTAURANT

PATRICIA CENTRE

CAFE & ROSES

MIETTE AVE.

MALIGNE TOURS

CONNAUGHT SQUARE

NUTTER'S

FREEWHEEL CYCLE

KONTOS RESTAURANT

JASPER MARKETPLACE

L & W RESTAURANT

VILLA CARUSO

YELLOWHEAD HWY.

To Old Fort
Point

CABIN CREEK RD.

WILLOW AVE.

PINE AVE.

CONNAUGHT DR.

93A

MOUNT ROBSON INN

MALIGNE LODGE

TEKARRA
LODGE

93

16

SCALE NOT AVAILABLE

MOON

Miette River

To Prince
George, BC

To Icefields Parkway and Banff (Banff National Park)

Take to the waters of Pyramid Lake in a canoe.

in 446 rooms. A large parking area for nonguests is located on Lodge Road, behind the golf clubhouse; you're welcome to walk around the resort, play golf, dine in the restaurants, and of course, browse through the shopping promenade—even if you're not a registered guest. On the lakeshore in front of the lodge is a boat and bike rental concession; canoes and kayaks can be rented for $18 per 30 minutes while bikes are $10 per hour. From the main lodge, a hiking trail follows the shoreline of Lac Beauvert and links up with other trails from Old Fort Point. To walk from town will take one hour.

MALIGNE LAKE AND VICINITY

Maligne Lake, one of the world's most photographed lakes, lies 48 km southeast of Jasper townsite. It's the source of the Maligne River, which flows northward to Medicine Lake and then disappears underground, eventually emerging downstream of Maligne Canyon.

The river was known to the natives as Chaba Imne, which translates to "River of the Great Beaver," but the name by which we know it today was coined by a missionary. After his horses were swept away by its swift-flowing waters in 1846, he described the river as being "la traverse maligne."

Driving up the Maligne River Valley to the lake is a 600-million-year-old lesson in geology that can be appreciated by anyone.

Maligne Canyon

As the Maligne River drops into the Athabasca River Valley, its gradient is particularly steep. The fast-flowing water has eroded a deep canyon out of the easily dissolved limestone bedrock. The canyon is up to 50 meters deep, yet so narrow that squirrels often jump across. At the top of the canyon, opposite the teahouse, you'll see large potholes in the riverbed. These potholes are created when rocks and pebbles become trapped in what begins as a shallow depression; under the force of the rushing water, they carve jug-shaped hollows into the soft bedrock.

An interpretive trail winds down from the parking lot, crossing the canyon six times. The most spectacular sections of the canyon can be seen from the first two bridges, at the upper end of the trail. In summer a teahouse operates at the top of the canyon. To avoid the crowds at the upper end of the canyon, an alternative would be to park at Sixth Bridge, near the confluence of the Maligne and Athabasca Rivers, and walk *up* the canyon (see "Hiking in the Maligne Lake Area," below). The **Maligne Lake Shuttle** stops at the canyon eight times daily. For reservations, call 780/852-3370; fare is $8 one-way from town. In winter, guided tours of the frozen canyon are an experience you'll never forget (see "Wintertime" below).

Medicine Lake

From the canyon, Maligne Lake Road climbs to

Medicine Lake, which does a disappearing act each year. The water level fluctuates due to a network of underground passages that emerge downstream in Maligne Canyon. At the northwest end of the lake, beyond where the outlet should be, the riverbed is often dry. In fall, when runoff from the mountains is minimal, the water level drops and, by November, the lake comprises of a few shallow pools. Natives believed that spirits were responsible for the phenomenon, hence the name.

Maligne Lake

At the end of the road, 48 km from Jasper, is Maligne Lake, the largest glacier-fed lake in the Canadian Rockies and second largest in the world. The first paying visitors were brought to the lake in 1929, and it has been a mecca for camera-toting tourists from around the world ever since. Once at the lake, activities are plentiful. But other than taking in the spectacular vistas, the only thing you won't need your wallet for is hiking one of the numerous trails in the area.

The most popular tourist activity at the lake is a 90-minute narrated cruise on a glass-enclosed boat up the lake to oft-photographed **Spirit Island.** Cruises leave in summer, every hour on the hour 10 A.M.–5 p.m., with fewer sailings in May and September; adult $32, child $15.50. Many time slots are block-booked by tour companies, therefore reservations are suggested. Rowboats and canoes can be rented at the Boat House, a provincial historic site dating to 1929, for $10 per hour or $45 per day. Sea kayaks go for $60 per day. The lake also has excellent trout fishing (Alberta's record rainbow trout was caught here), horseback riding, and whitewater rafting on the Maligne River. (For details on all the above, see "Other Recreation," below.) The cruises, boat rentals, and all activities are operated by Maligne Tours, 627 Patricia St., 780/852-3370. At the lake, Maligne Tours operates a souvenir shop and large café with a huge area of tiered outdoor seating overlooking the lake.

The **Maligne Lake Shuttle** runs from the Maligne Tours office at 627 Patricia Street, 780/852-3370, and from various hotels out to the lake six times daily through summer (three times daily in spring and fall).

CONTINUING EAST ALONG HIGHWAY 16

From Jasper townsite it's 50 km to the park's eastern boundary along Highway 16, following the Athabasca River the entire way. Beyond the turn-off to Maligne Lake, Highway 16 enters a wide valley flanked to the west by The Palisade and to the east by the Colin Range. The valley is a classic montane environment, with open meadows and forests of Douglas fir and lodgepole pine. After crossing the Athabasca River, 20 km from Jasper, the highway parallels six-km-long **Jasper Lake,** left as the last Ice Age ended. Along the lake are a number of viewpoints and picnic areas. At the lake's northern outlet, a plaque marks the site of Jasper House (the actual site is across the river from the highway). The next worthwhile spot is **Disaster Point,** a few km farther north. This is a great spot for viewing bighorn sheep, which gather at a mineral lick, an area of exposed mineral salts. Disaster Point is on the lower slopes of Roche Miette, a distinctive 2,316-meter-high peak that juts out into the Athabasca River Valley. Across the highway the braided Athabasca River is flanked by wetlands alive with migrating birds spring and fall.

Miette Hot Springs Road branches south from the highway 43 km from Jasper. This junction marks the site of **Pocahontas,** a coal mining town in existence between 1910 and 1921. The mine itself was high above the township, with coal transported to the valley floor by cable car. All buildings have long since been removed, but a short interpretive walk leads through the remaining foundations.

One km along Miette Hot Springs Road, a short trail leads to photogenic **Punchbowl Falls.** Here Mountain Creek cascades through a narrow crevice in a cliff to a pool of turbulent water.

Miette Hot Springs

After curving, swerving, rising, and falling many times, Miette Hot Springs Road ends 18 km from Highway 16 at the warmest springs in the Canadian Rockies. In the early 1900s, these springs were one of the park's biggest attractions. In 1910, a packhorse trail was built up the valley and the government constructed a bathhouse. The original hand-hewn log structure was replaced in the 1930s with pools that remained in use until new facilities were built in 1985. Water that flows into the pools is artificially cooled from 54°C to a soothing 39°C. Admission is $5.50 for a single swim or $7.75 for the day. It's open mid-May to mid-October, 10:30 A.M.–9 P.M., with extended hours of 8:30 A.M.–10:30 P.M. in summer. For more information, call 780/866-3939.

Many hiking trails begin from the hot springs complex; the shortest is from the picnic area to the source of the springs (200 meters). The springs is also home to the Ashlar Ridge Café, while adjacent are a restaurant and lodging.

HIKING

The 1,200 km of hiking trails in Jasper are significantly different than those in the other mountain national parks. The park has an extensive system of interconnecting backcountry trails that, for experienced hikers, can provide a wilderness adventure rivaled by few areas on the face of the earth. For casual day-hikers, on the other hand, opportunities are more limited. Most trails in the immediate vicinity of the townsite have little elevation gain and lead through montane forest to lakes. The trails around Maligne Lake, at the base of Mt. Edith Cavell, and along the Icefields Parkway have more rewarding objectives and are more challenging.

The most popular trails for extended backcountry trips are the **Skyline Trail,** between Maligne Lake Road and Maligne Lake (44.5 km, three days each way); the trails to **Amethyst Lakes** in the Tonquin Valley (19 km, one day each way) and **Athabasca Pass** (50 km, three days each way), which was used by fur traders for 40 years as the main route across the Canadian Rockies; and the **South Boundary Trail,** which traverses a remote section of the front ranges into Banff National Park (160 km, 10 days each way).

Before setting off on any hikes, whatever the length, go to the **Park Information Centre** in Jasper townsite or the Trail Office in the Icefield Centre along the Icefields Parkway for trail maps, trail conditions, and trail closures. To prevent overuse on trails that require an overnight stay in the backcountry, you *must* pick up a Wilderness Pass before heading out; $6 per person per night.

HIKES AROUND JASPER TOWNSITE

Pyramid Lake Loop
- Length: 17 km (5 hours) round-trip
- Elevation gain: 150 meters
- Rating: easy/moderate

Numerous official and unofficial hiking trails weave across the benchland immediately west of Jasper townsite. From the parking lot opposite the Aquatic Centre on Pyramid Lake Road, a well-marked trail climbs onto the benchland. Keep right, crossing Pyramid Lake Road, and you'll emerge on a bluff overlooking the Athabasca River Valley. Bighorn sheep can often be seen grazing here. If you return to the trailhead from here, you will have hiked seven km. The trail continues north, disappearing into the montane forest until arriving at Pyramid Lake. Various trails can be taken to return to town; get a map at the Park Information Centre before setting out.

Mina Lakes
- Length: 2 km (40 minutes) one-way
- Elevation gain: 60 meters
- Rating: easy

These two lakes lie on the benchland described above. The trailhead is the same as the Pyramid Lake Loop, except instead of keeping right, you'll need to take the first left fork, which traverses a typical montane forest of lodgepole pine, Douglas fir, and poplar before emerging at Lower Mina Lake. After a further 500 meters the upper lake is reached.

Patricia Lake Circle
- Length: 5 km loop (90 minutes round-trip)
- Elevation gain: minimal
- Rating: easy

This trail begins across the road from the riding stables on Pyramid Lake Road. It traverses a mixed forest of aspen and lodgepole pine—prime habitat for a variety of larger mammals such as elk, deer, and moose. The second half of the trail skirts Cottonwood Slough, where you'll see a number of beaver ponds.

The Palisade

- Length: 11 km (four hours) one-way
- Elevation gain: 850 meters
- Rating: moderate/difficult

The destination of this strenuous hike is the site of an old fire lookout tower atop a high ridge between the Athabasca River Valley and Pyramid Mountain. The trail begins from the very end of Pyramid Lake Road, crossing Pyramid Creek after one km then climbing steadily for the entire distance along a forest-enclosed fire road (take the right fork at the 7.5-km mark). Once at the end of the trail, it's easy to see why this site was chosen for the lookout; the panorama extends down the valley and across Jasper Lake to Roche Miette (2,316 meters).

The Whistlers

- Length: 8 km (2.5–3 hours) one-way
- Elevation gain: 1,220 meters
- Rating: difficultThis steep ascent, one of the most arduous in the park, is unique in that it passes through three distinct vegetation zones in a relatively short distance. (For the less adventurous, Jasper Tramway traverses the same route described here; see "Jasper Tramway" under "Sights in and around Jasper Townsite" above.) From the trailhead on Whistlers Road, 200 meters below the hostel, the trail begins climbing and doesn't let up until you merge with the crowds getting off the tramway at the top. The trail begins in a montane forest of aspen and white birch, climbs through a subalpine forest of Engelmann spruce and alpine fir, then emerges onto the open, treeless tundra, which is inhabited by pikas, hoary marmots, and a few hardy plants. Carry water—none is available before the upper tramway terminal. If you've taken the tramway, free guided hikes are offered around the summit area.

Old Fort Point

- Length: 6.5 km loop (2 hours round-trip)
- Elevation gain: 60 meters
- Rating: easy

Old Fort Point is a distinctive knoll above the Athabasca River, to the east of Jasper townsite. Although it is not likely a fort was ever located here, the first fur-trading post in the Rockies, Henry House, was located just downstream. It's easy to imagine fur traders and early explorers climbing to this summit for 360-degree views of the Athabasca and Miette Rivers. To get to the trailhead from town, take Highway 93A and turn left toward Lac Beauvert. The trail begins just over the Athabasca River. Climb the wooden stairs, take the left trail to the top of the knoll, then continue back to the parking lot along the north flank of the hill.

HIKING IN THE MALIGNE LAKE AREA

Maligne Lake, 48 km from Jasper townsite, provides more easy hiking with many opportunities to view the lake and explore its environs. To get there, take Highway 16 east for four km from town and turn south on Maligne Lake Road. The first three hikes detailed are along the access road to the lake; the others leave from various parking lots at the northwest end of the lake.

Maligne Tours, 627 Patricia St., 780/852-3370, organizes hikes led by knowledgeable guides along the Lake Trail (one hour; $10 per person) and into the Bald and Opal Hills (four hours; $40 per person). This same company provides transportation to the lake. The **Maligne Lake Shuttle** runs from downtown and some hotels out to the lake three to six times daily; $12 one-way.

Maligne Canyon

- Length: 3.7 km (90 minutes) one-way
- Elevation gain: 125 meters
- Rating: moderate

Maligne Canyon is one of the busiest places in the park, yet few visitors hike the entire length of the canyon trail. By beginning from the lower end of the canyon, at the confluence of the Maligne and Athabasca Rivers, you'll avoid starting your hike alongside the masses and you'll get to hike downhill on your return (when you're tired). To access the lower end of the canyon, follow Maligne Lake Road for 2.5 km to the warden's office, from where a one-km access road leads to Sixth Bridge. Crowds will be minimal for the first three km to Fourth Bridge, where the trail starts climbing. By the time you get to Third Bridge, you start encountering "adventurous" hikers coming down the canyon, and soon thereafter you'll meet the real crowds, bear-bells and all. Upstream of here the canyon is deepest and most spectacular. See "Maligne Canyon" under "Maligne Lake and Vicinity," above, for details of the walk starting from the *top* of the canyon.

Watchtower Basin
- Length: 10 km (3.5 hours) one-way
- Elevation gain: 630 meters
- Rating: moderate/difficultWatchtower is a wide, open basin high above the crowds of Maligne Lake Road. The trailhead is 24 km from Jasper townsite. All the elevation gain is made during the first six km, through a dense forest of lodgepole pine and white spruce. As the trail levels off and enters the basin it continues to follow the west bank of a stream, crossing it at km 10 and officially ending at a campground. To the west and south the **Maligne Range** rises to a crest three km beyond the campground. From the top of this ridge, at the intersection with the Skyline Trail, it is 17.5 km northwest to Maligne Canyon, or 27 km southeast to Maligne Lake. By camping at Watchtower Campground, day trips can be made to a small lake in the basin or to highlights of the Skyline Trail such as the Snowbowl, Curator Lake, and Shovel Pass.

Jacques Lake
- Length: 12 km (3–3.5 hours) one-way
- Elevation gain: 100 meters
- Rating: moderate

The appeal of this trail, which begins from a parking lot at the southeast end of Medicine Lake, is its lack of elevation gain and the numerous small lakes it skirts as it travels through a narrow valley. On either side, the severely faulted mountains of the Queen Elizabeth Ranges rise steeply above the valley floor, their strata tilted nearly vertical.

Lake Trail (Mary Schäffer Loop)
- Length: 3.2-km loop (1 hour round-trip)
- Elevation gain: minimal
- Rating: easy

This easy, pleasant walk begins from beside the Boat House, following the eastern shore of Maligne Lake to a point known as **Schäffer Viewpoint,** named for the first white person to see the valley. After dragging yourself away from the spectacular panorama, follow the trail into a forest of spruce and subalpine fir before looping back to the middle parking lot.

MARY SCHÄFFER

In the early 1900s, exploration of mountain wilderness areas was considered a man's pursuit. However, one spirited and tenacious woman entered that domain and went on to explore areas of the Canadian Rockies that no white man ever had.

Mary Sharples was born in 1861 in Pennsylvania and raised in a strict Quaker family. She was introduced to Dr. Charles Schäffer on a trip to the Rockies, and in 1889 they were married. His interest in botany drew them back to the Rockies, where Charles collected, documented, and photographed specimens until his death in 1903. Mary also became apt at these skills. After hearing Sir James Hector (the geologist on the Palliser Expedition) reciting tales of the mountains, her zest to explore the wilderness returned. In 1908, Mary, guide Billy Warren, and a small party set out for a lake that no white man had ever seen but that the Stoney Indians knew as Chaba Imne, or "Beaver Lake." After initial difficulties, they succeeded in finding the elusive body of water now known as Maligne Lake. In Mary's words, "There burst upon us. . . the finest view any of us have ever beheld in the Rockies. . . ." In 1915 Mary married Billy Warren, continuing to explore the mountains until her death in 1939. Her success as a photographer, artist, and writer were equal to any of her male counterparts. But it was her unwavering love of the Canadian Rockies—her "heaven of the hills"—for which she is best remembered.

Opal Hills
- Length: 8.2-km loop (3 hours round-trip)
- Elevation gain: 455 meters
- Rating: moderate

Turn left into the parking area beside Maligne Lake, then left again and continue to the top parking lot; this trail begins from behind the information board in the north corner. The trail climbs steeply for 1.5 km to a point where it divides. Both options end in the high alpine meadows of the Opal Hills; the trail to the right is shorter and steeper. Once in the meadow, the entire Maligne Valley can be seen below. Across Maligne Lake are the rounded Bald Hills, the Maligne Range, and to the southwest, the distinctive twin peaks of Mt. Unwin (3,268 meters) and Mt. Charlton (3,217 meters).

Bald Hills

- Length: 5.2 km (2 hours) one-way
- Elevation gain: 495 meters
- Rating: moderate

From a picnic area at the very end of Maligne Lake Road, this trail follows an old fire road for its entire distance, entering an open meadow near the end. This was once the site of a fire look-out. The 360-degree view takes in the jade-green waters of Maligne Lake, the Queen Elizabeth Ranges, and the twin peaks of Mt. Unwin and Mt. Charlton. The Bald Hills extend for seven km, their highest summit not exceeding 2,600 meters. A herd of caribou summers in the hills.

Moose Lake

- Length: 1.4 km (30 minutes) one-way
- Elevation gain: minimal
- Rating: easy

This trail begins 200 meters along the Bald Hills trail, spurring left along the Maligne Pass Trail (signposted). One km along this trail a rough track branches left, leading 100 meters to Moose Lake—a quiet body of water where moose are sometimes seen. To return, continue along the trail as it descends to the shore of Maligne Lake, a short stroll from the picnic area.

HIKES NEAR MT. EDITH CAVELL

Mt. Edith Cavell Road begins from Highway 93A and winds through a subalpine forest, ascending 300 meters in 14.5 km. Trailheads are located at the end of the road (Cavell Meadows Trail and a short interpretive trail) and across from the hostel two km from the end (Astoria River Trail). A third trailhead is on Marmot Basin Road where it crosses Portal Creek (Maccarib Pass Trail).

Cavell Meadows

- Length: 4 km (1.5 hours) one-way
- Elevation gain: 380 meters
- Rating: easy/moderate

This trail, beginning from the parking lot beneath Mt. Edith Cavell, provides access to an alpine meadow and panoramic views of Angel Glacier. The trail begins by following the paved Path of the Glacier Loop, then branches left, climbing steadily through a subalpine forest of Engelmann spruce and then stunted subalpine fir to emerge facing the northeast face of Mt. Edith Cavell and Angel Glacier. The view of the glacier from this point is nothing less than awesome, as the ice spills out of a cirque, clinging to a 300-meter-high cliff face. The trail continues to higher viewpoints and an alpine meadow which, by mid-July, is filled with wildflowers.

Astoria River

- Length: 19 km (6–7 hours) one-way
- Elevation gain: 450 meters
- Rating: moderate

Beginning opposite the hostel on Mt. Edith Cavell Road, this trail descends through a forest on the north side of Mt. Edith Cavell for five km, then crosses the Astoria River and begins a long ascent into spectacular Tonquin Valley. Amethyst Lakes and the 1,000-meter cliffs of the Ramparts first come into view after 13 km. At the 17-km mark the trail divides. To the left it climbs into Eremite Valley where there is a campground. The right fork continues following Astoria River to Tonquin Valley, Amethyst Lakes, and a choice of four campgrounds.

Maccarib Pass

- Length: 21 km (7–8 hours) one-way
- Elevation gain: 730 meters
- Rating: moderate

This trail is slightly longer and gains more elevation than the trail along Astoria River but is more spectacular. From 6.5 km up Marmot Basin Road, the trail strikes out to the southwest. It follows Portal Creek and passes under Peveril Peak before making a steep approach to Maccarib Pass, 12.5 km from the trailhead. The full panorama of the Tonquin Valley can be appreciated as the path gradually descends from the pass. At Amethyst Lakes it links up with the Astoria River Trail, and many options for day hikes head out from campgrounds at the lakes.

HIKES ALONG ICEFIELDS PARKWAY

Valley of the Five Lakes

- Length: 2.3 km (40 minutes) one-way
- Elevation gain: 60 meters
- Rating: easy

These lakes, nestled in an open valley, are small but make a worthwhile destination. From the

Jasper's backcountry holds a population of grizzlies.

trailhead, 10 km south of Jasper townsite along the Icefields Parkway, the trail passes through a forest of lodgepole pine, crosses a stream, and climbs a ridge from where you'll have a panoramic view of surrounding peaks. As the trail descends to the lakes, turn left at the first intersection to a point between two of the lakes. These lakes are linked to Old Fort Point by a tedious 10-km trail through montane forest.

Geraldine Lakes
- Length: 5 km (2 hours) one-way
- Elevation gain: 410 meters
- Rating: moderate

The first of the four Geraldine Lakes is an easy two-km hike from the trailhead (located 5.5 km along the Geraldine Fire Road, which spurs south off Highway 93A west of Athabasca Falls). The forest-encircled lake reflects the north face of Mt. Fryatt (3,361 meters). The trail continues along the northwest shore, climbs steeply past a scenic 100-meter-high waterfall, and traverses some rough terrain where the trail becomes indistinct; follow the cairns. At the end of the valley is another waterfall. The trail climbs east of the waterfall to a ridge above the second of the lakes, five km from the trailhead. Although the trail officially ends here, it does continue to a campground at the south end of the lake. Two other lakes, accessible only by bush bashing, are located farther up the valley.

Fortress Lake
- Length: 24 km (7–8 hours) one-way
- Elevation gain: minimal

- Rating: moderate

The trail to this seldom-visited lake straddling the Continental Divide begins from the Sunwapta Falls parking lot. For the first 15 km, the trail meanders along the east bank of the Athabasca River, then crosses it. Beyond the main bridge you'll need to ford the braided Chaba River, then continue southwest along the river flats for six km to the east end of Fortress Lake. The lake lies within British Columbia in Hamber Provincial Park. Its shores are difficult to traverse as they lack established trails.

Wilcox Pass
- Length: 4 km (90 minutes) one-way
- Elevation gain: 340 meters
- Rating: moderate

Views of the Columbia Icefield from the Icefields Parkway pale in comparison with those achieved along this trail on the same side of the valley as the Columbia Icefield Centre. This trail was once used by northbound outfitters because, 100 years ago, Athabasca Glacier covered the valley floor and had to be bypassed. The trail begins from the north side of Wilcox Creek Campground, three km south of the Icefield Centre. It climbs through a stunted forest of Engelmann spruce and subalpine fir to a ridge with panoramic views of the valley, Columbia Icefield, and surrounding peaks. Ascending gradually from there, the trail enters a fragile environment of alpine meadows. From the pass, most hikers return along the same trail, although it is possible to continue north, descending to the Icefields Parkway at Tangle Ridge, 11.5 km from the trailhead.

OTHER RECREATION

FAIR WEATHER

A number of booking agents represent the many recreation-tour operators in Jasper. **Jasper Adventure Centre,** in the lobby of the Chaba Theatre at 604 Connaught Drive, 780/852-5595, takes bookings for all the activities below, as well as for accommodations and for transportation to various points in the park and beyond. **Jasper Travel Agency,** in the railway station, 780/852-4400, offers a similar service. **Maligne Tours,** 627 Patricia St., 780/852-3370, operates all activities in the Maligne Lake area, including the famous lake cruise.

Mountain Biking

Bicycling in the park continues to grow in popularity: the ride between Banff and Jasper, along the Icefields Parkway, attracts riders from around the world. In additon to the paved roads, many designated unpaved bicycle trails radiate from the town. One of the most popular is the Athabasca River Trail, which begins at Old Fort Point and follows the river to a point below Maligne Canyon. Cyclists are particularly prone to sudden bear encounters–a few years ago a rider was pulled from his bike by a grizzly, within screaming distance of Jasper Park Lodge; make noises when passing through heavily wooded areas. The brochure *Mountain Biking Trail Guide* lists designated trails and is available from **Freewheel Cycle,** 618 Patricia St., 780/852-3898.

Horseback Riding

On the benchlands immediately behind Jasper townsite is **Pyramid Riding Stables,** Pyramid Lake Road, 780/852-3562. The stables offer one-, two-, and three-hour guided rides for $25, $43, and $65, respectively. The one-hour trip follows a ridge high above town, providing excellent views of the Athabasca River Valley. **Skyline Trail Rides,** at the Jasper Park Lodge, 780/852-4215, offers a one-hour guided ride around Lake Annette ($25 per person) and a 4.5-hour ride to Maligne Canyon ($70 per person). **Maligne Tours,** at Maligne Lake, offers three-and-a-half-hour guided rides through the alpine meadows of the Bald Hills for $60. Book at 627 Patricia Street, 780/852-3370.

Overnight pack trips consist of four to six hours of riding per day, with a few nights spent at a remote mountain lodge where you can hike, boat, fish, or ride. Rates start at $140 per person per day. For details, contact **Skyline Trail Rides,** 780/852-4215 or 888/852-7787; or **Tonquin Valley Adventures,** 780/852-1188.

Whitewater Rafting

The Athabasca, Sunwapta, and Maligne Rivers are run by a half a dozen outfitters. On the Athabasca River, the Mile 5 Run is an easy two-hour float that appeals to all ages. Farther upstream, some operators offer a trip that begins from below Athabasca Falls, on a stretch of the river that passes through a narrow canyon; this run takes three hours. The boulder-strewn rapids of the Sunwapta and Maligne Rivers offer more thrills and spills—these trips are for the more adventurous and also last around three hours. Most companies offer a choice of rivers and provide transportation to and from downtown hotels. Expect to pay $40–55 for trips on the Athabasca and $55 for the Sunwapta and Maligne. The following companies run at least two of three rivers: **Maligne Rafting Adventures,** 780/852-3370; **Raven Adventures,** 780/852-4292; **Rocky Mountain River Guides,** 780/852-3777; and **White Water Rafting,** 780/852-7238 or 800/557-7238. **Jasper Raft Tours,** 780/852-2665, floats the Athabasca River in large, stable inflatable rafts; adults $40, children $15.

For a different, more relaxing, and historically linked adventure, try a trip down the Athabasca River in a stable 10-meter voyageur canoe, similar to those used by early explorers and fur traders. These trips are offered by **Rocky Mountain Voyageur** starting at Old Fort Point and floating downstream for two hours. The cost, including transfers, is $50. For reservations, call 780/852-3343 or drop by any of the local booking agencies listed at the beginning of this section.

Fishing

Fishing in the many alpine lakes—for rainbow, brook, Dolly Varden, cutthroat, and lake trout, as well as pike and whitefish—is excellent. Guided fishing trips are offered by many outfitters. Whether you fish with a guide or by yourself, you'll need a national park fishing license ($6 per week, $13 per year), available from the Park Information Centre or On-line Sport & Tackle at 600 Patricia Street. Maligne Lake is the most popular fishing hole; in 1980, a 10-kg rainbow trout was caught in its deep waters, setting a provincial record.

Small motor boats are available from the Boathouse at Maligne Lake, 780/852-3370, for $70 per day, with rod and reel rentals extra. Guided fishing trips on the lake are offered by **Maligne Tours,** 780/852-3370; half day $125 per person, full day $170 per person. **Currie's Guiding,** 780/852-5650, offers trips to Maligne Lake (full day $160 per person) and to lakes requiring a 30–60 minute hike to access (from $140 per person for a half day). These rates include equipment and instruction. **Source for Sports,** 406 Patricia St., 780/852-3654, and **On-line Sport & Tackle,** 600 Patricia St., 780/852-3630, sells and rents fishing tackle and also have canoe and boat rentals.

Golfing

The world-famous **Jasper Park Lodge Golf Course** was designed by renowned golf-course architect Stanley Thompson. The course opened in 1925, after 200 men had spent an entire year clearing trees and laying out the holes to Thompson's design. Renovations were made in 1994, but the course plays as it did when it first opened. It is consistently ranked as one of the top 10 courses in Canada. The 18-hole championship course takes in the contours of the Athabasca River Valley as it hugs the banks of turquoise-colored Lac Beauvert. The 6,670-yard course is a true test of accuracy, and with holes named "The Maze," "The Bad Baby," and "The Bay," you'll need lots of balls. Greens fees for 18 holes vary with the season: $109 in summer, $89 mid-May to mid-June, and $69 in early May and from October 1 through to closing (usually mid-October). An electric cart is $32 per round. Golfing after 5 P.M. is $79 with a cart—a great deal during the long days of June and July. Other facilities include a driving range, club rentals ($28–42), a restaurant, and a lounge. Tee times can be reserved by calling 780/852-6090.

Indoor Recreation

Jasper Aquatic Centre, 401 Pyramid Lake Road, 780/852-3663, has an Olympic-size swimming pool; admission is $4.75. **Jasper Activity Centre,** next door, 780/852-3381, has squash courts, indoor and outdoor tennis courts, a climbing wall, a weight room, and an indoor skate park; admission $6.

WINTERTIME

Winter is certainly a quiet time in the park, but that doesn't mean there's a lack of things to do. Marmot Basin offers world-class alpine skiing; many snow-covered hiking trails are groomed for cross-country skiing; portions of Lac Beauvert and Pyramid Lake are cleared for ice-skating; horse-drawn sleighs travel around town; and Maligne Canyon is transformed into a magical, frozen world. Hotels reduce rates by 40–70 percent through winter and many offer lodging and lift tickets for under $70 per person.

Marmot Basin

The skiing at Marmot Basin is highly underrated. A huge injection of cash in recent years has meant even better facilities are offered and new lifts have opened up additional terrain. Lifts now take skiers into Charlie's Basin, a massive powder-filled bowl, and the opening of the Eagle Ridge Quad for the 2001/02 season will open up another two mountain faces. Local Joe Weiss saw the potential for skiing in the basin in the 1920s and began bringing skiers up from the valley. A road was constructed from the highway in the early 1950s, and the first paying skiers were transported up to the slopes in a Sno-Cat. The first lift, a 700-meter rope tow, was installed on the Paradise face in 1961, and the area has continued to expand ever since. Marmot Basin now has seven lifts servicing 400 hectares of terrain and a vertical rise of 890 meters. It doesn't get the crowds of Banff, so lift lines are uncommon. The season runs from early December to late April. Lift tickets are $44 for adults, $31 for seniors, $18 for children. (Through January tickets are just $31). Rentals are available at the resort or in town at **Totem Ski Shop,** 408 Connaught Drive, 780/852-3078. For more information on the resort, contact Marmot Basin Ski-lifts, 780/852-3816 or, for a ski report from Edmonton, 780/488-5909.

Buses depart three times daily for Marmot Basin from most Jasper hotels; $7 one-way, $12 round-trip. The first departure is 8–8:30 A.M.

Cross-Country Skiing

For many, traveling Jasper's hiking trails on skis is just as exhilarating as on foot. An extensive network of 300 km of summer hiking trails is designated for skiers, with around 100 km groomed. The four main areas of trails are along Pyramid Lake Road, around Maligne Lake, in the Athabasca Falls area, and at Whistlers Campground. A booklet available at the Park Information Centre details each trail and its difficulty. Weather forecasts and avalanche-hazard reports are posted here also.

Rental packages are available from **Source for Sports,** 406 Patricia St., 780/852-3654; **Spirit of Skiing** in the Jasper Park Lodge, 780/852-3433; and **Totem Ski Shop,** offering rentals, repairs, and sales at 408 Connaught Drive, 780/852-3078.

Maligne Canyon

By late December, the torrent that is the Maligne River has frozen solid. Where it cascades down through Maligne Canyon the river is temporarily stalled for the winter, creating remarkable formations through the deep limestone canyon. **Maligne Tours,** 627 Patricia St., 780/852-3370, offers exciting three-hour guided tours into the depths of the canyon throughout winter, daily at 9 A.M., 1 P.M., and 6 P.M.; adult $24, children $12.50.

ARTS AND ENTERTAINMENT

Theater and Cinemas

A local theater company, the Heritage Production Company, 780/852-4204, puts on two productions of historical interest in the Jasper Inn at 98 Geikie Street. The brave exploits of nurse Edith Cavell, for whom the park's best-known peak is named, come alive in a theater performance of *Edith Cavell Returns* each Sunday, Tuesday, and Thursday. Captured by German soldiers while assisting Allied troops in German-occupied Belgium during World War I, Edith Cavell was executed in 1915. The *David Thompson Story* tells the tale of one of North America's great geographers and his links to the Canadian Rockies. The plays cost adult $14, child $7 and are performed June–September, daily (except Saturday) at 8:30 P.M.

The **Chaba Theatre,** 604 Connaught Drive, 780/852-4749, shows first-run movies in its two theaters.

Bars and Nightclubs

The most popular nightspot in town is the **Athab,** in the Athabasca Hotel, 510 Patricia St., 780/852-3386, where bands play some nights. It gets

exploring Maligne Canyon in winter

pretty rowdy with all the seasonal workers, but it's still enjoyable; minimal cover charge. This hotel also has a large lounge and a bar with a pool table and a popular 5–7 P.M. happy hour. **Pete's,** upstairs, beside the Patricia Centre Mall at 614 Patricia Street, 780/852-6262, has a jam on Tuesday night and bands playing Friday –Sunday. The music varies—it could be blues, rock, or Celtic. The **De'd Dog Bar and Grill,** in the Astoria Hotel at 404 Connaught Drive, 780/852-3351, is a large, dimly lit sports bar with pool tables and plenty of locals drinking copious amounts of beer, especially during the 5–7 P.M. happy hour. Right downtown, the **Whistle Stop Pub,** in the Whistlers Inn, 105 Miette Ave., 780/852-3361, has great atmosphere with a classic wooden bar and memorabilia everywhere. You don't need to be a guest of Jasper's finest hotel, the **Jasper Park Lodge,** 780/852-3301, to enjoy the ambience of its three lounges: **Tent City** is a sports-style bar with a relaxed atmosphere; the **Emerald Lounge** is more intimate and has an outdoor terrace; while **Palisade's** is a winter-only bar attracting the skiing crowd each evening. Most of Jasper's other large hotels, including the Amethyst Lodge, Jasper Inn, and Marmot Lodge, also have cocktail lounges.

Shopping

Jasper certainly doesn't provide the shopping experience found in Banff, but a number of interesting shops beckon on rainy days. **Our Native Land,** 601 Patricia St., 780/852-5592, is a large shop chock-full of Indian arts and crafts produced by artisans from throughout western Canada. They also stock Inuit soapstone carvings from the Canadian Arctic. **Bearberry,** 612 Connaught Drive, 780/852-1112, features a good cross-section of Canadiana. Beyond the information center, **Pine Cones & Pussy Willow,** 308 Connaught Drive, 780/852-5310, is a little less tacky than your average souvenir shop, with furry toys and plastic rulers complemented by the works of local artists.

Within 100 meters of the information center is **Source for Sports,** 406 Patricia St., 780/852-4046, and the **Totem Ski Shop,** 408 Connaught Drive, 780/852-3078, both with a good stock of camping gear and other outdoor equipment.

Festivals and Events

Summer is prime time on the park's events calendar. The first weekend of June is the **Jasper to Banff Relay.** A month later, **Canada Day** celebrations begin with a pancake breakfast and progress to a flag-raising ceremony (in front of the information center) and a parade along Connaught Drive. Live entertainment and a fireworks display end the day. The **Jasper Lions Pro Indoor Rodeo,** on the second weekend of August, dates from 1933 and attracts pro cowboys from across Canada. Apart from the traditional rodeo events, the fun includes a mechanical bull, a children's rodeo, a casino, pancake breakfasts, the ever-popular stick-pony parade, and the crowning of Miss Jasper. Most of the action takes place in the arena at the Jasper Activity Centre, behind town on Pyramid Lake Road, 780/852-4622. The following weekend is the popular **Coureurs de bois.** Meaning "Runners of the Woods," this 10-km foot race is completed by around 150 runners in the tradition of early voyageurs, complete with plaid shirts and sashes. Call 780/852-5500 for details.

On the other side of the calendar, winter is not totally partyless—**Jasper in January** is a two-week celebration that includes fireworks, special evenings at local restaurants, a chili cook-off, discounted skiing at Marmot Basin, and all the activities associated with winter.

Park Interpretive Program

Parks Canada offers a wide range of interpretive talks and hikes throughout summer. Each summer night in the **Whistlers Campground Theatre** a different slide and movie program is shown. The theater is near the shower block. The **Wabasso Campfire Circle** takes place each Saturday night just before dusk; hot tea is supplied while various speakers talk about wildlife in the park.

Many different guided hikes are offered (all free) throughout summer; check bulletin boards at the Park Information Centre and campgrounds, or call 780/852-6176.

ACCOMMODATIONS

In summer, motel and hotel rooms here are expensive. Most of the motels and lodges are within walking distance of town and have indoor pools and restaurants. Luckily, alternatives to staying in $100-plus places do exist. Many private residences have rooms for rent in summer; two hostels are close to town (and many more are down the Icefields Parkway); bungalows are available that can be a good deal for families or small groups; and there's always camping in the good ol' outdoors. The park has nearly 2,000 campsites, and camping is virtually unlimited in the backcountry.

HOTELS AND MOTELS IN JASPER TOWNSITE

Aside from the famous Jasper Park Lodge, all accommodations discussed here are within walking distance of downtown Jasper. Rates quoted are for a standard room in summer. Outside the busy June–September, period most lodgings reduce rates drastically (ask also about ski packages during winter).

$50–100

Jasper's least expensive rooms can be found right downtown in the **Athabasca Hotel,** 510 Patricia St., 780/852-3386. The cheapest of the hotel's 61 rooms share bathrooms and are above a noisy bar, but the price is right—$55 s, $65 d. This hotel also has more expensive rooms, each with a private bathroom; $139 s or d.

$100–150

Right downtown is the 35-room **Astoria Hotel,** 404 Connaught Drive, 780/852-3351 or 800/661-7343, www.astoriahotel.com, a European-style lodging built in 1924 and kept in the same family since. All rooms have a fridge; from $145 s or d.

$150–200

On Connaught Drive southwest of downtown, **Mount Robson Inn,** 780/852-3327 or 800/587-3327, www.mountrobsoninn.com, was extensively renovated in the late 1990s and now has an air-conditioning unit in each room; $163 s or d.

Adjacent to the Mount Robson Inn is **Maligne Lodge,** 780/852-3143 or 800/661-1315, which features an indoor pool, hot tubs, a sun deck, and a restaurant. Rates for the medium-size rooms are $169 s or d while rooms in the new wing start at $189.

In a central position on Jasper's busiest corner is **Whistlers Inn,** 105 Miette Ave., 780/852-3361 or 800/282-9919, www.whistlersinn.com, which features spacious rooms and a rooftop hot tub; $171 s or d.

At the **Tonquin Inn,** at the northern edge of the townsite on Juniper Street, 780/852-4987 or 800/661-1315, www.tonquininnrockies.com, guests enjoy luxurious rooms, a beautiful indoor pool, an outdoor hot tub, and laundry facilities; from $174 s or d.

Behind the Tonquin Inn, the **Marmot Lodge,** 86 Connaught Drive, 780/852-4471 or 888/852-7737, features 100 modern and stylishly decorated rooms, many with mountain views. On the main level is a good restaurant. Some rooms and the indoor pool are fully wheelchair accessible. In summer, rates begin at $179 s or d, from $139 the rest of the year.

$200–250

Lobstick Lodge, 94 Geikie Ave., 780/852-4431 or 888/852-7737, www.mtn-park-lodges.com, has 139 extra-large, simply furnished rooms and a range of modern amenities including an indoor pool and an outdoor hot tub; from $204 s or d.

Amethyst Lodge, in a central location at 200 Connaught Drive, 780/852-3394, www.mtn-park-lodges.com, is named after a lake in the Tonquin Valley. It offers large air-conditioned rooms, an outdoor hot tub, and a restaurant; $204 s or d.

Jasper Inn, 98 Geikie St., 780/852-4461 or 800/661-1933, www.jasperinn.com, is a modern chateau-style lodging of brick and red cedar. Many rooms rooms have private balconies and over 100 are self-contained suites with kitchenettes and fireplaces. Other features include a large indoor pool, and an outdoor sundeck overlooking a Japanese rock garden. Rates range $210–260 s or d.

Jasper Park Lodge offers rooms and free-standing units in a variety of configurations.

Over $250
Sawridge Hotel, 82 Connaught Drive, 780/852-5111 or 800/661-6427, www.sawridge.com/jasper, offers 154 rooms built around a large atrium and indoor pool; rooms start at $259 s or d, discounted to $109 in the off season.

Charlton's Chateau Jasper, 96 Geikie St., 780/852-5644 or 800/661-9323, www.charlton-resorts.com, is one of Jasper's nicest lodgings. Rooms are large and the low ceilings give them a cozy feel. Downstairs is an excellent restaurant while up top is a rooftop sundeck; $300 s or d.

Jasper Park Lodge, 780/852-3301 or 800/441-1414, www.jasperparklodge.com, lies along the shore of Lac Beauvert, meaning "beautiful green" in French. This is the park's original resort and its most famous. It has four restaurants, three lounges, horseback riding, tennis courts, a championship golf course, and Jasper's only covered shopping arcade. The main lodge features stone floors, carved wooden pillars, and a high ceiling. The 446 rooms vary in configuration; some are modern while others are elegantly rustic. Most are in cottages spread around Lac Beauvert, each with a porch or balcony. Basic rooms start at $479 s or d, off-season rates begin at $149.

LODGES AND BUNGALOWS IN AND AROUND JASPER TOWNSITE

The earliest visitors to Jasper came by train, but as the automobile gained popularity in the 1920s, accommodations were built specifically to cater to visitors who arrived by vehicle. Typically, these "bungalow camps" comprised of a cluster of cabins set around a central lodge where meals were served and with no need for the railway were spread throughout the park. This type of accommodations remain in the park, a popular alternative for those don't need the luxuries of downtown Jasper. They are generally only open May to early October.

$50–100
Spread along a picturesque bend on the Athabasca River six km south of town is **Becker's Chalets,** 780/852-3779, www.beckerschalets.com. This historic lodging took its first guests over 50 years ago and continues to be a park favorite, with many guests coming back year after year. The original cabins still stand. Choose from inexpensive one-bed sleeping rooms ($80), moderately priced chalets each with kitchenette, fireplace, and double bed ($125, or $145 for those on the riverfront), and new premium units featuring all the modern conveniences, including color TV (from $205 per night). Becker's also boasts one of the park's finest restaurants.

The only accommodation of this type that falls into this lower price range is **Pine Bungalows,** 780/852-3491, on a secluded section of the Athabasca River opposite the northern entrance to town. Sparse but comfortable motel-style units with kitchenettes are $95 s or d, individual cabins with kitchens and fireplaces begin at $105.

$100–150

Bear Hill Lodge, 100 Bonhomme St., 780/852-3209, www.bearhilllodge.com, offers the only accommodation of this type in the townsite. Cabins are basic, but each has a TV, bathroom, and coffee-making facilities; $119–189 s or d.

One of the least expensive of a string of lodges immediately south of downtown is **Jasper House Bungalows,** four km south along the Icefields Parkway, 780/852-4535. It offers 56 rooms, including inexpensive sleeping units for $120; those with cooking facilities begin at $190.

Tekarra Lodge, 780/852-3058 or 888/404-4540, www.tekarralodge.com, is 1.5 km southeast of the townsite at the confluence of the Miette and Athabasca Rivers. Rooms in the lodge are $139 s or d; cabins, each with a kitchenette and wood-burning fireplace, begin at $159. Also on site is a casual restaurant open for breakfast and dinner, and bike rentals for guests.

Continuing south along Highway 93A from Tekarra Lodge, at the junction of the Icefields Parkway three km south of Jasper townsite, is **Alpine Village,** 780/852-3285, www.alpine villagejasper.com. This typical mountain resort is laid out across grassy gardens, just across the road from the Athabasca River. The older cabins have recently been renovated (from $140) while the new deluxe one-bedroom log cabins feature stone fireplaces and modern furnishings ($180). All units have a bathroom and kitchen. Open late April to mid-October.

Patricia Lake Bungalows, 780/852-3560, www.patricialakebungalows.com, is beside the lake of the same name, a five-minute drive north from Jasper along Pyramid Lake Road. Comfortable cottages with kitchens are $145–200 depending on the size. A number of very basic motel-style rooms are $75. Other facilities include a barbecue area and an outdoor hot tub.

Continue along Pyramid Lake Road from Patricia Lake and its impossible to miss the sprawling grounds of **Pyramid Lake Resort,** 780/852-4900 or 888/852-4900, www.pyramidlake resort.com, the only lodging away from town, besides Jasper Park Lodge, open year-round. Plenty of water-based activities and rentals, and interpretive program, and a large barbecue area make the resort a good choice for families; $149–239 per unit.

HOTELS, MOTELS, AND LODGES IN OTHER PARTS OF THE PARK

Icefields Parkway

A number of accommodations are strung out along the Icefields Parkway close to Jasper townsite (see above) while two more lie further south, along the parkway proper.

Historic **Sunwapta Falls Resort,** 780/852-4852, www.sunwapta.com, is 55 km south of Jasper townsite and within walking distance of the picturesque waterfall for which it is named. It features 52 units, all with televisions and some with kitchenettes and fireplaces. Out front is a self-serve restaurant popular with passing travelers and a quieter more relaxed restaurant and lounge upstairs. Rates start at $175 s or d. Open early May to mid-October.

Columbia Icefield Chalet, 780/852-6550, www.brewster.ca, part of the Columbia Icefield Centre, lies in a stunning location high above the tree line and overlooking the Columbia Icefield, 103 km south of Jasper townsite. It features 29 standard rooms, 17 of which have glacier views, and three larger, more luxurious corner rooms. Rates June–Sept. range $175–195 s or d, while the last week of May and the first few days in October rates start at $90. The facility is closed the rest of the year.

East of Jasper Townsite

Two accommodations east of the townsite are open in summer only. **Pocahontas Bungalows,** 780/866-3732 or 800/843-3372, is at the bottom of the road that leads to Miette Hot Springs; basic motel rooms are $80, while bungalows with kitchenettes range from $90 to $170. On site is a heated pool and restaurant.

Miette Hot Springs Bungalows, 780/866-3750, is within walking distance of the park's only hot springs. Motel units are $125 while bungalows start at $145.

Hinton

This medium-sized town lies along Highway 16, 19 km east of the park gate and 69 km east of Jasper townsite. Staying here provides an inexpensive alternative to staying in the park. The strip of motels, restaurants, fast-food places, and gas stations along Highway 16 is the place to start looking for a room.

All of the following are along Highway 16. Least expensive are the rooms available at **Pines Motel,** 780/865-2624, beside the golf course; $55 s or d.

The dowdy-looking **Big Horn Motel,** 780/865-1555, beside the Husky gas station, has surprisingly good rooms, some larger than others; $70 s, $75 d, kitchenettes an extra $10.

Holiday Inn Hinton, 780/865-3321, has a restaurant, an outdoor heated pool, and a fitness room with a hot tub. The 104 rooms are well furnished, and equipped with everything from hairdryers to Playstation games; rates start at $79 s, $89 d.

Hinton's newest accommodation is the **Ramada Hotel,** 780/865-2575, which features 55 comfortable rooms, a fitness room, and a spa facility; $96 s or d includes a light breakfast.

Black Cat Guest Ranch, 780/865-3084 or 800/859-6840, is a mountain retreat west of Hinton. All the rooms have private baths and views of the mountains. Horseback riding is available during the day, and in the evening, guests can relax in the large living room or hot tub. Meals are included in the rates or $133 s, $168 d. To get to the ranch take Highway 40 north for six km, turn left to Brûlé and continue for 11 km, then turn right and follow the signs.

Tonquin Amethyst Lake Lodge

The only backcountry accommodation in the park is Tonquin Amethyst Lake Lodge, 780/852-1188, www.tonquinadventures.com. The lodge is southwest of Jasper in the spectacular Tonquin Valley. Getting there involves a 23-km hike or horseback ride or, in winter, cross-country ski trip, from a trailhead opposite Mt. Edith Cavell Hostel. The original lodge was built in 1939, with more modern additions made in 1990, including a rustic dining room. Private cabins have wood-burning heaters, bunk beds, oil lanterns, and a spectacular view. The rate, $125 per person per night, includes accommodations, three meals, and use of small boats and fishing gear. Tonquin Adventures offers a number of well-priced packages, including riding into the lodge on horses. Rates are reduced in winter.

PRIVATE HOME ACCOMMODATIONS/ BED AND BREAKFASTS

At last count, Jasper had over 80 residential homes offering accommodations. Often they supply nothing more than a room with a bed, but the price is right—$40–80 s or d. Usually the bathroom is shared with other guests or the family; few have kitchens and only a few supply breakfast. In most cases, don't expect too much with the lower-priced choices. The positive side, apart from the price, is that your hosts are usually knowledgeable locals and downtown is only a short walk away. The Jasper Tourism and Commerce Information Centre has a board listing private home accommodations with rooms available for the upcoming night. Most have signs out front so you could cruise the streets (try Connaught, Patricia, and Geikie), but checking at the information center is easier. For a full listing that includes the facilities at each, write to Jasper Home Accommodation Association, P.O. Box 758, Jasper, AB T0E 1E0, or check out www.bbcanada.com/jhaa.html.

HOSTELS

Hostelling International operates five hostels in the park, but none right in downtown Jasper; the closest is seven km distant. A summer-only shuttle service runs between Calgary and Jasper, stopping at all hostels en route. To ride, you must have advance reservations for both the bus and hostel. A couple of privately owned shuttle services link the hostels in the immediate vicinity of Jasper. Make bookings for both accommodations and transportation through Jasper International Hostel, 780/852-3215.

Near Jasper Townsite

On the road to the Jasper Tramway, seven km from town, is **Jasper International Hostel,** which has 80 beds in men's and women's dorms, a large kitchen, a common room, showers, public Internet access, an outdoor barbecue area, and mountain-bike rentals. Members of Hostelling International pay $16, nonmembers $21. For hostel reservations, call 780/852-3215. In the summer months this hostel fills up every night. The front desk is open daily 8 A.M.–midnight. Cab fare between downtown Jasper and the hostel is $15, and the bus services charge $5 per person.

Maligne Canyon Hostel is on Maligne Lake Road, beside the Maligne River and a short walk from the canyon. Although rustic, it lies in a beautiful setting. The 24 beds are in two cabins; other amenities include electricity, a kitchen, and a dining area. Rates are $11 for members, $16 for nonmembers. For reservations, call 780/852-3215. Check in between 5 P.M. and 11 P.M. The hostel is closed on Wednesdayduring the months of October –April.

Mt. Edith Cavell Hostel offers a million-dollar view for the price of a dorm bed. It's 13 km up Mt. Edith Cavell Road, and because of the location there's usually a spare bed. Opposite the hostel are trailheads for hiking in the Tonquin Valley, and it's just a short walk to the base of Mt. Edith Cavell. The hostel is rustic but has a kitchen, dining area, and outdoor wood sauna. Members pay $11 per night, nonmembers pay $16. It's open mid-June to October and check in is 5–11 P.M. For reservations, call 780/852-3215.

Along the Icefields Parkway
Two hostels lie along Jasper's section of the Icefields Parkway. Check in is 5–11 P.M., but the main lodges are open all day. Reservations can be made at all major hostels or by calling 780/852-3215.

Athabasca Falls Hostel is 32 km south of Jasper townsite (at Km 198 from Lake Louise). It is larger than the one at Beauty Creek and has electricity. Athabasca Falls is only a few minutes' walk away. Members of Hostelling International pay $11, nonmembers $16.

Beauty Creek Hostel, 17 km north of Columbia Icefield (at Km 144 from Lake Louise), is nestled in a small stand of Douglas fir between the Icefields Parkway and the Sunwapta River. Each of its separate male and female cabins sleeps 12 and has a woodstove. A third building holds a well-equipped kitchen and dining area. Members $10, nonmembers $15. Open May–September.

CAMPGROUNDS

Near Jasper Townsite
Whistlers Campground, at the base of Whistlers Road, three km south of Jasper townsite, has 781 sites, making it the largest campground in the Canadian Rockies. It is divided into four sections; prices vary with the services available—walk-in sites $15, unserviced sites $17, powered sites $21, full hookups $24. Each section has showers. The campground is open May to mid-October. A further two km south is **Wapiti Campground,** which offers 366 sites and has showers; unserviced sites $16, powered sites $19. This is the park's only campground open year-round, with serviced winter camping $15 per night.

East of Jasper Townsite
East of the townsite, along Highway 16, are two smaller, more primitive campgrounds. **Snaring River Campground,** 17 km from Jasper on Celestine Lake Rd., is $10; **Pocahontas Campground,** 45 km northeast, is $13. Both are open mid-May to early September.

Along the Icefields Parkway
Wabasso Campground is along Highway 93A, 16 km south of Jasper townsite; $13. Traveling a further 20 km south, you'll find three campgrounds within 50 km. They are **Mt. Kerkeslin, Honeymoon Lake,** and **Jonas Creek Campgrounds.**

Columbian ground squirrels are common in all campgrounds.

Each is $10 per site, per night. **Wilcox Creek** and **Columbia Icefield Campgrounds** are within two km of each other at the extreme southern end of the park. Both are primitive campgrounds with toilets, cooking shelters, and fire rings; sites are $10.

OTHER PRACTICALITIES

FOOD

Coffeehouses and Cafés

Soft Rock Internet Cafe, in Connaught Square at 622 Connaught Drive, 780/852-5850, starts the day by dishing up plates of waffles topped with cream and your choice of fresh fruit for $4.50. If the cinnamon buns are still in the oven, you'll have to come back later in the day—they're gigantic! The variety of coffee concoctions here is mind-boggling, and prices are reasonable. It's open 7 A.M.–11 P.M. In the same vicinity, **Café & Roses,** 614 Connaught Drive (behind the first row of shops and up a nearby alley), 780/852-4445, is a small coffee shop away from the busy main street. **Truffles & Trout,** in Jasper Marketplace, corner Patricia and Hazel Streets, 780/852-9676, is a popular local hangout, with all the usual coffees, as well as boxed picnic lunches on offer. Across the road, **Nutter's,** 622 Patricia St., 780/852-5844, is another good pre-hiking stop, with a wide choice of goodies in bulk bins. **Spooner's,** in the Patricia Centre Mall at 610 Patricia Street, 780/852-4046, is a second-floor café with stunning mountain views and a good range of coffees and light meals. A couple of doors away, **Coco's Café,** 608 Patricia St., 780/852-4550, is another coffee-lover's meeting place. At the northern side of the downtown core is the **Bear's Paw Bakery,** 4 Cedar Ave., 780/852-3233, open daily from 6 A.M. It offers a great range of European-styled breads as well as cakes and pastries. **Dano's,** 604 Patricia St., 780/852-3322, will satisfy any ice cream or cappuccino cravings.

Cool and Casual

For pizza, you won't be able to miss **Jasper Pizza Place,** 402 Connaught Drive, 780/852-3225. It's a large and noisy restaurant with bright furnishings and walls lined with photos from Jasper's earliest days. Pizza from the wood-fired oven starts at $10.50 while smaller pita pizzas, perfect for a lunchtime snack, cost just $4.50. One of Jasper's oldest restaurants, **Papa George's,** in the Astoria Hotel at 406 Connaught Drive, 780/852-3351, has huge east-facing windows that take in the panorama of distant mountain peaks. Breakfast is $4–8, a traditional English afternoon tea served 2:30–4:30 P.M. is $7.50, while lunch and dinner feature burgers, pasta, and steaks; daily specials are $11–17 and include soup and salad. Hours are 7 A.M.–10 P.M.

Kontos Restaurant, 622 Patricia St., 780/852-3444, is a new addition to the Jasper dining scene. The menu is fairly standard, family-style dining with inexpensive lunch specials for $5 and dinner entrées ranging $10–21. (The bathrooms here are worthy of a special mention—they contain everything from sunscreen to singing birds). Kitty-corner, across Hazel Avenue, **L&W Restaurant,** 780/852-4114, appeals to a similar crowd with a small outside patio and plenty of greenery that brings to life an otherwise ordinary restaurant—a good place to take the family for an inexpensive meal.

Treeline Restaurant, 780/852-5352, high above town on the Whistlers, has, without a doubt, the best views in town. Daily breakfast and lunch buffets complement the à la carte menu while the Sunset Dinner package costs $50 including the gondola ride. Also out of town is **Pyramid Lake Resort Restaurant,** overlooking Pyramid Lake, 780/852-4900. Its small outdoor patio is a fine place to eat lunch.

Canadian

One of Jasper's best restaurants, **Becker's Gourmet Restaurant,** 780/852-3535, is five km out of town along the Icefields Parkway, but well worth the short drive. From this cozy dining room where the atmosphere is intimate or the adjacent enclosed conservatory, the views of Mt. Kerkeslin and the Athabasca River are inspiring. This restaurant is a throwback to days gone by, with an ever-changing menu of seasonal game and produce and the emphasis on a "mountain" style dining experience. With a bottle of wine expect to pay $100 for two. Becker's is also open for breakfast from 8 a.m.; the buffet costs $12.50.

Back in town, **Andy's Bistro,** 606 Patricia St., 780/852-4559, is an elegant eatery offering a wide choice of favorite Canadian dishes prepared with Swiss-influenced cooking styles. At the unique *stammtisch,* a large table, up to 10 diners can be seated at once, free to come and go as they please. It's the perfect place to mingle with fellow travelers. Entrées range $18–30 and it's open daily for dinner only.

The place to go for Alberta beef is **Tonquin Prime Rib Village,** on Juniper Street beside the Tonquin Inn, 780/852-4966, which specializes in charbroiled steaks and prime rib but also offers a good choice of seafood. Expect to pay from $20 for a hearty prime rib dish.

Upstairs at 640 Connaught Drive, 780/852-3920, is another popular steakhouse, **Villa Caruso,** with a number of open balconies offering great views across the valley. The restaurant itself has a modern, western-style decor, and a menu to match, with a wide variety of steak and ribs dishes from $18. But there's a lot more than steak on offer, including chicken, seafood, and pasta dishes.

Most of the larger accommodations have restaurants. **Walter's Dining Room** in the Sawridge Hotel, 82 Connaught Drive, 780/852-5111, features a menu of Alberta beef, rainbow trout, and British Columbia salmon in an elegant but relaxed atmosphere. They also do a breakfast buffet, but are closed for lunch. In the same vicinity, the **Inn Restaurant** in the Jasper Inn, 98 Geikie St., 780/852-3232, sits within a glass-enclosed atrium and features a menu of Alberta beef, ribs, fondue, and seafood. Entrées start at $15. Diners are offered complimentary limo service to the restaurant. The same menu is served in the just-as-elegant lounge for half the price.

Fiddle River Seafood Restaurant, 620 Connaught Drive, 780/852-3032, upstairs in Connaught Square, has fresh seafood, but expect to pay around $35–45 per person for a three-course meal. If you can't afford to eat here, at least stick your head in the door and admire the striking decor.

European

The best Greek meals in town are served at **Something Else Restaurant,** 621 Patricia St., 780/852-3850. Portions are generous, service is friendly, the prices are right, and you'll find plenty of alternatives if the Greek dishes don't appeal to you. Greek favorites are $11–16, pasta dishes $11–14, pizza from $10. It's open daily 11 A.M.–midnight.

Another Greek-influenced restaurant is **Palisades,** Cedar Ave., 780/852-5222. The menu offers a number of inexpensive vegetarian choices, pastas and pizza to $17, Greek specialties under $20, a massive T-bone steak for $22, and a $5 kids menu.

Miss Italia Ristorante, 610 Patricia St., 780/852-4002, upstairs in the Patricia Centre, features mountain views from tables indoors and out and colorful flowers throughout. Cooked breakfasts are $5–8. The rest of the day, pastas made fresh daily average $12, while Taste of Italy choices, featuring a sampling of cuisines from three regions, run $18.

The award-winning **Beavallon Dining Room** at Chateau Jasper, 96 Geikie St., 780/852-5644, ext. 179, offers an extensive menu emphasizing continental cuisine prepared by a Swiss chef. All the chairs are upholstered, and the blue tablecloths and wood-trimmed crimson walls provide an air of elegance—elegance you pay for. It's expensive—dinner main dishes range $22–34 The Sunday brunch—complete with live background music—features everything from pork tenderloin to smoked salmon.

Asian

The **Cantonese Restaurant,** 608 Connaught Drive, 780/852-3559, is the place to go for Chinese; combo specials are $9–13 and set menus for two start at $23. It's open daily noon–10 P.M.

Denjiro, 410 Connaught Drive, 780/852-3780, features a traditional sushi bar and eight tatami booths for eating the Japanese cuisine; combination dinners average $17 per person. It's open 5–11:30 P.M.

Jasper Park Lodge

The lodge offers a choice of casual or elegant dining in a variety of restaurants and lounges. **Obsessions,** in the Beauvert Shopping Promenade, has tempting French pastries, gourmet coffee, and homemade truffles and chocolates. Drinks and light snacks are served at the **Spike Lounge** overlooking the golf course. At lunchtime the smell of sizzling steaks from **La Terrasse** wafts across Lac Beauvert; this outdoor eatery is open only in summer. **Meadows Café,** downstairs in the shopping arcade, is open for a breakfast buffet 8–11:30 A.M. and then in the evening for a dinner buffet 5:30–9 P.M. The **Beauvert Dining Room** is a casual 500-seat eatery. It features a daily buffet breakfast and an eclectic dinner menu. The Sunday brunch, between 10:30 A.M. and 1:30 P.M. and cost $20, is especially popular. The **Moose's Nook,** with a rustic atmosphere, is a good place to enjoy traditional Canadian fare such as buffalo steak and salmon. It's open for dinner only, with mains from $18. The **Edith Cavell Room** is the finest fine-dining restaurant in Jasper. Its dark oak walls contrast with the white linens and large, bright windows overlooking Lac Beauvert and the mountains beyond. The classic cuisine is served with a French flair and price tag; if you need to ask the price, you can't afford it (the five-course table d'hôte menu is $62 per person). For all lodge restaurant reservations, call 780/852-6052. Food is also available in each of the lodge's three .

TRANSPORTATION

Getting There

Getting to Jasper by public transportation is easy, although the closest airport handling domestic and international flights is at Edmonton, 360 km to the east. The **VIA rail station** and the **bus depot** (used by both Greyhound and Brewster) are in the same building, central to town at 607 Connaught Drive. The building is open 24 hours daily in summer; the rest of the year Monday –Saturday 7:30 A.M.–10:30 P.M., Sunday 7:30–11 A.M. and 6:30–10:30 P.M. Lockers are available for $1 per day. Also here are a travel agent and car rental agencies.

Jasper is on the "Canadian" route, the only remaining transcontinental passenger rail service in the country. Trains run either way three times weekly. To the west the line divides, going to both Prince Rupert and Vancouver; to the east it passes through Edmonton ($116 one-

way from Jasper) and all points beyond. For all rail information, call 800/561-8630. Another rail option is offered by **Rocky Mountaineer Rail Tours,** 800/665-7245. This company operates a luxurious summer-only rail service between Vancouver and Jasper with an overnight in Kamloops (British Columbia). The one-way fare is $610 per person, with a $100 discount for travel in May and October.

Greyhound buses, 780/852-3926 or 800/661-8747, depart Jasper for all points in Canada, including Vancouver (three times daily, 12–13 hours, $99.19 one-way), Edmonton (five times daily, four and a half hours, $49.49 one-way) with connections to Calgary, and Prince Rupert (once daily, 18 hours, $132.57 one-way).

The only bus service between Jasper and Banff runs mid-April to the end of October, with buses continuing on from Banff to Calgary International Airport mid-May to mid-October. Buses depart the airport daily at 12:30 P.M. ($71 one-way to Jasper), pick up passengers in Banff at 3:15 P.M. ($51 one-way) and Lake Louise at 4:15 P.M. ($44 one-way), and arrive in Jasper at 8:20 P.M. The return service departs daily from Jasper Park Lodge at 12:50 P.M. and from the downtown bus depot at 1:30 P.M., arriving at Calgary airport at 9:30 P.M. Brewster also runs a nine-hour (one-way) tour between Banff and Jasper departing daily mid-April through October from the Banff and Jasper depots at 8 A.M.; if the bus picks you up at your lodging, departure time is earlier. The tour costs $89 one-way ($67 in spring and fall), $124 round-trip ($89 in spring and fall). The round-trip requires an overnight in Jasper. All of these bus services are operated by **Brewster,** 780/852-3332.

Getting Around

The **Maligne Lake Shuttle,** 780/852-3370, runs out to Maligne Lake 3–6 times daily ($24 round-trip) and will make drops at Maligne Canyon and Maligne Canyon Hostel ($8 one-way).

Rental cars start at $65 per day with 100 free kilometers. The following companies have agencies in town: **Avis,** 780/852-3970 or 800/879-2847; **Budget,** 780/852-3222 or 800/610-3222; **Hertz,** 780/852-3888; and **National,** 780/852-1117 or 800/387-4747.

Mountain bikes can be rented from: **On-line Sport & Tackle,** 600 Patricia St., 780/852-3630;

Source for Sports, 406 Patricia St., 780/852-3654; Freewheel Cycle, 618 Patricia St., 780/852-3898; and Beauvert Boat & Cycle, out at Jasper Park Lodge, 780/852-5708. Expect to pay $5–8 per hour or $15–28 per day. Freewheel Cycle leads a five-hour bike tour along Maligne Lake Road, but most of the hard work is done for you, as transportation is provided to the lake, allowing a two-hour downhill run on the bikes; $85 per person.

Cabs in town are not cheap. Most drivers will take you on a private sightseeing tour or to trailheads if requested; try Jasper Taxi, 780/852-3600 or 852-3146. Heritage Cabs, 780/852-5558, has a fleet of antique cars.

Tours

Brewster, 780/852-3332, offers a three-hour Discover Jasper tour taking in Patricia and Pyramid Lakes, Maligne Canyon, and Jasper Tramway (ride not included in fare). It departs April–October daily at 8:30 A.M. from the main bus depot; $42. Maligne Tours, 627 Patricia St., 780/852-3370, schedules a variety of tours, including one to Maligne Lake ($56, includes cruise). Jasper Adventure Centre, in the Chaba Theatre at 604 Connaught Drive in summer (at 306 Connaught in winter), 780/852-5595, operates a number of well-priced tours, including the following: Mt. Edith Cavell (departs 2 P.M.; three hours), Maligne Canyon (spring and fall only; departs 9:30 A.M. and 1 P.M.; three hours), and

Miette Hot Springs (departs 6 P.M.; four hours); $40 per person per tour. They also offer similar-priced tours taking in historical sites and local wildlife, as well as a mystery tour.

Air Jasper, 780/865-3616 or 877/865-3617, offers customized air tours from Hinton Airport, 69 km east of Jasper townsite; the cost is $110 per hour per person. Typically, an hour and a half airtime will get you as far as Columbia Icefield.

SERVICES AND INFORMATION

Services

The post office is at 502 Patricia Street, behind the Park Information Centre. Mail to be picked up here should be addressed General Delivery, Jasper, AB T0E 1E0.

Public Internet access is available two locations within Connaught Square Mall: More than Mail, 780/852-3151 and Soft Rock Internet Café, 780/852-5850. The former offers a wide range of other communication services including regular post, fax and copying facilities, a work area for laptops, international calling, and currency exchange. Internet access is also offered at the local library and at Jasper International Hostel.

The two Laundromats on Patricia Street are open 6 A.M.–11 P.M. and offer showers that cost $2 for 10 minutes (quarters).

The hospital is at 518 Robson Street, 780/852-3344. For the RCMP, call 780/852-4848.

Originally built as a home for Jasper's first superintendent, this historic building now houses the Park Information Centre.

Books and Bookstores

The small **Jasper Municipal Library,** on Elm Avenue, 780/852-3652, holds just about everything ever written about the park and has public Internet access. It's open Monday–Thursday 2–5 P.M. and 7–9 P.M., Friday 2–5 P.M., Saturday 10 A.M.–3 P.M.

Head to the Park Information Centre or the museum for a good selection of books on the park's natural and human history. Another good selection of literature can be found at **Jasper Camera and Gift,** 412 Connaught Drive, 780/852-3165. **Maligne Lake Books,** in the Jasper Park Lodge, has a good selection of coffee-table books.

Information

The residence of Jasper's first superintendent, a beautiful old stone building dating to 1913, is now used by Parks Canada as the **Park Information Centre.** It's right downtown in Athabasca Park on Connaught Drive, 780/852-6176. The staff provides general information on the park and can direct you to hikes in the immediate vicinity. They also handle questions for those going into the backcountry. **Jasper Tourism and Commerce,** 780/852-3858, also has a desk in the building, and the friendly staff never seems to tire of explaining that all the rooms in town are full. As well as providing general information on the town, they have a large collection of brochures on activities, shopping, and restaurants in town. In the far corner is the **Friends of Jasper National Park** outlet selling maps, books, and local publications. Look out for notices posted out front with the day's interpretive programs. The center is open in summer, daily 8 A.M.–7 P.M.; the rest of the year, daily 9 A.M.–5 P.M.

Jasper's weekly newspaper, **The Booster,** is available throughout town on Wednesday. As well as newsworthy stories, it includes a list of upcoming events, trail reports, (and a town map with funky little symbols highlighting the location of various "crimes"). **Wildlife** is an entertaining publication filled with stories of local issues and events; it's available freely throughout town.

For a list of park-related items available for sale, including publications and topographic maps, write to Friends of Jasper National Park, P.O. Box 992, Jasper, AB T0E 1E0, or call 780/852-4767. For more information on the park, write Superintendent, Jasper National Park, P.O. Box 10, Jasper, AB T0E 1E0; www.parkscanada.gc.ca/jasper. For general tourist information, write Jasper Tourism and Commerce, P.O. Box 98, Jasper T0E 1E0, or call 780/852-3858. The best commercial website related to the park is www.explorejasper.com, with lists of current events, current weather conditions, and loads of helpful links. A similar website is www.visit-jasper.com.

Jasper National Park Radio is on the AM band at 1490. For weather conditions in the park, call 780/852-3185.

Waterton townsite sits on a low-lying delta that extends into the deep waters of Upper Waterton Lake.

WATERTON LAKES NATIONAL PARK

INTRODUCTION

Everybody traveling to this small, rugged 526-square-km park does so by choice; tucked away in the extreme southwestern corner of Alberta, the park is not on a major highway or on the way to anywhere else. It's bounded to the north and east by the rolling prairies covering southern Alberta; to the south by the U.S. border and Glacier National Park in Montana; and to the west by the Continental Divide, which forms the Alberta/British Columbia border. The natural mountain splendor, a chain of deep glacial lakes, large and diverse populations of wildlife, an unbelievable variety of day hikes, and a changing face each season make this park a gem that shouldn't be missed on any trip to the Canadian Rockies.

The route to Waterton is almost as scenic as the park itself. From whichever direction you arrive, the transition from prairie to mountains is abrupt, almost devoid of the foothills that characterize other areas along the eastern slopes of the Canadian Rockies. Between the park gate and the small township of Waterton, two roads penetrate the mountains to the west. One ends at a large glaciated lake, the other at a spectacular canyon. The town is a smaller version of those in Banff and Jasper. Like those towns, Waterton holds a grand hotel built by the railway, a golf course, and a wide range of services. But the atmosphere here is very different.

See color map of Waterton National Park on page xiv.

PARK ENTRY

All visitors to Waterton Lakes National Park are required to stop at the park gate and buy a permit. A National Parks Day Pass is adult $4, senior $3, child $2 to a maximum of $8 per vehicle. It is valid until 4 P.M. the day following its purchase. If you're traveling beyond Waterton, a better deal is the annual Great Western Pass, good for entry into all 11 of western Canada's national parks; adult $35, senior $27 to a maximum of $70 per vehicle ($53 for two or more seniors). Annual passes can be bought at the park gate, or in advance by calling 800/748-7275 or online at the Parks Canada website, www.parkscanada.gc.ca.

THE LAND

Geology

Major upheavals under the earth's surface around 85 million years ago forced huge plates of rock upward and began folding them over each other. One major sheet known as the Lewis Overthrust forms the backbone of Waterton's topography as we see it today. It slid up and over much younger bedrock along a 300-km length extending north to Bow Valley.

Around 45 million years ago this powerful uplift ceased and the forces of erosion took over. About 1.9 million years ago, glaciers from the sheet of ice that once covered most of Alberta crept through the mountains. As these thick sheets of ice advanced and retreated with climatic changes, they gouged out valleys such as the classically U-shaped Waterton Valley. The three Waterton Lakes are depressions left at the base of the steep-sided mountains after the ice had completely retreated 11,000 years ago. The deepest is 150 meters. Cameron Lake, at the end of the Akamina Parkway, was formed when a moraine—the pile of rock that accumulates at the foot of a retreating glacier—dammed Cameron Creek. From the lake, Cameron Creek flows through a glaciated valley before dropping into the much deeper Waterton Valley at Cameron Falls, behind the town of Waterton. The town itself sits on an alluvial fan composed of silt and gravel picked up by mountain streams and deposited in Upper Waterton Lake.

Climate

Climate plays an active role in creating the park's natural landscape. This corner of the province tends to receive more rain, snow, and wind—much more wind—than other parts of Alberta. These factors, combined with the park's varied topography, create an environment where more than half the known species in Alberta have been recorded. Wind is the most powerful presence in the park. Prevailing winds from the south and west bring Pacific weather over the divide, creating a climate similar to that experienced farther west. These warm fronts endow the region with chinooks—dry winds that can raise temperatures in the park by up to 40°C in 24 hours.

One of the nicest aspects of the park is that it can be enjoyed in all seasons. Summer is great for the sunny windless days, fall for the wildlife viewing, winter for the solitude, and spring for the long days of sunlight as the park seems to be waking up from its winter slumber. Be aware, however, that many of the park's best sights and hiking trails lie at high elevations; some areas may be snowed in until mid-June.

Flora

Botanists have recorded 1,200 species of plants growing within the park's several different vegetation zones. In the park's northeastern corner, near the park gate, a region of prairies is covered in semiarid vegetation such as **fescue grass.** As Highway 5 enters the park it passes Maskinonge Lake, a wetlands area of marshy ponds where aquatic plants flourish. Parkland habitat dominated by **aspen** is found along the north side of Blakiston Valley and near Belly River Campground, while montane forest covers most mountain valleys and lower slopes. This montane zone is dominated by a high canopy of **lodgepole pine** and **Douglas fir** shading a forest floor covered with wildflowers and berries. An easily accessible section of this habitat is along the lower half of Bertha Lake Trail; an interpretive brochure is available at the Waterton Visitor Centre.

Above the montane forest is the subalpine zone, which rises as far as the timberline. These distinct forests of **larch, fir, Engelmann spruce,** and **whitebark pine** can be seen along the Carthew Lakes Trail. On the west-facing slopes of Cameron Lakes are mature groves of subalpine trees up to 400 years old—this oldest growth in the park has managed to escape fire over the centuries. Blanketing the open mountain slopes in this zone is bear grass, which grows up to a meter in height and is topped by a bright blossom often likened to a lighted torch. Above the tree line is the alpine zone, where harsh winds and short summer seasons make trees a rarity. Only **lichens** and **alpine wildflowers** flourish at these high altitudes. Crypt Lake is a good place for viewing this zone.

Fauna

Wildlife viewing in the park requires patience and a little know-how, but the rewards are ample, as good as anywhere in the Canadian Rockies. **Elk** inhabit the park year-round. A large herd gathers by Entrance Road in late fall, wintering on the lowlands. By early fall, many **mule deer** are wandering around town. **Bighorn sheep** are often seen on the north side of Blakiston Valley or on the slopes above the Waterton Visitor Centre; occasionally they will end up in town. **White-tailed deer** are best viewed along Red Rock Canyon Parkway. The park has a small population of moose, occasionally seen in lowlying wetlands. **Mountain goats** rarely leave the high peaks of the backcountry, but from Goat, Crypt, or Bertha Lakes you might catch a glimpse of one high above you.

The most common predators in the park are the **coyotes** that spend their summer days chasing ground squirrels around the prairie and parkland areas. For its size, Waterton has a healthy population of **cougars.** But these shy, solitary animals are rarely seen. Around 50 **black bears** live in the park. They spend most of the summer in the heavily forested montane regions. During August and September, scan the slopes of Blakiston Valley, where the bears can often be seen feasting on saskatoon berries before going into winter hibernation. Much larger than black bears are **grizzlies,** which roam the entire backcountry but are rarely encountered. Larger even still are **bison.** Although these prairie dwellers never lived in the mountains, they would have grazed around the eastern outskirts of the what is now the park. A small herd is contained in the **Bison Paddock,** just before the park gate.

Golden-mantled ground squirrels live on the Bear's Hump and around Cameron Falls. **Columbian ground squirrels** are just about everywhere. **Chipmunks** scamper about on

Bertha Lake Trail. The best time for viewing **beavers** is dawn and dusk along the Belly River. **Muskrats** can be seen on the edges of Maskinonge Lake eating bulrushes. **Mink** also live at the lake but are seen only by those with patience.

Two major flyways pass the park, and from September to November many thousands of waterfowl stop on Maskinonge and Lower Waterton Lakes. On a powerline pole beside the entrance to the park is an active **osprey** nest—ask staff to point it out for you. Waterton Heritage Centre has a great little checklist (free) for birders listing the 250 species recorded within park boundaries.

HISTORY

Evidence found within the park suggests that the Kootenay people who lived west of the park made trips across the Continental Divide 8,000–10,000 years ago to hunt bison on the plains and fish in the lakes. They camped in the valleys during winter, taking shelter from the harsh weather. But by around 1,500 years ago, they were spending more time in the west and crossing the mountains only a few times a year to hunt bison. By the 1700s, the Blackfoot—with the help of horses—had expanded their territory from the Battle River throughout southwestern Alberta. They patrolled the mountains on horseback, making it difficult for the Kootenay hunting parties to cross. But their dominance was short-lived. With the arrival of guns and the encroaching homesteads of early settlers, Blackfoot tribes retreated to the east, leaving the Waterton Lakes Valley uninhabited.

Oil City

It was Kootenai Brown, the valley's first permanent settler, who first noticed beads of oil floating on Cameron Creek. He and a business partner siphoned it from the water's surface, bottled it, and sold it in Fort Macleod and Cardston. This created much interest among the oil-starved entrepreneurs of Alberta, who formed the Rocky Mountain Development Company to do some exploratory drilling. At this stage the park was still a Forest Reserve; the trees were protected, but prospecting and mining were still allowed. A rough road was constructed through the Cameron Creek Valley, and in September 1901 the company struck oil

"KOOTENAI" BROWN

John George Brown was born in England in the 1840s and reputedly educated at Oxford University. He joined the army and went to India, later continuing to San Francisco. Then, like thousands of others, he headed for the Cariboo goldfields of British Columbia, quickly spending any of the gold he found. After a while he moved on, heading east into Waterton Valley, where his party was attacked by a band of Blackfoot. He was shot in the back with an arrow and pulled it out himself. For a time he worked with the U.S. Army as a Pony Express rider. One day he was captured by Chief Sitting Bull, stripped, and tied to a stake until his fate could be decided, but he managed to escape during the night with his scalp intact. Brown acquired his nickname through his close association with the Kootenay (today's preferred spelling) people, hunting buffalo and wolves with them until they had all but disappeared.

Brown married in 1869 and built a cabin by Upper Waterton Lake, becoming the valley's first permanent resident. Even though he had been toughened by the times, he was a conservationist at heart. When a reserve was set aside in 1895, Brown was employed as its first warden. In 1911, the area was declared a national park and Brown, age 71, was appointed its superintendent. He continued to push for an expansion of park boundaries until his final retirement at age 75. He died a few years later. His grave along the main access road to the townsite is a fitting resting place for one of Canada's most celebrated mountain men.

---

at a depth of 311 meters. It was the first producing oil well in western Canada and only the second in the country. In the resulting euphoria, a townsite named Oil City was cleared and surveyed, a bunkhouse and dining hall were constructed, and the foundations for a hotel were laid. The boom was short-lived. Drilling rigs kept breaking down and the flow of oil soon slowed to a trickle. A monument along the Akamina Parkway stands at the site of the well, and a little farther up the road at a roadside marker a trail leads through thick undergrowth to the townsite. All that remains are the ill-fated hotel's foundations and some depressions in the ground.

Waterton–Glacier International Peace Park
After becoming the valley's first permanent resident in 1869, Kootenai Brown began promoting the beauty of the area to the people of Fort Macleod. One of his friends, local rancher F. W. Godsal, began lobbying the federal government to establish a reserve. In 1895 an area was set aside as a Forest Reserve. Shortly after Montana's Glacier National Park was created in 1910, the Canadian government changed the name of the reserve to Waterton Lakes Dominion Park; it was later redesignated a national park. Many people followed the footsteps of Kootenai Brown and a small town named Waterton Lakes grew up on the Cameron Creek delta. The town had no rail link, so unlike Banff and Jasper—its famous mountain neighbors to the north—it didn't draw large crowds of tourists. Nevertheless, it soon became a popular summer retreat with a hotel, restaurant, and dance hall. The Great Northern Railway decided to operate a bus service from its Montana rail line to Jasper, with a stop at Waterton Lakes. This led to the construction of the **Prince of Wales Hotel.** Boat cruises from the hotel across the International Boundary were soon the park's most popular activity. This brought the two parks closer together, and in 1932, after much lobbying from Rotary International members on both sides of the border, the Canadian and U.S. governments agreed to establish Waterton–Glacier International Peace Park, the first of its kind in the world. The parks are administered separately but cooperate in preserving this pristine mountain wilderness through wildlife management, search and rescue operations, and interpretive programs. Peace Park celebrations take place each year, and the **Peace Park Pavilion** by the lake is dedicated to this unique bond. In 1979, UNESCO declared the park a **Biosphere Reserve,** only the second such reserve in Canada. In 1995 the park's importance was further recognized when UNESCO declared Waterton–Glacier International Peace Park a **World Heritage Site.**

SIGHTS AND RECREATION

Make your first stop the **Waterton Visitor Centre,** 403/859-2445, on the slight rise before descending to the village. Once in town, getting around on foot is the best way to explore. The **Waterton Heritage Centre,** 117 Waterton Ave., 403/859-2624, offers a small display area, with exhibits telling the story of park's natural and human history and a small gallery of paintings by local artists. A good variety of books are also sold. The heritage center is operated by the Waterton Natural History Association, which runs a variety of educational programs. The center is open May–September, 10 A.M.–5 P.M., until 7 P.M. in July and August. From the heritage center, wander south along the lakeshore to a large picnic area and the trailhead for the Waterton Lakeshore Trail (see "Hiking" below) or north to the **International Peace Park Pavillion** and stunning views across Emerald Bay to the Prince of Wales Hotel.

SCENIC DRIVES

Akamina Parkway

This road starts in the townsite and switchbacks up into the Cameron Creek Valley, making an elevation gain of 400 meters before ending after 16 km at Cameron Lake. The viewpoint one km from the junction of the park road is on a tight curve, so park off the road. From this lookout, views extend over the townsite and the **Bear's Hump,** which was originally part of a high ridge that extended across the lake to Vimy Peak (glacial action ultimately wore down the rest of the ridge). This section of the road is also a good place to view bighorn sheep. From here to Cameron Lake are a number of picnic areas and stops of interest, including the site of Alberta's first producing oil well, and a little farther along the road, the site of **Oil City,** the town that never was.

Cameron Lake, at the end of the road, is a 2.5-km-long subalpine lake that reaches depths over 40 meters. It lies in a large cirque carved around 11,000 years ago by a receding glacier. Mt. Custer at the southern end of the lake is in Montana. Waterton has no glaciers, but Herbst Glacier on Mt. Custer can be seen from here. To the west (right) of Custer is **Forum Peak** (2,225 meters), whose summit cairn marks the boundaries of Alberta, Montana, and British Columbia. Beside the lakeshore are enclosed information boards and concession selling light snacks and renting canoes, rowboats, and paddleboats ($17 for the first hour; $14 for additional hours). A narrow trail leads along the lake's west shoreline, ending after two km (40 minutes

Picturesque Cameron Lake lies at the end of the Akamina Parkway.

one way). Further on, grizzlies frequent the avalanche slope at the southwestern end of the lake, so hike with someone you can outrun.

Red Rock Canyon Parkway
The best roadside wildlife viewing within the park is along this 13-km road that starts near the golf course and finishes at **Red Rock Canyon.** The transition between rolling prairies and mountains takes place abruptly as you travel up the Blakiston Valley. Black bears (and very occasionally grizzly bears) can be seen feeding on saskatoon berries along the open slopes to the north. **Mt. Blakiston** (2,920 meters), the park's highest summit, is visible from a viewpoint three km along the road. The road passes interpretive signs, picnic areas, and Crandell Mountain Campground. At the end of the road is Red Rock Canyon, a water-carved gorge where the bedrock, known as argillite, contains a high concentration of iron. The iron oxidizes and turns red when exposed to air—literally going rusty. A short interpretive trail leads along the canyon.

Chief Mountain International Highway
This 25-km highway, part of Highway 6, borders the eastern boundaries of the park and joins it to Glacier National Park in Montana. It starts east of the park gate at **Maskinonge Lake** and climbs for seven km to a viewpoint where many jagged peaks and the entire Waterton Valley can be seen. The next stop, three km farther south, provides views of Chief Mountain, which has been separated from the main mountain range by erosion. The road then passes more spectacular viewpoints, Belly River Campground, and Chief Mountain.

Hours of operation at this port of entry are mid-May to the end of May, 9 A.M.–6 P.M., June to early September, 7 A.M.–10 P.M., early September to the end of the month, 9 A.M.–6 P.M. When the post is closed, you must use the Carway/Piegan port of entry, which is open year-round, daily 7 A.M.–11 P.M. It's on Alberta Highway 2 south of Cardston (or on Montana Highway 89 north of St. Mary, depending on your direction of travel).

From the border it's 50 km to St. Mary and the spectacular Going-to-the-Sun highway through **Glacier National Park.** The park's **St. Mary Visitor Center** is open mid-May to mid-October 8 A.M.–5 P.M., and until 9 P.M. in July and August. Alternatively, write Park Superintendent, Glacier National Park, West Glacier, MT 59936, USA, 406/888-7800, www.nps.gov/glac.

HIKING

Although the park is relatively small, its trail system is extensive; 223 km of well-maintained trails lead to alpine lakes and lofty summits affording spectacular views. One of the most appealing aspects of hiking in Waterton is that with higher trailheads than other parks in the Canadian Rockies, the tree line is reached quickly. Most of the lakes can be reached in a few hours. Once you've finished hiking the trails in Waterton, you can cross the international border and start on the 1,200 kilometers of trails in Glacier National Park.

The eight hikes detailed below comprise only a small cross-section of Waterton's extensive trail system. Most of the hikes climb to alpine lakes or viewpoints. Topographic maps (one map covers the entire park) are available at various outlets in town. If you are planning to stay overnight in the backcountry you must obtain a permit ($6 per person per night) from Waterton Visitor Centre or the park administration office.

Bear's Hump
- Length: 1.2 km (40 minutes) one-way
- Elevation gain: 215 meters
- Rating: moderate

This is one of the most popular short hikes in the park, and although steep, it affords panoramic views of the Waterton Valley. The trailhead is at the Waterton Visitor Centre, opposite the Prince of Wales Hotel. The trail switchbacks up the northern flanks of the Bear's Hump, finishing at a rocky ledge high above town. From this vantage point the sweeping view extends across the prairies and down Upper Waterton Lake to the northern reaches of Glacier National Park.

Bertha Lake Trail
- Length: 5.8 km (2 hours) one-way
- Elevation gain: 460 meters
- Rating: moderate

Bertha Lake is a popular destination with dayhikers and campers alike. The trail begins at the end of Evergreen Ave. near the far corner of Townsite Campground. For the first 1.5 km little elevation gain is made as the trail coincides with the Lakeshore Trail. Then the trail branches right and climbs steadily through a forest of lodgepole pine and Douglas fir along a well-maintained section to **Lower Bertha Falls**. Signs along this first, easier section correspond with the *Bertha Falls Self-Guiding Nature Trail* brochure available from the Visitor Centre. From here the trail passes **Upper Bertha Falls** and begins switchbacking steeply through a subalpine forest to its maximum elevation on a ridge above the hanging valley in which Bertha Lake lies. A trail encircles the lake. The backcountry campground on the lake's edge is one of the park's busiest.

Waterton Lakeshore Trail

- Length: 14 km (4.5 hours) one-way
- Elevation gain: minimal
- Rating: easy/moderate

This trail follows the heavily forested western shores of Upper Waterton Lake across the International Boundary to **Goat Haunt, Montana,** linking up with over 1,200 km of trails in Glacier National Park. Many hikers take the **Inter-Nation Shoreline Cruise Company** boat one-way ($12; call 403/859-2362) and hike the other. The boat dock at Boundary Bay, six km from town, is a good place for lunch. Park guides lead a hike along this trail each Saturday morning, making the return trip by boat; contact the visitor center for details. Hikers heading south and planning to camp in Glacier National Park must register at the Waterton Visitor Centre.

Crypt Lake Trail

- Length: 8.7 km (3–4 hours) one-way
- Elevation gain: 680 meters
- Rating: moderate/difficult

This is one of the most spectacular day hikes in Canada. Access to the trailhead on the eastern side of Upper Waterton Lake is by boat. The trail switchbacks for 2.5 km past a series of waterfalls and continues steeply up to a small green lake before reaching a campground. The final ascent to Crypt Lake from the campground causes the most problems, especially for those who suffer from claustrophobia. A ladder on the cliff face leads into a natural tunnel that you must crawl through on your hands and knees. The next part of the trail is along a narrow precipice with a cable for support. The lake at the end of

the trail, nestled in a hanging valley, is no disappointment. Its dark green waters are rarely free of floating ice, and the steep walls of the cirque rise over 500 meters above the lake on three sides. The International Boundary is at the southern end of the lake. A good way to avoid the crowds on this trail is to camp at the dock and set out before the first boat arrives in the morning. The **Crypt Lake Shuttle** leaves the marina daily at 9 A.M. and 10 P.M. for Crypt Landing, returning at 4 P.M. and 5:30 P.M.; $12 round-trip. Reservations are necessary in summer; call 403/859-2362.

Crandell Lake

- Length: 2.4 km (40 minutes) one-way
- Elevation gain: 120 meters
- Rating: easy

This easy hike to a subalpine lake from the Red Rock Canyon Parkway is popular with campers staying at Crandell Mountain Campground. The trailhead can be reached from within the campground or by noncampers along the Canyon

Crandell Lake

Church Camp access road. The lake can also be accessed from a trailhead seven km west of town along the Akamina Parkway. This trail is shorter (0.8 km) and follows a wagon road that was cut through the valley to Oil City.

Goat Lake Trail
- Length: 6.7 km (2 hours) one-way
- Elevation gain: 500 meters
- Rating: moderate

The first hour of walking from the trailhead at Red Rock Canyon follows the Snowshoe Trail along **Bauerman Creek** before branching to the right and climbing switchbacks through a mixed forest. The steep gradient evens out as the trail enters the Goat Lake cirque. The lake is a welcome sight after the uphill slog, its emerald-green waters reflecting the towering headwalls that surround it. Look for the lake's namesake on the open scree slopes west of the lake.

Carthew-Alderson Trail
- Length: 20 km (6–7 hours) one-way
- Elevation gain: 650 meters
- Rating: moderate/difficult

This hike linking the end of the Akamina Parkway to Waterton townsite can be completed in one long strenuous day or done with an overnight stop at Alderson Lake, 13 km from Cameron Lake. It leads through most of the climatic zones of the park and offers some of the best scenery to be had on any one hike. Most hikers begin at Cameron Lake. Transportation to the trailhead can be arranged through the **Park Transport Company** in the Tamarack Village Square ($7.50 one-way; 403/859-2378), which operates a hiker shuttle service to this and other trailheads in the park. From the Cameron Lake parking lot the trail climbs four km to **Summit Lake,** a worthy destination in itself. The trail then forks to the left and climbs steeply to Carthew Ridge. After rising above the tree line and crossing a scree slope, the trail reaches its highest elevation of 2,310 meters at **Carthew Summit.** The views from here are spectacular, even more so if you scramble up to one of Mt. Carthew's lower peaks. To the north is a hint of prairie, to the southeast the magnificent bowl-shaped cirque around Cameron Lake. To the south, the Carthew Lakes lie directly below, while glaciated peaks in Montana line the horizon. From this summit, the trail descends steeply to the Carthew Lakes, reenters the subalpine forest, and emerges at **Alderson Lake,** which is nestled under the headwalls of Mt. Alderson. The trail then descends through the Carthew Creek Valley and finishes at Cameron Falls in the townsite.

Vimy Peak
- Length: 12 km (5 hours) one-way
- Elevation gain: 825 meters
- Rating: moderate

Vimy Peak overlooks the townsite from across Upper Waterton Lake. It was once part of a ridge that extended across the Waterton Valley and was worn down by the relentless forces of glacial action. The trailhead is along the Chief Mountain International Highway, a half km from the Highway 5 junction. The initial six-km stretch is along the eastern bank of Lower Waterton Lake through forest and grassland. The trail then continues along the lake to Bosporus Landing opposite the town or climbs steeply to Vimy Peak (2,379 meters). The Vimy Peak trail actually ends at a basin short of the summit, which is still a painfully steep 40-minute scramble away.

OTHER RECREATION

Cruising to Goat Haunt, Montana

This is the most popular activity in Waterton. From the marina in downtown Waterton townsite, **Waterton Inter-Nation Shoreline Cruise Company,** 403/859-2362, runs scheduled cruises across the International Boundary to Goat Haunt, Montana, at the southern end of Upper Waterton Lake. The 45-minute trip along the lakeshore passes spectacular mountain scenery and usually wildlife. A half-hour stopover is made at Goat Haunt, which lies in a remote part of Glacier National Park and consists of little more than a dock and interpretive displays. You can return on the same boat or go hiking and return later in the day. If you are planning an overnight hike from here, you are required to register at the Wateron Visitor Centre before heading out on the lake. Another popular option is to take an early boat trip and walk back to town on the **Waterton Lakeshore Trail,** which takes about four hours. Boats leave the Waterton marina five times daily during summer. Fewer trips are made during May and September. The cruises operate until the end of September. Tickets cost $21 round-trip, $12 one-way, and you'll need to book ahead in summer. The same company operates a regular shuttle service to the Crypt Lake trailhead for $12 round-trip.

Fishing

Fishing in the lakes is above average with most anglers chasing brook and rainbow trout, pike, and whitefish. A national park fishing license is required and can be obtained from the Waterton Visitor Centre or any of the administration offices. The license costs $6 for seven days, or $13 for an annual permit.

Windsurfing

Winds of up to 70 kph attract hard-core windsurfers throughout summer and into fall. The winds are predominantly south to north, providing fast runs across Upper Waterton Lake from the beach at Cameron Bay. The lake is deep, keeping the water temperature low and making a wetsuit necessary. Read the warning signs at the beach before heading out.

Scuba Diving

On any given summer day, scuba divers can be seen slipping into the frigid waters of Emerald Bay. A steamer was scuttled in the bay in 1918. It had been used to haul logs and as a tearoom but now sits on the lake's floor, attracting divers who find it a novelty to explore a sunken ship so far from the ocean. No equipment rental is available in the park. The closest is at **Anderson Aquatics** in Lethbridge at 314 11th Street S., 403/328-5040, where you can also get your tanks filled. Full gear rental from Anderson is $50 per day, $75 for the weekend, including air fills. Through this shop, certification courses and field trips to Waterton Lakes are organized throughout the summer. Stop in on your way to the park for a rundown on all the dives, or ask at the Waterton Visitor Centre.

Golfing

The rolling fairways and spectacular mountain backdrop of **Waterton Lakes Golf Course** can distract even the keenest golfer's attention. The 18-hole course, designed by Stanley Thompson, is not particularly long (6,103 yards) or difficult, but the surrounding mountains and unhurried pace of play make for a pleasant environment. The course is four km north of the townsite on the main access road and is open June to early October. Its facilities include a rental shop, clubhouse, and restaurant serving sandwiches and snacks. A round of golf costs $28 during the day, dropping to $16 after 5 P.M. (which may have something to do with the healthy local bear population), or play as many rounds as you like in one day for $40. Club rentals are $7.50 and an electric cart is an additional $25 per round. For tee times, call 403/859-2114.

Windy Upper Waterton Lake is popular for windsurfing.

Horseback Riding

Just off the main park access road before town is **Alpine Stables,** 403/859-2462, which offers hour-long trail rides (starting on the hour 9 A.M.–5 P.M.) for $20. Two-hour Wildlife Habitat rides leave at 10 A.M. and 1 P.M. and cost $35. The three-hour ride, departing at 1:30 P.M., takes in the buffalo paddock on the edge of the prairies; $50.

When the Sun Goes Down

Interpretive programs are held nightly during the summer in Crandell Campground and at the **Falls Theatre** opposite Cameron Falls. Programs begin at 8:30 P.M., with special guest speakers appearing at the Falls Theatre Saturday night. Ask at the Waterton Visitor Centre or call 403/859-2445 for a schedule.

Being the biggest bar in town, the **Thirsty Bear Saloon** in the Bayshore Inn gets crowded. It pours happy hour daily 3–6 P.M., and a band plays two or three nights a week. It's open 11 A.M.–2 A.M. If it's a sunny afternoon, relax on the lakeside deck of the inn's adjacent restaurant with a cool drink. The **Rams Head Lounge** in the Kilmorey Lodge also has an outside deck with views of the lake, as well as a fireplace. Another downtown bar is the **Wolf's Den Lounge** in Waterton Lakes Lodge. In the Prince of Wales Hotel, the **Windsor Lounge** has panoramic views across the lake and live entertainment most nights.

Waterton Lakes Opera House, 309 Windflower Ave., 403/859-2466, shows movies daily at 7:30 and 9:30 P.M.

Wintertime

Winter is a quiet time in the park. Traffic on the roads is light, the Prince of Wales Hotel sits empty, the snowcapped peaks and abundant big game provide plenty of photographic opportunities, and a few trails are maintained for cross-country skiing. The main access road is plowed regularly and the Akamina Parkway is cleared to allow access to ski trails. Skiing in the park is usually possible from December to March, but conditions can change dramatically. Arctic fronts scream down from the north, and chinook winds from the west can raise temperatures by up to 20°C in an hour. Ski trails are set on weekends and the ski-touring opportunities are endless. Trails in the backcountry are not marked. Groups should carry avalanche beacons, be capable of self-rescue, and register with the warden before setting out. Ice climbing, snowshoeing, and backcountry winter camping are also popular. Winter camping is possible at Pass Creek, where you'll find a kitchen shelter, woodstove, and pit toilets. Three accommodations stay open year-round and offer all-inclusive winter packages. Gas may or may not be available in winter. Obtain trail information and weather forecasts at the park administration office on Mt View Road, open weekdays 8 A.M.–4 P.M., 403/859-5133. For information regarding backcountry skiing conditions and avalanche danger, contact the **Canadian Avalanche Association,** 800/667-1105.

ACCOMMODATIONS

HOTELS, MOTELS, AND LODGES

Waterton has a limited number of accommodations. Most start opening in May and will be full every night during July and August. By mid-October many are closed, with only the Kilmorey Lodge, Crandell Mountain Lodge, and Waterton Lakes Lodge open year-round. All accommodations are within the townsite, so walking to the marina and shops isn't a problem.

Under $50

One of the village's premier accommodations,

Waterton Lakes Lodge, at corner of Windflower Avenue and Cameron Falls Road, 403/859-2150 or 888/985-6343, www.watertonlakeslodge.com, has a small wing set aside for members of Hostelling International, or for those travelers willing to share living facilities. A total of 21 beds are spread through six rooms, with a maximum of four beds in any one room. Guests have use of all lodge facilities, including the Waterton Spa and Recreation Centre (for a small fee), tennis, and bike rentals, as well as a shared kitchen and bathrooms. Beds are $19.55 for members, $23.55 for nonmembers—a great deal. Check-in is after 4 P.M. and it's open mid-April to October.

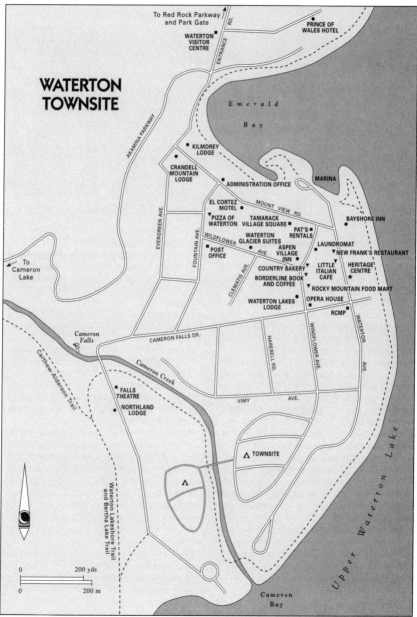

WATERTON TOWNSITE

To Red Rock Parkway and Park Gate

PRINCE OF WALES HOTEL

ENTRANCE RD.

WATERTON VISITOR CENTRE

AKAMINA PARKWAY

Emerald Bay

KILMOREY LODGE

CRANDELL MOUNTAIN LODGE

ADMINISTRATION OFFICE

MARINA

EL CORTEZ MOTEL

MOUNT VIEW RD.

PIZZA OF WATERTON

TAMARACK VILLAGE SQUARE

PAT'S RENTALS

BAYSHORE INN

EVERGREEN AVE.

FOUNTAIN AVE.

WILDFLOWER

WATERTON GLACIER SUITES

LAUNDROMAT

NEW FRANK'S RESTAURANT

To Cameron Lake

POST OFFICE

ASPEN VILLAGE INN

AVE.

CLEMATIS AVE.

COUNTRY BAKERY

LITTLE ITALIAN CAFE

HERITAGE CENTRE

BORDERLINE BOOK AND COFFEE

ROCKY MOUNTAIN FOOD MART

WATERTON LAKES LODGE

OPERA HOUSE

RCMP

WATERTON

Cameron Falls

CAMERON FALLS DR.

HAREBELL RD.

WINDFLOWER AVE.

AVE.

Carthew-Alderson Trail

Cameron Creek

VIMY   AVE.

FALLS THEATRE

NORTHLAND LODGE

TOWNSITE

Waterton Lakeshore Trail and Bertha Lake Trail

Upper Waterton Lake

0   200 yds

0   200 m

Cameron Bay

The Prince of Wales Hotel is the grandest of Waterton's accommodations.

$50–100

Kilmorey Lodge, Mount View Road, 403/859-2334 or 888/859-8669, www.kilmoreylodge.com, a historic inn on the shores of Emerald Bay, provides excellent value for money. From the lobby a narrow stairway leads up to 23 rooms tucked under the eaves, many of which have spectacular lake views. Each is furnished with antiques, and the beds have down comforters to ensure a good night's sleep. Downstairs is one of the town's finest restaurants, along with a lounge and gazebo for enjoying a quiet drink on those warm summer nights. The lodge stays open year-round. Rooms during summer start at $94 s or d, with more comfortable larger rooms from $130. Some rooms have lake views, but book in advance for these. Inexpensive packages are offered in winter.

The **El Cortez Motel** is one block from the main street on Mount View Road, 403/859-2366. It's an older, park-at-your-door motel with basic furnishings but no phones. Standard rooms are $70 s, $75 d, with some kitchenettes from $90.

Also in the same price bracket is **Northland Lodge,** 403/859-2353, www.northlandlodge.ab.ca, a converted house 100 meters south of Cameron Falls along a road of the same name. It features nine guest rooms, a large lounge with a TV and fireplace, and free coffee and tea. The two rooms that share a bathroom are $75 s or d while the remainder are $100 s or d.

$100–150

Across the road from the Kilmorey Lodge is **Cran-** **dell Mountain Lodge,** Mount View Road, 403/859-2288, www.crandellmountainlodge.com, a country-style inn dating to 1940. The lodge has seen many changes since it first opened with shared bathrooms and wood-heated water. Today each of the 17 rooms has a private bath and is beautifully finished with country-style furnishings, and out back is a private garden area. Two rooms are wheelchair-accessible. Rates are $116–178 s or d in the height of summer with reduced rates (from $84) the rest of the year.

The **Aspen Village Inn,** Windflower Ave., 403/859-2255 or 888/859-8669, offers large rooms for $126 s or d but is best noted for self-contained cottages which sleep up to eight for $160, an excellent deal for small groups. Also on the property is a barbecue area and kids playground.

A few dollars more than the Aspen Village Inn, the **Bayshore Inn,** Waterton Ave., 403/859-2211 or 888/527-9555, www.bayshoreinn.com, enjoys a prime waterfront location right on the main street. Amenities include private balconies, a hot tub, and an on-site restaurant and lounge. Rooms are $135 s or d for a basic room, $150 lake view.

$150–200

Two new accommodations, the first for many years, opened in the summer of 1998. The largest is **Waterton Lakes Lodge,** corner Windflower Avenue and Cameron Falls Road, 403/859-2151 or 888/985-6343, www.watertonlakeslodge.com, which is set on a 1.5-hectare site in the heart of town. All 80 rooms are large and modern, and each has mountain views. The lodge complex also holds Waterton Spa and Recreation Centre (free entry for guests), a restaurant, small cafe, and lounge. Standard rooms are $155–185, while those with kitchenettes range $190–240. It's open year-round.

The other new accommodation is **Waterton Glacier Suites,** on Windflower Avenue, 403/859-2004 or 888/527-9555, www.watertonsuites.com, featuring 26 luxurious rooms, each with a fireplace and whirlpool; $169–229 s or d.

Over $200

Waterton's most well-known landmark is the **Prince of Wales Hotel,** 403/859-2231 or 602/207-6000 (off-season), a seven-story gabled structure built in 1927 on a hill overlooking Upper Waterton Lake. It was another grand mountain resort financed by the railway, except, unlike those in Banff and Jasper, it had no rail link. It was built as part of a chain of first-class hotels in Glacier National Park, and is still owned by the company that controls those south of the border, Glacier Park Inc. (www.glacierparkinc.com). Early guests were transported to the hotel by bus from the Great Northern Railway in Montana. After extensive restoration inside and out, the hotel has been returned to its former splendor. Guests from the U.S. travel to the park in vintage touring buses. Rooms start at $205 s, $245 d, but some are pretty small. Lakeside rooms, with the best views, start at $285 s or d. The hotel is open mid-May to late September.

CAMPGROUNDS

Park Campgrounds

The park has three campgrounds holding a total of 391 campsites. They open only in summer, with winter camping permitted at Pass Creek, along the park access road. No reservations are taken, so to ensure a site, try to time your arrival to check-out time, which is 11 A.M. **Townsite Campground,** 403/859-2224, enjoys a prime lakeside location within walking distance of many trailheads, restaurants, and shops. Many of its over 200 sites have power, water,

and sewer hookups. The campground also offers showers and kitchen shelters. Sites are available on a first-come, first-served basis and fill up by early afternoon most summer days. Open late April to mid-October; walk-in tent sites are $15, unserviced sites $17, hookups $20-23. **Crandell Mountain Campground** is 10 km from the townsite on Red Rock Canyon Parkway. It has 129 unserviced sites ($13), flush toilets, and kitchen shelters. Open mid-May to mid-September. **Belly River Campground,** 29 km from the townsite on Chief Mountain International Highway, is the smallest and most primitive of the park's three developed campgrounds. It has pit toilets and kitchen shelters; sites are $10 per night. The later two campgrounds supply firewood but charge $4 per site to burn it.

Waterton also holds 13 backcountry campgrounds. Each has pit toilets, a cook shelter, and a water supply. Open fires are discouraged and are prohibited during periods of high fire danger; check with a warden. If you are planning to camp in the backcountry, you must obtain a Wilderness Pass from Waterton Visitor Centre or the administration office. Permits are $6 per person per night. Half of all sites can be reserved in advance ($10 per booking). Call 403/859-2224 for reservations. If your planned backcountry itinerary takes you over the border, ask at the information center about border-crossing regulations.

Commercial Campgrounds

Outside of the park, two private campgrounds take up the nightly overflow. **Waterton Springs Campground,** three km north of the park gate on Highway 6, 403/859-2247, has recently undergone massive renovations, including the construction of a large building holding modern bathroom facilities, lounge, general store, and a laundry. Also on-site is a fishing pond stocked with rainbow trout. Tent sites are $15, trailers and RVs pay $17–21. On Highway 5, five km east of the park gate, **Waterton Riverside Campground,** 403/653-2888, has powered sites, showers, and a barbecue on Saturday nights. Tent sites are $14, powered sites $17. Both these campgrounds close by the middle of September.

OTHER PRACTICALITIES

FOOD

Restaurants in the park offer a range of fare—from pizza and fast food to elegant dining. If you plan on cooking your own food, stock up before you get to the park. Groceries are available at the **Rocky Mountain Food Mart** on Windflower Avenue (open 8 A.M.–10 p.m.) and in the Tamarack Village Square on Mt. View Road. The Food Mart sells hot chickens—an easy and inexpensive camping or picnicking meal.

Cafés and Cheap Eats
For inexpensive breakfasts, homemade soups, delicious salads, and breads covered in homemade preserves head to **Borderline Book and Coffee** (also known as Pearl's), 305 Windflower Ave., 403/859-2284, where the indoor/outdoor tables are always busy. Next door is the **Country Bakery**, a city-style deli serving meat and fruit pies as well as a wide range of pastries. In the theater building on the corner of Windflower Avenue and Cameron Falls Drive is **Waterton Bagel & Coffee Co.**, serving up exactly that. **Gazebo Cafe on the Bay** in the Kilmorey Lodge serves light snacks and simple meals; seating is on an outdoor deck on the waterfront. It's open daily 10 A.M.–10 P.M.

For great pizza try **Pizza of Waterton**, 103 Fountain Ave., 403/859-2660, where they pile the dough with all kinds of meats, fresh vegetables, and a special savory sauce. It's open midday to midnight.

High Tea
Every afternoon between 2 and 4:30 P.M., the foyer of the Prince of Wales Hotel fills up as visitors descend on this historic landmark for High Tea. Scrumptious pastries, tea, coffee, and other beverages are served up on white linen at tables with the best view in town; $25 per person.

Restaurants
Little Italian Cafe, 113 Waterton Ave., 403/859-0003, is a great little restaurant serving up inexpensive Italian delights. All basic pasta dishes are priced under $12, but worth the extra bucks is Chicken Ranchesco ($17.50), a delicious chicken dish cooked with ham and sun-dried tomatoes. The Little Italian is also the best option for breakfast, with a full cooked breakfast from just $6.50. **New Frank's Restaurant,** 106 Waterton Ave., 403/859-2240, serves inexpensive Chinese food (from $7.50) and western food (from $9.50).

The **Kootenai Brown Dining Room** in the Bayshore Inn, 403/859-2211, overlooks Upper Waterton Lake and the mountains. Mule deer often feed within sight of diners. The food is excellent, especially the trout and beef dishes (from $15), and the view is free. The dining room is also open for a breakfast buffet ($12) and lunch. Hours are daily 7 A.M.–10 P.M. One of the most popular restaurants in town is the **Lamp Post Dining Room,** in the Kilmorey Lodge, 403/859-2334. It has all the charm of the Prince of Wales Hotel but with a more casual atmosphere and low prices to match. The mouthwatering menu offers appetizers starting at $4 and entrées ranging $14–26 (the French Rack of Lamb, $21, is a personal favorite). Leave room to finish with a delicious piece of homemade pie. The Lamp Post is open 7:30 A.M.–10 P.M.

The **Garden Court Dining Room,** 403/859-2231, is a formal restaurant in the Prince of Wales Hotel. Its high ceiling, views of the lake through large windows, and Old World elegance create a first-class ambience that is overshadowed only by the quality of the food. Prices are similar to any big-city restaurant of the same standard—expect to pay around $100 for two with a bottle of wine. If you are going to splurge, do it here. A large breakfast buffet every morning (6:30–9:30 A.M.) is worth trying if you won't be coming for dinner. Lunch is served 11:30 A.M.–2 P.M.; dinner 5:30–9:30 P.M. Reservations are required.

TRANSPORTATION

Getting There
The nearest commercial airport is at Lethbridge, 140 km away. Cars can be rented at the airport. The closest **Greyhound** buses come to the park is Pincher Creek, 50 km away. From the depot

*Cameron Falls is within easy
walking distance of the townsite.*

there, at 1015 Hewetson Street, 403/627-2716, you'll need to get a cab, which will cost around $55. Call **Crystal Taxi** at 403/627-4262.

Getting Around
The **Park Transport Company,** in Tamarack Village Square on Mt. View Road, 403/859-2378, operates hiker shuttle services to various trailheads within the park. Cameron Lake, the starting point for the Carthew-Alderson Trail (which ends back in town), is a popular drop-off point; $7.50 one-way. You could take one of these shuttles, then return on the bus later in the day if driving the steep mountain roads doesn't appeal to you. The company also offers two-hour tours ($25 per person) through the park and runs a local taxi service.

The **Crypt Lake Shuttle** leaves the marina regularly for Crypt landing; $12 round-trip. Reservations are necessary in summer; call 403/859-2362. **Pat's Rentals,** on Mt. View Road, 403/859-2266, rents mountain bikes (from $6.50

per hour, $32 per day) and motorized scooters ($18 per hour, $72 per day).

Tours
If you're in Calgary and interested in visiting the park but have a limited amount of time, consider a **Brewster** tour. The tour departs select Calgary hotels between 6:30 and 7 A.M., stopping at Head-Smashed-In Buffalo Jump before reaching the park. Around four hours is spent in the park, exploring town and its environs and traveling up to Cameron Lake. The return journey makes a stop at a historic foothills ranch. The tours run 12 hours and cost $98 per person. For reservations, call 403/221-8242.

SERVICES AND INFORMATION

Shopping and Services
The numerous tourist-oriented gift shops along Waterton Avenue are worth browsing through when the weather isn't cooperating. In the **Tamarack Village Square** on Mt. View Road, you'll find a good bookshop, a currency exchange, and a sports store selling camping gear and fishing tackle. The only **cash machine** in Waterton is in Pat's Rentals, also on Mt. View Road. The **post office** is beside the fire station on Fountain Avenue. **Itussiststukiopi Coin-Op Launderette** at 301 Windflower Ave. is open daily 8 A.M.–10 P.M. The closest **hospitals** are in Cardston, 403/653-4411, and Pincher Creek, 403/627-3333. The park's 24-hour emergency number is 403/859-2636. For the **RCMP,** call 403/859-2244.

Books and Maps
The **Waterton Natural History Association,** based in the Waterton Heritage Centre, 117 Waterton Ave., 403/859-2624, offers a variety of educational programs and stocks every book ever written about the park, as well as many titles pertaining to western Canada in general. It's open May–September, 10 A.M.–5 P.M.; longer hours in summer. Topographical maps of the park (one map covers the entire area) are available for $10.50 from the Waterton Visitor Centre, administration office, and Heritage Centre.

Information
On the main access road opposite the Prince

of Wales Hotel, the **Waterton Visitor Centre,** 403/859-2445, provides general information on the park, sells fishing licenses, and issues back-country permits. It's open June–August 9 A.M.–8 P.M., May and early September 9 A.M.–5 P.M.; closed the rest of the year. The park's administration office on Mt. View Road offers the same services as the Visitor Centre and is open year-round, weekdays 8 A.M.–4 P.M.; 403/859-2224. For more information on the park, write to Superintendent, Waterton Lakes National Park, Waterton Park, AB T0K 2M0. The Parks Canada web address is www.parkscanada.gc.ca/waterton. For general tourist information, www.discoverwaterton.com provides plenty current information and links to accommodations.

Often, wildlife viewing is best in the more remote parks of the Canadian Rockies.

LESSER-TRAVELED PARKS OF THE CANADIAN ROCKIES

The previous chapters have covered the better-known parks of the Canadian Rockies, but many other areas of special appeal are protected as provincial and wilderness parks. These parks give visitors the chance to enjoy the natural beauty and wildlife of the mountains away from the crowds associated with the national parks. They have no fancy hotels, golf courses, or shopping malls, and in some cases not even roads.

Seven provincial parks lie on the British Columbia side of the mountains. Mt. Robson Provincial Park, west of Jasper National Park, protects the highest peak in the Canadian Rockies. The Berg Lake Trail, which climbs to a high alpine lake at the base of Mt. Robson, is the most popular overnight hike in all the mountains. Mt. Assiniboine Provincial Park has no roads—guests fly in by helicopter to a small

lodge. The other provincial parks—Akamina/Kishinena, Elk Lakes, Height of the Rockies, Top of the World, and Whiteswan Lake—all have their own appeal and are well worth the effort required to reach them.

On the Alberta side of the mountains, three designated wilderness areas—White Goat, Siffleur, and Willmore—offer even more solitude. No horses or motorized vehicles are allowed within their boundaries; hunting and fishing are prohibited, as is all construction. This, ironically, gives these lightly traveled regions more protection than national parks. The drawback, and the reason so few people explore these areas, is that wilderness really means *wilderness,* sans roads, bridges, or campsites. With one exception at Willmore, no roads even lead to the areas' boundaries; the only access is on foot.

PROVINCIAL PARKS

AKAMINA/KISHINENA PROVINCIAL PARK

Bordering Glacier National Park (Montana, U.S.) and Waterton Lakes National Park (Alberta), this remote tract of 10,922 hectares protects the extreme southeastern corner of British Columbia. The park is named for its two main waterways, which flow southward into Montana. This was the main reason for the park's creation, as now, alongside Waterton Lakes National Park, entire watersheds of Glacier National Park are protected. The landscape has changed little in thousands of years, since the Kootenay rested in the open meadows beside Kishinena Creek before crossing the Continental Divide to hunt bison on the prairies.

The only access to the park is on foot from one of two trailheads. The most popular and easiest access is via Akamina Parkway in Waterton Lakes National Park (Alberta). From near the end of the road (the trailhead is signposted) it's a 1.5-km uphill slog to the park border, from where trails lead past stunning alpine lakes to the park's more remote corners. You can also access the area at the end of an unsealed road that leaves Highway 3 16 km south of Fernie (British Columbia). The road leads 110 km into the Flathead River Valley, where trails climb along Akamina Creek into the park.

Practicalities

Aside from a primitive campground beside Akamina Creek ($4 per night), the park has no services. Like all of British Columbia's provincial parks, Akamina/Kishinena is managed by the Ministry of Environment, Land and Parks, from a regional office at Wasa, north of Cranbrook. For further park details, write BC Parks, Kootenay District, P.O. Box 118, Wasa, BC V0B 2K0, 250/422-4200. The BC Parks website, www.elp.gov.ab.ca/bcparks, is another good source of information.

The nearest town is Fernie (pop. 5,100), out on Highway 3. It's traditionally been a coal-mining and forestry center, but the town has a great ski area, **Fernie Alpine Resort,** that is generally regarded as one of North America's undiscovered gems. Beside the highway, through town to the north, is **Fernie Visitor Info Centre,** 250/423-6868, www.city.fernie.bc.ca, where you can pick up a local Forest Service map of entire southwestern corner of British Columbia, including Akamina/Kishinena Provincial Park. Least expensive of Fernie's indoor accommodations is the **Raging Elk Hostel,** in a converted motel at 892 6th Avenue, 250/423-6811, www.ragingelk.com. An associate of Hostelling International, it provides all the usual facilities, including a communal kitchen and laundry. Rates range from $16 for a dorm bed to $45 for a double room with a TV. One of the better motels along the highway through town is **Park Place Lodge,** 742 Highway 3, 250/423-6871 or 888/381-7275, www.parkplacelodge.bc.ca, which features a restaurant and pub, a large courtyard surrounding a heated pool, and air-conditioned rooms for $80 s, $95 d. Up at the ski hill, halfway between Fernie and the turn-off to Akamina/Kishinena Provincial Park, the **Grizz Inn Sport Hotel,** 250/423-9221 or 800/661-0118, www.grizinn.com, is a favorite winter accommodation that is open year-round. It offers 45 modern self-contained units, an indoor pool, and a restaurant. Off-season rates start at $95 s or d. The best bet for campers is **Mt. Fernie Provincial Park,** 12 km south of town and four km north of the Akamina/Kishinena Provincial Park access road. Facilities are basic, but it's a pleasant setting and a short trail leads to a waterfall. Sites are $12 per night.

ELK LAKES PROVINCIAL PARK

This park encompasses over 17,000 hectares of rugged wilderness along the British Columbia side of the Canadian Rockies. Glaciers shaped the terrain here; their remnants can still be seen along the park's west border. The park lies adjacent to the southern border of Peter Lougheed Provincial Park in Alberta (see the "Kananaskis Country" chapter), but the only road access is from Highway 3, more than 120 km to the south. Head north for 35 km from Sparwood, between Cranbrook and the Alberta border, on a paved road to Elkford, then take an unpaved road for a further 87 km north into the park. From the main parking lot, a trail leads one km to Lower Elk Lake and another kilometer or so to Upper Elk Lake. At the lower lake, a narrow trail climbs 135 meters to a lookout. The stunningly beautiful upper lake is surrounded by steep snow-capped peaks, and several avalanche paths end right at water's edge. Fishing in the lower lake is productive for Dolly Varden and cutthroat trout.

Practicalities

The park's only facility is a primitive campground at the main trailhead. The nearest town is **Elkford,** a small coal-mining community 87 km south. The community has few services, but you'll find a small **municipal campground** within walking distance of downtown. On Front Street is **Elkford Visitor Info Centre,** 250/865-4614, a good source of park information. For further park information before arriving in the area, write BC Parks, Kootenay District, P.O. Box 118, Wasa, BC V0B 2K0, 250/422-4200, www.elp.gov.bc.ca/bcparks.

HEIGHT OF THE ROCKIES PROVINCIAL PARK

This long and narrow, 54,208-hectare park protects a 50-km-long section of the Canadian Rockies, including a 25-km-long stretch bordering the Continental Divide. The park lies entirely in British Columbia, bordered by Elk Lakes and Peter Lougheed Provincial Parks to the east and Banff National Park at its narrow northern reaches. It is accessible only on foot, and is not a destination for the casual day-tripper. Mountains dominate the landscape, with over 20 peaks—some of which remained unnamed until recently—rising over the magical 10,000-foot (3,050-meter) mark. They lie in two distinct ranges: the **Royal Group,** in the north, and the **Italian Group,** in the south. The dominant peak is 3,460-meter **Mt. King George,** in the Royal Group, which is flanked by massive hanging glaciers on its north- and east-facing slopes. Mountain goats thrive on all massifs, while the remote valleys are home to high concentrations of elk and grizzly bears.

The park can be reached from two directions.

Neither is signposted, so before setting out for the park, pick up a good map of the area at a local information center or Forest Service office. The following directions are intended only as a guide.

Connor Lake is the most popular destination in the south of the park. It is reached by passing through Whiteswan Lake Provincial Park (see below), then continuing along a rough logging road that parallels the White River to its upper reaches. (The most important intersection to watch for is 11 km from Whiteswan Lake; stay right, immediately crossing the river.) At the end of the road, a tortuous 72 km from Highway 93/95, is a small area set aside for tents and horse corrals. From this trailhead, it's an easy walk up Maiyuk Creek and over a low ridge to Connor Lake, where you'll enjoy great views of the Italian Group to the north and Mt. Forsyth to the southwest.

Small **Queen Mary Lake** lies in the western shadow of the impressive Royal Group. It is generally only the destination of those on horseback or mountaineers continuing into the Royal Group. To get there, turn off Highway 93/95 at Canal Flats and follow a logging road up the Kootenay River watershed. For the first 48 km, the road follows the Kootenay itself. Then it turns westward and climbs along the south side of the Palliser River a further 35 km to road's end. From this point, it's a 12-km hike up a forested valley, with numerous creek crossings, to the lake.

Practicalities

Primitive campgrounds lie on the shores of **Connor** and **Queen Mary Lakes.** An eight-person Forest Service cabin sits at the north end of Connor Lake. For cabin reservations and general park information, write BC Parks, Kootenay District, Box 118, Wasa, BC V0B 2K0, 250/422-4200, www.elp.gov.bc.ca/bcparks.

MT. ASSINIBOINE PROVINCIAL PARK

Named for one of the Canadian Rockies' most spectacular peaks, this 38,600-hectare, roughly triangular park lies northeast of Radium Hot Springs, sandwiched between Kootenay National Park to the west and Banff National Park to the east. It's inaccessible by road; access is on foot or by helicopter. A haven for experienced hikers, the park offers alpine meadows, lakes, glaciers, and many peaks over 3,000 meters to explore. The park's highest peak, 3,618-meter Mt. Assiniboine (seventh-highest in the Canadian Rockies), is known as the "Matterhorn of the Rockies" for its resemblance to that famous Swiss landmark. The striking peak can be seen from many points well outside the boundaries of the park, including Buller Pond in Kananaskis Country and Sunshine Village ski area in Banff National Park.

The peak is named for the Assiniboine people, who ventured into this section of the Canadian Rockies many thousands of years prior to European exploration. The name Assiniboine means "stone boilers"—a reference to these people's preferred cooking method. The mountain was sighted and named by a geological survey team in 1885, but the first ascent wasn't made until 1901.

Lake Magog is the destination of most park visitors. Here you'll find the park's only facilities and the trailheads for a number of interesting and varied day hikes. One of the most popular walks is along the Sunburst Valley/Nub Ridge trail. From Lake Magog, small Sunburst Lake is reached in about 20 minutes, then the trail continues northwest a short distance to Cerulean Lake. From this lake's outlet, the trail descends slowly along the Mitchell River to a junction four km from Lake Magog. Take the right fork, which climbs through a dense subalpine forest to Elizabeth Lake, nestled in the southern shadow of Nub Peak. From this point, instead of descending back to Cerulean Lake, take the Nub Ridge trail, which climbs steadily for one km to a magnificent viewpoint high above Lake Magog. From the viewpoint, it's just under four km, downhill all the way, to the valley floor. The total length of this outing is 11 km, and as elevation gained is only just over 400 meters, the trail can comfortably be completed in four hours.

Approaching the Park on Foot

Three trails provide access to **Lake Magog**, the park's largest body of water. The most popular comes in from the northeast, starting at Sunshine Village ski area in Banff National Park and leading 29 km via Citadel Pass to the lake. Not only is this trail spectacular, but the high

elevation of the trailhead (2,100 meters) makes for a relatively easy approach. Another approach is from the east, in Kananaskis Country. The trailhead is at the southern end of Spray Lake; take the Mt. Shark turnoff 38 km south of Canmore. By the time the trail has climbed the Bryant Creek drainage to 2,165-meter Assiniboine Pass, all elevation gain (450 meters) has been made. At 27 km, this is the shortest approach, but its elevation gain is greater than the other two trails. The longest and least-used access is from Highway 93 at Simpson River in Kootenay National Park. This trail climbs the Simpson River and Surprise Creek drainages and crosses 2,270-meter Ferro Pass to the lake for a total length of 32 km.

The Easy Way In

If these long approaches put visiting the park out of your reach, there's one more option: you can fly in by helicopter from the Mt. Shark Helipad, in the southern end of the Spray Lake zone of Kananaskis Country. Helicopter access is restricted to Wednesday, Friday, and Sunday and costs $100 per person each way, including a 30-pound per person baggage limit. **Alpine Helicopters,** 403/678-4802, operates the flights, but all bookings must be made through Mt. Assiniboine Lodge, 403/678-2883. If you're planning on hiking into the park, Alpine Helicopters will fly your gear in for $1.50 per pound. Alpine Helicopters, based in Canmore, charges $150 for a 30-minute flight-seeing trip over the park.

Camping and Accommodations

Lake Magog is the park's main facility area, such as it is. A designated camping area on a low ridge above the lake's west shore provides a source of drinking water and pit toilets. Open fires are prohibited. Sites are $5 per person per night. Also at the lake are the **Naiset Cabins,** $15 per person per night (book through the lodge). The more luxurious **Mt. Assiniboine Lodge,** 403/678-2883, email assinilo@telus planet.net, was built in 1928 by the Canadian Pacific Railway and is owned by BC Parks but managed privately. Sleeping up to 30 people in six rooms and six cabins, accommodations are rustic but comfortable, and the rate of $135 per person per day includes all meals.

Information
For further park information, write BC Parks, Kootenay District, P.O. Box 118, Wasa, BC V0B 2K0, 250/422-4200, www.elp.gov.bc.ca/bcparks. For information on the condition of trails leading into the park, drop by the Kootenay, Lake Louise, or Banff park information centers.

MT. ROBSON PROVINCIAL PARK

At the northern end of the Canadian Rockies, spectacular Mt. Robson Provincial Park was created in 1913 to protect 217,200 hectares of steep canyons and wide forested valleys; icy lakes, rivers, and streams; and rugged mountain peaks permanently blanketed in snow and ice. The park lies along the Continental Divide in British Columbia, adjacent to Jasper National Park, and shelters the headwaters of the Fraser River, one of British Columbia's most important waterways. Towering over the park's western entrance is magnificent 3,954-meter **Mt. Robson,** highest peak in the Canadian Rockies.

Highway 16 splits the park in two, and many sights of interest are visible from the highway. But you'll have to leave the car behind to experience one of the park's biggest draws; the famous Berg Lake Trail is strictly for hikers.

Flora and Fauna
The elevation differences within the park are as great as anywhere else in the Canadian Rockies, making for a great variety of flora and fauna. The main service center lies in a forested valley at an elevation of just 840 meters, right in the heart of the montane. The oft-photographed view of Mt. Robson from the visitor center is framed by a stand of trembling aspen across a cleared meadow, but the most common tree at this elevation is Douglas fir, which covers the valley floor. Western red cedar and hemlock thrive in damp sections of the park. As in the rest of the Canadian Rockies, the subalpine zone is dominated by Engelmann spruce and, at higher elevations, subalpine fir. The alpine zone in the park begins at around 2,300 meters.

In spring, black bears are often seen feasting on dandelions by the roadside, but their larger relative, the grizzly, rarely makes an appearance in the busy valley through which Highway

Mount Robson (3,954 meters) is the highest peak in the Canadian Rockies.

16 winds. Elk, moose, and mountain goats are also present, as are many smaller critters. Over 170 bird species have been identified, with the rare harlequin duck a special joy to watch as it passes though the park each spring.

History
Local Shuswap natives called Mt. Robson Yuhhai-has-hun ("Mountain of the Spiral Road") for its layered appearance. Historians guess that the peak's European name honors a member of the Hudson's Bay Company, though details of the christening have been lost to history.

Mountaineers were attracted to the challenge of climbing Mt. Robson in the early 1900s; the first official ascent took place in 1913 (the same year the park as we know it today was created). Led by Swiss guide Conrad Kain, the first ascent party was made up of members of the Alpine Club of Canada. Although this was the first official summit climb, the summit had been attempted four years earlier by the Reverend

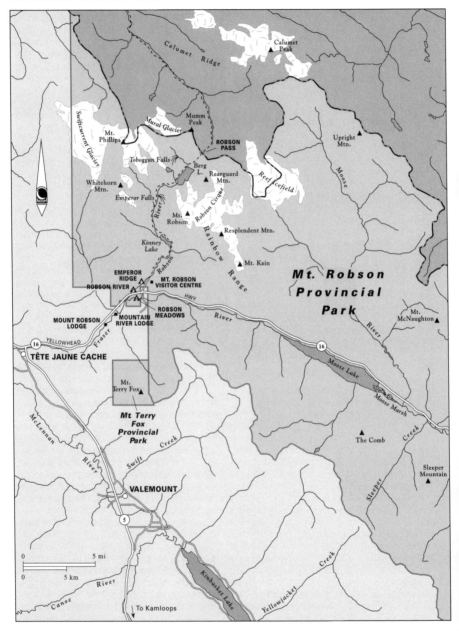

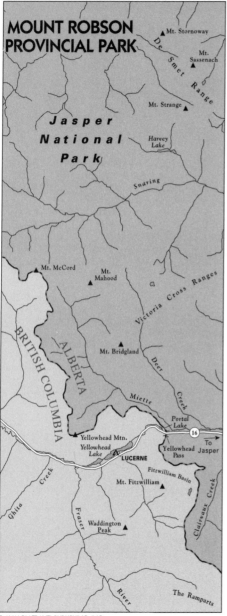

MOUNT ROBSON
PROVINCIAL PARK

Mt. Stornoway

Mt. Sassenach

De Smet Range

Mt. Strange

Jasper

National

Park

Harvey Lake

Snaring

Mt. McCord

Mt. Mahood

Victoria Cross Ranges

BRITISH COLUMBIA

ALBERTA

Mt. Bridgland

Deer Creek

Miette

Portal Lake

16

To Jasper

Yellowhead Mtn.

Yellowhead Lake

Yellowhead Pass

LUCERNE

Fitzwilliam Basin

Mt. Fitzwilliam

Clairvaux Creek

Ghita Creek

Fraser

Waddington Peak

River

The Ramparts

© AVALON TRAVEL PUBLISHING, INC.

George Kinney and friends. Kinney thought he'd made the summit, but he was climbing the summit ridge in a heavy fog; a cairn and a message recording the names of the members of Kinney's climbing team were later found on the ridge about 100 vertical meters from the top.

Roadside Sights

Highway 16 enters the park from the east at 1,066-meter **Yellowhead Pass,** on the British Columbia/Alberta border. It's the lowest highway pass over the Continental Divide. From the divide, it's 60 km to the park's western boundary and the visitor center. Just west of the divide, a rest area beside picturesque **Portal Lake** is a good introduction to the park.

Continuing westward, the highway passes long, narrow **Yellowhead Lake** at the foot of 2,458-meter **Yellowhead Mountain,** then crosses the upper reaches of the Fraser River. The Moose River drains into the Fraser River at **Moose Marsh,** a good spot for wildlife watching at the southeast end of **Moose Lake.** Moose often feed here at dawn and dusk, and waterfowl are present throughout the day.

Continuing west, the highway parallels Moose Lake; waterfalls on the lake's far side create a photogenic backdrop. As the road descends steeply to a wide, open section of the valley, it passes the main facility area, where you'll find a visitor center, campgrounds, a gas station, and a restaurant. On a clear day the panorama from this lump of commercialism is equal to any sight in British Columbia. The sheer west face of Mt. Robson slices skyward just seven km away across a flower-filled meadow. This is as close as you can get to the peak in your car.

If you're approaching the park from the west, you'll see Mt. Robson long before you reach the park boundary (provided the weather is co-operating). It's impossible to confuse this distinctive peak with those that surround it—no wonder it's known as the "Monarch of the Canadian Rockies."

Berg Lake Trail

- Length: 19.5 km (eight hours) one-way
- Elevation gain: 725 meters
- Rating: moderate/difficult

This is the most popular overnight hike in the Canadian Rockies, but don't let the crowds put

THE YELLOWHEAD STORY

Yellowhead is the name of a pass and lake within Mt. Robson Provincial Park, as well as a highway that crosses the continent as a northern alternative to the TransCanada. The name is attributed to a blond-haired trapper of French descent, who cached furs in the area. He became known as Tête Jaune, which translates as "Yellowhead." The French version of his name also lives on, for just outside Mt. Robson Provincial Park's western boundary lies the small town of Tête Jaune Cache.

you off—the hike is well worth it. Beautiful aqua-colored Berg Lake lies below the north face of Mt. Robson, which rises 2,400 meters directly behind the lake. Glaciers on the mountain's shoulder regularly calve off into the lake, resulting in the icebergs that give the lake its name. It's possible to traverse the trail's first section and return the same day; to get all the way to Berg Lake and back you'll need to stay in the backcountry overnight. Along the route are seven primitive campgrounds, including three along the lakeshore. Overnight hikers must register at the visitor center and pay a camping fee of $6 per person per night. Only 75 campsites lie along the trail. Bookings for these sites are taken at the visitor center or through BC Parks at 604/689-9025 or 800/689-9025. Book early as the quota fills quickly.

From the trailhead two km north of the visitor center along a narrow access road, the trail follows the Robson River 4.5 km through dense subalpine forest to glacially-fed **Kinney Lake.** There the trail narrows, crossing the fast-flowing river at the eight-km mark and climbing alongside it. The next four km, through the steep-sided Valley of a Thousand Falls, are the most demanding, but views of four spectacular waterfalls ease the pain of the 500-vertical-meter climb. The first glimpses of Mt. Robson come soon after reaching the head of the valley, from where it's a further one km to the outlet of Berg Lake, 17.5 km from the trailhead. The first of three lakeside campgrounds is two km from this point.

While the panorama from the lake is stunning, most hikers who have come this far will want to spend some time exploring the area.

From the north end of the lake, trails lead to Toboggan Falls and more mountain views, to the head of Robson Glacier, and to Robson Pass, which opens up the remote northern reaches of Jasper National Park.

If the uphill walk in seems too ambitious, contact **Robson Helimagic,** 250/566-4700, which makes helicopter drop-offs at Robson Pass from Valemount every Monday and Friday; $155 per person (minimum four). Another option for those inexperienced in backcountry travel is a guided hiking package with **Mount Robson Adventure Holidays,** 250/566-4386. The three-day, two-night trip is $500 per person, or fly in and hike out over the same period of time for $860 per person.

Other Hikes in the Park

Aside from the busy trail to Berg Lake, the park holds only two other established trails. The shortest of the two ascends the slopes of 2,458-meter **Yellowhead Mountain.** From the trailhead across the rail line at Yellowhead Lake, it's a steady climb through subalpine forest to the first viewpoint at the one-km mark. Another three km and a total elevation gain of 720 meters brings you to flower-filled meadows and panoramic views extending east to the Continental Divide and west to the Selwyn Range. Allow two hours each way for this hike.

The other option is the 13-km (each way) **Fitzwilliam Basin Trail,** which requires an overnight stay in the backcountry. Elevation gain is 950 meters, so it's a fairly demanding trail. From the trailhead on the south side of Highway 16, three km east of Lucerne Campground, the trail climbs steadily for six km to the confluence of Rockingham and Fitzwilliam Creeks. Although easy to follow, the remaining seven km along the northern slopes of 2,911-meter Mt. Fitzwilliam are rough going. After ascending a steep ridge the trail all but dissipates, but many camping spots can be found in the wide lake-filled basin.

Other Recreation

Mount Robson Adventure Holidays, based at Mt. Robson Adventure Centre (by the visitor center), 250/566-4386 or 800/882-9921, conducts a number of "gentle adventure" tours within the park. These include rafting ($39), canoeing on Moose Lake ($45), and a guided hike to Kinney Lake ($45). The adventure center is also home to a unique mini-golf layout decorated with native plants and wood carvings. **Mount Robson Whitewater Rafting,** 250/566-4879 or 888/566-7238, runs the Class III rapids of the Fraser River, with a portage around Rearguard Falls; $65 includes lunch. Some of the Jasper rafting companies also offer this trip, with transportation from Jasper included.

Flight-seeing is available in Valemount, 20 km west then 22 km south on Highway 5 from the visitor center. **Premier Air,** 250/566-4901, offers fixed-wing flight-seeing over the area for $75 per person for 40 minutes, $135 for 70 minutes. **Robson Helimagic,** 250/566-4700, charges $155 per person for a 36-minute helicopter flight up to and around Mt. Robson.

Park Campgrounds
Within the park are four campgrounds with road access. The park operates three of these. Closest to the visitor center is **Robson River Campground,** while across the road is **Robson Meadows Campground.** Both have flush toilets and showers but no hookups; $17.50 per site. In the east of the park is the more rustic **Lucerne Campground,** where sites are $12. **Emperor Ridge Campground,** 250/566-8438, is a commercial facility right behind the visitor center; $18 per site including hot showers but no hookups.

Robson Shadows Campground, five km west of the visitor center, 250/566-9190, is part of Mt. Robson Lodge. It also has showers but no hookups. Sites are $14.50 per night.

Lodges
The park has no indoor accommodations, but two lodges lie just outside the park's western boundary and motel accommodations are available 44 km to the southwest in Valemount.

Mountain River Lodge, four km west of the visitor center, 250/566-9899 or 888/566-9899, www.mtrobson.com, is in a delightful setting right alongside the Fraser River. The main lodge holds five rooms each with a different character, a balcony, and private bathroom. The rates of $80–100 s or d include a cooked breakfast. A self-contained riverfront cabin costs $90 per night.

One km beyond Mountain River Lodge is the turn-off for **Mount Robson Lodge,** 250/566-4821 or 888/566-4821. A variety of recreational activities, including whitewater rafting can be organized for guests, and meals are available. Rates in the free-standing cabins range $75–125 s or d.

Information
At the park's western entrance, **Mt. Robson Visitor Centre,** 250/566-9174, features informative natural-history slide shows, an evening interpretive program, and trail reports updated daily. Hikers and climbers can pick up detailed trail descriptions and topographical maps ($11) at the center. Hours are mid-June to mid-September, daily 8 A.M.–8 P.M.; mid-May to mid-June and mid-September to mid-October, daily 8 A.M.–5 P.M.; closed the rest of the year. Another source of information is BC Parks' Mt. Robson Area Office, P.O. Box 579, Valemount, BC V0E 1Z0, 250/566-4325, www.elp.gov.bc.ca/bcparks.

TOP OF THE WORLD PROVINCIAL PARK

This wild and remote 8,790-hectare park lies beyond Whiteswan Lake Provincial Park (see below), a rough 52 km from Highway 93/95 (turn off the Whiteswan Lake access road at Alces Lake). You can't drive into the park, but it's a fairly easy six-km (two-hour) hike from the end of the road to picturesque **Fish Lake,** the park's largest body of water. The trail climbs alongside the pretty Lussier River to the lake, which is encircled with Engelmann spruce and surrounded by peaks up to 2,500 meters high. The hike to the lake gains just over 200 vertical meters and makes a good day trip. Trails from the lake lead to other alpine lakes and to a viewpoint that allows a good overall perspective on the high plateau for which the park is named. Fish Lake is productive for cutthroat trout and Dolly Varden.

Practicalities
Bring everything you'll need–there are no services within the park. Camping is possible at one of four designated areas for $5 per person, or you can stay in the large cabin nestled in trees beside Fish Lake ($15 per person). For park information and trail conditions, contact BC Parks, Kootenay District, Box 118, Wasa, BC V0B 2K0, 250/422-4200, www.elp.gov.bc.ca/bcparks.

WHITESWAN LAKE PROVINCIAL PARK

Access to this popular British Columbia park is from Highway 93/95, 50 km south of Radium Hot Springs and 28 km north of Skookumchuck. From a signed turnoff, an unpaved logging road takes off east into the mountains, leading first to 1,994-hectare Whiteswan Lake Provincial Park, then to Top of the World Provincial Park (see above). The road climbs steadily from the highway, entering Lussier Gorge after 11 km. Within the gorge, a steep trail leads down to **Lussier Hot Springs.** Two small pools have been constructed to contain the odorless hot (43°C)

Whiteswan Lake

water as it bubbles out of the ground and flows into the Lussier River. Within the park itself, the road closely follows the southern shorelines of first **Alces Lake** then the larger **Whiteswan Lake.** The two lakes attract abundant bird life; loons, grebes, and herons are all common. They also attract anglers, who come for great rainbow trout fishing. Both lakes are stocked and have a daily quota of two fish per person.

Practicalities

The main road skirts the lakes and passes four campgrounds; $12 per site, no showers.

For park information, contact BC Parks, Kootenay District, Box 118, Wasa, BC V0B 2K0, 250/422-4200, www.elp.gov.bc.ca/bcparks.

WILDERNESS AREAS

SIFFLEUR WILDERNESS AREA

This remote region on the Alberta side of the Canadian Rockies lies south of Highway 11, which crosses west-central Alberta between Rocky Mountain House and Saskatchewan River Crossing, in Banff National Park. It is completely protected from any activities that could have an impact on the area's fragile ecosystems. That includes road and trail development; no bridges have been built over the area's many fast-flowing streams, and the few old trails that do exist are not maintained. Elk, deer, moose, cougars, wolverines, wolves, coyotes, black bears, and grizzly bears roam the area's four main valleys, while higher, alpine elevations harbor mountain goats and bighorn sheep.

The main trail into the 412-square-km wilderness begins from a parking area two km south of the Two O'Clock Creek Campground at Kootenay Plains (see the special topic **Kootenay Plains**). The area's northeastern boundary is

a seven-km hike from here. Even if you're not heading right into Siffleur, the first section of this trail, to Siffleur Falls, is worth walking. Along the first section, the trail crosses the North Saskatchewan River via a swinging bridge, then at the two-km mark crosses the Siffleur River, reaching the falls after four km (allow 70 minutes one-way). These are the official "Siffleur Falls," but others lie further upstream at the 6.2-km and 6.9-km marks. Once inside the wilderness area, the trail climbs steadily alongside the Siffleur River and into the heart of the wilderness. Ambitious hikers can continue through to the Dolomite Creek Area of Banff National Park, finishing at the Icefields Parkway, seven km south of Bow Summit. Total length of this trail is 68 km (five to seven days). Another access point for the area is opposite Waterfowl Lakes Campground in Banff National Park. From here it is six km up Noyes Creek to the wilderness area boundary; the trail peters out after 4.5 km and requires some serious scrambling before descending into Siffleur. This trail—as with all

KOOTENAY PLAINS

To appreciate them one must breathe their breath deep into the lungs, must let the soft winds caress the face, and allow the eye to absorb the blue of the surrounding hills and the gold of the grasses beneath the feet. Here the air is sweeter, drier, and softer than anywhere I know, and here the world could easily be forgotten and life pass by in a dream.

—Mary Schäffer, 1905

The Kootenay Plains—a unique area of dry grasslands in the mountains—is one of the Canadian Rockies' more special spots. As Mary Schäffer noted during her historic journey north to Maligne Lake, to gain full appreciation of the plains you must leave the road and pause in their midst.

The climate on the plains is the warmest in the Canadian Rockies. Vegetation such as June grass and wheat grass, usually associated with the prairies of southeastern Alberta, thrives here. Low snowfall and regular chinook winds make the area prime wintering grounds for elk, mule deer, bighorn sheep, and moose. For thousands of years, the Kootenay peoples would cross the mountains from the Columbia River Valley to hunt these mammals and the bison that were then prolific. Over time, the fearsome Peigans pushed the Kootenay westward and claimed the plains as their own. Today two Indian reserves can be found on the plains, but they are mostly used and protected as ecological reserves, lying at the southern end of Abraham Lake and beside Highway 93, 28 km east of Saskatchewan River Crossing (Banff National Park).

others in the wilderness area—is for experienced hikers only.

Practicalities

Two O'Clock Creek Campground lies two km from the park's main trailhead in Kootenay Plains Provincial Recreation Area. It is a primitive facility, with a picnic shelter and drinking water. Sites are $11 per night.

For more information contact Alberta Environ-ment, Main Floor, 9945 108th St., Edmonton, AB T5K 2A6, 780/944-0313, www.gov.ab.ca/env.

WHITE GOAT WILDERNESS AREA

White Goat comprises 445 square km of high mountain ranges, wide valleys, hanging glaciers, waterfalls, and high alpine lakes. It lies north and west of Highway 11, abutting the north end of Banff National Park and the south end of Jasper National Park. The area's vegetation zones are easily recognizable: subalpine forests of Engelmann spruce, subalpine fir, and lodgepole pine; alpine tundra higher up. Large mammals here include a large population of bighorn sheep, as well as mountain goats, deer, elk, woodland caribou, moose, cougars, wolves, coyotes, black bears, and grizzly bears.

The most popular hike is the **McDonald Creek Trail**, which first follows the Cline River, then McDonald Creek to the creek's source in the heart of the wilderness area. McDonald Creek is approximately 12 km from the parking area on Highway 11, but a full day should be allowed for this section as the trail crosses many streams. From where McDonald Creek flows into the Cline River, it is 19 km to the McDonald Lakes, but allow another two full days; the total elevation gain for the hike is 1,224 meters. Other hiking possibilities include following the Cline River to its source and crossing Sunset Pass into Banff National Park, 17 km north of Saskatchewan River Crossing, or heading up Cataract Creek and linking up with the trails in the Brazeau River area of Jasper National Park.

Practicalities

White Goat Wilderness Area has no services and is for experienced hikers only. For more information, contact Alberta Environment, Main Floor, 9945 108th St., Edmonton, AB T5K 2A6, 780/944-0313, www.gov.ab.ca/env.

WILLMORE WILDERNESS PARK

Willmore Wilderness Park is a northern extension of Jasper National Park. It lies south and west of Grande Cache, a small town on Highway 40 between Hinton and Grande Prairie.

The 4,600-square-km wilderness comprises mountains and foothills and is accessible only on foot, horseback, or, in winter, on skis. It is totally undeveloped—the trails that do exist are not maintained and in most cases are those once used by trappers. The park is divided roughly in half by the Smoky River. The area west of the river is reached from Sulphur Gates. The east side is far less traveled—the terrain is rougher and wetter.

The park is made up of long, green ridges above the tree line and, farther west, wide passes and expansive basins along the Continental Divide. Lower elevations are covered in lodgepole pine and spruce, while at higher elevations the cover changes to fir. The diverse wildlife is one of the park's main attractions; white-tailed and mule deer, mountain goats, bighorn sheep, moose, elk, caribou, and black bears are all common. The park is also home to wolves, cougars, and grizzly bears.

The easiest way to access the park is from Sulphur Gates Provincial Recreation Area, six km north of Grande Cache on Highway 40 and then a similar distance along a gravel road to the west. Those not planning a trip into the park can still enjoy the cliffs at **Sulphur Gates** (formerly known as **Hell's Gate**), which is only a short walk from the end of the road. These 70-meter cliffs are at the confluence of the Sulphur and Smoky Rivers. The color difference between the glacial-fed Smoky River and spring-fed Sulphur River is apparent as they merge. One of the most popular overnight trips is to Clarke's Cache, an easy 16-km hike to the remains of a cabin where trappers once stored furs before taking them to trading posts further afield. A good option for a day trip for fit hikers is to the 2013-meter summit of **Mt. Stearn** from a trailhead 3.5 km along the access road to Sulphur Gates. The trail begins by climbing alongside a stream through montane, then subalpine forest, and then through open meadows before reentering the forest and forking and rejoining. The official trail then climbs steeply and continuously to Lightning Ridge (10 km one-way), but an easier summit is reached by heading up through the grassed slopes to a summit knob, 6.5 km and 1,000 vertical meters from the road; allow 6–6.5 hours for the round trip.

Practicalities

Anyone planning an extended trip into the park should be aware that no services are available, most trails are unmarked, and certain areas are heavily used by horse-packers. Three outfitters—**Sherwood Guides and Outfitters,** 780/922-2266; **U Bar Enterprises,** 780/827-3641; and **Wild Rose Outfitting,** 780/693-2296—offer pack trips into the park; expect to pay around $150 per person per day, all-inclusive.

More information and topographical maps are available from the **Natural Resources Service** office on Shand Avenue, Grande Cache, 780/827-3356 or in advance from Alberta Environment, Main Floor, 9945 108th St., Edmonton, AB T5K 2A6, 780/944-0313, www.gov.ab.ca/env. The book *Willmore Wilderness Park,* published by the Alberta Wilderness Association, is available in Grande Cache at **Grande Books,** in the Pine Plaza Shopper's Mall on Hoppe Avenue.

Grande Cache

This town of 4,400, the most remote in the Canadian Rockies, is at the gateway to Willmore Wilderness Park and is surrounded by total wilderness, offering endless opportunities for hiking, canoeing, kayaking, fishing, and horseback riding. It perches on the side of Grande Mountain above the Smoky River, which flows from its source in Jasper National Park through Willmore Wilderness Park, eventually joining the Peace River and draining into the Arctic Ocean.

The first Europeans to explore the area were fur trappers and traders, who cached furs near the site of the present town before taking them to major trading posts. At one point there was a small trading post on a lake south of town on Pierre Gray Lakes; its remains are still visible.

Grande Cache is a planned town. Construction started in 1969 in response to a need for services and housing for miners and their families working at the McIntyre Porcupine Coal Mine. The town was developed 20 km south of the mine to maintain a scenic environment.

For great views of the surrounding area, consider climbing **Grande Mountain.** It's a steep trail, gaining 730 meters of elevation in 3.5 km (allow 90 minutes one-way), but from the summit, the view across the Smoky River Valley to the Rocky Mountains is spectacular. The trail follows a power line the entire way to the peak and is easy to follow. To get to the trailhead, head northwest of town one km and turn right at the cemetery gate. Park, walk along the road to the power line, veer right, and start the long slog to the summit. The lakes south of town are good for exploring by canoe. They harbor large populations of waterfowl and are good for fishing; rainbow and brook trout, whitefish, and arctic grayling are commonly caught. Many of the forestry roads are suitable for mountain biking; **Grande Cache Adventure Sports,** 780/827-3764, rents bikes.

Grande Cache Practicalities
Most motels are busy in summer so make reservations in advance. On the highway through town, **Big Horn Motor Inn,** 780/827-3744, is the best value. Each room has a fridge, some have kitchenettes, and a laundry and restaurant are on the premises; $40–50 s, $50–60 d. Also along the highway is **Alpine Lodge Motel,** 780/827-2450, $50 s, $60 d; and **Mountain Village Motel,** 780/827-2453, which charges the same for basic but modern rooms. Overlooking the plaza is the **Grande Cache Hotel,** 780/827-3377, www.grandecachehotel.ab.ca, which has 44 standard rooms and a few suites, a restaurant, and a lounge with country bands on weekends; $65 s, $69 d.

Marv Moore Campground, 780/827-2404, has semiprivate, well-treed sites and showers,

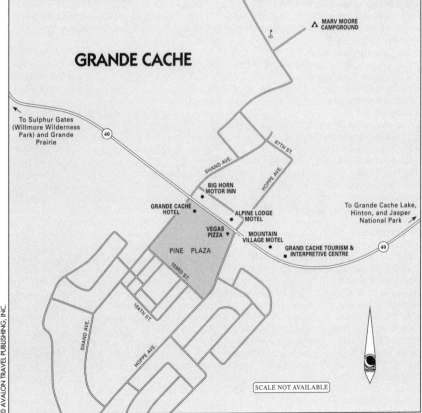

GRANDE CACHE

To Sulphur Gates (Willmore Wilderness Park) and Grande Prairie

MARV MOORE CAMPGROUND

97TH ST.
SHAND AVE.
HOPPE AVE.

BIG HORN MOTOR INN

GRANDE CACHE HOTEL

ALPINE LODGE MOTEL

VEGAS PIZZA

MOUNTAIN VILLAGE MOTEL

PINE PLAZA

GRAND CACHE TOURISM & INTERPRETIVE CENTRE

To Grande Cache Lake, Hinton, and Jasper National Park

103RD ST.
104TH ST.
SHAND AVE.
HOPPE AVE.

SCALE NOT AVAILABLE

kitchen shelters, and firewood; unserviced sites $13, hookups $15. It's at the north end of town off Shand Avenue. Alberta Environment campgrounds are located at regular intervals the entire length of Highway 40. Of special note are the ones at **Sulphur Gates Provincial Recreation Area,** north of town, which makes a good base for exploring Willmore Wilderness Park, and at **Grande Cache Lake,** five km south of town, which has good swimming, canoeing, and fishing. Sites at both areas run $10 per night.

On a clear day, the view from **Mountainview Cafe,** in the Grande Cache Hotel, is worth at least the price of a coffee. Soup and sandwich lunch specials are around $6 and pizza and pasta dishes start at $8. A dining room in the hotel opens at 5 P.M.; dinner entrées range $12–16. Call 780/827-3377 for reservations and information. **Vegas Pizza and Spaghetti House,** 207 Pine Plaza, 780/827-5444, is an inexpensive place to go for a meal; portions are large and the atmosphere pleasant.

The **Grande Cache Tourism and Interpretive Centre** 780/827-3300 or 888/827-3790, is outstanding, not just considering the size of the town that it represents, but for the wealth of information contained within it. It's easy to spend at least an hour in the two-story complex, with displays that include the human history of the region, local industry, stuffed animals, tree identification, and one on Willmore Wilderness Park. Other features include an information desk, gift shop, and large deck from where views extend across the Smoky River Valley to the highest peaks of the Canadian Rockies. It's open in summer daily 9 A.M.–7 P.M., the rest of the year Monday–Friday 8:30 A.M.–4:30 P.M.

BOOKLIST

NATURAL HISTORY

The Atlas of Breeding Birds of Alberta. Edmonton: Federation of Alberta Naturalists, 1992. Comprehensive study of all birds that breed in Alberta with easy-to-read distribution maps, details on nesting and other behavioral patterns, and color plates.

Busch, Robert H. *The Wolf Almanac*. New York: Lyons & Burford, 1995. A detailed analysis of the wolf, from its evolution as a distinct species to the issues surrounding breeding wolves as pets. Includes 12 pages of color plates.

Gadd, Ben. *Handbook of the Canadian Rockies*. Jasper: Corax Press, 1995. The latest edition of this classic guide is in color, and although bulky for backpackers it's a must-read for anyone interested in the natural history of the Canadian Rockies.

Gray, D. M. and D. H. Male. *Handbook of Snow*. Toronto: Pergamon Press, 1991. Comprehensive guide on everything you ever wanted to know about snow but didn't ask because no one else would have known either.

Hallworth, Beryl and C. C. Chinnappa. *Plants of Kananaskis Country*. Calgary: University of Calgary Press, 1997. An incredibly detailed book, encompassing over 400 species of flora, complete with color plates and illustrations. It could be used in the field anywhere in the Canadian Rockies.

Hare, F. K. and M. K. Thomas. *Climate Canada*. Toronto: John Wiley & Sons, 1974. One of the most extensive works on Canada's climate ever written. Includes a chapter on how the climate is changing.

Herrero, Stephen. *Bear Attacks: Their Causes and Avoidances*. New York: Nick Lyons Books, 1995. Through a series of gruesome stories, this book catalogs the stormy relationship between people and bruins, provides hints on avoiding attacks, and tells what to do in case you're attacked.

Lauriault, Jean. *Identification Guide to the Trees of Canada*. Markham, Ontario: Fitzhenry & Whiteside, 1989. Makes tree identification easy through drawings of leaves, and maps detail distribution of species.

Patterson, W. S. *The Physics of Glaciers*. Toronto: Pergamon Press, 1969. A highly technical look at all aspects of glaciation, why glaciers form, how they flow, and their effect on the environment.

Rezendes, Paul. *Tracking and the Art of Seeing*. Charlotte, Virginia: Camden House Publishing, 1992. This is one of the best of many books dedicated to tracking the North American mammals. It begins with a short essay on the relationship of humans with nature.

Scotter, George W. *Birds of the Canadian Rockies*. Saskatoon: Western Producer Prairie Books, 1990. Description of most recorded species including habitat and habits. Color photos.

Scotter, George W. *Wildflowers of the Canadian Rockies*. Edmonton: Hurtig Publishers Ltd., 1986. Color plates of all flowers found in the mountain national parks. Chapters are divided by flower colors, making identification in the field easy.

Sharp, Robert P. *Living Ice: Understanding Glaciers and Glaciation*. Cambridge, England: Cambridge University Press, 1988. A detailed but highly readable book on the formation, types, and results of glaciers.

Slinger, Joey. *Down & Dirty Birding*. Toronto: Key Porter Books, 1996. A hilarious but practical look at the art of bird-watching, with sections of text such as "How to steer clear of people who think bird-watching is better than sex."

Vacher, André. *Summer of the Grizzly.* Saskatoon: Western Producer Prairie Books, 1985. True story of a grizzly bear that went on a terrifying rampage near the town of Banff.

Whitaker, John. *National Audubon Society Field Guide to North American Mammals.* New York: Random House, 1997. One of a series of field guides produced by the National Audubon Society, this one details mammals through color plates and detailed descriptions of characteristics, habitat, and range.

Wright, William H. *The Grizzly Bear.* Originally produced by the University of Nebraska Press in 1909 and reprinted many times since, this book was authored by a hunter turned naturalist whose change of attitude through a lifetime of association with bears is very poignant.

HUMAN HISTORY

Barnes, Christine. *Great Lodges of the Canadian Rockies.* Calgary: W. W. West Inc., 2000. This book delves into the history of the many famous mountain lodges—such as the Banff Springs Hotel and Jasper Park Lodge—and lesser-known but equally interestingly historic accommodations. Includes many historic photos.

Hart, E. J. *Jimmy Simpson: Legend of the Rockies.* Banff: Altitude Publishing, 1991. Details the life of one of the most colorful of the pioneer outfitters in the Canadian Rockies.

Jenness, Diamond. *The Indians of Canada.* Toronto: University of Toronto Press, 1977. Originally published in 1932, this is the classic study of natives in Canada, although his conclusion, that they were facing certain extinction by "the end of this century" is obviously outdated.

Lavallee, Omer. *Van Horne's Road.* Montreal: Railfare Enterprises, 1974. William Van Horne was instrumental in the construction of Canada's first transcontinental railway. This is the story of his dream, and the boomtowns that sprung up along the route. Lavallee devotes an entire chapter to telling the story of the railway's push over the Canadian Rockies.

McMillan, Alan D. *Native Peoples and Cultures of Canada.* Vancouver: Douglas & McIntyre, 1995. A comprehensive look at the archeology, anthropology, and ethnography of the native peoples of Canada. The last chapters delve into the problems facing these people today.

Marty, Sid. *Men for the Mountains.* New York: Vanguard Press, 1979. Written by a park warden, this book tells the story of those who lived in the Canadian Rockies and the risks and adventures involved.

Marty, Sid. *Switchbacks: True Stories from the Canadian Rockies.* Toronto: McClelland & Stewart, 1999. This book tells of Marty's experiences in the mountains and of people he came in contact with in his role as a park warden. Along the way he describes the way his experiences with both nature and fellow humans have shaped his views on conservation today.

Sandford, R. W. *The Canadian Alps: The History of Mountaineering in Canada.* Canmore: Altitude Publishing, 1990. Complete human history of the Canadian Rockies from the earliest explorers to first ascents of major peaks.

Schäffer, Mary T. S. *A Hunter of Peace.* Banff: Whyte Museum of the Canadian Rockies, 1980. This book was first published in 1911 by G. P. Putnam & Sons, New York, under the name *Old Indian Trails of the Canadian Rockies.* Tales recount the exploration of the Rockies during the turn of the century. Many of the author's photographs appear throughout.

Scott, Chic. *Pushing the Limits.* Calgary: Rocky Mountain Books, 2000. A chronological history of mountaineering in Canada, with special emphasis on many largely unknown climbers and their feats, as well as the story of Swiss guides in Canada and a short section on ice climbing.

Smith, Cyndi. *Off the Beaten Track*. Jasper: Coyote Books, 1989. Accounts of women adventurers and mountaineers and their impact on the early history of western Canada.

Touche, Rodney. *Brown Cows, Sacred Cows*. Hanna: Gorman, 1990. The story of the development of Lake Louise ski area as told by a former general manager.

Whyte, Jon. *Indians in the Rockies*. Banff: Altitude Publishing, 1985. Written from firsthand experiences, this is an excellent insight into the first humans to live in the Canadian Rockies.

RECREATION

Daffern, Gillean. *Kananaskis Country Trail Guide*. Calgary: Rocky Mountain Books, 1997. Two volumes cover all the official and unofficial trails in Kananaskis Country.

Helgason, Gail, and John Dodd. *The Canadian Rockies Bicycling Guide*. Edmonton: Lone Pine Publishing, 1986. Details 60 bicycling routes using simple maps and road logs.

Kane, Alan. *Scrambles in the Canadian Rockies*. Calgary: Rocky Mountain Books, 1992. Routes detailed in this guide lead to summits, without the use of ropes or mountaineering equipment.

Kariel, Herbert G. *Alpine Huts in the Canadian Rockies, Selkirks, and Purcells*. Canmore: Alpine Club of Canada, 1986. Covers the history of all huts in the Rockies, with current access routes and status and descriptions of nearby peaks to climb.

Kunelius, Rick, and Dave Biederman. *Ski Trails in the Canadian Rockies*. Banff: Summerthought, 1981. Detailed guide to cross-country skiing in all national parks of the Canadian Rockies.

Patton, Brian, and Bart Robinson. *The Canadian Rockies Trail Guide*. Banff: Summerthought,

1992. This regularly updated guide, first published in 1971, covers all hiking trails in the mountain national parks.

Potter, Mike. *Fire Lookouts in the Canadian Rockies*. Banff: Luminous Compositions, 1998. This book specializes in hikes to fire lookouts. Trail descriptions are detailed, and each is accompanied by the history of the lookout and those who have staffed them.

Potter, Mike. *Backcountry Banff*. Banff: Luminous Compositions, 1992. This book's title is a little misleading, for included are many shorter trails that can be enjoyed by everyone. Includes logged distances and readable trail description of over 100 hikes in Banff National Park.

OTHER GUIDEBOOKS

Hempstead, Andrew. *Moon Handbooks: Alberta and the Northwest Territories*. Emeryville: Avalon Travel Publishing, 2001. A beautifully written travel guide to the province of Alberta, including the gateway cities of Calgary and Edmonton, and the Northwest Territories.

Hempstead, Andrew, and Jane King. *British Columbia Handbook*. Emeryville: Avalon Travel Publishing, 2000. From Vancouver to Victoria, from the Canadian Rockies to the wild northlands along the Yukon border, this book covers Canada's westernmost province extensively.

The Milepost. Bellevue, Washington: Vernon Publications. This annual publication is a must-have for those traveling through western Canada and Alaska. The maps and logged highway descriptions are incredibly detailed. Most northern bookstores stock *The Milepost*, or order by calling 800/726-4707.

PERIODICALS

The Canadian Alpine Journal. Canmore, Alberta. Annual magazine of the Alpine Club of Canada with articles from its members and climbers from around the world.

Canadian Geographic. Ottawa: Royal Canadian Geographical Society. Bimonthly publication pertaining to Canada's natural and human histories and resources.

Equinox. Markham, Ontario. This bimonthly publication looks at Canada's natural world and humanity's relationship with it.

Explore. Calgary. Bimonthly publication of adventure travel throughout Canada.

FREE CATALOGS

Alberta Accommodation Guide. Alberta Hotel Association. Lists all hotel, motel, and other lodging in the province. Available at all Tourist Information Centres or by calling 800/661-8888.

Alberta Campground Guide. Alberta Hotel Association. Lists all campgrounds in the province. Available at all Tourist Information Centres or by calling 800/661-8888.

Accommodations. Tourism British Columbia. Lists all accommodations, including commercial and provincial campgrounds in the province. Available at all Visitor Information Centres or by calling 800/663-6000.

Tour Book: Western Canada and Alaska. Booklet available to members of the Canadian or American Automobile Associations.

REFERENCE

Daffern, Tony. *Avalanche Safety for Skiers & Climbers.* Calgary: Rocky Mountain Books, 1992. Covers all aspects of avalanches including their causes, practical information on how to avoid them, and a section on rescue techniques and first aid.

Guide to Manuscripts: The Fonds and Collections of the Archives, Whyte Museum of the Canadian Rockies. Banff: Whyte Museum of the Canadian Rockies, 1988. This book makes finding items in the Whyte Museum easy by providing alphabetical lists of all parts of the collection.

Johnson, Leslie. *Basic Mountain Safety from A to Z.* Canmore, AB: Altitude Books, 2000. Everything you need to know about safety in the mountains, including a large section on camping.

Karamitsanis, Aphrodite. *Place Names of Alberta.* Calgary: University of Alberta Press, 1991. An ongoing toponomy project. Volume 1 alphabetically lists all geographic features of the mountains and foothills with explanations of each name's origin. Volume 2 does the same for southern Alberta's geographical features.

INDEX

GLACIERS

GOLF COURSES

HIKING TRAILS

HIKING TRAILS (continued)

SKIING/SNOWBOARDING

WATERFALLS

ABOUT THE AUTHOR

Andrew Hempstead has spent many years exploring, writing about, and photographing the Canadian Rockies. He has been writing since the late 1980s, when, after leaving a promising career in the field of advertising, he took off for Alaska, linking up with veteran travel-writer Deke Castleman to help research and update the fourth edition of *Alaska-Yukon Handbook.*

In addition to this book, he is the author of *Moon Handbooks: Alberta and the Northwest Territories* and *Moon Handbooks: Vancouver;* is coauthor of *British Columbia Handbook* and *Australia Handbook;* and has contributed to subsequent editions of *Alaska-Yukon Handbook* (Moon Travel Handbooks). Andrew has also traveled to New Zealand multiple times on assignment to write and photograph for Moon Travel Handbooks and The Guide Book Company. He is a contributing writer to *Road Trip USA* (Avalon Travel Publishing) and Microsoft's *Automap,* and his work has appeared in *National Geographic Traveler.* He has also traveled purely for pleasure through most of the United States, Europe, the South Pacific, and India.

When not working on his books, Andrew is happiest hiking, fishing, golfing, camping, and enjoying the simple pleasures in life, such as sitting on his deck with a nice cold beer and watching the sun set over the mountains. He calls Canmore, Alberta, home.

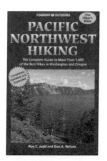

MOON HANDBOOKS

provide comprehensive coverage of a region's arts, history, land, people, and social issues in addition to detailed practical listings for accommodations, food, outdoor recreation, and entertainment. Moon Handbooks allow complete immersion in a region's culture—ideal for travelers who want to combine sightseeing with insight for an extraordinary travel experience in destinations throughout North America, Hawaii, Latin America, the Caribbean, Asia, and the Pacific.

WWW.MOON.COM

Rick Steves shows you where to travel and how to travel—all while getting the most value for your dollar. His Back Door travel philosophy is about making friends, having fun, and avoiding tourist rip-offs.

Rick's been traveling to Europe for more than 25 years and is the author of 20 guidebooks, which have sold more than a million copies. He also hosts the award-winning public television series *Travels in Europe with Rick Steves*.

WWW.RICKSTEVES.COM

ROAD TRIP USA

Getting there is half the fun, and Road Trip USA guides are your ticket to driving adventure. Taking you off the interstates and onto less-traveled, two-lane highways, each guide is filled with fascinating trivia, historical information, photographs, facts about regional writers, and details on where to sleep and eat—all contributing to your exploration of the American road.

"Books so full of the pleasures of the American road, you can smell the upholstery."
~ BBC radio

WWW.ROADTRIPUSA.COM

TRAVEL✦SMART®

guidebooks are accessible, route-based driving guides focusing on regions throughout the United States and Canada. Special interest tours provide the most practical routes for family fun, outdoor activities, or regional history for a trip of anywhere from two to 22 days. Travel Smarts take the guesswork out of planning a trip by recommending only the most interesting places to eat, stay, and visit.

"One of the few travel series that rates sightseeing attractions. That's a handy feature. It helps to have some guidance so that every minute counts."
~San Diego Union-Tribune

guides are for campers, hikers, boaters, anglers, bikers, and golfers of all levels of daring and skill. Each guide focuses on a specific U.S. region and contains site descriptions and ratings, driving directions, facilities and fees information, and easy-to-read maps that leave only the task of deciding where to go.

"Foghorn Outdoors has established an ecological conservation standard unmatched by any other publisher."
~Sierra Club

WWW.FOGHORN.COM

CiTY·SMaRT™

guides are written by local authors with hometown perspectives who have personally selected the best places to eat, shop, sightsee, and simply hang out. The honest, lively, and opinionated advice is perfect for business travelers looking to relax with the locals or for longtime residents looking for something new to do Saturday night.

There are City Smart guides for cities across the United States and Canada, and a portion of sales from each title benefits a non-profit literacy organization in its featured city.

www.travelmatters.com

User-friendly, informative, and fun: Because travel *matters*.

Visit our newly launched web site and explore the variety of titles and travel information available online, featuring an interactive *Road Trip USA* exhibit.

also check out:

www.ricksteves.com

The Rick Steves web site is bursting with information to boost your travel I.Q. and liven up your European adventure.

www.foghorn.com

Visit the Foghorn Outdoors web site for more information on the premier source of U.S. outdoor recreation guides.

www.moon.com

The Moon Handbooks web site offers interesting information and practical advice that ensure an extraordinary travel experience.

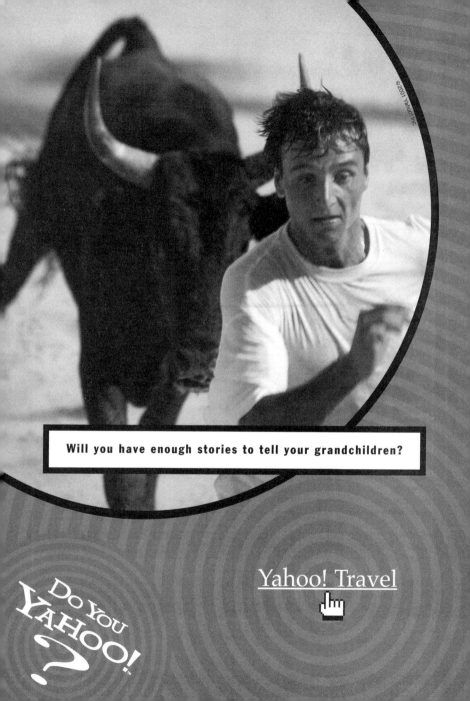

Will you have enough stories to tell your grandchildren?

U.S.~METRIC CONVERSION

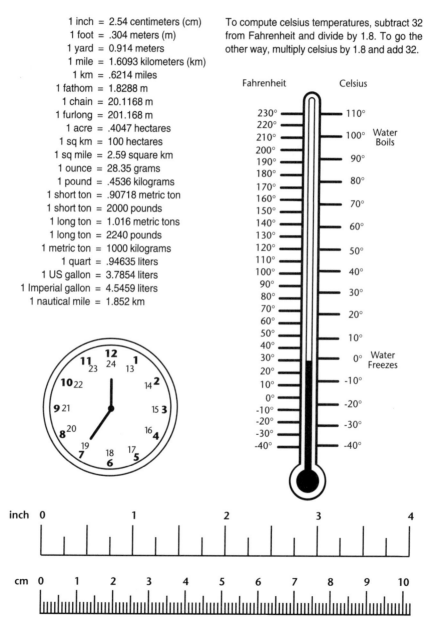

1 inch = 2.54 centimeters (cm)
1 foot = .304 meters (m)
1 yard = 0.914 meters
1 mile = 1.6093 kilometers (km)
1 km = .6214 miles
1 fathom = 1.8288 m
1 chain = 20.1168 m
1 furlong = 201.168 m
1 acre = .4047 hectares
1 sq km = 100 hectares
1 sq mile = 2.59 square km
1 ounce = 28.35 grams
1 pound = .4536 kilograms
1 short ton = .90718 metric ton
1 short ton = 2000 pounds
1 long ton = 1.016 metric tons
1 long ton = 2240 pounds
1 metric ton = 1000 kilograms
1 quart = .94635 liters
1 US gallon = 3.7854 liters
1 Imperial gallon = 4.5459 liters
1 nautical mile = 1.852 km

To compute celsius temperatures, subtract 32 from Fahrenheit and divide by 1.8. To go the other way, multiply celsius by 1.8 and add 32.

Fahrenheit   Celsius

230°   110°
220°
210°   100°   Water
200°   Boils
190°   90°
180°
170°   80°
160°
150°   70°
140°   60°
130°
120°   50°
110°
100°   40°
90°
80°   30°
70°
60°   20°
50°
40°   10°
30°
20°   0°   Water
10°   Freezes
0°   -10°
-10°
-20°   -20°
-30°
-40°   -30°
                  -40°

inch 0   1   2   3   4

cm 0   1   2   3   4   5   6   7   8   9   10

Banff 17,18 M
       T W H

Swiss village Inn. 4/8 lms
    $130   7 GST
           3 AHT
           x 17.
    inn of banff.   0

#9253835   #9253835
inn.ofbanff.com $145.60

(Cancelled)

Jasper F S

Astoria   4 days   #V47698
                                     astoriahotel.com
2 dbls $168

Lake Louise Inn   22,23. S M. 3 dys.   www.lakelouiseinn.com
                                          #6313
2 dbls 159. ind. 1780⁸ include breakfast.

hotels.
  1-864-762-4122

banfflakelouise.com
→ activities and attractions.   1-866-762-4122

B.C. Golden.